Also by Cyra McFadden

THE SERIAL

Rain or Shine

Rain or Shine

A FAMILY MEMOIR

Cyra McFadden

Secker & Warburg
London

First published in England 1986 by
Martin Secker & Warburg Limited
54 Poland Street, London W1V 3DF

Copyright © 1986 by Cyra McFadden

British Library Cataloguing in Publication Data

McFadden, Cyra
  Rain or shine: a family memoir.
  1. West (U.S.)—Social life and customs
  I. Title
  978'.032'0924   F595.2

  ISBN 0-436-27580-5

Grateful acknowledgment is made to Warner Bros. Music
Inc. for permission to reprint an excerpt from "Don't Fence
Me In" by Cole Porter. © 1944 (Renewed) Warner Bros.
Inc. All Rights Reserved. Used by Permission.

Printed and bound in Great Britain by
Biddles Ltd, Guildford and King's Lynn

FOR KENT

Acknowledgments

Without the help of my brothers Terry and Tom Taillon, who gave me access to our father's files and scrapbooks, I could not have written this book. They have my gratitude as well as my love.

Rain or Shine

Cy Taillon

INTRODUCTION

When my father died, in April of 1980, newspapers in the West compared him with John Wayne. "Cy Taillon was more than a rodeo announcer," said the writer for the Miles City *Star* in Miles City, Montana, "like John Wayne was more than an actor. Each became an embodiment of an ideal, a spokesman for a quality of life and a way of living it." America was younger when my father left his family's North Dakota farm and Wayne left the football field of the University of Southern California, the writer continued. "It took men of iron will, stout hearts and sensitive manner to tame her. Stubborn men who spoke their minds and minded what they spoke. Times have changed, so has America. And so has rodeo."

He's right about America and rodeo. My father never changed, not in his loyalty to Western values. When his Denver house was burglarized of two hundred dollars' worth of appliances several years ago, he told the Denver *Post*, "I plan to have an armed resident in the house with orders to shoot first and argue later."

Cy was at the top of his profession then. In fact he was the top, with no competition for his title "Dean of Rodeo Announcers," an accolade accorded him by the rest of the rodeo world and almost always attached to his name. Once a rakehell, he'd been respected and respectable for thirty years: well paid, happily married, a family man and a householder. But inside him, beneath his custom-tailored Western jackets, beat the heart of a cowboy. No one stole his toaster while he was out on the road, if he could help it, and walked away intact. A shotgun shell or two should handle the problem nicely.

We were not speaking to each other then. His blue-eyed darling as a child, named after him, dressed like him as a wrong-sex, unusually short cowboy, I'd grown up, moved away from Montana, moved away in heart and mind from my father and shoot first, argue later. I had a couple of degrees, a divorce behind me and a second marriage; a suburban California house; belonged to the ACLU; took part in San Francisco peace marches while my half brother by my father's second marriage was fighting in Vietnam and my father editorializing from the crow's nest, the rodeo announcer's booth, in support of the war.

The last time we'd seen each other, he and I argued about racial intermarriage, hippies, Catholicism as the one true religion and what to have for dinner. We were at an elegant San Francisco Chinese restaurant. My father insisted that we both eat chow mein. I was full of self and my new sophistication and didn't want to sit at the same table with a man who'd order chow mein at Kan's. Especially a man in kangaroo-skin cowboy boots, nipped-in Western suit and diamond pinkie ring.

We were obnoxious in equal proportions, but my father won. He had a voice that could fill a football stadium without amplification, and he was picking up the check.

So he went back to embodying the West while I went back to ACLU meetings. We exchanged letters in which we discussed politics and each other's character defects. Then we exchanged no letters at all, keeping track of each other through relatives, waiting for the other to heal the rift. Cy Taillon's daughter, I am as stubborn as he was. We loved each other, missed each other, and made ourselves miserable, and this went on for years, time for our grievances to harden into granite.

I rankled at a distance about the form my father's letters took, when I was still receiving them. He sent me a carbon of the letters he wrote his entire family. It was a large family. He always sent me the blurry last carbon.

His own grievances predated our quarrel about San Francisco

and whether or not it was part Sodom, part Gomorrah. As a child, I used to meet my father on the rodeo circuit in the summers, in Billings or Miles City or Lewiston, traveling by Greyhound bus, a label pinned to my shirt: "If bus isn't met deliver to Cy Taillon, fairgrounds." On each such occasion, he marched me off instantly to a beauty shop to have a permanent wave, frustrated beyond tolerance that no matter who did what to me, and no matter how much he paid for it, my hair refused to curl. He wanted a daughter who looked like Shirley Temple. Instead, he had a sulky, waiflike child who looked more like Oliver Twist.

The afternoon before we met for dinner at Kan's, he'd made one more attempt. "Go get your hair done," he said, and gave me twenty dollars. At the beauty shop in his San Francisco hotel, a hairdresser tormented me into a lofty bouffant. I felt freakish, and it didn't help our relations that my father was once again disappointed. "I give up," he said when he saw me. I had to put on my dark glasses. Crying, I had been taught long ago, was for sissies.

We were a long time reconciling, and when reconciliation came, it came on my father's terms. He was sick and demoralized after a small stroke. A letter turned up in my mailbox, on his flamboyant stationery, with its cowboy hat, microphone and lariat logo and the legend: "Cy Taillon, Master of Ceremonies and Rodeo Announcer, with records unequaled for consecutive engagements." He wrote that he'd been hoping for a move from me for years, feeling that "any desire to communicate" should originate with me because he was blameless in our estrangement.

I raged at his tone of injured merit; thought about how he always told reporters he had two children, my two half brothers, Terry and Tommy, and not three; remembered every hurt, every slight, and how, when Cy finally left his tempestuous marriage to my mother, he quickly began the process of erasing me from the record of his life along with her.

When we were together, he sometimes slipped and called me "Pat." I was the living reminder that he'd once slept with her, caroused with her, been deeply and destructively in love with her. Respectability had come late and hard to him. I remembered the person he'd been—dazzling, reckless, a drunk.

The day his letter came, I phoned him, and the voice that had made him famous resonated over the line. Majestically, he told me that if I apologized, he was willing to forgive me. He was, he said, incapable of holding a grudge.

We had nine years to make our peace before cancer killed him. I wrote a book during that time, was interviewed by reporters myself and began to tell the ones who asked me where I got my odd name that my father invented it. He was Cy Taillon, Dean of the Rodeo Announcers and living Western legend.

That he was pleased, Terry and Tommy assure me. He also kept articles that I wrote and sent and newspaper pieces in which I mentioned him. What he wrote me was that he was pleased my book was doing well but that the attention paid to it surprised him. He was a writer, too, for Western periodicals, with files full of fan letters. He'd never received as much press as I did, for what was after all a short book. I must have a very good press agent.

In the summer two years after he died, I went back to Montana. This time I went to Great Falls, where my father died and my two brothers live. (I'm dropping "half brother" at this point because we're related not just by blood but by our complicated love for our father.) There I went on a pilgrimage of sorts with Terry, then thirty-seven and a rodeo announcer himself.

Cy was dead. My stepmother, Dorothy, was dead. My mother was failing and close to dying. Even more than Terry did, I felt cut loose from my life as I'd known it until then because my husband of twenty years had died the December before.

In Terry's new Buick Skylark, named "Ol' Sorrel Top," we headed for the Miles City Bucking Horse Sale, the last of Cy's unequaled consecutive engagements. Though Miles City has a celebrated rodeo, our real reason for the trip was to spend time together and to build a bridge between our vastly different lives.

Forty-four-year-old woman, widowed, an urban dweller; kid brother, now grown up and graying, big, barrel-chested, a cowboy. To make the trip and the bridge building go more smoothly, Terry set the car on cruise control and stopped only at crossroads bars.

The road from Great Falls to Miles City heads south across barren, empty country. We peeled away the miles with Jack Daniel's for me and Black Velvet for Terry, while Willie Nelson sang old Hank Williams songs on the tape deck. After spending most of his

life on the road, traveling with Cy and then making the circuit himself as a bronc rider, Terry is an expert in dead-animal identifica-
tion, needing only a blot on the highway, a bit of entrail or a couple
of tail feathers, to say authoritatively, "That's your coney" or
"That's your magpie."

He said little else as we rolled along, other than "How do you
like all this nothing?"

I said it was beautiful nothing. I'd missed it. I also said I wished
my husband could have seen it.

"He's seeing it now," Terry said. Full of Jack Daniel's and strong
feeling, I had to jam on my dark glasses again.

I did not believe that my dead husband, a man without a religious impulse, was hovering over the road to Miles City and listening, with Terry and me, to Willie Nelson. I also knew that Terry
not only believes in heaven, he knows it looks just like Montana.

This book is a memoir of my father's life on the rodeo circuit,
his marriage to my mother and my effort to understand the ways in
which I am their daughter, who left the West and the world of rodeo
behind, full of fear and loathing, to find that Cy Taillon's imprint
was indelible. The first writing he ever published was satire; so was
mine. We look alike, more so as I get older. Like my father, I love
the road show, packing a bag, heading off somewhere or nowhere,
traveling light, never looking back over my shoulder. All three of
Cy's children, my brothers and I, have the rhythm of the road
throbbing in our inner ears, seductive and disorienting if we have
to stay in one place for long.

Recently, a friend pointed out to me something obvious I had
not realized and found mildly clinical. The daughter of the man
with a pipe organ in his throat, a voice that filled me with awe and
thrilled audiences, I gravitate toward men with deep, resonant
voices. The last time I spoke to him, I knew Cy was dying because
his voice on the phone was thin, the cancer having attacked his
vocal cords, and the voice was the man. Without it, there would
have been no Cy Taillon, no outpouring of tributes when he died,
no Dean of Rodeo—a sport that grew more respectable as my father
did—championing it articulately, insisting that cowboys were
professional athletes instead of hell-raising gypsies.

Our problem with each other was that I loved the hell-raising gypsy who had disappeared, as the years went by, behind reputation and money, the stability of his second marriage and his increasingly John Wayne–like views of how the world should work.

He thought men should be manly, in the traditional Western mold. Women should be their better halves, a role my mother found less than congenial. Male children should call their fathers "sir" and toe the line like West Point cadets. Daughters should defer to them, in matters of politics, religion and what to order from a Chinese menu. Their hair ought to curl.

I became respectable too, though I never deferred to Cy about much of anything, but like him, and like my mother, I prefer the night lights and the bright lights to the daylight, moving restlessly down the road to staying put. It's hereditary, I excuse myself, and fight the pull of the road, the cowboy bars and the signs I pass driving across California, going to visit a friend or carry out a writing assignment: "Oakhurst Rodeo, Saturday and Sunday."

That's going to be a good one, I think. Rowdy and dusty. No sixty-thousand-dollar-a-year All-American saddle-bronc riders. No NBC television cameras. Instead, heat and beer and animal smells, and cowboys from miles around convening in a small town to ride their hearts out and the seats of their pants off. I grip the wheel and keep going only because whoever is announcing, it won't be my father, and unless it's Terry, who says it can't be done, no one will ever preside over the crow's nest with the same style and presence.

Rodeo goes on, better attended and more popular all the time. My brothers' lives go on, and mine does, and through us, our father's name; it's still difficult to pay for a drink, in a Western bar, if your last name is or once was Taillon. But when the Miles City *Star* headlined its editorial: "The Voice of the Bucking Horse Sale is Stilled," it marked not only the end of a man but the end of an era.

Rodeo won't have another senior statesman. Popular mythology aside, there aren't that many gentleman cowboys, perhaps because the gentleman part rubs against the grain, and though some of them are good at what they do, the announcers who now travel my father's old routes aren't in his one-man category. They lack his showmanship and his patrician style.

In Sparks, Nevada, on my way home from Montana, I watched

the movie *The Electric Horseman* on television in my air-conditioned motel room, still suspended between Miles City and San Francisco, my old life and the one I lead now. I'd seen it before, but this time it stirred me, with its elegiac theme of a West once wild and now paved over, once free-spirited and now tame.

Sunny, the broken-down cowboy hero, was reminiscing about his days as a rodeo rider and about Clark Wembley, an announcer with a "voice like runnin' molasses." He made the cowboys, winners and losers, feel special, Sunny says. He encouraged them.

Clark Wembley was Cy Taillon, I knew, and I remembered one of my father's surefire crowd pleasers, a line that rumbled out from the booth over big- and small-town arenas and was followed, after a still moment, by thunderous noise. "Ladies and gentlemen, this cowboy's only pay this afternoon is your applause."

Though the crowd had heard this staple of his repertory a hundred times, and so had I, it always brought us to our feet clapping until our hands ached.

Cy and Pat Taillon in the early years of their marriage

ONE

When they were young, my parents believed they were indestructible, so fast and flashy nothing could touch them. Cy was a lady-killer, a small, natty man whose riverboat-gambler good looks struck women down like lightning bolts. My mother, the former Patricia Montgomery, was a vaudeville dancer, the star of the St. Louis Municipal Opera in the late twenties. When she married Cy, she turned trick rider in the rodeo equivalent of halftime shows. You can take the girl out of show biz, but you cannot take a little girl from Little Rock, or Paragould, which is close enough, and turn her into a house pet.

At least not Pat, with her performer's ego, her longing to shine. Tiny-waisted and white-skinned, her black hair slicked to her cheekbones in sculptured spit curls, she was Cy's equal in recklessness, matching him drink for drink, seduction for seduction, irrational impulse for irrational impulse. Together they shot off sparks and left behind scorched earth, and if they ever thought about how their travels might end, they didn't waste much time on sober reappraisal.

They had more pressing concerns, the main one how to get to the next town with little money, a child and hangovers. My father's schedule took him from Butte, Montana, to Salt Lake City, Utah, from Puyallup, Washington, to Baton Rouge, Louisiana, and sometimes the travel time was a couple of days. We lived in a 1937 blue Packard, spending endless, viciously hot days in it going from Canada to New Mexico and back up to Wyoming, Utah and Idaho—wherever there were rodeos. We slept in that car, ate breakfast, lunch and dinner in it, sang along with the Sons of the Pioneers in it, quarreled in it. My parents must have made love in it, when I was asleep and the Packard parked behind the bleachers in some small-town fairground, waiting for daylight and the rodeo. Between them, there was a strong erotic pull. They walked with their hips touching and had flaming fights over each other's real and imagined flirtations.

Raised on a North Dakota farm, one of nine children of a French Canadian family, Cy had been a law student, a self-taught musician who led dance bands and played in movie-theater pit orchestras, a boxer and a radio personality in Billings and Salt Lake City. In both towns, he was a celebrity, known as "The Singing Announcer" because until a tonsillectomy put an end to this facet of his career, he sang with his bands.

The huge leather scrapbooks he kept all his life document some of these successes; but he claimed triumphs in everything he did, telling a writer for a trade paper called *Hoofs and Horns*, early in his rodeo career, that he'd won a Golden Gloves championship when he was boxing and given a recital at Carnegie Hall as a child prodigy violinist.

How much of that interview is true, I don't know, nor do I think Cy did. For much of his life, he was engaged in the game of inventing himself—adding to what was true what was desirable, stirring counterclockwise and serving up the mix. He must have swallowed much of it himself.

What is fact is that after leaving law school with a theatrical troupe, he ended up, in his early twenties, in Great Falls, where he became a radio announcer and moonlighted as a musician. His hillbilly band, reported the Great Falls *Tribune*, drew 14,600 letters to the local radio station in six and a half weeks. This was roughly half the population of Great Falls at the time. It must have been a letter-writing town.

After two months in St. Paul, Minnesota, as "announcer and entertainer," Cy came back to Great Falls, and in 1929 was leading a trio during the dinner hour at the Hotel Rainbow and picking up other band jobs around town. "The Green Mill gardens, dinner and dancing resort on the paved extension of Second Avenue North, will be formally opened tonight. Eddie Stamy will be director of the orchestra that will play for at least four dances a week. Cy Taillon, Minneapolis, who handles the drums, violin, bells, piano, and most anything else, is charged with providing the sweet numbers."

"Cy Taillon and his orchestra will entertain you again at the Crystal Ballroom . . . Featuring 'The Crystal Ballroom Red Jackets.' "

"Tree Claim Park presents Cy Taillon and his 'Rocky Mountaineers.' Master of Ceremonies, Waddie Ginger, Admission 50 cents."

To the list of instruments he played, another ad for a resort added xylophone, banjo and "relatively smaller string instruments."

The woman who became Cy's second wife got her first glimpse of him during those days. She was a schoolgirl. He was playing one of the twin pianos in the window of a music store. Their eyes met, she told me, and it was Romeo and Juliet, only more intense. If my mother got in their way for twelve years, that was only because Dorothy was fourteen at the time. My father also had his hands full with other women.

A personal archivist, Cy kept copies of every letter he ever wrote, including one to the city attorney of Great Falls in those years. A woman was harassing him, he complained, accusing him of being the third party in a "spiritual triangle" and fathering her three children by remote control. "Further proof she is hopelessly irrational," he wrote, "is her obsession that I have money."

In my teens, I met a woman who knew Cy in Great Falls. "He was the most beautiful man who ever lived," she said. "You don't look very much like him."

She wasn't rude so much as disappointed. I offered to say hello to him for her.

"He wouldn't remember me. There were too many of us. I'll tell you what, though, say hello for the Willis sisters and let him wonder which one."

The student's pilot license Cy took out in 1933 lists his age as

*Cy in the mid-1940's, at the time he was doubling for
Robert Taylor*

twenty-five, weight 139 pounds, height five feet seven and three-
quarters inches, hair black and eyes gray-green. It doesn't describe
the movie-star handsomeness of his regular features, his olive skin,
his wavy black hair and those eyes—as slate green as the ocean, and
when he was angry, as cold.

He looked enough like Robert Taylor to double for him, later,
in the riding scenes of the movie *Billy the Kid.*

Rodeo stock producer Leo Cremer tapped him for the crow's
nest in the early thirties. Cy left radio for what he said was a three
months' leave and never went back. Cremer was famous for his Brahma bulls, whose average weight was three-quarters of a ton: Black
Devil, Yellow Jacket, Deer Face, Tornado, Joe Louis, Dynamite.
He also had good instincts when he signed my father, despite Cy's
reputation as a hard drinker and man-about-town.

Because he'd been attracted to it since his childhood, "Roman riding" the horses on the family farm, Cy was a natural for rodeo. He'd mainly swallowed a lot of dust. After he broke a shoulder, he gave up any ambition to be another Casey Tibbs.

He had cards printed, giving his address as the Mint Cafe, Great Falls, and offering "a New Technique in Rodeo Announcing."

A rodeo announcer keeps up a running commentary on the cowboys and the way they fare in the events, calf roping, Brahma-bull riding, bareback and saddle-bronc riding and, more recently, team roping. Cy was the best, a showman who could play a crowd the way he played stringed instruments, by instinct and with perfect pitch. At the piano, he held to the theory that the more keys you used, the better you played. At the mike, he also used the equivalent of all the pedals. "Ladies and gentlemen, this next waddie broke his wrist and three ribs down in Abilene a few weeks ago, and now he's back in competition. That's called courage in my book. Tiny Rios out of Tulsa, Oklahoma, on a mean hunk of horseflesh called Son of Satan. . . . Let's give him a little encouragement."

From his law school days, when he won prizes in debate, he had a sophisticated vocabulary. He used it, never talking down to his audience of cowboys, stock producers and their wives, ranchers and rodeo-loving kids. Nor did he often forget a cowboy's name, or where he came from, or how he fared in previous rodeos, no matter how chronic a loser the cowboy. So they loved him, even when he borrowed their prize money or their wives. He always paid the money back, and the wives straggled home, moony but unrepentant, on their own.

The reviews began to come in early. Cy never got a bad one, any more than he ever took an unflattering photograph, or if there were any, they never wound up in his scrapbooks, a researcher's nightmare because he clipped articles without the name of the newspaper or magazine and frequently without the date. Sometimes he clipped only the paragraphs that mentioned his name, which he underlined. The articles describe him as silver-voiced, golden-voiced, gold-and-silver-voiced, crystal-voiced, honey-voiced. They talk about his clear, bell-like voice. They run out of adjectives and call him the Voice.

In them, he's also spare, handsome and hard as nails; lean, wiry and a natty dresser; suave and dapper; the man who knows rodeo; the possessor of an encyclopedic memory. Said one writer, consigned to anonymity by my father's clipping methods, "Taillon keeps the show going like a golf ball swatted down a concrete highway."

Rodeo was used to announcers who treated the sport as a Wild West show, part vaudeville, part circus. Cy dignified it, with his ten-dollar words, his impeccably tailored, expensive suits and his insistence that the cowboys were professional athletes. When he intoned "Ladies and gentlemen," women became ladies and men became gentlemen; the silver-tongued devil in the announcer's box, as often as not a rickety structure over the chutes and open to the rain, spoke with unmistakable authority. In a world where pretending to be an insider earns the outsider dismissal faintly underlined with menace, he counted as a working cowboy, though he earned his living with his mouth rather than his muscle.

Like the contestants, he lived from rodeo to rodeo, making just enough money to keep us in gas and hamburgers. He worked in all weather: heat, cold, freak rainstorms that turned arenas into mudholes. If he had extra money, everybody drank, and when we rented a room in a motor court, a luxury, cowboys bunked on the floor with their saddles for pillows. Despite his slight frame, he never hesitated about piling in when there was a fight; you had to get through him to get to somebody bigger, and because he was light on his feet and fast with his fists, few made it. Someone wading into my father also had to take on my mother, not one to sit on the sidelines letting out ladylike cries of dismay. A hundred-pound woman can do substantial damage with teeth, fingernails and a high-heeled shoe, and Pat had an advantage going in. No man would hit her back, though she was swearing ripely and trying to maim him, because no self-respecting Western man hits a lady.

The bars were my parents' living rooms. We spent our nights in them, our mornings in the Packard or a motor court—with Cy and Pat sleeping off their headaches and begging me to stop that goddamn humming—and our afternoons at the Black Hills Round-up or the Snake River Stampede, rodeos that blur into one.

A newspaper photo of the Taillon family "at home" in a Colorado motel, 1937

Pat sat in the bleachers, if she wasn't trick riding. I sat in the crow's nest with Cy, sometimes announcing the Grand Entry or the national anthem for him or testing the p.a. system. "One two three four, testing testing testing." I wanted to be a movie star. Cy said you had to start somewhere.

The high point of those afternoons, for me, was when Cy played straight man for the rodeo clowns, who sometimes railed at him because he wouldn't allow off-color material, the crude jokes that were a staple. Not present just to entertain, the clowns also divert the bulls or horses when a rider is down. The cowboys and the crowd love and respect them. So did I, and when my father bantered with them from the stand, he took on added luster.

Pinky Gist and his two mules, Mickey and Freckles, George Mills, John Lindsay, the great Emmett Kelly and a dozen others—sad-faced men in baggy pants, absurdly long shoes and long underwear, out in the arena, and my father aiding and abetting them:

"Eddie, there are ladies present here today. Would you mind pulling up your pants?"

"Sure, Cy." Eddie did a flawless double take, pulled his pants up and doffed his porkpie hat to my father. When he lifted the hat, his pants fell down again, revealing long johns with a trapdoor.

"I'm sorry, Cy. I was asleep in the barrel over there and a train hit me. It tore the buttons off my suspenders."

"That wasn't a train, Eddie," Cy said, kingly at the microphone. "That was a two-thousand-pound Brahma bull, and there's another one coming out of the chute right now."

Eddie screamed hoarsely, stumbled across the arena, clutched at his pants and fell over his shoes. "I wondered why I never heard the whistle."

No matter how many times I heard these routines, they never paled for me. Such is the power of early-childhood conditioning that I still love slapstick; mine is the lone voice laughing at a club act in which the comic gets hit with a pie.

I'm less taken with exhibition roping. The great trick-rope artist on the circuit was Monty Montana, a handsome man who could do anything with a rope, including roping Cy Taillon's daughter. On my father's command, I pretended to be a calf; bolted through a string barrier and into the arena; ran like mad until Monty lassoed me, ran down his rope, threw me and tied me. He never hurt me. The crowd loved it. I hated it.

Not to be upstaged, Pat sometimes followed with her breakneck trick riding—headstands at the gallop, vaulting to the ground from a standing position in the saddle. She was so fearless that the cowboys gathered at the fence to watch her, wondering if this would be the night Cy's crazy wife killed herself.

I still have part of her trick-riding costume, a red Spanish bolero with white scrollwork, silver spurs with tooled-leather straps and canted-heel boots. The full-sleeved white satin shirt disappeared, as did the high-waisted red pants that would fit a twelve-year-old boy. Pat's life in those years is recorded in a few bits of her rodeo wardrobe, her own mutilated scrapbook, in which she also obliterated the supporting cast, and not much else.

Constants from those countless rodeos: the smell of sweat and horses that rose out of the open stalls, just below the booth; the fine dust that floated over the arena, powdering evenly cowboys, animals, the crowd, my father's suit and his pointy-toed boots; the haze of cigarette smoke over the stands; the whinnying of horses, the bawling of calves and howling of dogs, left in pickup trucks out in the parking lot.

Always present too were the high voices of women, wives and girlfriends and rodeo groupies, the "buckle bunnies" who were, and are still, the wives' natural enemies. They set the standards of female dress, with their starched curls and their pinkish pancake makeup, ending in a line at the chin. The buckle bunnies wore tight frontier pants and tooled-leather belts, into which they tucked their nailhead-studded shirts. One who was always around, and whom I admired, had a belt with beads spelling out her name, just above her neat rump: "Bonnee."

As for the wives, they were a tight-knit and wary bunch, sitting in the stands afternoon and night, watching their husbands compete and watching the single women through the smoke from their cigarettes. Those that had children left them sleeping in the trailers, and protected their primary interests. Cowboys then, and cowboys now, bear watching.

If the rodeo was in some two-dog town, we might be there for only one daytime and one evening performance, and then it was back on the road again, with a tour of the local bars in between. These had a certain classic similarity—a jukebox playing cowboy songs about lost love and lost illusions, beer signs with neon waterfalls and on the wall the head of a deer with brown glass eyes.

Such bars did not bother to throw kids out, and so we played the pinball machines, or listened to the bragging and the laughter, or put our heads down on the table, among the shot glasses and beer bottles, and slept. Because slot machines were legal in Montana and Nevada, I liked the bars there best; they weren't legal for children, but who was watching? In Helena, Montana, with money I pried loose from my mother by practiced nagging, I won a jackpot. The quarters poured through my hands and onto the floor, a silver river of money.

No one would have thrown me out of the bars whatever I did,

Cyra in cowboy gear at about age two

because I was Cy Taillon's daughter, his namesake, a miniature version of Cy in my own hand-made boots and my Stetson.

Bartenders served my ginger ale with a cherry in it. Cowboys asked me to dance to the jukebox, and asked Pat if she knew my father had himself another little gal. Expansive on bourbon, Cy sat me on the bar and had me sing "Mexicali Rose." I have no voice, and hadn't then, but what I lacked in musicality, I made up for in volume. I could also imitate my father at the mike, booming out: "The only pay this cowboy is going to get tonight . . ." and other crowd pleasers.

Not only did rodeo people live like gypsies, traveling in an informal caravan from town to town; my father and I looked like gyp-sies, both dark-skinned to start with and tanned by the sun pound-ing down on us, both with dark hair and high cheekbones. Mine softened as I grew older. Cy's became more pronounced, until, just before he died, the flesh receded from the bone. Once, when I was ten, and he and I were having lunch in the Florence Hotel in Mis-soula, Montana, a woman asked to take a snapshot of us. She was from out of town, she said, and we were the first Indians she'd ever seen. We posed for her in front of the Florence's corny Indian mu-rals, palms raised in the B movie "how" sign.

All of which I took for granted, when our family lived on the road, as the way everyone lived, though a social worker might have taken a dim view of it and I already knew at least one person who did. It was normal to have a dapper, charming father whose public

An early publicity photo of Pat

self bore little resemblance to the private Cy, the one who drank too much and flared into an alcohol-fueled temper. It was normal to have a trick-riding, ex-chorus-girl mother who still did dancer's limbering-up exercises every morning, sinking into splits and sitting on the floor spraddle-legged, bending her head first to one knee and then to the other. "You better stay in shape when you grow up," she told me as I watched, "because a woman's looks are all she's got."

It was normal to spend days and nights at the rodeo, listening to Cy's molasses voice and the voices of the cowboys, jawing, swearing and bantering with each other, smelling leather, calves in their pens and horse manure; to sit high above the bleachers in the announcer's stand and all but melt with love and pride when, on cold nights, Cy took his jacket off and put it around me.

It wasn't just normal to live in a Packard, it was classy. A Packard was still a classy car when it was ankle deep in hamburger wrappers. Some rodeo people pulled trailers and thus had the equivalent of houses, but most drove pickups or the kind of cars which, if they were horses, would have been taken off and shot.

I also believed then that Pat would stay spirited and taut-bodied forever, like a young racehorse, and that my father, whenever he wanted to, could make himself invisible. He told me that he could, but not when anybody was watching, and in the somewhat deflected way he always told the truth, he was telling it then.

T W O

A few blocks from my San Francisco apartment, a shop sells high-fashion cowboy boots. Custom-ordered from Texas, in lizard, they cost $1,500. The same shop sells stovepipe jeans to tuck into the boots, sterling and turquoise belt buckles and Ralph Lauren's idea of Western wear.

The shop thrives, though there are no cowboys here, and so do similar shops in Beverly Hills, where on quaintly named Rodeo Drive, one sees pencil-hipped, forever blond TV producers in cowboy regalia, coke spoons dangling from the gold chains around their necks.

The West has been reinterpreted by Clint Eastwood, and nothing is more chic on the hills of San Francisco than a pickup truck. But I worry. Does anyone tell the rhinestone cowboys they'll never get the look right until they have broken every major bone in their bodies? That if they wear needle-toed cowboy boots for long, they'll soon have feet as misshapen as a ballerina's, corn-ridden appendages that look like tubers and hurt like hell when the boots come off? That real cowboys don't wear tinted aviator glasses; they either disappear behind ink-black lenses or squint into the sun through eyes red as pickup-truck taillights?

Does anyone warn the owner of a creamy new Stetson that throwing a cowboy hat on the bed is bad luck? The next bronc will throw you on the same shoulder you broke competing in the bareback event in Cheyenne. Your wife will get tired of watching soap operas on TV, in the motel, while you're being stuck together with steel pins again, and leave you, taking the kids, the truck and Bob, your Aussie dog. Your creditors will close in; many broken-down bronc riders have few other finely honed skills except spitting for distance.

Or so it was once. Now some cowboys on the circuit are MIT graduates or alumni of two years in Nepal with the Peace Corps. A few are black, finally staking out their claim on what has until recently been an all-white segment of mythic America. San Francisco has a gay rodeo, though it's not sanctioned by the Professional Rodeo Cowboys Association, and though one brings up the subject in, say, the Cowboys Bar in Great Falls and then backs slowly, slowly out the door.

When Cy started out on the circuit, riders were mostly farm boys like himself, aspiring cowboys who harassed the horses on the family spread until they got their big break at Frontier Days in Fargo, or Waco, or Mandan. Some of them were fifteen but lied and said they were eighteen, some were veterans of thirty-five so full of steel by then you could pick them up with a magnet. Young or old, after a few lifetimes passed in seconds on the backs of horses named Powder River or Tailspin Terror, they walked like arthritic old men. Then as now, a few died. "Don't worry about it if the ambulance pulls out of the fairgrounds and the siren is going," Cy told me. "You start your worrying when they don't bother with the siren."

Though rodeo claims a good safety record, compared with other sports and considering the number of participants in it, injuries tend to be impressive. Horses roll on the riders they've bucked off, crushing ribs. To drive their point home, they trample them. Careering around the ring, when a rider is down, a bronc kicks with the force of a heavy-gauge shotgun.

Brahma bulls not only gore their fallen riders but have a knack for finding the soft flesh of the groin.

You can get hurt before you even get out of the chute, trying to get a saddle on a bronc that crushes your leg against the chute wall as easily as bending a straw.

Compared with cowboys, pro football players, in their helmets and padding, are at no more physical risk than chess players. So routine are injuries no one mentions the trivial, the cracked ribs and broken collarbones, and the riders don't cater to them: when my brother Terry was thrown and got his teeth rammed through his lower lip years ago, Tommy mopped up the worst of the blood, packed Terry's lip with ice and pushed his face back into something resembling a human face. Terry got on his next horse and rode.

Children are taught to be stoic before they're taught to feed themselves. Get your finger slammed in a car door at the fairgrounds and an embarrassed parent will swoop down on you. "For heaven's sake, will you stop that bawlin'! You can't get yourself in a lather over every whipstitch."

None of which matters, eternally taped ribs or wives clean out of patience, if you love the road. Cy loved it because he was fiercely independent; he'd sooner starve, he said, than work for somebody else. Pat loved it because it led away from Paragould, Arkansas, and poverty. I loved it because it was the life I knew. By my third birthday, I had logged 150,000 miles, occasion for an AP wirephoto captioned: "She Sees America."

It is inaccurate to say we saw America. What we saw was the western half of the country, the straight highways that shimmer in the heat across Nevada and Utah, the small-town fairgrounds where the rodeo was usually part of a country fair or paired up with a carnival. We saw hundreds of cafes called the Stockman's, the Wagon Wheel or the Gold Nugget, all of them serving mashed potatoes with an ice-cream scoop and offering you your choice of dessert, orange sherbet or orange sherbet. We saw hundreds of bars that still set the standard, for me, of a decent place to buy a bourbon-and-branch (in Montana, called a whiskey ditch).

A bar should be cool and dark, a cave hollowed out of the heat, and it should have a rail, ideally brass, where you can hook your boot heel, the better to settle in and ponder life. The bartender should greet you with "How're you folks today?" and then leave you alone; or if he knows you from other Frontier Days, "Cy, you old son-of-a-gun, how you been keepin'?"

No fake stained glass, no Perrier, and if the bar serves food, no friendly-puppy waiters crying, "Hi! My name is Roger. I'm your serving person tonight."

A decent bar will produce a napkin for a lady, one with cheerfully crass cartoons on it, possibly the only napkin in the place. The cartoons will feature steatopygic women wearing no underpants and surprised by a high wind. Caption: "Just Bummin' Around."

There should be the summer smell of beer sprinkled with salt, the pleasant reek of sour mash bourbon, a rack with Planters peanuts in bags you have to rip open with your teeth, another rack with nail clippers and one with key chains: "Souvenir of Puyallup, Washington." A waitress is optional, but if there is one, her name should be Velma.

Walk out of such a bar on a hot day, into the glare of the street, open the doors of your car, with its melting tires, and you'll get an idea of what it's like to burn in hell.

These are some of the big-time rodeos Cy announced year after year: the Rodeo de Santa Fe, Santa Fe, New Mexico; the Snake River Stampede, Nampa, Idaho; the Pike's Peak or Bust Rodeo, Colorado Springs, Colorado; the Southwestern Exposition and Rodeo, Fort Worth, Texas; the Canadian Western Stock Show and Rodeo, Edmonton, Alberta. The small-time ones all took place, in my memory, in the same smoldering town with a ratty arena and a bar called The Last Roundup.

From the Black Hills Roundup in Belle Fourche, South Dakota, most years, we went to Cavalier, North Dakota, just across the border from Manitoba, and the farm where my father grew up. His father, Eli Taillon, and his mother, the first white child to be born in Pembina County and the former Philomine Dumas, still lived there. Born in 1870, she lived to be eighty-seven and left twenty-one great-grandchildren. Until my generation, it was a good Catholic family.

A tiny woman, Grandma Taillon still made her own lye soap in a boiling kettle in the yard; refused to "hook up to the electricity," so that the farmhouse, at night, swam in the shadows cast by kerosene lamps; killed chickens with fearsome skill. Preparing for Sunday dinner, she grabbed a hen by the neck and swung it in circles until its neck and its will to live gave out. Shrieks and the beating

he "golden-voiced" Cy at the mike

of wings and the figure of my grandmother, upright and still except for her implacably whirring arm. I tried to behave myself at her house.

Of Cy's nine brothers and sisters, all but two had left the farm and its backbreaking days. Uncle Henry worked it, and Aunt Ida, ageless in her great bulk, presided over the kitchen. A sea beast thrown up on land, Ida wore dresses the size of tents, made of printed sacking, and bedroom slippers with the tops of the toes cut out. Though she made shy overtures to me, I thought of her as made of the same dough as the bread she baked every day, soft, white and repulsive, and hurt her feelings by whining for store bread instead. Child of the truck stops, I hated farm food, especially those all too fresh chickens, and longed for french fries cooked in rancid grease.

We never stayed in Cavalier more than a few days. Pat was bored before the car came to a stop in front of the house, feeling correctly that she was out of place there. A woman who never could master the swivel-handled potato peeler, she had nothing to contribute in the way of usefulness, and no one called on her to rattle out a barrage of tap steps or do splits up a wall. Nor did anyone else on the farm own a fitted cosmetics case or wear white lounging pajamas. Grandma Taillon and Ida knew nothing about either lip brushes or lounging.

"Go talk to Ida, damn it," Cy said when Pat complained. She and I exchanged horrified looks.

Thirty years later I became curious about Ida, but she was dead and it was too late to ask her why she never left home, never married, spent her own eighty-seven years at the pump handle and over the wood stove. I am left with her obituary and what it reveals about her lifetime of duty and hard work: charter member of the Tongue River Homemakers Club; 4-H leader; member of the Tongue River Sewing Circle, the American Legion Auxiliary, the Pembina County Pioneer Daughters, St. Bridget's Catholic Church and its Altar Society.

A patchwork quilt she made for us tells the same plain tale. With twenty varieties of fancy stitch, none repeated in the whole, the quilt is the work of a woman who loved her needle. But it's meant for utility, not beauty. The odd-shaped pieces of fabric are homely, cut from the sleeve of a worn cotton work shirt, a pair of whipcord pants or a flannel shirt. How Ida must have longed to cut just one sleeve off one of my mother's silk blouses or one cuff off her bell-bottomed satin pants, to feel the slippery stuff under her needle.

Pat and I were both outsiders on the farm because the language spoken there was mostly Canadian French. Cy spoke it. We neither spoke nor understood it. Much of the time, during those visits, Cy was hidden away, helping my grandmother take care of his father.

Grandfather Taillon was nearly deaf. All communication with him took place by shouting in French, and since he rarely came out of his downstairs room, from which there issued forth bellows and thumps, I thought he was mad. In several visits to Elm Croft, the farm's name, I saw him only a few times, a gaunt old man with Cy's strong cheekbones, yellowed gray hair and hawk's eyes. Though he spoke to me kindly, if unintelligibly, Cy quickly took him back to his room, seeming embarrassed by him and shooing him down the dark hall with what sounded like threats and invective. I think he must have wanted me to think of my grandfather as a gentleman landowner instead of a wild-looking old man, an apparition in long underwear.

Always, Cy's pattern was to treat things as grander than they were, as if the reality would compromise him. When he made me a gift of his ordinary violin many years later—or rather lent it to me, because he soon took it back—he insisted that it was a Stradivarius.

Nonetheless, he loved Elm Croft and the Red River valley in which it was situated, the flat, loamy fields surrounded by woods, the swimming hole with its heart-stopping rope swing and the farm animals, especially the horses.

Mechanization came late to the farm, and its horses were working animals that pulled threshers and bundle wagons for the haying. When Cy was growing up they also pulled the buggy, the light cutter, the sleigh and the Taillon brothers, who skied the frozen ditches in the winter, towed along at bone-rattling speed behind Old Ned, Cy's favorite. Ned, he wrote in an article called "Once a Farm Boy," was a roan weighing 1,250 pounds, "of uncertain lineage, with some Percheron blood."

In the same piece, he writes about the life of the place, the grueling hard work, the rosary his mother recited every night in French, with the family and the neighbors kneeling around her, and the joys of informal evening musicales. The family had its own orchestra of self-taught musicians, with all the children playing instruments—"fiddles, guitars, piano, xylophone, auto-harp, trumpet and drums"—except for Ida. She never learned to play, Cy notes, because she was too burdened with cooking and housekeeping chores.

With the other Taillon boys, he fished in the neighboring streams, hunted in the woods for bush rabbits, partridges and coyotes and ice-skated on the frozen Tongue River in the winters, when the temperatures dropped as low as sixty below zero. He played his fiddle and acted as a caller for square dances in farmhouses "where the musicians would usually stand in a doorway between two rooms filled with sweating and stomping revelers."

Elm Croft couldn't hold him. How can you keep a boy like Cy down on the farm after he's seen Fargo? But it formed him, so that the farm boy remained even when a reporter was describing him as "blasé and full of adjectives as a circus advance man." Resplendent in a satin Western shirt, boots and cowboy hat, on one of those visits he once took me out to the barn, where a colt had just been born. He had me smell its breath. "Sweet as new hay," he said. "Sweet as a baby's."

Yet he seemed happy to have left the place when we were back on the road again, with the world framed by the windshield. Shaking the dust of Cavalier off his feet, Cy merely traded it for different dust, but for him the dust of the rodeo arena was like greasepaint for actors. It had seeped through his skin; he missed it painfully when we were away long. In the winters, when there were no rodeos, he drank with more determination, got into more trouble—the infinite varieties of it having to do with money and women—and was dangerous to be near, volatile and looking for a fight. His restlessness was that of a bucking horse in the chute. My mother's mood wasn't markedly better.

A former chanteuse, as well as the tap-dancing sensation of St. Louis, Pat had a throaty contralto voice. She had no range at all but could have turned "Onward, Christian Soldiers" into a torch song. I remember her singing "Don't Fence Me In" along with the radio. "Let me ride thru the wide-open country that I love . . . Don't fence me in."

It could have been their theme song. I made the back seat of the car into a nest and filled it full of clothes, books, blankets and my collections: matchbooks, bar napkins, rodeo programs and swizzle sticks. They left laundry in towns all over the circuit because they were too impatient to wait for it to be ready; threw the windows and the door open when we slept in motor court cabins, to let in fresh air and cowboys looking for a place to bunk; seemed to think walls and a ceiling would cave in and smother them; rarely made it all the way through a movie. "Come on, now." My mother dragged me up the aisle, still riveted to Yvonne De Carlo, and out of the theater. "I can't stand to stay cooped up in this place."

Somebody usually picked up the laundry anyway, settled our bar bill and paid off the irate owner of the Drop Inn when we left his motor court at dawn, ahead of schedule and the bill. Film crews have retinues who follow them on location, sweeping up rubble and settling damage claims. Cy and Pat attracted a retinue of their own, loners drawn to them as a glamorous couple and admirers who saw themselves reflected in their high shine.

It was a thankless job, in their case. They didn't really care about bills and laundry or about orderly lives. But for the most patient of the loners, it eventually paid off.

Meanwhile we rolled along in the Packard, hell-bent for Dallas, Fort Worth, Baton Rouge and Alabama City. We had our classy car, and gas money. We could sing three-part harmony to "San Antonio Rose." We had the Brahma bull by the tail.

THREE

My mother once told a friend why she left Paragould, Arkansas. "I got tired of grits." Paragould is poultry-raising country. Cold in the winters, it swelters in the summertime. A few years ago, a Deep South heat wave killed off the chickens by the thousands. An Arkansas cousin wrote that they were "keeling right over, already roasted," while in Little Rock, nearby, that same summer, one man shot and killed another over holes made in a plastic wading pool.

At sixteen, Nedra Ann Montgomery fled the climate and the cuisine and departed Arkansas for St. Louis, where she changed her name to Patricia. "Pat Montgomery" would look better on a marquee. Her mother, Minnie Mae, had died of tuberculosis at forty-five, leaving "Baby Sister" in the care of her older sisters, Lucille, Hester, Cleo and Ila Mae. A brother, Rudolph, was in reform school. Their father, Brown Montgomery, was the town drunk and, according to another cousin, Clifton, "mean as a weasel."

Brown was the engineer for the city waterworks. Widowed, he spent his time drinking corn whiskey, tending the boiler at the Paragould power plant and shooting at anything that moved, including Clifton. As a child, Clifton was dispatched to fetch Brown home for Sunday dinner. He remembers with clarity a discussion between them punctuated with blasts from a 12-gauge shotgun.

Because Brown had once been a railroad man, his children could ride the trains on free passes. Nedra Ann got on the train in Paragould, with no one's permission, no profession and no prospects, and got off in St. Louis reborn as Pat Montgomery, dancer and singer; or, as she preferred to call herself, "soubrette."

The next sister up the line, Ila Mae, never forgave her. "Oh no, Baby Sister couldn't settle for honest work as a fry cook."

My mother had always danced, Ila Mae told me in our last conversation before she died. My aunt made it clear she hadn't changed her views on the subject of life upon the stage. "She used to get on an old box, or a tub, or anything she could, and just dance her head off. And she'd say, 'Someday they're going to have to pay to see me.' My brother would laugh, and she'd say, 'Gimme some pennies.' Well, they didn't have one penny between them, you know. But there she was, dancing on some old box out in the backyard like a fool."

Pat got a job modeling for a department store and found work at night as a chorus girl in a less prestigious theater across the street from St. Louis's finest, the Fox. But she had lean times at first, and I suppose she lived then the way poor girls like her have always lived when they came to the city, that she found a man, or men, to serve as her protector while she took her bearings. Souvenirs of her St. Louis days were still among the thin rag endings of her personal possessions thirty years later: a carnelian dinner ring hidden in the back of a drawer, a note reading "After the show, I sure do hate to wait!," a papery pressed gardenia.

Whatever she found in St. Louis, and despite Ila Mae's having followed her there to keep a custodial eye upon her, she didn't go home to Paragould for years, not until she could go back in style. Nor did she attend her father's funeral when he died, widely unmourned. Brown had remarried. His sixteen-year-old second wife had buck teeth. Brown tormented her by telling everyone that Lily could eat an apple through a knothole.

Because Pat was five feet two, she was a "pony," the shortest dancer in a chorus line and the one positioned at the end. She caught the attention of the Fox Theater management anyway and soon moved across the street to its glittering variety show. Vaudeville was flourishing in the mid-twenties. The Fox, Ila Mae recalled, was "really a high-class place, with a big orchestra pit down below, and the orchestra would rise up on a platform. They had all these gorgeous costumes, and beautiful music, and comedy, tap dancing . . ."

Soon the Fox featured Miss Pat Montgomery—"And Can She Sing and Tap!"—as female lead. Cousin Clifton, twelve years old then, rode the magic train to St. Louis, with his mother, to see my mother perform. At the end of her big solo number, the audience pelted her with bouquets. Said Clifton, remembering, "I swear, I thought it was raining roses."

In rapid order, her star on the rise, Pat auditioned as a singer with the Municipal Opera, was hired and became "specialty featured artist." She joined the Missouri Theater's Missouri Rockets— "One of the Finest, Most Versatile Choruses to Ever Set Foot Behind Footlights." She went off to New York with Ernie Young's Revue in the chorus of a production called *Rain or Shine*.

The Revue didn't dazzle New York, but my mother was there long enough to antagonize her four sisters, who thought it was time she settled down, by sending them a postcard: "Have hit the big time." The others were all sensibly married by their late teens, and all were devoted to grits. Only Ila Mae had pursued a career—as a fry cook.

Like Cy, Pat invented herself, with energy and imagination. She rapidly learned to wear stylish clothes, lost her Arkansas accent and became expert at cosmetics. When she finished working with her sable brushes, her pots and jars and hand mirror, her thin upper lip was the top half of a heart, her eyebrows two horizontal commas. Her own eyebrows, she banished, to conform to an ideal of beauty. If thine eyebrow offend thee, pluck it out.

Vain beyond common sense, she thought her size 7 feet were too large and crammed them into size 5½ shoes. I have seen her cry because they hurt so much by the end of an evening, and I have seen Cy pick her up in his arms and carry her to the Packard, wobbling on the high heels of his cowboy boots. It wouldn't have occurred to either of them that Pat could take her shoes off, not when they flattered her ankles and made her look taller, and it wouldn't have occurred to me, either. I shared my parents' highly developed sense of what is important.

Pat was so consistent about this that her scrapbook, like my father's, is a patchy record of her career. She clipped and pasted as selectively as he did and even scratched out other faces in photos. Why should she read about or look at photos of anyone but herself?

What evidence that more or less survived shows that she danced at Billy Rose's Golden Horseshoe, having moved on to conquer Chicago, as well as less glamorous nightclubs. These have names such as the Four Aces (with its Famous Four Ace Band of Rhythm) and the Golden Pumpkin, "The Most Beautiful Chinese Cafe in the World." Signing on with Ernie Young again, she played the Oriental Village at the Chicago World's Fair, where, for reasons that cannot be reconstructed, the group elected to perform something called *Spanish Nights*. The Revue also played the provinces.

A snapshot on which she wrote "My Al, Minot, North Dakota, 1931" preserves the flavor of those tours. A dusty Plymouth sits in

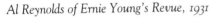

Al Reynolds of Ernie Young's Revue, 1931

Pat on the road in Helena, Montana, 1931

a field, with a line of sagging tents in the background. On the Plymouth is a placard: "Ernie Young's Productions, Featuring Al Reynolds, Chicago's Favorite Son. 50 PEOPLE!" "My Al" leans on the car, looking jaunty in a sport coat, impeccable white shirt and pale striped pants. In front of that tent city in a field, he's dressed for Ascot.

"Always kicking!" reads the caption on another snapshot, this one of my mother braced against a telephone pole in the middle of nowhere, showing off her extension. In still another, she does splits at the top of a flagpole. Caption: "Was it shaky up here? Oh boy and how!" Her good cheer seems unflappable, even when she's waving around in a high wind.

Then she met Cy Taillon, and after a twenty-four-hour courtship, married him. They must have looked at each other and instantly recognized their similarities: two peacocks in a world of mud hens.

Cy was announcing the 1931 Montana State Fair, in Great Falls. Pat was part of the featured entertainment, Ernie Young's road company. The tour was a vacation, she told reporters, before she went off to a starring engagement on Broadway. Enthralled, the Great Falls paper printed her picture, Cy's picture and the headline: "Radio Announcer Weds Revue Girl."

In St. Louis, Ila Mae got a telegram. "She didn't explain anything, just said they were married and that was it. My brother Rudy said, 'Oh my God, a radio man. They're as bad as actors. She'll never settle down, she'll dance and dance the rest of her life.' " Ila Mae wired back: "Baby Sister and Cy, Good luck."

They needed it, because as the best man at their wedding later observed, with unconcealed satisfaction, "they didn't have enough sense between them for a good plow horse."

I have said my parents attracted a retinue, people drawn to their specious glamour; they seemed to give off light, noise and gaiety, like a house in which there is a perpetual party going on, and people gravitated to them and stayed. The one who stayed longest was Roy Qualley, my father's friend and self-appointed caretaker.

Eleven years older than Cy, Roy was also from a big family and a farm, this one in Decorah, Iowa. In old photos, the farmhouse springs out of the flat expanse surrounding it like some strange out-cropping. Unsoftened by a single tree, a sprawling carpenter gothic house high off the ground on its foundation, it looks like a model made of cardboard.

Roy's grandparents immigrated from Norway, changing the spelling of their name. Kvale became Qualley. In photos, the family is unsmiling; they all have Roy's stolid, level gaze, parents and children alike looking resigned to hard work, the monotonous mid-western landscape and virtue as its own reward. While they shared little in terms of temperament, Roy and Cy shared a common background and the urge to escape from it.

Roy's nickname was Old Honest Face. It was he who paid the bar bills, extricated my hot-tempered, bantamweight father from fistfights and saw that Cy made it to the radio station most mornings. Square and stocky, already balding by the time he reached his twenties, he had delivered newspapers in Great Falls, sold encyclopedias door to door in Spokane and mined gold in the hills above Helena.

A lifelong self-improver, he clipped from a 1927 Spokane newspaper Mussolini's Efficiency Precepts:

Master your body and mind.
Concentrate on the one thing before you.
Get seven hours' sound sleep.
Never stay in bed after the instant of awakening.
Read the newspapers while dressing.
Shave: I am anti-whiskers.
Drink a glass of milk for breakfast.

The lure of gold brought Roy out West, and once, he struck it. With a partner, he hit what was reported as "an important strike of high-grade gold ore," but something went wrong and the mine and the dream got away. Undaunted, he staked out another claim and clipped another newspaper story that must have held out promise to him: "In His Prison Cell, Convict Turns Sand into Gold — The Secret of the Medieval Alchemists Rediscovered."

Ila Mae thought Cy and Roy met in some Great Falls boardinghouse. Both lived in numbers of them, old houses converted into hotels and catering to single men. She also thought Cy invested in one of Roy's mining ventures, though money, as Roy liked to say, burned a hole in Cy's pocket. He invested it mainly in goodwill. However the connection developed, they were tightly if oddly linked.

Roy worked out on barbells at the YMCA. He took business school correspondence courses and read books on nutrition and hair growth. Cy drank, caroused and still had more hair than he needed.

Roy saved every receipt. Cy was thirty-five before he had a bank account.

Roy said severely that all Cy thought you could buy with money was a good time. Cy said of Roy, "He tried to keep me on the straight and narrow path, and I did his fast living for him. He got to hear about it, and it saved him a lot of money and the wear and tear on his physique."

Theirs was a reciprocal exchange, and when my mother came along, she got Roy as part of the package, inscribing a photo of herself, wearing clinging silk and an ankle bracelet: "To Roy, the Best Pal in the World." Now Roy had not only my father to keep on the straight and narrow but also Pat, who showed a cheerful preference for the wide and convoluted.

He must have liked the amplified job duties. Like Ila Mae, Roy was a born heel snapper, one of the sheep dogs among us who like to nip at other people's ankles and herd them into line. In another throwback to early conditioning, I can recognize a heel snapper on sight, in or out of uniform, with or without brass buttons.

"Somebody has to do it," such people generally defend themselves. In this instance, Roy was right. Put two careless people together, and the damage increases disproportionately—more debts, more broken glass and more threats of lawsuits for alienation of affections. When Leo Cremer, a big, benign man known as a steady hand with horses, contracted with my father to announce rodeos for him, he tried to get my parents to stop doing their imitation of Scott and Zelda. But the life of the circuit, which Pat embraced enthusiastically, didn't help. Unlike their Rodeo Drive imitators, tall

Pat as a young chanteuse

in the saddles of their Mercedes, real rodeo cowboys aren't known for their consumption of white wine and soda.

Rocketing along from rodeo to rodeo, Pat and Cy drove the car they owned before the Packard, a Ford sedan painted yellow. Always, they posed with it in the background of snapshots, the way another couple might have posed on their front porch.

Tireless in her efforts to rehabilitate my mother, Ila Mae had moved from Arkansas to Great Falls to be near them. Now she teamed up with Roy in disapproving mightily of their lives. Perhaps because she was unofficial title holder for world's cleanest woman, she wasn't taken with their style of traveling. "You should have seen that car of theirs. It was *filthy,* and that yellow color showed up every speck of dirt. All those clothes of theirs were stuffed in the back, piled right up to the ceiling. They couldn't be bothered with suitcases, they just threw everything they owned in the back

Ila Mae at about eighteen

seat and went off. Pat drove if Cy was drunk, and she drove like a cowboy, or a maniac." To Ila Mae, the two were one and the same.

She was bitter about life in general. Her husband had run off with another woman, who caught his eye over the grave at a funeral. She'd lost her only child in infancy. There she was, working as a waitress, thirty years old and secondhand goods. Men were lustful beasts, and it didn't improve her state of mind that Baby Sister cottoned to the creatures. "Pat, or whatever you call yourself now," she wrote, in care of Rodeo Headquarters, Deer Lodge, Montana, "always remember our body is a Temple and God means for us to keep it sweet and clean. You showed it off on the stage all those years, *that's enough*."

From her account of my parents, and cousin Clifton's, I see the six years of their marriage before I was born as a frenetic silent movie—the yellow Ford smoking out of some small town, with creditors, love-stricken saddle-bronc riders and faithful Roy Qualley in pursuit; loud quarrels and impassioned reconciliations; a supporting cast of Other Women, Other Men. Pat and Cy competed in sexual conquest as they competed in everything else.

Two small people with enormous egos, they loved each other but needed the reassurance to be found in numbers, the proof that marriage hadn't dimmed their separate luster. When Cy parked Pat on the farm in North Dakota one summer, the better to cut his own wide swath on the circuit, she seduced every able-bodied man for miles. "The only thing you told me not to do," she drawled at Cy when he came back to get her, summoned by his mother, "was smoke in the barn."

Says another cousin, also visiting the farm that summer, "That girl was a living fireball."

Briefly, after this episode, my parents made an attempt at conventional domesticity. They set up a small apartment in Billings, Montana, where Pat kept house and cooked dinners Cy rarely came home at night to eat. He was flying small planes again, too restless to remain earthbound.

Pat teamed up with a male dancer and opened a dance studio. It became a huge success. But it closed a few months after it opened.

"Some jealousy developed between Cy and her business partner," Ila Mae said discreetly. "I don't remember just what it was all about." Pat gave up both the apartment and the studio and joined Cy on the road.

Ila Mae had married again, to a gentle, round-faced clothing

A newly married Ila Mae with her second husband, Wiley Gosney

salesman named Wiley Gosney, and also moved West. Their own apartment in Great Falls became my parents' mail drop and the place where they bunked when they weren't on the road.

This proved a trial for Ila Mae. She could lecture my mother about cleanliness and its proximity to godliness, and how "undies worn twice aren't very nice." The two couples could share expenses. But Cy tended to disappear for two or three days at a time, coming home when the poker game finally wound down, and docile Wiley, who stayed good-humored even when told to wash his hands ten times a day, was in Ila Mae's view too sorry for Pat and too ready with his ironed, starched handkerchief. Pat became pregnant. Ila Mae had a good reason to ask that they find a place of their own.

Unlikely candidates for parenthood, Cy and Pat made the best of it. They took two rooms in a boardinghouse, with the second for a nursery. I was born, another newsworthy event to the Great Falls *Tribune*. They started a scrapbook for me. Scrapbooks, in my family, are a way of life. You may have nothing else, but you've got your press clippings.

In two weeks, we were on the road again. Where Cy went, Pat was going, with or without a baby. Either she knew better, by now, than to send him off on his own, or he knew enough to insist that she come with him.

Soon I was big enough to be outfitted like a Western Barbie doll and had a role in their long-playing drama. I played what my mother called Little Pat and Cy called Little Cyra and my aunt called "the poor little thing."

And I had a glorious time, as unofficial mascot of the rodeo, from Canada to New Mexico, though my parents sometimes forgot momentarily that I existed. After a long night larking in the bars in Cheyenne, Wyoming, they once left me sleeping in a motor court bed, packed up and headed for the next rodeo. Seventy miles out of town, they had to turn around and go back.

"The poor little thing needs regular hours and good food & training," Ila Mae wrote, in letters that sometimes tracked us down weeks after they were written. Sometimes I stayed with her for a few weeks or a month and got all three of these things, as well as

...ra at the time she was considered the unofficial mascot of the rodeo circuit

scrubbed inhumanly clean. They held little appeal for me. Mild Wiley watched me chafe under her regime and sometimes intervened. "For Chrissake, let the kid wear her cowboy hat." He only got us both in trouble.

FOUR

"One time I came home, and here was boots and saddles and every-thing else on the sun porch, and you were in my bed, and Cy and Pat had took off again." At seventy-five, Ila Mae sounded as irate, despite the intervening years, as she must have that afternoon in 1940 or so. The problem with Baby Sister, she said, was that she'd never had proper training herself. "The older girls wouldn't let her do anything. I did it. I stood on a box and made pies."

When my mother stood on a box, she danced, and I doubt that her motherless childhood had much to do with it. No one was less suited to pie baking. On the rare occasions when we had a room with a kitchenette and Pat cooked, the food was inedible. Food didn't interest my mother. She'd have preferred to take a pill in order to stay nourished and not waste time better spent kicking up her heels.

If she sewed a button on a shirt for Cy, she stuck herself with the needle and bled on it. She was a copious bleeder.

Refusing to learn the right way to pull a cowboy's boots off for him, she faced Cy and tugged, instead of standing with her back to him and straddling his outstretched leg. He swore. Pat rocked his foot back and forth in her hands and swore back at him. When the boot came off, she hurtled across the room, caught up in the mo-mentum.

She was a soubrette, not a housewife, and if Cy sometimes forgot it, Pat never did. In our household, what mattered was style, not substance.

They were passionate about clothes, both of them. Pat had a fur coat, made of beaver tails and known as her mink, and dozens of hats that I loved to try on. She claimed that her swirling, bright dresses were made in Paris, France. On the road, in the heat, she wore high-heeled shoes that showed off her legs and wide-legged shorts. In her wardrobe, there were no pastels; she saw life, and herself, in primary colors.

So did Cy, who customarily wore satin and sateen shirts in the colors of parrot feathers, narrow-legged Western pants and the fanciest boots he could find. Straight out of bed in the morning, he pulled them on. He looked peculiar, since he slept in shorts and undershirt, but with his boots on, he was nine feet tall in his own eyes and in mine. It took me twenty years to realize my father was a small man.

Shoes hurt his feet. He owned a pair of black cowboy boots for funerals.

Not left out of all this sartorial splendor, I had my own black felt cowboy hat with white trim and a chin strap, gabardine pants and plaid shirts, neckerchiefs with silver slides and my own tooled boots, the first pair I owned a few inches long. Years later, Cy had these bronzed for me. They came back from the mail-order house that turned them into bookends with a printed card enclosed: "Baby's First Shoes."

How and if these clothes were ever paid for, I don't know. On one desperate occasion, when we needed gas and had no money, we pulled into a one-pump gas station and filled up. Coached by my parents, I used the bathroom, stayed in for a while as a diversionary tactic, then bolted out and jumped on the running board of the already moving Packard. We must not have paid for the gas, because the red-faced attendant ran after us for a short distance, yelling at us.

I suppose my mother's finery was left over from her chorus girl days, a kind of dowry. Cy must have purchased his with charm and credit.

Nor do I know how they paid for all the studio photographs they had taken, recording for posterity the latest additions to our wardrobes. Though Roy said money burned a hole in Cy's pocket, it rarely traveled that far between his hand and the bar. Pat was a two-fisted drinker. Cy was a drunk, charming and good-humored when sober, combative and cold-eyed when full of bourbon.

Their fights began to heat up. Her makeup case on her lap, Pat sat in the passenger seat of the Packard, spitting on a sponge and putting pancake makeup on her black eyes. She'd banged herself up, she told me, bumping into something in the dark.

Those fights were the private side of their lives together. Cy disappeared and reappeared, when we were anywhere as long as a few days, throwing the door of a room open late at night with a bang that woke me and set my heart racing with anticipation. They shouted at each other until Pat hurled herself at Cy like a terrier. They wrestled, lurching back and forth across the room in a parody of the way they danced, bodies locked together. Before I learned not to intervene, I wrapped myself around Cy's pant leg. He reached for his belt buckle.

Belt buckles the size of salad plates are cowboy fetishes. Gold, silver or both, they are awarded as prizes in major rodeos and put up as security for loans. When Cy took off his belt, I knew he was going to use it on my backside, but matters rarely reached that point. All he had to do to reduce me to whimpering panic was reach for the buckle.

When the fight was over and we were all in bed, I heard Cy crying. He was trying to do something, he told my mother, about his "complex."

It wasn't pride alone that kept Pat from cutting and running. She loved Cy with the kind of love that motivates kamikaze pilots. As much as they fought, whittled away at each other's egos and competed for the limelight, they took fierce pride in their respective prizes: the fireball of a woman who stood on the stage in a rainstorm of roses, the darkly handsome man other men liked and other women pursued.

They had a child, for whose affection they also competed. Behind their surface glamour, they were equally insecure. Cy still had to scratch for engagements. Pat had come home from her last tour with a dance company with her tail between her legs. Having ridden the bus nonstop from New York to Great Falls, she ended up on Ila Mae's doorstep. "Half dead, and the dirt beneath her fingernails. I said to her, just wash your hands and go to bed. She must have slept for two, three days."

Between them, they owned a car, not yet paid for, their clothes and a couple of saddles. Together they stood, however shakily, and divided they fell. So they made up their quarrels in bed, and in the morning faced the world again over a table in some coffee shop, joking with the waitress and ordering French toast for me as a signal that the good times were beginning again.

In the car, to get back in my good graces, Cy turned into an affectionate father and a good buddy again, instructing me on the finer points of rodeo: how it was the only authentically American sport. How cowboys had to be tougher than any other athletes. "Put a football player on one of Leo's bucking horses, and there wouldn't be enough left of him to send home to his poor old mother." Why Brahma-bull riders should be small. "They're like jockeys. They've got to be light, because the bigger the man, the slower the reflexes." How misguided it was of outsiders to think the sport was cruel, an attitude that rankled my father all his life.

Bucking horses were born to buck. They liked nothing better than the chance to make some cowboy wish he'd gone into selling insurance. Why weren't the bleeding hearts worried about the riders?

The silver and honey voice spoke only to me, and I forgot the night before and began to think about the next rodeo. If there was a carnival playing the same fairgrounds, Cy would toss me a long strip of free tickets. He had connections. I spent some of the best evenings of my life riding Ferris wheels.

Less happily, we might arrive in town to find "Uncle Roy" Qualley waiting for us. Working a mining claim when he wasn't traveling as a salesman, Roy wasn't in tandem with us as often anymore, but his relationship to our family confused me anyway. I knew Ila Mae was married to Wiley. I still thought of her as married to Roy. It had something to do with their parallel world views.

"Leave the baby with me if you're going to go chasing around the countryside forever," Ila Mae kept urging my parents. Her strong card was my health. I had "spells" of vomiting, was too thin, with sharp knees and sharper collarbones, and couldn't gain weight. I needed liver, spinach and homemade rolls.

Roy was shy with me and issued no edicts about my upbringing, but he doled out dimes and quarters and weeks later expressed dismay that I hadn't saved them. A penny saved was a penny earned. From little acorns mighty oaks grow. He held no brief for investing your capital in slot machines.

Aware that I had to start school soon somewhere, I was afraid Ila Mae would prevail. The last time I'd stayed with her, she'd stripped me naked on the front porch of her apartment building when I came in from the yard, so I wouldn't track dirt into the house. The phrase didn't exist then, but I still consider this child abuse.

That summer started out as another freewheeling season on the circuit. Between rodeos, to keep body and soul together, Cy announced air shows and amateur nights in small-town movie theaters, did some carnival barking—as a personal favor, he explained, to one of the carnies, who was also French Canadian—and took us to Leo Cremer's ranch in Big Timber, Montana, where we rode, fished and played poker. For a few weeks, we lived with a couple named Pearl and Earl in a Billings boardinghouse, which had a resident German shepherd and was generous with the raisins in the tapioca. When we bought a small trailer, no bigger than a pup tent, I knew the purchase meant we were prospering.

Cy told people that he had a "handle on my complex." He wasn't drinking for weeks at a time, intervals when my mother also stopped singing "Stormy Weather" endlessly, her theme song when she had a radio program in St. Louis. They were talking about settling down in Billings for part of the year; I could start school, Cy would work in radio again and Pat would open another Studio of the Dance. Cy said she might be too out of shape. Pat slid into vertical splits up the side of a door frame to prove she wasn't, one of her more startling acrobatic feats.

But she wasn't always kicking that summer, her feistiness intact but her physical vitality dimmed. Afternoons, she lay in bed with a wet washcloth on her forehead, complaining of headaches. Ila Mae rode the bus to Billings and conferred with Cy behind closed doors. The two voices rose and tangled, while I pushed my statues of horses around, in the next room, and tried to eavesdrop.

After one of these conferences, Cy stalked past me, announcing that he was on his way to get drunk. "Poor little thing," Ila Mae said, following on his heels and gathering me into her arms. For something productive to do, she took me off to the bathroom and attacked the skin on my elbows with a pumice stone.

Pat was the beauty of the five Montgomery girls, though studying her photographs, I cannot tell how much of her beauty was nature and how much art. While Ila Mae was also small, dark and vivid, her prettiness was sharp-edged, her animation born of nervous energy. She washed. She sewed, turning out the drab dresses neither my mother nor I ever wore, made of "goods" that would last longer than either of us. She put up jams and jellies, stored winter clothes in mothballs and in the spring, hung them out on clotheslines to air. She sat me down and taught me how to hem tea towels in neat little whipstitches, though I proved to be a bleeder like my mother, and though no matter how neatly I sewed, Ila Mae ripped the hems out and made me do them over again.

Idle hands were the devil's work, she said, and took on the job of my religious education, also neglected. I had to learn to love Jesus, who had died for my sins.

A picture called "The Sacred Heart" hung in Ila Mae's spare bedroom, over the bed I slept in when I visited her—Jesus with reproachful brown eyes, chest open at the sternum, and his exposed heart dripping a single drop of blood. The Sacred Heart gave me nightmares, though it was intended to inspire me to right living and piety, and I threw tantrums over sleeping in the same room with it. "About Cyra's disposition hope it has improved for she has plenty of room," noted one of Ila Mae's letters.

Doctors came to the boardinghouse, carrying black bags, attended Pat, and then drew blood samples from me. She had the headaches. I got stuck with the needles and resented it. The summer that began so promisingly was fading into confusion, tension and the misery of staying in one place for weeks at a time. Ila Mae came and went, telling me to keep my voice down, stay out from underfoot and pray for improvements of my character. God knew everything I did. *Everything.* Not a sparrow falleth, nor a child with a smart mouth on her sass her aunt.

Cy came and went, drunk as often as he was sober. Pat came

and went. Despite orders to stay in bed, she got dressed, put on her makeup, pulled a cloche hat over her spit curls and went dancing with Pinky, a friend from the old days. They were going down to the Club, they said, for a little fun and a Chicken Snack. While Pat dressed, Pinky sat on the bed and sang for me "I Don't Want to Set the World on Fire."

Pinky had pink cheeks, pink clothes and pink cotton candy hair. Ila Mae said she wasn't any better than she should be.

Toward the end of the summer, Cy got the first two-day rodeo he'd been hired for all summer, somewhere in eastern Montana. Pat and I went with him. The second night, because I caught "walking pneumonia," we had to go back to Billings. There my parents had their last fight, probably exacerbated by their worries about money.

I watched it from the distance imposed by a high fever, not greatly alarmed. They always fought; they always made up; they were a matched pair, like two pintos with similar markings. The fight took place in the trailer, and I watched with detachment the steps of their familiar, intricate dance.

I fell asleep. In the morning, Cy was gone and my mother was still dressed. She looked at me with the same detachment I had felt the night before and began to rummage in the mess she and Cy had made of the trailer, digging for my jacket. We were going to see Pearl and Earl, she said, so she could use the telephone in the boarding-house.

Privately as well as publicly, Cy's every gesture had flair. Liberating himself from Pat and the wreck of their marriage that night, he unhitched the trailer from the Packard and drove away. He'd "gotten hitched." Now he got unhitched.

Pat made her phone call, and the following day, Roy Qualley came to Billings and performed an act just as tidily symbolic. With the trailer hitch he had brought along, he attached our house on wheels to his own car and hauled us away.

Roy Qualley as a young man in Great Falls, Montana

FIVE

Thus began the next phase of Pat's life, and Cy's, and my introduction to normal living, as opposed to traipsing around on the rodeo circuit. Roy had been in love with my mother for twelve years, he told Ila Mae—biding his time, waiting for the marriage to self-destruct and breathing our exhaust. He'd had time to plan our moral reform.

Pat must have been moved by his patience and his inarticulate longing. She filed for divorce, and within two weeks after Cy signed the papers, married the best man at her first wedding. No more living in a car or in the trailer, which vanished almost as soon as Roy unhitched it. We moved into a small house in Missoula, Montana, where Roy had a job with a wholesale candy and tobacco company and began to learn the ropes of what he called, grimly, "staying put, like sane people."

With his life savings, he took Pat shopping. In Lucy's Furniture Store, in an afternoon, they picked out a living-room suite, consisting of a beige sofa and matching armchair, both high on brass casters, both ponderous and both covered with the same kind of indestructible plush that is used to cover stuffed animals. They bought a Formica dinette set, slippery and cold to the touch, in mouse gray. They chose the china and silver plate that remained unused, thirty-seven years later, when Roy died.

It wasn't genteel to eat off the good china unless entertaining visiting heads of state. We used humbler dishes and graduated, in the fifties, to Melmac. Roy got us a plastic-handled set of knives, forks and spoons with Wrigley's bubble gum premiums.

For my room, they bought a bed, a bureau and a desk, at which I could apply myself to my schoolwork. I had a good mind, Roy told me, but like Cy, I was a grasshopper instead of an ant. With hard work, I could still aspire to ant status.

He put away our childish things, our boots and saddles. We saw no more of Pinky or my mother's other few remaining friends from the old days. We saw as little of Cy as the law allowed. While he was still my biological father, with visiting rights, this was a technicality. A father was the man who brought you up, not the handsome hell-raiser who breezed into town once in a while, on his way somewhere else, and left you "high-strung" for a week. Cy's very existence threatened Roy.

When Pat handed me over to him on the doorstep of the house, with Roy standing silently at her side, the old electricity between them hung in the air, heavy and palpable. They were still in love with each other, their divorce and Pat's second marriage another technicality. I had never heard of sex and I felt the tension between them. Roy felt it, and he had heard of sex.

There must have been hell to pay when the door closed, as there was when my mother got one of Cy's letters addressed to "Dear Cyra Sue and Pat." These, Roy tore open and shook out energetically to show us that no check for child support was enclosed. He also pointed out the obvious, that money doesn't grow on trees.

As a law student in North Dakota, Cy published his first piece of writing, a satire on the Charleston that begins:

> The Charleston is the name of a new form of physical exercise which is practiced on the ballroom floor, in fraternity and sorority houses, or in any place that a mental delinquent happens to become imbued with the desire to execute its intricacies for the amusement of those about him. This violent exercise, which is called a dance, differs from popular previous dance steps in that it requires more dexterity and less intelligence . . .

His prose style hadn't changed much when he began writing to Pat almost daily, ostensibly about my welfare. It was still flamboyant and stylish, full of posturing for her benefit but calculated not to offend Roy, the silent partner in their correspondence, who all but dusted those letters for fingerprints.

He also kept them all. Roy kept everything. Upstairs, in the succession of houses we rented, were the usual domestic trappings. The basements were archaeological sites, embedded with layer upon layer of letters, documents, old candy-order forms; age-whitened Life Savers and fancy boxes of petrified chocolates; every discarded item of clothing any of us ever owned; frayed inner tubes and snow shovels without handles, single surviving gloves of a pair, blankets turned into fine lace by moths. Roy was so compulsive a saver that when Pat threw something away, an old *Reader's Digest* or a soup can full of bacon grease, he went out to the garbage can in the alley, retrieved it and squirreled it away down in the basement.

Bacon grease, he believed, made roses grow to the size of cabbages, knowledge withheld from the general public by the fertilizer companies. We had no rosebushes, but we had our underground bunker full of bacon grease, and mice.

They ate the old chocolate, as well, but they didn't eat Cy's letters, probably because they were difficult to swallow. From Big Timber, where his return address was a friend's car dealership, he sent us a newspaper clipping from a Salt Lake City paper, showing a pretty eighteen-year-old with coyly downcast eyes nibbling on a pencil and contemplating her ballot for an election. "It was rather difficult to talk on the telephone to you the other night, as the young lady pictured on the enclosed was well within hearing distance." Hoping to be hired by one of Salt Lake City's radio stations, he continues, "I occupied myself with assisting at the mortuary." There he worked his magic on the mortuary owner's daughter. "I had informed her that I had no intention of again being married. Under these circumstances, she took enough phenobarbital, morphine and another kind of tablet to kill several persons."

A hardy creature, Miss Winifred L. pulled through, but not without leaving a hysterical suicide note addressed to Cy. "Under these circumstances, I thought it best to leave Salt Lake City."

In another letter, this one from California, he talks about enlisting in the Army so that he can choose his own branch of service instead of being drafted and says that if he's too old for the Aviation Corps, he'll join the Marines. "I would appreciate your reaction as Cyra's mother."

He mentions being delinquent in his child support, which he hopes to pay when he can sell the Packard, "a necessity that breaks my heart." He tells us about radio jobs promised and of rodeos for which he was almost hired before the "machinations" of some other announcer. He signs himself "Yours" and notes in a postscript, "Haven't had even a glass of beer in more than a *month!*"

Brilliantly manipulative, at once genuine and self-serving, these letters must have played chords on my mother's heartstrings. Into them, Cy tucks a picture of a lion cub, for me, and "a brochure with the finest explanation of Christ for a little youngster that I have ever seen. I happened to chance upon it at the mortuary."

Roy notwithstanding, he drops his guard now and then. Pleading to see me before he goes into the service, he tells Pat, "If I should become a casualty, several problems might be solved." I would inherit his service insurance. My mother would be freed of "our situation." All things considered, he might be worth more to both of us dead than alive.

How could Roy have competed with Cy's swagger and dash, or convinced himself that once he married Pat, the two of us would transfer our powerful affections? Though Cy would not agree to adoption, Roy changed my last name to his. He loved me, he told me, as if I were his own flesh and blood. He provided for me, according to his own ideas about what children need to prepare themselves for a world that rewards the deserving and punishes the slothful: brown oxfords instead of cowboy boots, a wholesome diet instead of hamburgers, indoctrination in the theory that whatever the task at hand, you attacked it with disproportionate zeal.

No chore was so routine, so trivial, that you could not compound it, washing the same window and polishing it with a chamois until the glass was so spotless you thought you were buffing thin air. Mowing the lawn in swatches that went up and down, back and forth, and then diagonally, though the grass cried out for mercy and could no longer be seen by the human eye. Sanding and varnishing the wooden panels of the family station wagon until you were hallucinating from inhaling varnish fumes. I still cannot wash a window without seeing Roy's red, sweating face on the other side and his finger tapping on the pane, pointing out an invisible smudge.

Work might not give you pleasure but it gave you dignity, which was better than bouquets thrown at your feet. Pat was a lost cause; her idea of hard labor was shaving her legs. My character, or lack of it, was not yet irreversibly determined; I could still be rescued. If only Cy wouldn't keep writing those letters, with plaintive requests that I write back in care of a bar in some cow town, and would stop turning up in Missoula, still nine feet tall to me in his boots and hat, the brim pinched jauntily into a Cheyenne roll. Stubbornly, I preferred boots to oxfords, rodeos to Lutheran vacation Bible camp, neither a camp nor a vacation.

Never one to shirk from duty, Roy found my re-education trying. The fly in the bacon grease was that I had "bad blood," my legacy from Cy.

His marriage to Pat, a consummation devoutly wished, was even more profound a disappointment. Briefly, she convinced herself that security was what she wanted most. She traded passion for it. She relinquished her footloose life, and Cy, for the plain, worshipful suitor who was his antithesis. Almost at once, she changed her mind, writing to Cy and receiving his letters through a post office box after Roy began opening all her mail. When she and I went grocery shopping, she phoned Cy from pay phones. In the back of her closet, she kept a suitcase packed and ready. Before a year was out, she grabbed it, and me, and got on a train. Cy had sent her the money to meet him in Denver, Colorado.

That last act of defiance determined the course of the rest of Pat's life. Whether she acted out of sheer wickedness, as Ila Mae said, or because conformity stifled her, or because of the pull of her feeling for Cy, she paid for it for forty years. The high-spirited colt no one could break, not even Cy, broke herself.

The compost heap that was our basement contained the history of that flight, which I knew little about because in Denver, my parents left me with relatives and took off for those few weeks by themselves. That Roy filed for divorce is on record; the document is intact, pain evident through the legal boilerplate. That Ila Mae got on the bus yet again and came to Missoula to be by Roy's side, I could have guessed. No one loved a melodrama more than she did, nor another piece of evidence that the world reserved suffering for those who least deserve it.

In the best of times, Ila Mae's letters are full of bankruptcies, house fires and illness beyond the reach of modern medicine. "The dr. says he's never seen anything like it, you wouldn't recognize him if you met him on the street, guess it's in God's hands now, he can't weigh more than seventy five pounds." Or: "Poor thing, well guess its for the best. She's out of this vail of tears now."

My aunt saw the world through morose-colored spectacles. If no one she knew was the victim of something sufficiently horrible, she included in her letters clippings from the newspaper: children abandoned by their mother, an old woman robbed on the street, a car wreck in which six people burned to death. Across the front of these enclosures, she scribbles, "Isn't this *terrible?*"

Solidly in Roy's corner, as Baby Sister burned down the barn again, she rose to new heights of outrage, bombarding my mother with two letters daily.

Dear Pat, just rec your card; Roy called me last nite I was so shocked that it has made me sick.

Ila Mae's health, it was a family conviction, was a fragile thing, her every breath drawn in torment. A lesser woman couldn't have borne it, much less kept on believing in God and putting up her own bread-and-butter pickles.

I am so disgusted with you to think you & Cy would try & pull something over on Roy . . . I have all ways stood by you when you left Cy for less. But this time I could beat your head off . . . You would have fit if you hadn't got your divorce from Cy so you could marry Roy Then to treat him this way: You aren't a child any more: I think you have back bone of jelly fish.

In the throes of emotion, my aunt always leaves out articles and punctuation.

Pat it isn't funny breaking a person heart and some day you are going to find that out . . . If you go back with Cy I will never visit if you live with him 100 yrs for he doesn't like me & I don't like him if I never see him again will be too soon . . .

Her threat not to visit again might have been a miscalculation, but she wound up with a zinger. "Some day Pat your turn will come to reap what you are sewing." There are a dozen of these letters, all in what Ila Mae would have called the same "vain," as well as more letters from Pat's other sisters, mobilized from campaign headquarters in Great Falls, and a letter from her old friend Pearl in Billings.

This one scolds her at length and then suggests she buy Ila Mae a fur coat: "They're so comfortable for this cold country. It would last for years." Ila Mae, Pearl adds as an afterthought, isn't well, and furthermore, she's a grand sport.

Long-distance phone calls, in those days, were still reserved for major life upheavals, too expensive for casual chat. When she phoned Pearl with the news about Pat, my aunt must have thriftily covered a second subject, the effect of Montana winters on an invalid.

No fur coat materialized as a thank-you for pointing out the path of righteousness. Cy was out of work again, broke again and drinking again. He and my mother must have made love again and fought again, caught up in the patterns of provocation and response that impose themselves upon a long marriage, grooves worn deep because they have been traveled so often.

Pat collected me and came home to Missoula, getting off the train, as she had when she left Arkansas all those years before, transformed. Her illusions were gone, and her fire. A soldier gone AWOL and now back in the trenches, she consigned herself to her second marriage.

Before their meeting in Denver, Cy had been a pariah in our new household. Now he became evil incarnate in boots. I was told not to mention his name.

He had joined the Army, Roy said. With luck, we'd never lay eyes on him again. I absorbed this information and had more spells, severe enough to warrant doctors, more needles and a health regime imposed by Roy.

The main feature was chewing every mouthful of food thirty times to "get the good out of it." Pat was also supposed to chew thirty times, to set a good example. Since we both cheated, Roy sat at the head of the dinette-set table, his eyes worried and watchful, and led us out loud in unison chewing. One, two, three, four . . . fourteen, fifteen, sixteen. The leaves changed color while we sat over a single dinner. Snow covered the ground. Spring came, and summer, followed by fall again. Or so it seemed to me, rhythmically revolving my jaw. Put cottage cheese on fork. Lift fork to mouth. Chew for eternity, while the earth rotates and your lifetime passes.

A health-food fanatic before health food was chic, Roy believed in the digestive tract the way some people believe in the one true path to the Buddha. Whole classes of food, everything I liked, would "repeat on you." French fries coated your stomach with grease, which never "passed"; it just sat there, turning you into a human grease trap. Not only should you eat an apple a day, you should eat the whole thing, core, seeds and stem. Briefly, before it proved unenforceable, Roy insisted that when ingesting oranges and bananas, you should eat the peel.

Harder to endure were his noon-hour tours around the Paxson Grade School playground in the station wagon, making sure I was wearing my snow pants. His method of curing head colds involved "sweating it out of you" with a portable heater and every blanket in the house. He doled out cod-liver oil by the shot glass. He believed in the healthy properties of fresh air.

Winter and summer, we left our bedroom windows open eight inches. At the end of my bed, October through February, would be a drift of new snow.

Worst of all was the mail-order house long underwear he made me wear, a peculiar peach color. Changing into gym bloomers in the school locker room was an exercise in humiliation, one more reason why I was miserable at school.

My speech was then an imitation of Cy's, inflated and full of big words, that made me seem a wizened, pretentious adult, whose only other conversational mode was swearing. Neither vocabulary served me well as an icebreaker with either teachers or kids my own age.

I could already read, also considered eccentric, but read from the last page to the first, the result of long exposure to Burma Shave signs. Thank God no one in Missoula then had heard of dyslexia. Roy would have found a homegrown cure for it.

His anxiety about my health, I know now, originated in something real. If I romanticize Pat and Cy's life together, their great love and greater talent for destructiveness, I can't romanticize the venereal disease my mother contracted before I was born and for which she was being treated that last summer in Billings. It ruined her own health and made the family keep a worried eye on me.

Pat's post office box notwithstanding, Roy early on managed to intercept her letters from Cy. The parts of them he chose to read aloud, he read to her. The paragraphs he chose not to read, he x'd out, with thick, angry black lines. Some of these letters explain Pat's mysterious illness.

"My report came back from the State Board of Health yesterday and supplementing the report of the local pathologist, it was entirely *negative*. Both made Kahn tests in addition to Wassermanns so it would seem quite conclusive that not even the slightest possibility exists that I had ever been exposed." He goes on to beg her for the results of the latest blood tests done on me. Guilt and worry about us both, he says, have given him a great deal of hell.

Venereal disease was considered so shameful then that Roy's and Ila Mae's anxious letters back and forth about Pat's condition used a code word for it: malaria. How her illness must have stigmatized my mother, tying a bell on her as a moral leper. How it must have strengthened Roy's hold over her, the authority of a stern parent over a child.

Only Cy sympathized, and refused to judge her, and Cy could no longer be part of her life. The Denver fling had driven that reality home. It also drove Pat home to Roy, prepared to lie in the bed she had made for herself.

To my Dear Wife Pat.
May all our Days be
as happy as this one Love Ray.

LEE STUDIO
OCONTO, WIS.

10-19-41

S I X

Plain men who marry beautiful women worry. With opportunity
ever at hand, will they be betrayed? Jealous of Cy before the Denver episode, Roy had his answer. It filled him not just with anguish
but with an increased sense of injured merit. "To my dear wife
Pat," he had inscribed the picture of himself he gave my mother
on their wedding day. "May all our days be as happy as this
one." Now he tore the picture in half, in front of us both so that I
would be aware of my mother's perfidy. Later he retrieved it from
the garbage and saved it, as he saved his copy of the divorce complaint.

Paragraph II: "That ever since said marriage the plaintiff has
been a good and faithful husband and has performed and discharged
all of his marital duties and obligations, but that the defendant, totally disregarding the solemnity of her marriage vows, did volun-
tarily and wilfully commit adultery in that defendant engaged in
sexual intercourse with one Cy Taillon."

For years it puzzled me that Roy so carefully preserved evidence
of his humiliation. His pack-rat tendencies alone do not explain it.
What does is that in the early years of their marriage he saw his claim
to Pat, awarded him for years of single-minded devotion, as tenuous.
She would leave him, if not with Cy, with some other man, and
when she did, Roy would be left with something—pride-saving proof
that he was the injured party.

None of us would be allowed to forget this, ever. If insufficiently impressed with my mother's appalling lack of rectitude, I might tap-dance to the same tune.

The torn and patched portrait, the divorce papers and the scolding letters from Ila Mae were also saved for me, hoarded against the day I would renounce Cy. Roy believed he was engaged in a tug-of-war for both Pat's soul and mine. He could not stop tugging long after Cy let go of his end of the rope.

Dear Cy,

    I haven't answered your last letter because I've been doing a lot of thinking.

    I realize now that you and I could never be together again with any kind of Harmony, too much water has passed under the bridge; but couldn't live with you for almost twelve yrs. without having a lot of memories, and our having Cyra made those memories harder to forget, but I am forgetting them and I know its best for all concerned.

Written in pencil on lined paper, this letter is a rough draft. Though it is signed "Pat," the handwriting is not my mother's but Roy's.

    I like my home here with Roy and he has been very good to both Cyra and I and the fact that I am ——— ——— proves that he has my interest and happiness at heart.

My guess is that Roy planned to dictate this letter to Pat, or stand over her while she copied it, when he could think of the right words to fill in the blanks. My mother now conducted all of her affairs, without exception, through her second husband and life manager.

He made her weekly appointment at the beauty parlor, drove her there, waited for her in the car and drove her home. She gave him the grocery list and he did the shopping, abolishing another pretext for her to leave the house and come within dialing distance of a pay phone. When she went bowling Tuesday nights, let out of her cell for an exercise period, Roy and I went along with her. Since

Pat was allowed to bowl only on Ladies' Night, an assignation at the alleys was unlikely. Roy was taking no chances.

He enlisted me in these security precautions, taking me aside and questioning me closely soon after he got home from work. Had Pat talked to any strange men while he was gone? Any man we knew? Any men? If she'd talked to anyone on the telephone, what had she said? He tried for casualness while he conducted these interrogations, but a smiling tormentor is still a tormentor. I remained tight-lipped and wary even when he threw in the promise of an ice-cream cone after dinner.

Half a dozen times a day, he phoned Pat from work, making sure she was still nailed to the floor. My mother took to leaving the bathroom door open while she was on the toilet, offending my sensibilities. I think she did this because it gave her an extra second or two to hitch up her pedal pushers and sprint for the insistently ringing telephone.

Sometimes she and I sat on the front porch on hot afternoons, enjoying a Missoula pastime, watching the lawn sprinklers. Neighboring housewives sat on their front porches too, visiting back and forth and offering my mother the limited social exchange of "Hot enough for ya?" We never had to wait long before the wood-paneled station wagon slowly rounded the corner on patrol. Finding no strange car in the driveway, Roy sometimes rolled down the window, waved and told us he was "just passing by" on his delivery rounds.

Other days, he pulled his hat well down over his eyes, looked neither left nor right and drove on. Now almost totally bald, and self-conscious about it, Roy never went out without a hat. Apparently he thought that if he pushed it down far enough, we couldn't see him.

Evenings we gathered around the radio. Roy lay on the sofa with his arms folded tightly across his chest and his eyes closed. Pat sat in the matching overstuffed chair, chain-smoking Lucky Strikes, and looked at some point in the middle distance. I lay on my stomach on the rug, doing homework.

We looked like a *Saturday Evening Post* cover, the family gathered round the Philco, listening to "The FBI in Peace and War," but this homey tableau was no more realistic than most. We talked not at all. Pat yawned now and then, out of boredom. Roy brooded, or slept, or pretended to sleep while he watched her through almost closed eyes. I tried to look busy over my arithmetic workbook while elaborating on my favorite fantasy: Cy coming to the door, with the Packard waiting at the curb, and taking me back to Billings, or Butte, or anywhere there were rodeos.

He needed me with him, he would explain to my mother and Roy, because he had so much work announcing he couldn't handle it all alone. I was a top hand at the mike and could work the

Pat, Cyra and Roy in Missoula, Montana

crow's nest almost as well as he could, maybe better in a few years when I'd had more experience. So long, and we'd write from the road.

Next reel, me at the microphone, at a night rodeo, high above the arena. I'm spinning out long silk strings of words, like my father. I'm emanating the same star quality. I have new boots, since my old ones don't fit anymore. My hair flows down my back, beneath my white Stetson, and back in its element it is naturally curly. This gives me such a marked resemblance to Margaret O'Brien that everyone who sees me says I'm the spitting image. They're all amazed that they overlooked it before.

Caught up in this scenario, I went off to brush my teeth at eight o'clock dazed as a sleepwalker, and when I was in bed, left the door of my room open so that I could hear the doorbell. It never rang, except at the behest of a Jehovah's Witness or the Fuller Brush man, from whom Pat was afraid to accept the free sample in case Roy thought it evidence of intimacy.

After that first year of their marriage, my mother and Roy went nowhere as a couple and invited no one. A town the size of Missoula has few secrets. Pat's flight with Cy and Roy's cuckoldry had enlivened the party lines over a long, otherwise dull winter. They hadn't been a brilliant success in small-town society even before scandal made matters worse.

Social life in Missoula revolved around card parties, a few couples invited for bridge, highballs and small sandwiches, cut on the bias for elegance and filled with olive-pimento cheese spread. Pat went to these gatherings grudgingly. She hated bridge and played badly. Roy had once enjoyed them, but he did not enjoy being the object of curiosity and pity; and if they'd toughed it out and accepted invitations, they'd have had to reciprocate.

They had played host for their own card party only once. The three of us spent a tense afternoon getting ready. Roy complained about Pat's sloppy housekeeping and her sandwich-cutting technique, pressing the bread down hard with outspread fingers and then sawing between them. The gluey white bread retained the imprint of her fingertips; each sandwich had craterlike squashed places in it.

Pat pursued the logic of the pecking order by yelling at me. In the interest of fairness, I had assigned myself the job of counting all the nuts in the paper nut cups to be sure that each guest got exactly the same number and nobody got more cashews than anyone else. Throughout these preparations, the air vibrated with our respective grievances and hurt feelings.

An hour into the soiree, Pat bungled a bridge hand. Roy addressed the guests on the subject of her shortcomings as card player and housewife, smiling an awful smile that included us all in the joke. My mother took these comments in the spirit in which they were intended, jumped to her feet and upended the card table into his lap.

Nut cups, scorepads, pencils, highballs, sandwiches and bridge mints scattered. So did the guests, thanking Pat and Roy for the lovely evening. The party lines must have hummed nonstop the next day.

Because friends' mothers did not throw tantrums and embarrass people, it hardened my heart against her that mine did. I was judgmental as only children are judgmental. I was desperate to conform to Missoula social norms. I was also too young to know that all parents embarrass all children, if by no overt act, by breathing.

The "good dishes," the green-stemmed wine and water goblets Pat and Roy had picked out together, the silver plate for twelve in its chest—gradually, all were relegated to the backs of the kitchen cupboards, there to gather dust for thirty-five years. The two of them gave no holiday open house with Tom and Jerries served from the cut-glass punch bowl. They invited no friends for supper, so they never needed the mahogany-veneer drop-leaf table in the living room. Roy put an ad in the newspaper and sold these things. Bit by bit, he let go of his own cherished fantasy, the backlit vision of domestic life with Pat he must have clung to throughout all those lonely years in the boardinghouses.

In early snapshots of him is a Roy I never met. He parts his already thinning hair in the middle, slicks it down, smiles dashingly and puts an arm around each of two pretty women in flapper dresses. He poses in the bathtub of a boardinghouse, while one friend scrubs his back with a long-handled brush and another, playing the butler, offers him a bottle of beer on a tray. He visits Yellowstone Park with friends, in an open touring car, strikes pugilistic poses in his boxing clothes and holds up strings of trout he caught. He looks happy.

The yellowing old photos trace his transformation until he became the man my mother met, prematurely middle-aged before he was thirty. He doesn't smile anymore but stares at the camera with a severe, humorless gaze. His body thickens and seems to take on gravity, a body not just heavier but somehow closer to the ground. What the photos don't tell me is what changed him, why he grew old and disappointed while still young.

All the adults I knew—neighbors, teachers, the man behind the grocery store counter—admired Old Honest Face. They told me how hard he worked and how good he had been to my mother and me. I should be grateful to him, they said, for treating me, a child not his own, as if I were his flesh and blood.

I endured these lectures shifting from one foot to the other, felt guilty for not being as grateful as people thought I ought to be and heard a faint undercurrent in all such tributes, the animosity people feel toward goodness that carries with it the whiff of self-congratulation. It won Roy admiration, but it didn't win him affection.

Cy, the reprobate, had hundreds of friends. Roy, virtue personified, had none, with the exception of Ila Mae, a kindred spirit. She visited us so often the intervals between visits seemed shorter than the visits themselves. Arriving on the Greyhound bus, for she and Wiley could not afford a car, she brought preserves, pickles and implacable good intentions.

She took over the kitchen and cooked all our meals, thereby, she suggested to Pat, staving off Roy's and my imminent starvation. She unearthed the chenille bedspreads we never used from the cedar chest, aired them on the clothesline and put them on the beds. "Now isn't that nicer, Patty?" She scrubbed the kitchen walls and woodwork with ammonia and water, bringing on one of her migraine headaches.

"You shouldn't have done it," Roy said. "Not with your health."

"Well, I had to, Roy," Ila Mae said in a small voice, from her bed of pain. She managed to imply that Pat's housekeeping was so bad we were about to be shut down for health code violations.

At dinner, she urged Roy to have third helpings. If there was one thing she loved, she said, it was to see a hungry man eat. Anyone who worked as hard as Roy deserved a good hot supper at the end of the day, and given her many other onerous responsibilities, who knew when she'd be back and he'd get another one?

Roy took her shopping for things she thought our household needed. They came home with a furry cover for the toilet seat, a flowered plastic cover for the toaster and one for the mixer. Ila Mae believed in covering things with other things: beds with bedspreads, chair arms with doilies, my mother with more clothes.

Pat's usual at-home costume was shorts or pedal pushers and a blouse with the bottom rolled up and knotted above her trim bare midriff. Ila Mae bullied her into the housedresses she ran up on her sewing machine, indestructible garments cut like flour sacks. Pat looked self-conscious and uncomfortable, like a dog children have dressed in doll clothes.

The way we were living, my aunt frequently announced, made her just sick. So did an endless list of other things—the inhumanity of man toward man, children who sassed, the absence of a butter knife on a butter plate—but in Pat's lackadaisical housekeeping she saw a chance both to do her Christian duty and to get her own back. No one had ever pelted Ila Mae with roses. It seemed unlikely that anyone ever would. She wasn't the Montgomery sister who'd been the "Toast of St. Louis" and she had few prospects of becoming the "Toast of Great Falls." Even her husband didn't appreciate her.

Gentle Wiley, once the most tractable of men, had learned to resist all attempts to improve his character by practicing passive resistance, paying no more attention to Ila Mae's nagging than to a dog barking somewhere way off in the distance. He spent his time at home barricaded behind his newspaper with a forbidden can of beer within easy reach. He no longer washed his hands on command.

Ila Mae and Pat on an icy sidewalk during one of Ila Mae's frequent visits to Missoula

Only Roy praised Ila Mae, admired her and held her up as an example to Pat. He fussed over her health. He gorged himself on her cooking ostentatiously, knife and fork flying to the accompaniment of blissful grunts, so that Pat didn't miss the point: Good Man Eating Good Meal Cooked by Good Woman. At the bus depot, when Ila Mae headed back to Great Falls, he told her that he couldn't thank her enough for everything she had done.

Ila Mae always said she only wished that she could have done more. She began to write to Roy in care of the candy company, private letters that stressed their mutual bond of sympathy. "Please Roy tear this letter up don't take it home," she begins one such missive, but she was appealing to the wrong man.

Ila Mae's letters in that period fill a good-sized box that once held overshoes. She wrote once a day and sometimes twice, in her usual breathless style and on any piece of paper that came to hand, including the backs of letters she had received herself. Waste not, want not. For material, she had Pat's infidelity with Cy to chew over, an event that could not be overanalyzed. She had her own frail health and Wiley's illness as well. In his mid-thirties, he'd had a stroke and was at death's door, she narrates, though his condition seems to exasperate more than worry her. She had her own romance with Roy's brother Vin.

Consummated or unconsummated, the product of her imagination or a real love affair—the details are missing, in the interest of discretion or because there weren't any—this passion flowered from one of her visits to us when Vin was visiting too.

Vin was a bachelor. Though he came to Montana looking for work, he spent his month or so with us lying on the sofa, drinking beer and snapping dish towels at Pat's rump, an entertainment that infuriated her but sent both Vin and Roy into fits of high-pitched whinnying. He was no charmer, in my opinion, since he had little use for children other than as beer bringers, but Ila Mae found him more attractive than I did.

It would seem hypocritical of her to chastise Pat for a love affair and then indulge in one herself. But my aunt's extramarital adventure, her letters make clear, bears no resemblance to Pat's whatsoever, since Ila Mae's was divinely ordained. "Some how I have a Feeling that God intended for Vin & I to meet for God knows we couldn't help it."

Though written English fought her all the way, she gave Cy stiff competition as a masterful manipulator. Writing to Roy, tirelessly stirring up domestic unrest, she sought not just to conquer but to divide.

Monday morning

Dear Roy:
Well how are things going better I hope. Roy, Pat hurt my feelings when I got ready to leave she never even as much said thanks all she said was, she was glad that I came over,

ask Vin for he was there. But I know how you felt about it:
for as I told you that I will all ways help you In any way That
I can. any time. You just let me know.

    I know she was glad when I left.

    The dinner at the restaurant was very nice & She was
nice as she could be . . .

"As nice as she could be" is a conventional phrase. Ila Mae
somehow gives it the subtext "which we both know isn't very nice
at all."

Wiley is in such condition I called the Dr. have appointment for 8 this evening he is going to have ex ray somehow
I know that we will have to give up the House before Long
& I just can't go back to his mother's to live. I will let you
know how things turn out.

Finally comes the main business at hand:

. . . Pat has written to Hope about Cy calling all the time &
Hope is such cat that she has spread it all over town. I told
Pat long ago that you can't trust her. Please Roy don't tell
her any thing I tell you because I know you are right & will
all ways do the right thing.

"Cy calling all the time . . ." The words must have detonated
within Roy like a bomb. He could intercept letters and destroy them.
Must he also have the phone ripped out? Surround our bungalow
with a moat? Hire a team of sharpshooters trained to fire at anybody
wearing a cowboy hat? Leaving him reeling in the shock waves, Ila
Mae winds up briskly.

. . . Will let you know how Wiley comes out he looks half
dead.

Busy though she was fanning all those flames, Ila Mae did not
neglect my mother's moral guidance or mine. To Pat, she wrote:

"Pat dear you have such lovely home & the grandest husband I pray to God to help you & keep you good sweet & loyal all ways." And to me: "Hello Susie have you been good little girl. Remember when you are naughty that God puts a mark on the Board."

She closes with the promise that she is going to send me "nice Bible book." I doubt that I so much as looked at the pictures. To my well-intentioned aunt, I owe my continuing resistance to all forms of religious belief. Though her own faith was genuine, and though she believed that godliness was next to cleanliness, she instilled in me the conviction that God, like Ila Mae and Roy, was a keeper of old scores, the type cowboys would say had Himself a burr under His saddle.

SEVEN

Wiley recovered and went back to selling men's clothing at Strain Bros. department store, where he got a little respect as "our Mr. Gosney." Vin went back to Wisconsin, without Ila Mae. She wrote Roy that she would not have gone with him even if he'd asked. My mother and stepfather went on with the accommodation that would become a long marriage. Inscrutable, I once considered it, but I am now older and I do not think of marriages as scrutable.

Theirs made as much sense as any. Pat was childish herself, incompetent at the practical business of living and saddled with a young child. She needed refuge and may have thought of it as temporary, from one day to the next, until the days added up to years and she no longer thought of it at all. Roy was used to disappointment: the gold strike, when he was a miner, that somehow made someone else rich, the innocent schemes for self-improvement he pursued—business school correspondence courses, health food and miracle vitamins, potions and unguents for growing hair—that led nowhere and left him unchanged. His marriage to my mother was just one more.

Roy never gave up trying to reverse his baldness. It pains me still that I once humiliated him by giving him a pair of military brushes for Christmas. He opened the package, then left the room, choking out that I'd done it now and this time I was going to catch it. Pat laughed helplessly. I wondered what I had done and why he did not like my gift. It wouldn't help matters now if I could explain to Roy that I didn't see him as bald because I didn't see him at all.

While I had not seen Cy for months either, he still held me in the same thralldom and his distant star eclipsed Roy. The parent on the scene making the rules cannot compete for glamour with the one who is not there, and when the rules include chewing each mouthful of food thirty times, there is no contest.

Nor could Roy compete with Cy in knowing how to charm me, though he longed for my affection and tried hard to win it. He gave me a watch for my birthday, a gift he could ill afford. Cy sent a telegram, delivered to our front door by messenger, and dazzled me; I knew of no other child who had ever received a telegram. "Isn't that just *typical*," said Ila Mae, who was there. "Scaring us all like that. I thought sure it was from Wiley, and his mother had passed away."

For Christmas, Roy gave me the bicycle I'd longed for, second-hand but lovingly repainted, and had to watch while I exclaimed over it briefly, set it aside and went back to pawing over Cy's gift, a package full of smaller packages. Individually wrapped, these contained every food I loved and was no longer allowed to eat: a tall jar of stuffed green olives, the kind I used to fish out of my parents' martinis; animal crackers; Kraft's caramels; marshmallows; Tootsie Rolls; a dozen Hershey bars. Roy's face told me that before I had taken a bite out of these, he could hear my teeth starting to rot.

Cy's letters came, addressed to me. A man was entitled to write to his daughter, if not to his ex-wife, so Roy reluctantly let the mail go through. Though I could read them perfectly well myself, Pat helpfully volunteered to read these letters to me and was less puzzled than I was, I'm sure, by such information as: "In the event you are interested, I haven't had a date in the last two and a half months. I tried keeping company with a girl in Salt Lake City but despite the fact that I am continually lonesome as Hell for someone . . . I haven't been able to make a go of it and despite myself have been drawn into a shell from which it is difficult to emerge."

He was bouncing around the country again, finding little work and hard up. From Tucson, and Phoenix, and a dozen other western towns, he wrote letters, ostensibly to me, about prospects and re-versals. "Next week, M-G-M begins the filming of *Apache Trails* here and I hope to obtain work on that until my shows get under way." "I was offered a show at St. Louis for March 25–April 1st but I guess my price was too high as I have not heard from them." "It will be necessary for me to dispose of the car in some manner which I hope to determine within the next few days. There remains a balance of $272.20 and I do dislike to lose an investment of $1300.00 because of that amount. Yet . . . I have to have some cash to go on until February unless something breaks in the meantime."

He didn't get the job as a movie extra. He didn't get the radio announcing job he wanted at a small station in Harrisonburg, Vir-ginia. He left a job as a ranch hand because "the situation there became practically unbearable" and holed up on another ranch owned by a friend, to "get out the scores of letters incident to lining up my itinerary for this, my final year in this game."

Desperate, he finally sold the Packard, in Salt Lake City, for a few hundred dollars. It broke his heart, he wrote, and it also broke Pat's. Reading this news to me, she cried.

The midnight-blue Packard had been our announcement to the world, and ourselves, that we Taillons were winners. It had style, that ephemeral thing Pat and Cy valued above all else. It repre-sented the old, footloose high-roller days, and no sensible Plymouth station wagon, its fenders and hood a muddy maroon, could inspire the same pride of ownership. That Cy would part with it was un-thinkable.

Roy, Pat and I all knew that Cy could not have brought himself to sell the car unless he was flat broke. Only Roy found that knowl-edge heartening. Though Cy enclosed a crisp fifty-dollar bill, in par-tial payment of overdue child support, the money was not as welcome as the news that "the Big Shot," as Roy called Cy, was in a tailspin and rapidly losing altitude.

My parents' divorce agreement, unusual at the time, provided that each had custody of me for six months of the year. Pat was to take me for the school year, Cy for the summers and school vaca-tions.

My spending school vacations with him was impractical, since he was usually thousands of miles away. Summers were also out of the question. He was working rodeos then, and in Roy's and Ila Mae's views, couldn't take care of me properly. Still spindly and neurasthenic, I could not survive three months of hard travel, hamburgers and Hershey bars. So I saw Cy only when he came through Missoula. Because these visits were infrequent, and because Cy staged each like a Broadway play, they became big events not just for me but for Missoula, anticipated with as much interest as the opening day of deer-hunting season.

Missoula is a pretty town with numerous virtues. Spectacle and diversion are not among them, unless one counts watching car crashes at an intersection called "Suicide Junction." Cy's appearances were at least as exciting, and nobody died.

Forbidden by Roy to come to our house anymore, he picked me up at Paxson Grade School. I knew he was in the building before I actually saw him because he stopped in at the principal's office to find out which classroom I was in. Through the office secretary, or a miscreant kid putting in detention time, word leaked out the door that some cowboy movie star was in our midst.

Next came the sound of Cy's boot heels down the hall, accompanied by pairs of other feet. In the course of his progress from the first floor to the second, he'd picked up a retinue. Trotting behind him were the principal, female teachers and kids who were supposed to be somewhere else. All that was missing was a marching band playing "I Love a Parade."

I'd hear his unmistakable baritone, pitched for the bleachers, telling how he'd always wanted to teach school himself, because there was no job like it. Oh, not for the material rewards, maybe, but for the satisfaction.

Finally he stood in my classroom door, handsome as Gary Cooper, in his whitest hat and nattiest Western shirt and narrow-legged pants, with his beautifully manicured hands resting on an enormous silver and gold belt buckle. "Cy Taillon," he introduced himself, lifting his hat to my teacher, who looked breathless. On one of these occasions, he got a spontaneous round of applause from the third grade.

Manic with joy at seeing him again, I was anxious to leave school

Cyra (first row, second from left) in her skinned-back-pigtails stage

and have him to myself, but not Cy, surrounded with admirers. He let himself be persuaded to give an informal talk about rodeo, the only all-American sport, while the principal beamed and took a seat and thought this was his own idea. "I guess you've heard about enough," Cy said, at intervals. "No, no," screamed his rapt audience.

He'd seen what looked like a fine instrument through the open door of the music room, Cy mentioned. He played a little piano himself. Soon he was installed on the bench putting the old upright through his rendition of "Springtime in the Rockies," heavy on trills suggesting birdsong. He captured everyone within range of his voice, roughly the southwest quadrant of Missoula, with stories of his travels across America, the grandest country in the world. He had us all, kids and adults, jumping through hoops.

Cy was not being paid for this performance, but things were slow on the circuit and an audience was an audience. He would have gladly done two shows, called a square dance and then pitched War Bonds in front of the PTA. Appreciation was the little bottle labeled "Drink Me" whose elixir made him tall, taller, taller still.

By the time I finally got him out of there, by threatening to have hysterics, he had a date with the red-haired music teacher to discuss my buried talent for music (still buried so deep it has never surfaced); an ink stain on his middle finger from signing autographs with a school pen; a satisfied flush under his suntan. The music teacher believed Cy had always wanted to be a concert pianist—if only he could have had lessons, instead of being entirely self-taught. The principal knew Cy thought being principal of Paxson Grade School the noblest of callings. The girls in the class all wanted to grow up to be Miss Rodeo America and the boys champion bronc riders.

Was everybody happy? Everybody except my father, who deflated visibly when we were by ourselves and the performance was over. Demonstrating that he was not bound by Roy's relayed injunctions, he took me out for greasy food. He told me how much he'd missed me and read the report cards I'd saved up for him. But he was restless, gazing out the car windows as we sat in the drive-in parking lot, not even bothering to flirt with the car hop.

He asked me about my mother. How was her health? Did she have headaches anymore? How was she wearing her hair now? Did she still sing that damned song all the time around the house? He meant "Stormy Weather," Pat's staple along with "Rain or Shine." She was fond of songs about love under assorted climatic conditions.

Before he dropped me the block from home Roy permitted, Cy gave me a letter for her, with instructions to deliver it when Roy was not around. It was nothing to do with Roy, he said, just news about old friends.

I gave him the letter Pat had tucked into my lunchbox, uneasy because I was sure that Roy would not approve and that he would find out. He missed nothing, my stepfather, no invisible speck on a freshly washed window, no blade of grass left standing on a lawn mowed so closely it looked as if it had been cropped by sheep, no subversive act of Pat's or mine, real or suspected.

Sometimes I stared at him absentmindedly. "I know what you're thinking," Roy was inclined to announce on such occasions. Whatever it was, he didn't like it and repaid my stare with odd forms of reprisal. Most unbearable was no reading other than school books, enforced by night raids to make sure I wasn't reading by flashlight under the covers. Second most unbearable was helping clean out the garage, a useless undertaking consisting of shifting piles of things, the overflow from the basement, from one damp, spider-infested corner to the other. As a middle-aged adult, I have yet to live in a house with either a garage or a basement.

What form Pat's punishments took, I don't know, since house arrest does not permit many embellishments. Whatever the risk, she continued to stay in touch with Cy by whatever means she could contrive.

In 1942, a few months before he enlisted in the Army Air Corps, Cy wrote Pat a three-page typewritten letter advising her to have an abortion. Her own letter to him, appealing to him for advice, had followed him around for weeks, from temporary address to temporary address. It filled him with confusion, coming "as a considerable additional shock to those of the past few years." He had no right to enter into any decision she might make, he wrote, but he was full of concern for her state of mind—"It is the grossest kind of an injustice to bring an unwanted child into the world"—and her health. "You are still taking treatments and if you intensify these again as you did before, there is a great possibility that your health will be impaired to a great extent. Moreover, in consideration of the fact that this condition of yours continues to persist, you will be taking a tremendous chance for the baby. Do you think it would be fair to subject an unborn one to the chance?"

They were lucky with me, he says, in that my periodic tests do not indicate any disease. Pat cannot count on being as lucky a second time.

His usual eloquence trails off into near-incoherence: "Regardless of what our actual feelings toward each other may be—or, regardless of what may develop in the future—if you do feel as you have indicated, and, in consideration of all that you are going through now . . ."

Beginning "Dearest Pat" and ending "All my love," this is my father's valedictory letter to my mother. It hints at their continuing longing for one another while acknowledging that he has no further claim on her. "In the light of your quickly chosen circumstances, I really have no right to make any further suggestions regarding you or your relationship to me." It tells her that "the thoughts that your letter aroused in my mind are far too involved to write." Write him as soon as possible with regard to her decision, Cy pleads; he will always be of any help he can be to her. But he was letting go of her at last. Whether she had the baby or not, Pat was pregnant by Roy. There could be no more tangible proof that she was his wife now.

No baby was born. My mother's medical condition may have made it possible for her to have a legal abortion, or she may have made the private arrangements women then and now contrive to make if they are desperate enough. I don't know, either, whether she ever received Cy's letter or whether Roy intercepted and withheld it. All I do know about her pregnancy is that Ila Mae was never consulted. Had she been, another boot-box would have bulged with her counsel on the subject, along with privileged information on what God thought about it.

Later that year, Pat had a nervous breakdown. I was told she was visiting Ila Mae. She was actually in a sanitarium called Warm Springs. A ceaseless flow of letters from Ila Mae harangued Roy about feeding me properly and seeing that I went to Sunday school, discussed Pat's "malaria" as the cause of her emotional problems and blamed Cy for her physical and moral deterioration. "Before she met him she was sweetest thing ever lived." Ila Mae hadn't thought so at the time but she wasn't a slave to foolish consistency.

Roy should "keep chin up," she told him, and enclosed a note for Pat telling her to think of Roy and do everything the doctors ordered, "for they know what's best for you."

My mother's sister Lucille also wrote to her, from the Wisconsin dairy farm where she lived with her second husband. Her first had been a Filipino railroad engineer named Pedro Magatutu, a union that must have raised eyebrows back home in Paragould. Pedro was seduced by the music of the rails, and vanished. Lucille settled down with Henry and the dairy herd. "You make Roy happy and *forget* the past,"she wrote Pat. "I know about the haphazard life you've led, & dear was it worth it? I'm lots older than you and I want you to be happy with Roy as I am with Pa. It takes a man with a little more age & yes common sense to make a woman appreciate her good fortune."

Did Pat hear, in her sisters' words of comfort, their mutual belief that she was being punished for her sins? Her therapy involved drugs, spinal taps and something called "brain waves"; she must have been ready to believe it.

Once in the two months she was gone, she phoned, reassuring me that she was all right, only having such a swell time with Ila Mae that she was staying longer. She also told me to be good, one of those parental injunctions she rarely uttered. She'd been on the receiving end of it too often.

No uncritical expression of love and sympathy came from Cy this time, for no one told him about Pat's breakdown, though Lucille's letter mentions that she and Pa have heard from him. "Cy writes us he may join the Army, just where he belongs." The family's consensus was that he was in no way involved, other than as a guilty bystander.

While my mother was gone, Roy and I made a qualified peace with each other. He lectured and scolded me less. I tried harder to please him, aware that something I did not understand was causing him pain and worry. In return for my grudging efforts at housekeeping, he granted me an allowance for the first time, a quarter a week. All his life, Roy carried a change purse, an old-fashioned black leather pouch with a clasp that opened with a snap. Doling out my allowance, he opened it slowly and deliberately, shook it to inspect its contents and then handed over the two dimes and a nickel with care, as if the coins were breakable.

What money Roy earned, he earned for six-day weeks of hard work, and though he managed to put a little aside, he never had more than he needed. The trouble he had parting with it was commensurate with the trouble he had getting hold of it in the first place.

It puzzled me, his insistence that even a penny was precious, worth stooping to pick up from the sidewalk. It angered Roy that he could not get it through my head that money was not manufactured inside slot machines and that before it ended up carelessly scattered up and down a bar, the shiny silver dollars and the crumpled bills, someone had to earn it. I thought money fell out of the sky, he said, like Cy, and would end up the same way, broke and a bum, unless my quarters went into the bank he gave me and stayed there.

They went in, but they came out as fast. I had learned to work the coins out through the slot on top, armed with determination and a table knife I kept hidden underneath my mattress. An adult lifetime later, I still feel guilty when I spend money and guilty when I save it, caught between two powerful object lessons.

What money buys, Roy taught me, is security. What it ought to buy, Cy taught me by example, is self-respect, that fragile intricate form of it that people understand only when they have no security whatsoever. The ethic of the rodeo circuit was that if you won prize money for an event, you paid some less fortunate cowboy's entry fees in the next event. You also saw to it that he could hold his head up in the bar after the rodeo, which meant not buying a drink but buying a round and leaving the bartender the change. The money was a loan, but a loan that would never be called in.

The ethic around our household in Missoula was that self-respect came only at the price of honest labor. A handout, however well meant, degraded the receiver. In those post-Depression years of the early forties, tramps appeared at our screen door sometimes, asking to cut firewood, or mow the lawn, in exchange for a meal or a dollar. They terrified Pat, but Roy had forbidden her to turn them away, no matter how shabby they were.

Tell them to come back in the evening, he made her promise. If they did, he found some job for them and showed them where we kept our tools in the garage. He never stood over their shoulders while they did some task that did not really need doing, or conducted an inventory of the tools before they left. When the man came to the back door again, Roy met him with change purse in hand. "Here's your wages," he said gravely, and shook hands.

My father and my stepfather both understood dignity. They only understood it differently, a matter of temperament. Both were midwestern farm boys who left home and came out West, where there was room for ambition. Both fell in love with Pat, whose attraction for them must have been that she embodied no trace of girl-next-door, unless you happened to live next door to a burlesque house. They were more alike than they knew, and had my mother not come along, they might have remained friends until they were old men, Roy riding the tail of the comet, Cy grateful for the ballast.

EIGHT

As good as his word, Cy enlisted in the Army Air Corps. Friends had urged him to somehow remarry my mother in order to avoid the draft, he wrote to me, but he was outraged "at the apparent fact that someone would think that I would use the subterfuge of hiding behind the skirts of any woman to escape an obvious duty." "Subterfuge" sent me to the dictionary at school, to look up the word. Cy's letters frequently sent me burrowing through the dictionary, educational fallout from his letter-writing style.

He was ready to dispute with anyone "that I should fall into the category of being a coward," a thought that would have occurred to no one, not even Roy, who'd ever seen my bantamweight father pile into a fight. I was proud of him and terrified. From the way Roy and Ila Mae talked about Cy's joining the Army, I had the strong impression that he'd get killed, at least if he had enough decency left in him to do the right thing for once.

The months before he was assigned to duty were the worst months of his professional life thus far. Rodeo job after rodeo job fell through because of cancellations. The country had other things on its mind, and without the Packard, Cy had to travel between the few announcing jobs he scraped up on crowded wartime trains. While this was expensive, he wrote, it was still cheaper than trying to run a car in the face of gas and rubber shortages.

To keep body and soul alive, he went back to Salt Lake City in the hope of getting a job at the Remington plant there, but he could not hold out for the two or three weeks it took to get hired and so signed on as a track laborer at an ordnance plant, for sixty-five cents an hour. He said the job saved him money on manicures.

What money he did not need to live on, and he was living cheaply, he'd send on to Pat to buy school clothes for me. Though Roy kept pointing out that Cy was a deadbeat, who owed him hundreds of dollars in child support, he took his obligation seriously at that point, and when he could not send cash—always the crisp new bills he liked to carry instead of worn ones—he at least worried about it. Again he mentioned the $10,000 in service life insurance he was assigning to me. He too seemed to think it likely I would collect. The drifty, demoralized summer behind him had left him pessimistic about his prospects in general.

An old shoulder injury, the result of his last attempt at bronc riding, kept Cy out of combat. As he'd feared, he was too old to be a pilot, a major disappointment. For all his posing and posturing, his idea of serving his country involved more than the public relations slot he soon found himself in. He sent clippings of himself, dapper in uniform, leading dance bands and acting as m.c. for bond drive evenings and air shows. As usual, he underlined his name, frequently misspelled, in case I managed to miss it while reading the photo captions. Letter after letter, he fumed about being on the sidelines of the war and vowed not to give up on being assigned to combat duty. Having failed other tests of manhood, in others' eyes and his own, he longed for another, one he knew he would pass.

Then his letters stopped coming, an unprecedented and alarming lapse. Though my own letters were less frequent than Cy's, though I saw him briefly and seldom and though I was settling into my new life with my mother and Roy, I basked in the certainty of my father's love. He sent me birthday telegrams and Christmas boxes full of things that were associated, in my mind, with the old days. He still addressed me as Taillon instead of Qualley, though Pat instructed me to write him that she could call me anything she wanted. He wrote me every two weeks, even when I didn't write back or wrote the letters children write when they are rebelling against an emotional claim: Dear Dad, How are you? I am fine. I got a B in spelling. P.S. My mother says to tell you she needs the money and send it.

Never had he stopped writing, no matter where he was or what was happening to him. As the months went by, I began to believe that he had been killed.

Even in peaceful Missoula, reminders that there was a war on were constant. At school, we took up collections to buy War Bonds. At home, Roy started a Victory garden, digging up our backyard and planting carrots, potatoes and onions, "good keepers" in case our food supply was cut off. A skillful farmer, he grew so many vegetables that we could supply our neighbors and still have enough to stockpile in a dank corner of the basement, smelling of earth and filling me with horror. I saw a lifetime ahead of eating cooked carrots.

Like everyone else, we saved flattened tin cans, cooking fat and string. When kids asked why the soldiers needed cooking fat and string to fight the Germans, no convincing answers were forthcoming. Adults didn't seem to know either. It was all part of "the war effort." We got the impression that they considered the question smart-alecky if not treasonous.

Ours not to question why. Ours to compete over who could make the biggest string ball and thank our lucky stars we weren't the children of Europe, who were being bombed and starving. When the March of Time newsreel at the Wilma Theater showed air raids, the cylindrical bombs dropping from the bellies of the planes, a girl I knew, at the movies with her parents, screamed that we were all going to be killed, a possibility that visited itself upon me as her parents led her, sobbing, up the aisle.

I caught her fear. The sight of a plane in the clear skies over Missoula turned me weak-kneed and made me lose bladder control. In bed, I heard the snarling engines in the newsreels again and waited for the explosion that would blow us all to smithereens.

Don't be ridiculous, Pat and Roy said, standing in the doorway of my room when nightmares made me cry out. Nobody was going to bomb South Central Avenue. The war was a long way away. We were winning it.

Kids who'd lost their older brothers came to school silent and swollen-eyed and suffered the awkward, unctuous sympathy of the rest of us. The newspaper announced additions to the list of "Gold Star Mothers." Evenings, the kids on my block were shooed out into our front yards while our parents listened to the news on the radio. When we were called in again, to sit down to supper, they were in no mood to tolerate complaints about the ration-coupon fare.

The adults knew more than they were telling us, it was clear, and maybe what they knew was that we weren't winning at all. We were losing. Still no letters from Cy; I knew he'd been sent into active combat, as he longed to be, someplace where the bombs were falling.

"You do what your father tells you," Pat said to me over the dinner table one night, backing Roy up on some point of contention between us, such as the palatability of turnips. "My father's dead," I said, and burst into noisy sobs that were both self-dramatizing and born of real fear. Only the vehemence with which Pat denied it convinced me otherwise. My outburst caused the blood to drain out of her face and make her hands shake, so that she couldn't steady the match to light her cigarette.

Roy pushed back his chair and left the kitchen table. I bolted from it too, and in my room went back to work rolling string, superior heavy cord that Roy brought home for me from the candy company. It came on packing crates, he said, and if I kept up the good work, rolling it nice and tight like that, I might get a prize from the War Department.

I had the awards ceremony planned out in my mind, complete with a band and a famous general presenting me with the plaque. It pleased me to think how the people who found me an oddity, too fond by half of ten-dollar words, would have to revise their opinions and apologize or not get a seat in the auditorium.

When I'd last heard from my father, he'd been stationed in New Jersey. I wrote him a long, patriotic letter that would reach him somehow, I thought, if he were on some secret mission but still alive. I wrote him again, and again, and when I could find nothing to write, sent him newspaper clippings, content irrelevant; the point was an excuse to ask Pat for a stamp. I changed my tune and wrote dramatic letters berating him for not writing to me anymore, his very own daughter, the best string saver in Missoula. No answer over the weeks. I wrote him that I had a fatal disease and was dying. Weak as I was, and despite how hard it was to hold a pencil, I wanted to say goodbye.

Though Cy knew this was hokum, concern about my health must have been at the back of his mind constantly. He called Pat, late at night after I was in bed. She told him I was just fine, and what was it to him? He told her that he was getting married again. He must have stopped writing because he was afraid to break this news, not to me, but to her.

Pat's replay of this conversation to me was flat and don't-give-a-damn. She couldn't remember the woman's name, she said, and offered no information except that she was twenty-eight. An old maid.

My reaction was outrage that Cy hadn't consulted me. I made up a form to send him regarding my future stepmother: name, date of birth, height, weight, hair color, color of eyes, hobbies, favorite movie star, health (good? average? excellent?) but I lost my nerve before I mailed it.

They were already married by the time I met Dorothy, the girl who had seen Cy playing one of the twin pianos in the window of a Great Falls music store, when she was fourteen, and told a girl-friend, "Someday I'm going to marry him." The story was one newspapers loved and reprinted for thirty years.

An Army nurse, Dorothy had masses of auburn hair, a volup-tuous body supported on short, thick legs, and enormous green eyes, extraordinary eyes that seemed to fill up her entire face. They glis-tened as if with tears all the time and gave her a wistful expression even when she smiled. She emphasized them with emerald-green eye shadow and a heavy black line on each upper lid.

Her hair was shoulder-length and artfully curled. She wore styl-ish, fitted gabardine suits, never slacks, and high-heeled backless pumps, called "Spring-o-lators," always color-matched to the rest of her clothes, heavy pancake makeup and jewel-toned pillbox hats. Her earrings matched everything else, her perfume preceded her into a room, and young as she was, she had adopted a notion of el-egant style, furred, hatted and gloved, suited to a much older

Dorothy Cosgriff in her high school years

woman. One thing you could say for her, she said of herself, was that she knew how to dress.

I'd never seen anyone as glamorous as Dorothy and was stunned. She must have been taken aback by Cy's rail-thin, somber daughter, dark-skinned, pigtails pulled so tight they made my own eyes look slanted. Having prepared for our meeting by reading etiquette books in the Missoula library, I greeted her with "It's a pleasure to make your acquaintance."

This did not get our relationship off to the smooth start I had intended, but nothing I could have said or done would have improved matters much. For Dorothy, I was evidence that my mother existed; that she had been Cy's wife for twelve years; that while Cy could sever every other tie, he had a child by a former show girl whose own beauty and style had made her a celebrity in Dorothy's hometown. I was the hard fact that interfered with the mythmaking of perfect love, burning uninterrupted with a true flame since the piano player and the schoolgirl locked eyes through the music store window.

The two of them were staying at Dorothy's parents' house in Great Falls, home on leave, when I went to visit, riding the bus as I'd always ridden the bus to catch up with Cy somewhere or other. The Cosgriff family, Dorothy's parents and a sister living at home, took me in warmly. They were a close, devoutly Catholic bunch, one with whom Cy must have felt at home, and they seemed to have enough of everything to go around and extend to me, rooms, beds, delicious food and tolerant good humor. If they also found me exotic, a gnome inclined to oratorical flourishes, they were kind about it. They were getting used to Cy's oratorical flourishes and willing to get used to mine.

Dorothy took my hair out of the pigtails and rolled it up on metal curlers. Like all previous efforts to curl my hair, hers failed. The reason, she told Cy and the rest of the family, was that I had impossible hair, as straight and fine as a cat's. She let me rummage around in her jewelry box and gave me a pair of earrings she no longer wore because they matched a dress she no longer had. I had no use for earrings but knew she meant the present as a goodwill gesture and was so effusive in my thanks I must have unnerved her again. Letting me try on one of her uniforms, she pointed out that her own waist was so small it almost fit. My mother had a really tiny waist too, I said, and got a look from Cy that created a wind-chill factor in the warm room. When he and I sat side by side on the sofa later that same night, Dorothy came into the room, ignored a pair of empty armchairs and wedged herself between us.

"Dorothy, for god's sake," Cy said, at once amused and irritated. I moved over so that the three of us were not squeezed together but felt like an inadvertent troublemaker again.

I went back home to Missoula a day later, and with some childish impulse to wound, regaled Pat with praise of Dorothy, her auburn hair, her green eye shadow, her diamond engagement and

wedding rings and her Spring-o-lators. I told her about the photo
I'd seen of her in her nurse's uniform, carrying the American flag
at the head of a parade. To my disappointment, Pat asked no questions at all, nor showed any interest in this monologue. Only when
I produced the plastic button earrings Dorothy gave me did she be-
tray curiosity. She took the earrings over to the kitchen window and
turned them over in her hands, examining them as if they were jig-
saw pieces.

Whether by remarrying, or drying out, or both, Cy had re-
deemed himself in Ila Mae's eyes. She had seen him and Dorothy
when they were in Great Falls, my aunt wrote to my mother, and
"Pat you wouldn't recognize him he different man, handsome as
dog." The drying out was Dorothy's doing. "He hasn't had single
drink for mos. She said it was either the bottle or her take his choice.
They don't any of them touch a drop, any of her people." This was
a miracle and proof of God's grace, as Ila Mae had told Cy to his
face. As for Dorothy, she had to give her credit. Before she came
along, he was headed "straight for gutter."

I was sixteen or so when Dorothy gave me her own account of
Cy's reform. She had not only made him swear that he would never
take another drink, but on their wedding night had insisted that he
get down on his knees and pray to God, for help in keeping his word,
before he climbed into bed. She and I were in a motel room in Puyallup, Washington, waiting for Cy to come back after announcing
a night rodeo. When he appeared, I could not look him in the eye
and snapped on the television set.

The scene stays in my mind still, hilarious and disturbing as a
Thurber cartoon. In it, Cy kneels beside the bridal bed in his boxer
shorts and his cowboy boots.

Some women believe that the right woman, loving and resolute
enough, can dry out a drunk and turn a lady-killer into a happily
monogamous husband. In my view, this is like believing you can
win at three-card monte. Yet with Cy and Dorothy, I saw it happen.
My father became a man I barely knew, a new Cy impeccable in his
starched uniform, clear-eyed and confident, within months after
their marriage.

He walked differently. His old swagger had given way to a brisk,
military step compromised somewhat by his bowed legs but impres-

sive anyway. His manners with Dorothy were courtly; he opened car doors for her and held her coat, each of these acts ceremonious. To me, he observed that ladies did not sit with one ankle perched on the other knee and that there were also places well-brought-up little girls did not scratch. When I swore in his presence, he threatened to wash my mouth out with soap. Shades of Roy and Ila Mae. I was amazed.

Through laser looks and a stiffening of his body, as he sat behind the wheel of a car or on the sofa in Dorothy's parents' living room, he let me know that our old lives were now off-limits in conversation. "Remember . . ." I would begin, or "We used to . . ." and there would emanate from Cy what felt like a blast of cold air, freezing out both reminiscence and me.

The same cold draft chilled us all when Cy addressed me as "Pat," a mistake he corrected in the same breath but that left him flustered and Dorothy annoyed each time it happened. How much or how little Dorothy knew about Cy's first marriage, the powerful attachment, the destructive behavior and the refusal to acknowledge that it was over, she knew enough to feel threatened. If mentioning Pat was unavoidable, my mother was "Her." "You'd better call Missoula and let her know when Cyra's coming home." The pronoun came out of my stepmother's mouth with backspin on it. Without having it spelled out for me, on my short and infrequent visits, I knew that Dorothy felt the sooner I was back on the bus, the better.

Soon after the marriage she resigned her commission, while Cy, unwilling to be outranked by his wife, went into Officer Candidate School. Dorothy became pregnant. My brother Terry was born, the event marked by a printed announcement headed "Taillon Stampede" and listing the doctor in attendance as the Arena Judge and the nurses as Pickup Riders. Along with everyone else on their mailing list, I got this announcement and glued it into my scrapbook, beside clippings about my mother's bowling league. It was the first piece of mail from Cy for nearly a year.

Ila Mae wrote, full of goodwill toward the reconstituted Taillons and breathless about the baby. Cy was sorry now that he had named me after him, she said. Otherwise Terry could have been Cy

Jr. Always practical, she suggested that since "Cyra funny name any-way as I have all ways said," the problem could be solved if Roy and Pat changed my name. Her suggestion was Minnie Mae, after my maternal grandmother, who was "living saint until God took her to be angel."

Longing to see the new baby, I got my chance at last. Cy was stationed in Oakland, California, and was coming home, briefly, to get Dorothy and Terry. He'd found an apartment, no easy task in wartime. Before they left, he called and arranged for me to visit the family in Great Falls. I went, and through no fault of mine or any-one else's, became a burden on Cy and Dorothy's marriage that both of them deeply resented. During that week, Pat had her second nervous breakdown. This one was so severe she was sent back to the hospital at Warm Springs immediately.

Behind the closed doors I had learned to associate with trouble, Cy talked to Roy on the telephone. Afterward, in the upstairs bed-room of the Cosgriffs' house, he and Dorothy shut themselves away for hours, conferring over the crisis. The room was thick with smoke from Cy's cigarettes, his remaining vice, when he emerged to tell me that I was coming along with him, Dorothy and Terry to Oak-land. He had the grace to tell me what was going on this time, though I dimly understood "nervous breakdown." Roy was too up-set himself to take care of me, he said. He also agreed with Cy that the cause of Pat's illness was overwork. "She had to go and start another damned dance studio."

Several months before, Pat had launched "Patricia's School of the Dance" on the ground floor of a moving and storage company in Missoula. It offered tap, ballet and exercise classes for what ads forthrightly called "fatties" and was an instant success.

The money must have come from Roy, not a large investment in that it involved only rent and equipping the place with mirrors, ballet barres and exercise mats. It must have been large to him, and how my mother talked him into freeing her from her captivity, as well as backing her financially, I can't imagine.

That Cy was remarried may have had something to do with it, in that he no longer posed so grave a threat. It may have occurred to Roy that having married his dream woman, the glamorous show girl, he had turned her into a household drab. Hidden under a bushel, or one of Ila Mae's housedresses, Pat's light cast no luster on him. Whatever negotiations took place behind the scenes, Patricia's School of the Dance opened with fanfare.

The Daily Missoulian ran my mother's press release, the same one she'd used when she opened her Billings studio years before. It outlined her theatrical career, with flourishes, and included a high-minded statement about Dance and the Whole Child. We held an open house for prospective customers, with iced tea and bakery cookies. Old publicity pictures of Pat filled the big window facing the street: Pat in a feathered headdress doing the splits, Pat waving from the door of an airplane, "en route to further studies in Paris." Had she really been to Paris? I asked her, dying to hear all about it. That's what it said, didn't it? she snapped.

By the end of her first month, she had so many students, kids taking tap after school and their mothers sweating through acrobatic routines mornings and evenings, she had to hire an assistant instructor, a high school girl who had mastered the time step and could lead Beginning Tap, over and over, through "East Side, West Side."

Roy kept the books at the studio and spent all his evenings there. I reported to the place after school and ran errands, among them checking out library books on ballet for Pat. She knew virtually nothing about it but was teaching it anyway. Her students mainly learned to stand on one leg and point their toes.

I loved the school. One large bright room with a hardwood floor, it smelled of sweaty rubber mats and floor polish, the ammonia with which Roy and I cleaned the mirrors, and take-out food. With no time to go home for dinner, the three of us ate in the partitioned-off office at the front, on Roy's secondhand wooden desk. Though Roy claimed he went out for hamburgers and milk shakes only because no drive-ins offered take-out spinach, he loved the greasy food he preached was poisonous and fell on it with as much appetite as my mother and I did. Scratch a food faddist and you'll find a man whose erotic fantasies center on french fries.

Still slim and supple, no longer isolated from the world outside our bungalow, Pat turned into a beauty again. My mother was one of those women who can dazzle one day and the next look plain, gray-faced and lifeless. In retrospect, I can reconstruct the periods before her breakdowns by remembering how she looked. Light went out of her face a little at a time, as if behind her eyes she were pulling down a shade. As a child, I hadn't learned to read the signs and had no clue. So when her second bout of mental illness shattered her, life upended itself without warning. With my father and his new family, I left Great Falls in a few days, on a train packed tight with servicemen and headed for California.

The four of us had two seats. Dorothy sat in one holding Terry, whose restless crying rose up with the crying of other babies. I sat in the other, watching the landscape go by until the overhead lights dimmed and it was black outside. Cy stood for the whole trip in the crowded aisle, holding on to the overhead baggage rack and refusing to trade places with either Dorothy or me. His notion of chivalry dictated that he stand for eighteen hours or so while his wife and children sat.

My parents' shared-custody agreement, a cousin told me later, had resolved a deadlock. Neither parent wanted full-time responsibility for me. In fact, neither wanted custody. Cy wanted to pursue his rodeo career. Pat wanted to pursue the fantasy that she was still a show girl despite her marriage to Roy. They weren't enlightened but self-centered.

Wasn't that a fine kettle of beans? the cousin asked. Didn't it just make me want to shake the two of them until their teeth rattled?

Of course it did, but memory is selective. One couldn't live with it if it weren't. I prefer to remember my mother all dazzle and snap, leading her dancing classes at the studio while I gloried in gilt by association. I prefer to remember Cy swaying in the aisle on that trip to Oakland, gallant and asleep on his feet.

NINE

The apartment in Oakland, dark and smelling of mildew, was in the basement of a stucco house on a hill. The rent for it was extortionate, Cy complained, wartime profiteering on the part of our landlady, who lived upstairs, scolded every time we turned on our radio and threatened to evict us when I picked plums from the tree in the backyard. She didn't mind if they rotted unpicked, or if birds ate them, only if tenants' children did.

Without my being there, Cy, Dorothy and Terry would have been cramped in their three rooms. Cy's soldier's pay had to stretch farther than my father and his new wife anticipated. They had no privacy and countless practical problems, from putting me in school somewhere to getting along without a car, never easy in California. Because our hill was so steep, Dorothy could push Terry's buggy down it to shop, but not up again. She had to wait on the corner for Cy to come home on the streetcar, in the evenings, with her buggyload of baby, laundry and groceries.

Far harder on her, the apartment teemed with mice. Dorothy was in terror of them. I wasn't, and when she and I were at war with one another, I could always pretend that I had seen a mouse. It gave me a satisfying sense of power to see her standing on a kitchen chair, white-faced and helpless—my powerful stepmother reduced to powerlessness. She and I had quickly arrived at the relationship we never substantially altered. With equal vehemence, we detested each other.

So jealous of Cy she resented even the fraction of his affections I claimed, Dorothy was a setter of snares. In her version of our skirmishes, she made heroic efforts to please her stepdaughter. I failed to appreciate these efforts, or appreciate them enough, or appreciate them in the proper way, impossible because there was no proper way. "I'm not angry, I'm only hurt," was her litany.

"I'm not hurt, I'm only angry," I screamed back at her, and caught hell from my father for "sassing back." Like most men, Cy hated what he called "a cat fight," friction between women. His un-Solomon-like solution was to join in the shouting himself, until the landlady wielded her gavel, a broom handle, and brought us all to order by pounding on her kitchen floor, our kitchen ceiling.

Dorothy escalated our hostilities every chance she got. I became ever more resentful and cagier, as good at provoking her as she was at provoking me. She spent a lot of time on that kitchen chair, cowering from imaginary mice, and was subjected to worse forms of terrorism. Carrying the baby across the room, I got good at faking a stumble and making it look as if I were about to drop him on his head.

This hateful behavior I look back on without guilt because I was up against an equally unprincipled opponent. What affection I can find in my middle-aged self for Dorothy is based on what a worthy enemy she was, how determined and how inventive. I got up the Irish in her, she said, but what I really brought to flower in her was tactical genius. One has to respect the domestic Desert Fox who never deploys the same weapons in the same place or repeats the same maneuver.

I had few clothes with me in Oakland, only those I would have needed for a few days of visiting in Great Falls. Ila Mae's handiwork, these clothes were dowdy even at Our Lady of Lourdes, the Catholic school at the foot of the hill where Cy enrolled me. Other girls my age wore skirts and sweaters, he noticed, when he escorted me there on his way to the Army base in the mornings. I alternated among three skimpier versions of the housedresses Ila Mae made for Pat, cotton print sacks cut like those worn by early female missionaries.

As tight as money was in the household, my fashion-conscious father insisted Dorothy buy me a pleated plaid skirt and matching sweater.

Dorothy set out on this mission alone. With unerring instinct, she picked out an outfit that made me look even more sallow and wizened than I already looked, the skirt two sizes too large and so long it came to the top of my socks, the sweater a yellow-green never seen in nature, seldom in art. My skin took a greenish sheen from it even under the low-wattage light bulbs our landlady made us use.

Cy looked at me and registered the same despair he had felt when he paid ten dollars for a permanent wave and my hair didn't bend. His expression told me he had a hopeless case for a daughter: deck her out in a brand-new green sweater, and the whole kid turned green.

Dorothy told me how much these clothes had cost and the trial-by-streetcar she had gone through to buy them. All that money, and all that work, and one could tell from my sour look that I didn't like them. It just went to show that as far as I was concerned, she could do nothing right.

As soon as I put on that sweater and skirt, I knew they made me look like an organ grinder's monkey. I also knew it was politic to make a show of appreciation and launched into one fit for a cast of thousands. I jumped up and down, squealed, hugged Dorothy, hugged Cy, hugged Dorothy again. I said the skirt was the most beautiful skirt in the world and the sweater was even prettier. I claimed to want to sleep in these clothes, so that we would never be parted. Oh thank you thank you thank you thank you. I concluded with a clog dance meant to convey wild excitement.

My stepmother watched. Her shoulders sagged and a pair of perfect tears spilled from her luminous green eyes. "You know," she said, "even if you don't like a present somebody gives you, you could pretend to be grateful."

That I remember this incident, so far in the past, is a sign of arrested development. I do remember it, and after thirty-five years, compulsively thank telephone solicitors for calling.

Our time in Oakland must have passed slowly for Cy and Dorothy as it did for me. Cy was just one more lieutenant, and the man hated being one more anything. Dorothy, a gregarious young woman, was far from her friends and family, trapped in a basement with a new baby, a loathsome stepdaughter and mice. Only Terry, blond, sunny-tempered and sturdy, thrived. The world's prize baby, in Cy's view, Dorothy's and mine, he made us into a family of sorts, in spite of ourselves, because we all thought of him as under our care and joint proprietorship. At Our Lady of Lourdes, I got into a fist-fight with a girl who claimed her baby brother was walking before he was.

There, too, I was baptized as a Catholic at my own insistence. Frantic to conform, as usual, I had undergone a conversion of epic proportions, complete with religious visions lifted from *The Song of Bernadette* and an inner voice announcing I was destined to be a saint. When I wrote home about it, the baptism caused proportionate religious hysteria on my Aunt Ila Mae's part, and prompted one of the few letters Roy ever wrote me.

In his surprisingly elegant hand, he informed me that no matter how much holy water the priests and nuns had made me drink, I was a Lutheran. While he had no religious faith of his own, Roy knew all about "mackerel snappers" just as he knew all about house cats. Cats jumped on your chest and sucked out your breath while you were asleep. Catholics sucked out your soul, sold it on the soul market and turned the proceeds over to the Pope.

Ila Mae changed church affiliations frequently because she and the minister differed on some fine point of theology. Her restless quest stopped short of Catholicism, however, and she also wrote furious letters to Cy and Dorothy, more letters to me. In mine, she pointed out that Catholicism was for foreigners and I had been born right here in the U.S. of A.

I must have known that the Catholic Church and I were just one of those things, and that when I went back to Missoula, it would be all over between us. Certainly I threw myself into my new faith the way one hurtles into doomed love affairs, with such excessive-ness the nuns at school were alarmed rather than pleased. I prayed for hours at a time, in front of the statues in the chapel; genu-flected deeply upon entering and leaving the pews, as if taking a curtain call; told my rosary beads at recess and lunchtime, while every-body else ate. I had a brown-bag lunch but was fasting. No oppor-tunity for a pietism got by me. I was ready with "Bless you" before anyone within miles thought of sneezing.

Though Cy looked at his prospective saint askance too, he arranged for my baptism, and never one to miss an opportunity, asked his CO from the base to be my godfather. I do not remember that imposing gentleman's name because I never saw or heard from him again.

Because of my prayers, I felt sure at the time, the war finally ended. Cy took me to downtown Oakland, the streetcar we rode inching through the crowds in the street, to see the victory celebration. Confetti poured down on us from the tall buildings. Car horns blared. Men pounded my father on the back, because he was in uniform, and weeping women kissed him. Caught up in all that emotion, I had a satisfying cry too. Somewhere in the back of my mind was a release from the fear I had felt back in Missoula—that Cy would die in the war, that bombs would fall on the peaceful town, that there was no such thing as safety anymore, or sameness.

I was right about the "sameness" part. In a few weeks, I was back in Missoula again, my temporary family and I having made another long train ride home. And while Missoula was intact, not bombed into oblivion, my mother wasn't.

Though she'd been withdrawn sometimes before, I'd never seen her so old-looking and dispirited. She padded around the house in bedroom slippers, incurious about the time I had been away. Patricia's School of the Dance was empty, I could see through the dusty windows, except for the ballet barres that still lined the walls. No sign out front, no mirrors, no rubber exercise mats on the floors. Roy must have sold the fittings secondhand and closed the place while she was in the hospital at Warm Springs.

At first I wondered if Pat missed the school, then if she remembered that there had been one. She moved around now in a fog of her own making, smiling when she sensed that a response of some description was called for, picking up small objects—ashtrays, copies of the *Reader's Digest*, pots and pans—and then putting them back where she got them. She seemed to be keeping herself busy, but the busy work accomplished nothing and her monotonous slow pacing led nowhere. Roy told me to be nice to her and made an exhausted effort to be nicer to her himself.

Why it takes so many years to forgive one's parents their failings and sympathize with their disappointments, I cannot explain. Nor do I know why that sympathy comes so much harder than the tolerance one summons easily for friends, or strangers. All of Roy's long life, I thought of him as a tyrant, my mother his helpless victim. Now I know he was a victim of their marriage as much as she was, a man who didn't miss the brass ring but had the misfortune of catching it.

My stepfather must have lain awake nights, during those years, comparing the fantasy of Pat to the damaged woman sleeping in the other room. He must have felt he had two children, my mother and me, neither one loving him and neither really his. He was subject to night terrors, bad dreams that made him cry out so loudly, I would get out of bed and wake him up.

To stall off the moment when I would leave him alone again, Roy told me about these nightmares in detail. Large animals sprang onto his back and dug their claws into him; no matter how he struggled, he could not shake them off. Gaping pits opened in front of the station wagon while he drove around Missoula replenishing vending machines. Someone close to him died, in dream after dream. Roy stood at the graveside, grieving deeply, but did not know who lay in the coffin.

From Wisconsin came word that his brother Vin actually had died, of bronchial flu. A sister wrote a long letter describing his last hours in the hospital and the funeral arrangements. "The casket was a very lovely one. The pillow was a sort of ashes of roses color and a third of the cover was too and a little in the scarf over the casket. You see he was so dark & thin we didn't want him to lay on white or cream."

Roy sat up all night, for a week, reading this letter over and over again. In the mornings, I'd find him in the same chair in the living room, the lights all on and cigarette smoke dense in the air. So superstitious he'd make a U-turn and drive around the block rather than let a black cat cross his path, my stepfather must have blamed himself for Vin's death, believed that his nightmares had been prophetic. If he fell asleep and dreamed the same dream again, someone else might die, one of the few other human beings to whom he felt connected.

What little he revealed of himself served only to make him more opaque. We lived, when I was ten years old, in a house that had two bedrooms facing the street, North Avenue East. In mine one winter evening, I sat on my bed reading, in my Montgomery Ward catalogue mail-order underwear. Roy drove past, coming home from work, hurtled into the house and my room and stood there, still with his hat on, red-faced and wild-eyed. On his forehead, a vein pulsed.

He snatched up a blanket and threw it over my spindly form. "My God, woman," he shouted. *"Are you mad?"*

What quirk of his sexual nature led him to see a forty-pound child, in peach-colored cotton vest and knickers, as Susanna tempting the elders? What other quirk caused him to express his outrage in language that might have come from Edgar Allan Poe? My stepfather remains as much a mystery to me now as he was then, a man whose mind resembled the curious hodgepodge he had created in our basement.

I have a copy of a book he sold door to door in 1921, *The Standard Dictionary of Facts*. He must have studied it extensively himself and had chosen to underline "100 A.D., The Huns Migrate Westward" and "1834, Robert Peel, Premier, Difficulties in Canada."

I have representative volumes from his library on baldness remedies, cancer cures and the diagnostic talents of the lower bowel. Also heavily underlined is a book entitled *Making Yourself Taller*.

Though I have moved numbers of times myself, I have carted along Roy's canvas boxing shoes, in case I ever need them; a leather miner's apron and a Life Saver display rack from the candy company—useless artifacts, all of them, and impossible to discard. I keep expecting them to unravel for me that dour, inscrutable man who wanted to be taller, and hairier, and no doubt happier.

I leave him behind, for the moment, with his impracticable dreams and his night terrors, in order to catch up with Cy: but my stepfather will be back. Roy Qualley was tacked as closely to Cy Taillon's heels as his shadow.

TEN

In 1945, after his discharge from the Army, Cy set out on the rodeo circuit again. He had promised Dorothy that when the war was over he would get a steady job, the kind that came with a regular paycheck, and that the family would settle down somewhere. No more gypsying; she had his word on it. In its place, security and a life that made sense.

He could no more have kept this promise than squeezed his feet into shoes without complaining that they pinched intolerably. My father was destined to announce rodeos the way other people are born cellists or water diviners. Keeping regular hours and leading a normal life, he would have vaporized, like the wicked witch in *The Wizard of Oz*, leaving nothing behind but gray ash and a pair of cowboy boots.

Whatever her preference in the matter, Dorothy went along with his change of heart, becoming an expert packer of suitcases, spending her evenings in motel rooms, with the baby, while Cy was at the fairgrounds orchestrating the roar of the crowd. Blessed with more sense than Pat had, she imposed the condition that Cy come straight home after the rodeo.

My newly respectable father did. For the first time in his life, he welcomed domesticity instead of finding ways to avoid it. He opened the first bank account he ever had and stayed out of the bars, which meant he had money to deposit in it.

That first year on the circuit after the war was as lean as the prewar years. Cy's itinerary for 1945 shows few bookings and entire weeks followed by the notation "To be announced at a later date."

He was on his way to a successful career notwithstanding. After 1946, and the Great Falls air show disaster, these itineraries run to three double-spaced pages, the rodeos so close together he had to fly, rather than drive, between some of them.

You can still hear firsthand accounts of this event over a whiskey ditch at the Cowboys Bar, across from the fairgrounds where it took place, and if you linger there long, you will. Calling itself a bar and museum, the Cowboys is lined with rodeo photos and populated with the former riders in them. These men, soft-bellied but with handshakes you can feel in your shoulder blades, reminisce about favorite Brahmas as if they were much-loved household pets. They also reminisce about what proved to be the turning point in my father's life on the circuit.

Pete Logan, another announcer, described it in a tribute he wrote, for *World of Rodeo and Western Heritage*, when Cy retired. Noting that his longtime colleague "left indelible footprints along the long and lonely rodeo road," Logan tells what happened that afternoon in a style that suggests he would have also made a first-rate documentary filmmaker:

> August, 1946. Great Falls, Mt. A hot August afternoon. Within seconds it got much hotter.
>
> For some reason known only to God, the Air Force decided to fly three fully fueled airplanes past a grandstand that was occupied with no less than ten thousand people. An Air Force person was to comment on this as the rodeo waited. Without warning the planes collided. Bits and pieces of metal started falling. One plane ploughed into a race barn not three hundred yards from the grandstand and exploded, killing horses and people. A second one crashed into a hillside less than a quarter mile away and exploded. The third was able to stay airborne and stagger back to the Air Force base.
>
> The Air Force person froze, unable to say a word. Cy im-

mediately took over and calmly explained that there was no danger now. And as the heat from the burning plane, the awful smell of death permeated the atmosphere, the people remained pretty much as they were, transfixed at the horror of what they had seen. The slightest suggestion of uncertainty or panic would have resulted in the death of scores of humanity. A then 17-year-old girl remembers bits of metal falling by her, with tiny sparks falling in her hair, the heat from the burning gasoline, and thru it all, hearing Cy talking to them.

Perhaps it was the same woman who told me her own version of this tale, a few summers ago, and in the course of it issued the definitive statement on Cy's voice. "I don't know what God looks like," she said, "but I know what He sounds like."

His presence of mind brought my father a citation from the Air Force and masses of publicity. Newspapers all over the country ran the story and his picture; intrigued with the strikingly handsome man with the profession no one outside the West had ever heard of, they also ran sidebars discovering rodeo. Bookings began to pour in, not just for rodeos but for public events of all kinds. After all the lean years of eating more dust than steak dinners, Cy was established.

At least he was established in most people's eyes. After the Great Falls air show disaster, he sent me a clipping. The story notes breathlessly: "In addition to his announcing experience he has been a theatrical producer, vaudeville performer, songwriter, dance musician, amateur boxer, airplane pilot and radio producer." Written beside this list is an addition only Roy Qualley could have made—"& Bum," it reads.

Westerners love a hero, and when the hero is one of their own, a cowboy, their pride does not diminish in a small matter of four decades. On trips back to Great Falls now, I size up the fairgrounds and wonder how such a small place could have held ten thousand people. I listen to eyewitness accounts of that afternoon and ponder their discrepancies. As the bourbon flows, the number of people killed increases, the explosion virtually wipes out Great Falls and my father remains at the mike while flames lick at the wooden announcer's stand.

I swallow my skepticism, along with the drink I am never allowed to pay for. As my father's daughter, I should know that mythmaking has its own logic.

I also know less about Cy, at that point in his life, than do the tale tellers, for just when he stepped to center stage, I drifted off into the wings and our long estrangement began. While I still joined Cy, Dorothy and Terry on the circuit from time to time, or spent a school holiday with them in Great Falls, I was never part of my father's household again after Oakland. As was inevitable, after his remar-

Cy, Tommy, Dorothy and Terry on the road between rodeos

riage the father and the child of his first marriage began to grow apart.

Cy had two sons now, two future cowboys. My brother Tommy's birth in 1947 occasioned another announcement in the form of a mock rodeo program, reproducing the logo from Cy's letterhead. The Second Performance of the Taillon Stampede noted that Tommy Louis was the brother of the previous world champion baby boy, Terry James. Along with the Arena Director, the Pickup Riders and the Judges (Cy's mother and father), this edition lists Mr. and Mrs. Cy Taillon as Producers and Cy Taillon as Announcer. Cy thus managed to get his own name in print twice.

He had his pretty second wife, who had transformed his life and made him infinitely happier. So domestic she made up motel beds in the mornings, with neat hospital corners, Dorothy was the wife my mother had refused to be, the woman behind the man instead of the one constantly stepping in front of him.

He had both the freedom of the road and a place to call home, the Cosgriff house in Great Falls. The family made its base there during the thirty days a year or so they weren't traveling.

Cy's voice boomed through that house and his proprietary presence filled it. His previous addresses had been boardinghouses, motels and favorite saloons. In Dorothy's mother's house, he enjoyed comforts ordinary to other people, extraordinary to Cy, such as beds without lumps in them, home cooking and full-sized bars of soap in the bathroom. His mail was waiting for him there, instead of bouncing from General Delivery in one town to General Delivery in the next.

Best of all, none of these things threatened to curb his independence because the house was not Cy's own. He could come and go, unencumbered by anything but his luggage. No one expected him to run errands or take down the storm windows; his arrival was an event, another personal appearance. My father never walked into a room, anywhere, without expecting faces to turn toward him and at least a silent round of applause. If one read a magazine when he was present, or listened to *Amos 'n' Andy* rather than to Cy, he sulked.

He knew no more drunken nights and unspeakable mornings.

Nor did he start the day rummaging for enough change to put a few gallons of gas in the car. With his career thriving, Cy had become an astute businessman, acting as his own agent, commanding high fees. The first year he needed a tax accountant, he passed the news on to me, and thus to Pat and Roy, in Missoula. He was so busy now, he wrote, he could not keep track of his complicated financial situation.

Roy took the opportunity to deliver an address on the subject of Cy's unpaid child support. He never tried to collect this money, because he found it more satisfying that Cy owed it, but when Cy sent me a crisp new twenty-dollar bill for Christmas, Roy placed a personal lien on it. He opened a passbook savings account for me, at the First National Bank in Missoula, and soon had cause for more anger and indignation. No banking laws prevent minors from drawing their money out of savings accounts and investing it in Fred Astaire movies.

I would have preferred one of Cy's old Christmas boxes, full of stuffed olives and animal crackers. Cy didn't know about this because we knew less and less about each other. When I came to visit him, infrequently, we were taken aback by how the other had changed and how the familiar had become strange.

As I grew, I stayed thin and became gawkier, the kind of pre-adolescent poltergeist who can't move about without tripping over her own feet. From across a room, I could cause Dorothy's Hummel figurines to fall off their shelves. My hands were too big for the rest of me and hung at the ends of my wrists like a pair of empty gardening gloves. They were shaped like Cy's meticulously manicured hands, but his were deft, while what I did with mine, mainly, was drop things.

Immune to the sulfurous-smelling anti-acne cream Dorothy bought me, I broke out in blotches; was a demonstration model of nervous tics and twitches; still cried when spoken to sharply. In Cy's view, accurate in this case, I was also freakishly bookish. Normal twelve-year-old girls, by way of making conversation, did not recite "Hiawatha." After I confessed to Terry, who blew the whistle on me out of astonishment, that I had always been afraid of horses, my father knew no blood ties existed between us. My strongest memory

Cyra in Missoula at about age twelve

of him then is Cy staring at me, with his heavy black eyebrows raised. He must have been trying to figure out who I was.

He seemed as alien to me. For years, Cy shared with champion bronc rider Casey Tibbs the title "World's Best-Dressed Cowboy." This accolade, awarded him by the Western Clothiers Association, my father earned with his wardrobe of dozens upon dozens of cowboy hats: soft grays and beiges, black, white and mossy green. Twenty color-coordinated outfits accompanied him on the road, Western suits made for him by a tailor in Denver out of fine, lightweight gabardine. Dorothy packed them all in layers and layers of tissue paper, so they emerged from suitcases without a wrinkle. His cowboy boots were also custom-made, of kangaroo skin. Cy had found that kangaroo skin was the softest of leathers, he told reporters. Now he could wear nothing else.

His shirts crackled with starch when they emerged from their own tissue-paper clouds. He held his tie in place with a diamond horseshoe stickpin fashioned from his mother's wedding ring. His best kangaroo-skin boots had gold- and silver-inlaid heels, and a leather hanging bag made for him by a fan had his profile at the mike tooled into it and the legend "Cy Taillon, World's Greatest Rodeo Announcer." Even his tuxedos, he told the Denver *Post*, were custom-tailored and Western-cut. The former peacock in the bright satin shirts had adopted his own version of quiet good taste.

NO NO

At the curb in front of the Cosgriff house was the latest of his Buick Roadmasters. By 1959, Cy was driving 65,000 to 80,000 miles a year. By 1971, he had worn out nine of these cars as well as ten Cadillacs. Before he announced his last rodeo, he had put another half dozen cars out to pasture—in Western parlance, tuckered out.

One of these Roadmasters was salmon pink and silver, with my father's initials on silver plaques on the doors. At thirteen, I took

No

A teenaged Cyra leaning against the Buick Roadmaster in front of the Cosgriff family home, 1954 its 1953 Oldsmobile

Rocket 88

Cy Taillon, "World's Greatest Rodeo Announcer"

it for a spin around the block, at his insistence, and almost put us both through the windshield when I stepped on the power brakes. Cy said I drove like my mother and asked if she had put me up to killing him.

He was a fixture, by then, at all the big rodeos with the romantic names, the Snake River Stampede, the Pike's Peak or Bust Rodeo, the American Royal Horse Show and the Calgary Stampede, as well as thirty smaller ones a year. By the late fifties, he estimated that 87,000 people had heard him announce. When he began presiding over rodeos on national television, the number shot up, and he received requests for signed photos, as if he were a movie star.

Announcing in Madison Square Garden, he even impressed an eastern sportswriter and got a good if condescending review, one that suggested he was not as provincial as New Yorkers might expect: "His diction is excellent and he speaks gentlemanly English with a faint touch of Westernism."

We went nowhere, when I traveled with the family, where my father was not lionized and where people did not crowd around him, dogging his gold and silver heels and hanging on his every word. To these people's amazement, he remembered all their names from one year to the next, cowboys, local rodeo officials, fans and without exception, reporters. No wonder it irritated Cy that I would not wear cowboy boots anymore; that I'd as soon watch television in the motel as sit through every performance he gave; that when I did go, while he enthralled the rest of the rodeo crowd, I sat in the grandstands and read.

Out of necessity, I had ceased to be a satellite spinning in his orbit. So there he was, with his rodeo-loving sons, his tireless press agent of a wife and a daughter who looked like him, was named after him and had decided "seen one rodeo, you've seen them all."

Public speakers always find themselves preoccupied with the face in a crowd stretched into a yawn. Mine must have been that bored face Cy picked out, blandly disengaged except when a calf got its neck broken in the calf-roping event.

On these occasions, infrequent though they were, I registered moral outrage. Rodeo was cruel, I said. This attitude my father could not tolerate, not from me, not from journalists and, most of all, not the self-righteous, lily-livered SPCA.

Cy no longer "cussed." He made an exception for misguided critics of the sport that was his life as well as his livelihood. In a piece he wrote for *Western Horseman*, he tells of trying to convert some SPCA officials, at a rodeo in Chicago, "to my honest belief that any cruelty in the game applies more to the contestants than to the stock." Bucking horses did not work over five minutes a year and "enjoyed the greatest freedom of any animal." Thousands of calves and steers "were slaughtered every day, without a sporting chance, in order to provide meat for our tables. . . ." As for injuries, "a ratio of about ten contestants were injured for any animal hurt in any way."

Soon after the Chicago rodeo began, a quarter horse burst out of the chute without a buck-jump. "Attaining great speed, it veered sharply to the left and exploded into the concrete wall from which it rebounded with an obviously broken neck: With tongue lolling grotesquely, the animal gave a few convulsive jerks and was dead."

From the crow's nest, the Voice of the West announced that this animal was merely stunned. "I also expressed the hope that it would soon recover."

The audience, including the SPCA inspectors, was not convinced. It booed and hissed. Cy ducked behind the chutes for a desperate consultation with the stock producers.

The dead horse had been dragged out of the arena, in full view of the hostile crowd. Later in the rodeo, notwithstanding, my father announced that it had been "frightened or confused by the lights" and was once again in perfect health. Into the arena charged a similar horse, flummoxing the Chicagoans, who couldn't tell one horse from another. "We went on to complete one of the most enthusiastically received performances of the entire engagement."

My rodeo heritage aside, my heart still goes out to the steer when the rope snaps taut around its neck. I wince when the rider jumps from his horse, runs down the rope and twists its neck in a hammerlock. But I have come to accept the sport on its own terms and keep my remaining objections to myself. Call this craven if you will. Then ponder what might have happened to a daughter of Manolete, at the bullring in Madrid, who was moved to wail, "Oh, the poor bull."

ELEVEN

In an old "Red Ryder" cartoon panel, the strip's creator, Fred Harmon, has Red say to Cy Taillon, "It wouldn't be a show without your silver-tongued palaver." I'm sure my father liked the exposure and that he took exception to the word "show." A major concern of his, as he refined and developed his style at the mike, was that rodeo develop a more dignified image as well. It was a sport, not a carnival act, and it behooved everyone who had anything to do with it—sportswriters, fans and contestants alike—to remember that.

Bronc riders and record-time ropers, a modest lot, rarely wave their hats at the crowd or give each other "high fives" at the end of a ride. Any who did would have felt the cutting edge of Cy's silver tongue.

The reporter who wrote about colorful buckaroos putting on a daredevil Wild West show soon had a wrathful Cy on the other side of his desk, his expensive boots parked on it and his voice making the paper clips rattle. Rodeo belonged on the sports page, not in the entertainment section, and the correct term was "rodeo athletes," not "cowpokes."

The fan who caught up with him to tell him he and the wife thought those hands sure could ride was set straight. Rodeo contestants were not ranch hands but professional riders and ropers.

"They have developed such skill with rampaging livestock," Cy thundered at a writer for a Fort Worth newspaper, "that the average ranch hand would be licked hands down in competition with them." Putting an ordinary ranch hand in the rodeo arena, in fact, would be like "letting a sandlot baseball player in the World Series."

The writer had said in print that cowboys were cowboys, not athletes. When my father got through with him, he published a follow-up column deciding that he "just possibly was wrong."

Cy wore the Western equivalent of Savile Row tailoring because he wanted to look like a man presiding over a major sports competition rather than like a barker for Annie Oakley or Wild Bill Hickok. He pioneered the "straight man" style of announcing, even when the cowboys themselves told him he sounded like a storefront lawyer, because he thought the old style of cornball comedy from the crow's nest was an affront to both competitors and audience. Says Pete Logan, who began announcing rodeos the year after Cy did, "At times he was stubborn, uncompromising and difficult, but always a dedicated professional. He was acutely aware that his conduct and appearance reflected on our profession." Thus he set standards that those who followed him had to have "if they ever expected to get out of the bushes."

Much of the impetus for these reforms, I am certain, came from Dorothy, who turned Cy into a gentleman by being a lady, unmistakable as anything but one, in a world that divided women into two categories. One was what my brother Terry calls "twinks, scuzzbutts and squirrels," rodeo groupies. The other was good ol' gals, female counterparts of their Western men.

Good ol' gals wore jeans and boots. They hauled horse trailers as handily as they hauled their husbands from a bar, or someone else's bed, and had what Dorothy called "mouths on them." They could tell dirty stories, drink men twice their body weight under the table or ride a breakneck barrel race.

Dorothy stuck to dresses and high-heeled shoes, though there are no heels high enough to traverse a rodeo grounds and end up smelling like a rose. She never laughed at a dirty joke, much less told one, and had a way of causing the joke teller to wither and mutter, "No offense intended." In her mink-stoled and perfumed wake, gentility followed, trotting to keep up.

So did the old-fashioned gallantry cowboys accord "ladies" and grudging deference from members of her own sex. Somehow my stepmother spent her long married life on the circuit without its rough-and-tumble rubbing off on her. Instead, she rubbed the rough-and-tumble off the circuit, and Cy. It was a point of pride with her that the house the family eventually bought in Denver showed "no trace of any Western influence." Neither did Dorothy, she emphasized to an interviewer in Sydney, Australia, where Cy announced the riding events at the Royal Easter Show. While she professed to love rodeo, she disliked Western dress, would never wear it and made only one concession to it. This was to wear clothes made in the same fabric as her husband's suits. "The dress I wear merely complements his outfit."

No cowboys bunked on the wall-to-wall carpet in that house in the suburbs of Denver. My father's collection of Western bronzes was consigned to the den. It could have been the house of a branch bank manager or a dentist.

The sport was changing along with Cy, rubbing off its rough edges. Back in 1945, a group of rodeo contestants had founded the Cowboys Turtle Association, so named because they had been so slow in seeing the need for it and getting it started. The organization was a union of sorts, its intention to cut riders and ropers in on a fair share of the profits.

Before the Turtles, promoters could stage rodeos and skip out with the gate. Contestants' entry fees were not added to the prize money for an event; the cowboy paid for the privilege of risking life and limb, while the promoters scooped in both his entry fees and the money fans paid to pass through the turnstiles.

The organization became the Rodeo Cowboys Association and eventually the Professional Rodeo Cowboys Association, which now regulates all phases of the rodeo profession. One of its rules is that entry fees must be added to the prize money. Though he may have to enter ninety or a hundred rodeos a year, sometimes competing in two on the same day, a top cowboy can keep himself in Holiday Inns, Levi's and orthopedic surgeons. If he's a champion, and his kids don't insist on enrolling in rodeo school in Henryetta, Oklahoma, or Clovis, California, an all-American bronc rider can put them through Yale.

These gains came hard, over the objections of the producers. The producers hired Cy and issued his contracts—more often than not, in the form of a handshake—and signed his paychecks. Because his sympathies were with the cowboys, he joined the RCA anyway and promoted it from the beginning. One cowboy who approved wrote the following poetic tribute: "Cy Taillon tossed his Stetson aside / And kissed the girls goodbye. / This is one big show he can't announce, / But he's workin' it high."

Numbers of more formal testimonials followed. Over Cy's desk, in later years, was a display of awards, including one from International Rodeo Management naming him the 1966 "Rodeo Man of the Year." My father rode tall in the saddle in the eyes of money men and cowboys alike.

How could we find common ground anymore, when he became such an estimable personage, his daughter and the Voice of Rodeo? Never a shy wood violet, Cy now took himself seriously indeed. He became an avatar of traditional American values and a pre–Ronald Reagan symbol of political conservatism. He grew cocksure of his judgment even when it made little or no sense, as when, though a Republican, he voted for John F. Kennedy "to show that Catholics aren't prejudiced."

He claimed intimacy with the rich and powerful, beginning sentences with "When I went fishing with Ike Eisenhower last summer . . ." or "I've been in touch with Lyndon about that, and he told me confidentially . . ." His name-dropping made me writhe. So did Dorothy's claim, in the press, that my father's most notable characteristic was his modesty.

In Denver, he ran a Captain Queeg–like tight ship. All hands on deck for an early breakfast, permission to go ashore viewed with suspicion, liberties canceled for infractions. As what I still think was a mildly rebellious adolescent, I managed to break every rule in his book when I was around and inspire the issuing of new ones. Cy once woke me out of a sound sleep to point out my lack of consideration for others, in the form of a single hair in the sink.

No one is purer in thought, word and deed than a reformed rake-hell. No one is as insufferable. Cy now expected hero worship, but he was not going to get it from me, and what he got instead were reminders that I had known him for a long time and did not look upon him as a candidate for Mount Rushmore.

Nor had time altered my relationship to my old antagonist, Dorothy. No longer the insecure young woman I thought of as my wicked stepmother, she was still doing a convincing imitation. She had gained weight, had a matronly quality now and dyed her hair its former auburn. What had not changed was that she still resented my existence, as evidence of my mother's existence. In actuality, she explained to me once, I didn't exist.

She reasoned as follows. Cy was Catholic. My mother wasn't. If Cy had married outside the Church, he hadn't really married. If there was no first marriage, there could be no child born of it.

With the test of this syllogism standing there, living, breathing and marveling, some accommodation had to be made. It stopped short of the reality principle. I think my stepmother convinced herself that my attachment to the Taillons was the result of a mix-up in the record-keeping procedures of Deaconess Hospital.

With Terry and Tommy, I was on more tolerant ground. They thought me prissy. I considered them a pair of roughnecks. We formed close ties despite all this, probably because they too were riddled with faults, and heard about them. Scatter them thousands of miles apart, and the children of the same family remain an affinity group. Growing up, always, is a matter of "us against them," and in relation to Dorothy and Cy, my brothers and I were the "us."

All three of us were proud of our father and longed for his good opinion. All of us fell short of his standards and ignited his short fuse. I fought him with words, the torrents I could produce as part of his genetic legacy to me. As a teenager, Terry once fought him physically.

Coming in late one night, he found his small, stainless-steel father waiting for him in the kitchen. The two enacted the universal father/son scene: Where have you been? You've got your mother worried half to death.

Strapping teenage son: She can go to hell . . .

Cy escorted Terry out to the backyard to discuss their differences. He had not lost his skills as a Golden Gloves boxer. Says Terry, "The next thing I knew, I was on my back, looking at the stars. He really Powder Rivered me."

According to the code of the West, one does not disparage motherhood, or its embodiment, Mother. Whatever the law in the rest of the land, we lived under that code, with Cy keeping a boot on the back of the neck of the lawless element. He revised the code as he went along but never its underlying tenet: thou shalt honor thy father the rodeo announcer, or encounter his ire, backed up, if necessary, by one hell of a punch.

He was impossible, I thought then, a tyrant. I still think so but give him credit for consistency.

My mother had done battle with Cy toe to toe, as incendiary-tempered as he was and as fond of a good brawl. Far more intelligent than Pat was, Dorothy employed guerrilla tactics, tears and wounded feelings. These always won the day because Western men hold the unexamined belief that they "can't stand to see a woman cry."

They believe this about themselves because they learned it from their mothers. For the same reason, they believe that women are the weaker sex, that men are their strong protectors and that a man's house or mobile home is his castle. These inculcated attitudes leave Western women a lot of room to wield the power behind the saddle, without appearing to come anywhere near it. My stepmother knew this intuitively, and in her traditional femininity, her furs, bangles and beads, must have been more terrible to Cy than an army with banners. You can't challenge a lady to come out and fight like a man.

I fought with my father because I wasn't a lady, I was a teenager and thus a rolling gland. I fought with him because while I did not miss Cy the reckless drunk, I missed the Cy who had been fallible. I fought with him because he was bigoted against Jews, blacks, Easterners, intellectuals, hippies, draft resisters, Democrats, city dwellers and sopranos.

I liked to listen to opera on the radio. Cy called it "caterwauling" and imitated the female singers in falsetto.

The more he believed his own press, and saw himself as exemplar of the best of America, the more he railed against what he saw as the worst, anything that did not fall within the narrow confines of his values. What was most maddening was that he thought of himself as the model of tolerance, some of whose best friends were hippie Jewish sopranos. Arguing with him was tilting at a wind-mill of rectitude, and one always ended up unhorsed. Over the telephone, my father once drove me into an incoherent, stuttering rage. He waited it out and asked me if there were psychiatrists in Missoula.

Cy's politics and his all-round conservatism were not unusual in his part of the world and still aren't. In a coffee shop in Montana just a few years ago, I heard one man in cowboy boots tell another that England ought to "stop pussyfooting around and bomb the liv-ing shit out of the Falklands."

I leaned over the leatherette booth between us and asked why. He told me that you had to stop the Commies somewhere, little lady, and apologized for having said "shit."

I knew I was home, and felt the same mixture of helpless affec-tion and anger I often felt toward Cy. Most people live with vacil-lation and doubt. Men like my father have no doubts and never vacillate: the natural order of things is as clear to them as their fa-vorite trout streams, or the Rocky Mountain air, and on the cloud-iest day, they can still see forever.

What Cy saw was a landscape of immutable certainties, one I have sometimes longed to rest my eyes upon as he did. Always seeing himself as acted upon, rather than acting, he was a stranger to the paralyzing emotion I know best, vague, all-purpose guilt. I drag quantities of it around, like a suitcase full of bricks. My father once spelled out his version of self-blame in a letter to me.

He was not only at odds with me just then but disappointed in my brothers. "I am probably unfortunate," he wrote, "in being a most sensitive person and having an all encompassing love for those I had a part in creating."

I stopped visiting Cy. He stopped visiting and calling me. He collected more accolades, and made more money, and became still better known. I went about my own life, reading about him more often than I saw him. For source material I had the private museum for which my stepfather Roy served as curator, the mentions of Cy that came over the teletype machines at *The Daily Missoulian*, where I was known as a copyboy, and the clippings Ila Mae sent.

In our Missoula house was a large wooden desk where no one ever wrote a check or affixed a stamp to a letter; its function was to serve as one more hollow log where Roy could stuff things. In its drawers, along with thousands of pipe cleaners, a massive collection of No. 2 pencils and, eventually, thirty-seven years' accumulation of unopened junk mail, Cy's onetime best pal stuffed articles torn out of magazines and every scrap of print about Cy he could get his hands on.

He pushed these into the backs of the drawers, burying them under the pipe cleaners. I rummaged for and found them. Such was the strength of Roy's mysterious obsession that he kept tracking Cy long after I left home, tearing the one-line listing out of *TV Guide* when Cy announced rodeos on national television, unconsciously imitating Cy by underlining my father's name.

The great river of letters Ila Mae wrote, going for the record in Sheer Volume of Personal Correspondence, had Cy as their major subject—every sighting in Great Falls, every bit of malicious gossip she could glean from unnamed sources. "Heard something wrong with Cy, he losing His Voice. Their trying to keep it hush but he in trouble now. The paper said he was taking vacation, he really have operation at the Mayo Clinic."

My mother seemed to have forgotten Cy at last, as she had forgotten so much else, but as his status as living Western legend grew, no one else who'd ever met him seemed immune to my father's fascination. Even my high school teacher collected clippings for me, asked to be introduced to him someday and told me how they'd heard him, sometime, somewhere, and never forgotten his mighty Wurlitzer voice.

My sense of his powerfulness increased, and my determination not to become fixed on him, ever again, as the pole star. Not only had that misconception caused me pain in the past, I could see its effects on my mother.

The large Taillon family boasts a great many cousins, one of whom has her own theory about why my father and I quarreled so long and bitterly and why, after I was fifteen or so, I had to take his all-encompassing love for his children on faith. Her reason is less cerebral than mine are.

"Don't you know what you did to cross Cy?" my cousin Sis asked me. "All of a sudden, you shot up and got taller than he was."

TWELVE

It took him twenty years, but my father finally managed to arrange an annulment of his marriage to my mother, thereby ratifying his long, stable marriage to Dorothy. Pat had been a youthful mistake. Dorothy was the helpmeet and full-time companion for whom Cy always came first, and my father adored her.

She traveled the circuit with him, though it meant leaving Terry and Tommy, whom she also loved with fierce possessiveness, in charge of housekeepers much of the year. She selected his clothes, color-coordinating them as relentlessly as she did her own. Without complaint, she lived out of suitcases and motel rooms, spent the rest of her time in automobiles, traveling the same roads year after year, and became as skilled a promoter of Cy's business interests as he was.

Typical of their marriage was that my stepmother never learned to drive. She merely came along in the passenger seat while Cy steered their joint course. Even Ila Mae approved of her vocation as the woman behind the man and expanded on it in one of her treatises on marriage. "I always say it important for man to be king, thats the way it has always been with Wiley and Me, for God created he woman out of mans rib. The man came first Remember That Pat."

Her attitude would have come as news to Wiley, but he wrote no letters and issued no rebuttals. Instead, he spent his days trying to become invisible, keeping his nose in the sports pages, his feet off the ottoman and his head off the crocheted doily over the back of the chair. If he left shoe-polish smudges on the upholstery and hair-oil stains on the doilies, it wasn't for lack of trying to pass through his own household without a trace.

My uncle sought not earthly rewards, nor pie in the sky when he died, but domestic tranquillity. He might as well have aimed at being the first men's clothing salesman on the moon. His hundred-pound spouse had the stamina of a jockey, the eye-hand coordination to snatch a speck of dust out of the air before it settled on one of her end tables and an insatiable appetite for reform. In this, the world stubbornly continued to defy her, going its own untidy way. Crime raged in the streets. Promiscuity grew rampant. Drugs ravaged America's youth. Wiley shed cigarette ash on the carpet.

Ila Mae wrote on, her pen the weapon she wielded against chaos. Her stream-of-consciousness prose reveals her vision of the interconnectedness of all things, sometimes with alarming clarity. "Two young girls were robbed & stabbed here that worked at the taco treat, they caught the men. One blessing they didn't rape them. Know what I would do if I got my Hands on them, Wiley have cold he leave filthy Kleenex all over the Place."

All the years he had been married to my mother, Ila Mae thought of Cy as the Prince of Darkness. Now that he was successful, and happily remarried, and no longer a drunk, his former sister-in-law reinstated him back into the human race, and ever magnanimous, appointed herself his best friend and spiritual adviser.

My father rarely called her and never went to see her. She interpreted his neglect as proof of their indissoluble bond, intimacy so profound it threatened Dorothy. "Cy was here and he didn't come to see me, guess Dorothy wouldn't let him. Her sister say he always asks about me. For he know I always have good cup of coffee for him if he need somebody to talk to." She had advice ready to serve up with the cream and sugar. Dorothy should stop dying her hair, Cy was ruining his feet in those cowboy boots and my brothers were going to end up in jail if he did not stay home with them more often. Teenage hoodlums were the product of "broken homes."

Cy never came around to profit from this wisdom. It accumulated, doing no one any good, until Ila Mae bundled it off to us in Missoula. She must have known her constant reminders of Cy caused unrest in our household but attributed to herself only the purest of motives. "Know Susie would want to know about Cys throat, she could send him a get well card & maybe a letter."

I'm sure my mother did not want to be reminded of Cy at all, or to hear about Dorothy, the paragon. Roy could have taken no pleasure from Ila Mae's description of Cy's house in Denver, which she had never seen but described as rivaling the Taj Mahal. Her misinformed medical bulletins upset me and got Roy's hopes up until Cy turned up on television again, the voice as sonorous as ever, the man as dapper and handsome. When it came to malicious mischief, my law-and-order aunt was a repeat offender.

Cy and I lived at such physical and emotional distance from one another by then that I knew almost as little about him as Ila Mae did. My visits were occasions for friction, my view of my father the blinkered view of an adolescent in revolt against a parent who overwhelmed me. Terry and Tommy knew another Cy entirely, and loved him so much less critically, their adult lives are memorials to him.

I found him heavy-handed on the reins, and bucked, and reared, and finally bolted out of his reach. My brothers found in him the model of a Western man, with the perfect mix of toughness and tenderness, and as soon as they were old enough, took to the circuit as rodeo cowboys. They knew his hard anger too, but looked upon it as strength; could have chosen lives outside the rodeo but never considered it; believe that while none of us can ever measure up to our father's stature, we were privileged to see the mark made on the wall.

The father Terry and Tommy grew up with instructed them in the deft and serene art of fly fishing. He taught them to put out a line as lightly as a sigh and to smell a trout swimming in some dark eddy, smugly assuming it is going to die of old age. He spent their thousands of hours on the road together teaching them about wildlife. Both my brothers can spot a mountain goat on a mountain-goat-colored rocky promontory or an eagle so high overhead it looks like a wren. Accurate within a few hours, they can predict the first snowflake of winter from the quality of a chill in the air.

Terry, Cy and Tommy

Both are dead shots. Though Cy's passion was fishing, he saw to it they learned to hunt, because in Montana hunting is not only a rite of manhood but a means of filling the larder. At a cousin's house in Billings a few years ago, the dinner entrée was antelope tacos. Terry had shot the antelope, and split an elk with a hunting buddy the past winter, and took great glee in telling me what I was eating. He was reminding the sister from San Francisco who she really was and where she really came from. The antelope tacos were good but greasy. We washed them down with quarts of orange soda pop.

Tommy stores Cy's files, his scrapbooks and copies of the articles he wrote for Western publications. In them our father reminisced about favorite horses, adventures on the rodeo circuit and his love for wild birds. Sentimental articles, written in Cy's literate, ornate style, they brought him more recognition and more fan letters. My brothers tell me that the wild birds he wrote about ate out of Cy's hand.

We are children of the same man, the three of us, but of different memories, and when we're together now, we spend much of our time trying to make those memories mesh, living testimony to the staying power of his presence. The public Cy looms as large, still written about frequently years after his death.

That Cy, the rodeo announcer, never missed an engagement. In health or shaking in his boots with a fever, he turned up at the microphone and routinely gave a performance that earned a standing ovation. As an especially lyrical reporter put it, "He can fairly make you hear the cling-clang of spurs, the snap of leather, the furious snorting of the bronc demons as they come kicking, leaping, swirling out of the chutes defying any man to stay aboard."

The remarkable part of this description is that Cy made the reporter hear all these things in a newspaper office, a week in advance of the show.

Long after he became successful, he would drive all night to appear at a small-time rodeo because his being there guaranteed a crowd. Cy said he chose his profession because he wanted to be his own boss. In reality, he worked for the sport he loved, so slavishly that he rarely took time off.

He caught colds working in downpours in roofless announcer's booths, sweated in heat waves without loosening his tie or taking off his jacket and went out to the fairgrounds two hours before a performance to study his program notes, intent on coordinating the flow of events seamlessly. There he also made rounds, shaking hands with veteran cowboys, meeting the green kids riding in their first rodeos and wishing them luck. His compendious memory tucked away their names and histories. The green cowboy plummeted out of the chute on a bronc demon to the sound of Cy's voice, introducing him as glowingly as if he were a champion.

His closest rival for the rodeos that meant big money and prestige was Pete Logan, whom Cy respected as another dignified professional. Cy never tried to move into Logan's territory, Logan wrote, though "he has had several chances at me I am sure." Not only would doing so have been unethical, but "Cy [never] tried to replace anybody that was doing his job."

The onetime rounder had become principled, hardworking and reliable, a man whose handshake was as good as his signature on a contract. If he seemed pompous to me, swollen beyond recognition with pride, he would have argued he had earned that pride. The early years of Cy's life were a trajectory toward crash and burn, alcoholic drifting and a marriage that threatened to destroy him with its violent emotional extremes. He climbed out of the rubble determined never to look back.

From my vantage point as part of my father's past, I resented the extent of that resoluteness. I might have been more sympathetic to it had I been able to look upon my mother's course as its alternative. Though she functioned more or less normally for periods of weeks or months, by the time I was in high school the fogs closed in again without warning. Pat wandered off into them, in the clutch of private misery that put her out of Roy's reach and mine. During one of these withdrawals, she dug her old, cracked Samsonite suitcase out of the basement, packed it with odds and ends of her clothing and sat in a chair, waiting, as if the Missoula house were the Milwaukee Railroad depot downtown, near her former School of the Dance, and she were ready to go wherever the next train would take her. She came out of her lassitude to struggle with Roy when he took the suitcase away from her, more roughly than was necessary.

From Great Falls, Ila Mae assumed responsibility for her medical care, genuinely concerned about Baby Sister, taking her usual pleasure in a crisis. She pelted us with the names of doctors and clinics, legal expertise—"There would be no public hearing no one would have to know about it, just be signed by a Judge"—and pep talks urging Pat to cooperate in her own healing. "The treatment have to be given in closed ward hospital where they have special trained nurses for it . . . so Pat don't you think if you could be cured six weeks would be worth it . . . Some times we have to do things we don't want to."

Roy, Ila Mae and Wiley

My mother's breakdowns embarrassed Roy, as did all information about the family that became known outside it, lumped together as "washing your dirty laundry in public." He waited the latest illness out, forbidding me to talk about it, raging and weeping if it went on long. I marched back and forth to school and to my job at *The Daily Missoulian*, removing myself from a situation I felt powerless to change, protected by my own isolating fog. Ila Mae scolded. And scolded.

"Dr. Layne is a very brilliant man & he has gone out of his way to be helpful in this case. Roy, bring her, I would take her my self, I could do all the talking for her."

I don't think Roy ignored my aunt so much as he no longer heard her. Too many letters, over too many years, fell through the mail slot in our front door twice a day, filled every crevice in the house and exceeded his capacity to absorb them. Roy was like a soldier in combat who had learned to sleep through machine-gun fire.

Trivial or consequential, Ila Mae's letters are one long letter, really, no installment ever complete. She folded up her sheaf of blue-lined sheets, put all those words in an envelope and sealed it. Irresistible impulse seized her, and on the outside of it, she scribbled a recipe: "One can potato soup condensed, 1 can milk, handfull of cheese cheddar, mix well, shredded wheat, bake. I serve with jello mold fruit cocktail in it."

We heard about every head cold, every dish Ila Mae washed and every insight that came to her as she struggled to make sense of human existence: "I always say God have a plan," she wrote when she had some painful dental work done. "My gumbs hurt so bad today tho don't ask me what it is."

We knew about every change in the weather in Great Falls, Montana, over forty years. Ila Mae took blizzards as personally as she took holdups at the Taco Treat, as visitations upon her by a malevolent universe.

When the spring thaws came, she raised her voice in seasonal rhapsodies. The crocuses pushed through the ground, the birds sang and her arthritis no longer troubled her. "This winter so long I thought God trying to kill me."

Her never-ending letter testifies to the need to chronicle one's life, lest its events have no significance beyond oneself, and the trouble with them is that in our household they turned into cries of "Wolf!" so familiar they lost the power to mobilize the villagers.

Ila Mae's health preoccupied her, the migraine headaches that run in the family, arthritis and a painful chronic ailment described only as "My Colon." As frequently as she switched from one church to another, she went from doctor to doctor. Her search wasn't for one who could cure her as much as it was for the one doctor who would understand how much she suffered, who would set aside whole afternoons for her visits and pick up his telephone each and every time she called.

"I in Hell and He out playing golf," she wrote when one doctor defected from his full-time responsibility. She intended to sue him, because, for once, she wasn't going to take it lying down.

The woman downstairs would testify in court that she'd seen Ila Mae that day looking half dead. Ila Mae had demanded her medical records, which would have kept the few copying machines in Great Falls busy until both plaintiff and defendant had died of old age. A new doctor took the place of the target of her wrath and created a diversion. He performed surgery on My Colon, apologizing on behalf of the entire medical profession that it hadn't been performed long ago. My aunt wrote that "they took out practically the whole Thing." The fragment remaining still hurt, though not as much as that source of indescribable torture, her bridgework.

Roy telephoned Wiley, while Ila Mae was in the hospital, and sent flowers that "set him back" ten dollars. My mother listened to the detailed bulletin he relayed to us with one of her almost invisible eyebrows raised. Pat had stopped wearing makeup and now had a face that was a clean slate, whatever went on behind it unwritten for anybody else to read. Her raised brow bone was as eloquent as if she'd stuck her tongue out and told us what she thought of her sister's latest brush with the Grim Reaper.

I assumed that nothing much went on in my mother's mind and that she had somehow unplugged it, so that the clatter of life going on around her was barely perceived background noise, elevator music. I thought the woman I remembered had burned herself out and had no joy left in her, and no memories, and certainly no traces of Miss Patricia Montgomery, St. Louis's bright star of the stage.

Pat outraged me, when I was a junior in high school, by proving

Cyra's high school graduation photo, Class of '55

just how wrong I was. A date picked me up to take me to a movie. He arrived half an hour early, and from my bedroom, as I hurtled into my clothes, I heard my mother's low voice, talking about how hot it was for April and what a suntan she was getting, just sitting out in our backyard.

She sounded social and relaxed. The boy guffawed at something she said. I snagged a stocking, tried to put my neck through the arm-hole of my dress and jerked the curlers out of my bangs. Frantic with anxiety, I made my entrance. My mother had pulled up her blouse and was showing my date her smooth brown back, with the white band of her bra bisecting it, while he looked on grinning foolishly.

I dragged him out of the house and jumped into his car before he could open the door. "Your mother's really something," he said when he came around to his side.

"You shut up," I said.

Though both would have been as shocked as I was, and would have let my mother the exhibitionist hear about it, I never told Roy or Ila Mae about this incident. I didn't warn them that the show girl was still in there, and that she still had a high kick left in her. I kept my own counsel, not because I was kind, but because I was thrown so badly off balance.

I had burst out, "Mother!" Pat looked at me with amusement and no apology at all. Lazily, she tucked her blouse in, said she hoped we had a nice time and trotted out her honeyed southern drawl to tell my escort, "Nice meeting y'all."

What made me want to kill her on that occasion, I know now, was that she had a powerful sexual edge on me. An aged crone in her forties, my mother could call up her former seductive self effortlessly, a genie out of the bottle, and make her nubile daughter vanish from sight, print summer dress, Cuban-heeled shoes, Fire and Ice lipstick and all. Worse, she thought this was funny.

Now that I am her age then, I remember this scene with pride in Pat, and a whiff of middle-aged envy. Her second marriage turned the living fireball into a cowed creature who no longer knocked over bridge tables when belittled beyond tolerance, and whose dancer's body had lost its taut-muscled definition. Obeying the rhythm of her illness, she checked in and out of Roy's life and mine like a weary salesman checking into another cheap hotel, indifferent to the decor and the company in the dining room.

She could still transfix that teenaged boy with the baring of her suntanned back and her husky drawl, the low murmur that turned talk about the weather into an intimate treatise on the pleasure principle. As that unworthy audience for her female magic observed, when Pat chose to be she was still really something.

THIRTEEN

At eighteen, shortly after my freshman year in college, I got married. My mother and Roy gave me a steam iron. Ila Mae gave me two sets of sheets and pillowcases she had trimmed with embroidered borders, a lecture on sex along the lines of "we all have to do things we don't want to do sometimes" and two dozen blank thank-you note cards. Cy walked down the aisle as stiffly as if he were nailed to a board, after a sharp exchange between us in the anteroom of the Lutheran church in Missoula. I was wearing a white knit dress, a white satin pillbox hat and white satin pumps with three-inch heels. I loomed above Cy, who told me that I wobbled when I walked in those things and seemed to want me to take them off and make my journey to the altar stocking-footed. He must have thought I should make some concession since he couldn't wear his cowboy hat.

Roy boycotted the wedding. I had asked my father to give me away instead of asking him. He wouldn't come at all, he said, because I had shamed him so cruelly by this act of repudiation he couldn't face people. Nor would he ever set foot again on the same ground, hallowed or otherwise, with Cy.

Ila Mae and Wiley brought Pat, who took one of her rare stands against Roy's authority by telling him she would attend whether he came with her or not. For the occasion, she resurrected a rose silk dress that must have been twenty years old but still had flair, even though it was tight for her and had the only shoulder pads left in Montana. A neighbor gave her a home perm that turned her hair, mostly gray by now, into tight corkscrews. She made up her face and crammed her feet into ancient alligator pumps with open toes.

She looked very pretty, I told her as I pinned on her gardenia corsage. My mother smiled with great sweetness and apologized for her hands, holding them out for me to inspect. Her fingernails were clipped short, and as they had been for many years, were without nail polish. She said she had wanted to "do" them but had no manicure tools anymore. Did I know what had happened to the set Cy gave her, in the red leather case?

I said it didn't matter and wondered when she had last seen that manicure set. I also knew what had happened to it. Anything Roy knew that Cy had given either of us disappeared, sooner or later. We had both learned early on not to ask what had become of "junk" like missing manicure sets or plastic statuettes of horses.

Pat and Dorothy met for the first time at that wedding. They introduced themselves to one another politely enough but could not conceal their mutual curiosity. Dorothy stared at my mother's thirties dress, the two round spots of rouge on her cheeks and her Little Orphan Annie permanent wave. My mother turned her good child's open gaze on Dorothy, in her mink stole and kelly green everything else.

Neither matched the other's image of her old rival for my father's love, a contest that never really existed other than in my stepmother's mind. Pat expected the auburn-haired nurse I had described so effusively as a child. Dorothy expected the face that had launched a thousand bronc riders. They looked at each other as if neither could believe her own eyes, two women thickening into middle age who had in common only that they had married the same man. When they weren't staring at each other, they stared at Cy, who was frozen with discomfort, as if searching for some clue to his inexplicable tastes.

Of the dearly beloved gathered together, only Ila Mae enjoyed that somewhat forlorn wedding, my leap into the idea of normalcy that prevailed at the time. Many of my high school friends were already married. Some of them had babies. Instead of pursuing acting careers, they were settling for what was possible, and greeted with warm approval in Missoula, and seemed smugly happy in their roles as young housewives. At her request, I had given one of them a rolling pin as a shower present; she wanted a new kind that one filled with ice water because it made flakier piecrust.

In the back of my mind, I knew mine was a mismatch, and walked through the ceremony, head held high, as if I were auditioning for a role I knew I would not get. My father and my bridegroom, my college drama professor, looked down upon each other, neither of them impressed by the other's credentials, and Cy played father of the bride with bristling irritation. For Dorothy and Pat, the other woman was the Ancient Mariner, though disappointingly devoid of glittering eye. Instead, my mother looked mildly out from beneath her horizontal-comma eyebrows, drawn on with the old painstaking care, and as it usually did, Dorothy's mascara ran.

That left Ila Mae to rejoice in the ceremony, which vindicated her formative role in my upbringing. I was being sensible, for once, instead of following Pat into the world of greasepaint and loose morals. I wouldn't be exposed to the rodeo circuit anymore and so wouldn't relapse into swearing when I wasn't showing off my vocabulary, like Cy. Though he had earned back Ila Mae's good opinion by becoming respectable, she still thought plain speech was good enough for the Bible and ought to be good enough for him.

Before my new husband and I drove away in a shower of rice, my aunt passed on to me her accumulated domestic wisdom, standing on her toes so that she could look me in the face or at least in the chin. I was to remember who was the boss, never send shirts to the laundry, save the ends of bars of soap and press them together to make new bars, and when I no longer needed the diapers, hem them and use them for dish towels. I was not pregnant. Ila Mae was looking ahead.

My husband learned in her parting address to him that I was clean about my person, made my own clothes on my Singer sewing machine and could learn to cook if I put my mind to it. I had eaten good food at her table all those years, and so knew what it was. If my household management was so inept at first that he needed expert help, she was just a phone call away and would be there before he could say "too much starch in the collars." Into his jacket pocket, because I was carrying a nosegay rather than a purse, she tucked her recipe for icebox rolls.

Though it did not last long and caused as much pain as most failed marriages, mine freed me, finally, from my family. It removed me physically from my mother, whom I loved but whose custodianship Roy expected me to share, all the while pretending that Pat wasn't ill and needed no custodianship. By staying home from my wedding, and staging a noisy weeping scene behind his closed bedroom door while I was in my own room getting dressed in something old, something new and something borrowed (my bridegroom would slide on the blue garter, for the flash camera of the photographer), Roy hardened me against further emotional appeals he might make. He had a legitimate claim on me. It wasn't the claim he was making, one that precluded all other loyalties and that I had been resisting with more assertiveness as I got older.

He had raised me as Qualley. On my eighteenth birthday, I took back my legal name, Taillon.

As for Cy, my marriage elevated me, in my view, to parity with him. It proclaimed that I was an adult, who could do what I liked without his consent, and for whom another man was more important than he was. For the satisfaction I took in shooing my father off to the wings, for once, instead of being ushered into them myself, I was willing to master my aunt's icebox rolls and give up my career as the next Helen Hayes.

My husband and I moved to Oregon. Though none of us was in a league with Ila Mae, my mother, Cy and I kept in touch through letters. I rambled on cheerfully about married life, which wasn't cheerful in the least. My mother wrote about large events in her life, such as a new refrigerator. The refrigerator was the first major household purchase she and Roy had made since they'd set up housekeeping, in one afternoon, at Mr. Lucy's furniture store fifteen years earlier. Ila Mae's comment on this acquisition, when Pat wrote her about it too, was "too bad it had to be a Kelvinator."

Cy sent me twenty-five-dollar checks on birthdays and on the birth of my first child, and the unreadable last carbons of his sched-

Cyra

ules and his letters to the whole family. I had not seen him for two years when I made a last visit to him and Dorothy in Denver. Now that I regarded my father as an equal, I regarded Dorothy as an equal too and met her hostility head-on. Under the guise of girl talk, we sat in her spotless kitchen, over coffee, and skewered each other like chickens for the barbecue.

Dorothy told me how pretty I'd be if I ever learned to dress and if my skin ever cleared up. I told my overweight stepmother about the terrible metabolic curse I was under, how I stayed thin no matter how much I ate. I sighed and added that I guessed I was just like my father.

While we never tired of this sniping, and both perversely enjoyed it, Cy did, in a hurry. He turned his coldest green look upon me, one that could have frozen Lake Michigan in July, and got the same cold look back. It told him that his anger no longer turned me into a whimpering heap. Having no way of knowing that a nervous tic pulsed in my eyelid, he tried impressing his daughter into the deference due him.

At dinner one night, when there were guests present, he brought a bottle of Chianti to the table with a white napkin draped over his arm, ceremoniously pulled the cork and announced that he would pour it after it had time to breathe. I suggested maybe he should keep an oxygen tank around, in case the wine didn't start breathing on its own.

He itemized how much everything in the house had cost and showed me Dorothy's Grand Baroque sterling silver, "the most expensive pattern made." I thanked him warmly once again for his most recent twenty-five-dollar birthday check.

He told me he now drove Cadillacs, rather than Buicks, because he had "a certain image to maintain." I told him I thought Cadillacs were ostentatious and for a split second thought my father was going to swing on me.

Similarly, Dorothy gained no admiration from me through her own steady stream of self-praise, a conversational style she may have picked up from long intimacy with Cy. For modesty's sake, these compliments were always attributed to others. The man who laid the wall-to-wall carpet had urged Dorothy to become a professional decorator; he had never met anyone with her color sense. Someone had stopped her on the street in San Francisco to tell her how nice it was to see an elegantly turned-out woman for a change.

Years later, also in San Francisco, my stepmother startled me and a nearby table of diners with the most singular of these spontaneous tributes. Her gynecologist, she announced loudly, had said to her, "Mrs. Taillon, you have the uterus of a young girl."

My father and Dorothy were equally unimpressed with me, a young woman with intellectual pretensions and a pugnacious set to the jaw. It never occurred to Cy that I had his temperament, as well as his bone structure. He and Pat had taught me never to run or even walk away from a fight, a rule of life still dear to writers of Western songs, and neither had thought to mention that I need not go out looking for one.

What angered Cy most in me was what he knew was also true of himself: that he was stubborn, demanded unqualified love from others and found it hard to forget, impossible to forgive. What angered me most about Cy was his rigidity, his total lack of warmth. Put my arms around him, and I was hugging a telephone pole. We kept our distance after that visit because father and daughter knew we had the same inflated pride, as well as the same cheekbones, and what we saw when we looked at each other made us both flinch.

I had to ask Cy for two hundred dollars when I fled my bad marriage. This wasn't the hardest part of extricating myself from it, but it was far from the easiest. He sent the money promptly, suggested that I live with a cousin in San Francisco while I was getting on my feet financially and emotionally, and filled two single-spaced pages with "if you had listened to your older and wiser father in the first place . . ." That he was right this time made his pointing out the obvious almost unbearable.

Cy announced the Grand National Western Livestock Exposition, in the San Francisco Cow Palace, for thirty-one consecutive years. The Cow Palace is a cavernous building shaped like a giant Quonset hut on the southern margins of the city, the rodeo a prosperous one whose main sponsor, for years, has been Winston cigarettes. A jumping-horse competition gives the proceedings an overlay of proper English classiness. Banners and flags fill the huge hall, floats are lowered from the ceiling and at the Grand Opening ceremonies rodeo dignitaries come out at the full gallop on horses doubly weighted with the silver on their saddles, bridles and stirrups. The cowboys who walk or limp away from the various events as PRCA champions have won as much as eighty thousand dollars for the year, as well as glory.

The riders and ropers at the Cow Palace are the best. The buckle bunnies are the prettiest, in their pearly cowboy hats and sprayed-on Western shirts and pants. Their boots are meant for dancing the two-step, after the rodeo, rather than riding. Their pink mouths open to let out piercing shrieks of "Ride 'em, cowboy! Hang in there, baby!"

Behind the arena and the chute area, where the vendors sell beer and hot dogs, the livestock exhibitors scrub bulls the size of small buildings with brushes and soapy water, rub them down as carefully as if they were fragile Chippendale chairs and await the judges with the clipboards, who'll get down on their hands and knees and inspect their entries from every angle. They're looking for perfect conformation, and Prime-grade flesh on the heavy bones, but it's a fair guess that when one is inspecting the undercarriage of such an animal, it gets a few points for having a friendly attitude.

The massive Winston scoreboard prints out times and scores electronically. When the honor guard rides out with the flags of the United States and California, their black horses have sparkle dust on their rumps, and the audience that applauds is saluting superb horseflesh along with all else for which America stands. Hats over their hearts, the crowd stands erect and still for the playing of "The Star-Spangled Banner," watching a faceted, reflecting ball revolving in the ceiling. It's the same lighting effect, but not the same crowd, one would find in a disco.

My father loved the Cow Palace rodeo, commanding the lavish spectacle and filling the enormous space with his voice from an announcer's stand almost lost in the vastness.

He liked descending on the big city in his latest Cadillac and taking up residence in his hotel just off Union Square. If people on the street did a double take at the sight of the small man in the Western suit, high-heeled boots, big hat and diamond horseshoe stickpin, they were simply struck by his fine clothes and good looks. He paraded fur-stoled and hatted Dorothy on his arm, fragrant in a cloud of perfume, as if the two of them owned the San Francisco sidewalks and no doubt wondered why I hung behind, studying department store windows.

The Cow Palace board of directors included some of the city's prominent citizens, fine men Cy was proud to call his friends. The proprietors of his favorite restaurants recognized him from year to year, as they could hardly have failed to do, and Cy gave them both his patronage and tickets to the rodeo, expensive box seats he produced with a flourish. I also got free tickets, and one year shared a box with two Chinese cooks from Johnny Kan's and an Italian waiter from Fior D'Italia.

That was the year Cy deposited me in a downtown beauty salon to have my hair done before I appeared out at the Cow Palace. As I shook hands with the members of the board of directors, big, hearty men, I was miserable with self-consciousness under my bouffant, which looked as if it should have swallows nesting in it.

San Francisco was the high point of the circuit for Dorothy too. It was sophisticated, and unlike Chicago or Dallas, did not reek of the stockyards. Most of all, she liked the sidewalk flower stands, where my father bought violets for her furs. The city to which I had moved nonetheless alarmed them. Even before the hippies came along in their madras bedspreads of many colors, it had a reputation for both hedonism and excessive liberalism. It was full of interracial couples and homosexuals. I was involved with a man who was thirty-two years old and had never been married.

The dress code Dorothy remembered fondly, from years ago, no longer existed. Hatted and befurred women were the exception, not the rule, and Dorothy sighed for San Francisco's lost elegance.

The shape of my life further alarmed them. I picked them up one night in my male friend's old Volkswagen, veteran of so many spray-paint jobs, ranging from beige to army green, it was now mottled like army camouflage. I lived in a neighborhood not in the guidebooks, in an apartment above a grocery store reached by three flights of odorous stairs. I had joined a "Communist front organization," the ACLU. Cy was deeply relieved when he determined that I still used my married name.

I was too busy supporting myself and a child to be looking for fights anymore, especially not with my father. We fought constantly anyway, over whether the city I had embraced was or was not a cesspool. We fought over the man I would later marry, who never bought clothes and always needed a haircut.

"Your father's a short man," he said to me as we drove home from the rodeo one night. "You always talk about him as if he were a six-footer."

"Not short, *medium* height," I said. I thought I was abnormally tall, a giantess, and that this explained why I could look down on the top of Cy's hat.

I separated the man and the Western myth long enough to quarrel with Cy definitively, with such lingering wounds we did not see each other, and wrote no letters, for nearly eight years. In the early sixties, he and Dorothy came to San Francisco for the Cow Palace engagement as usual. They called me a day before they were about to leave. I rushed from the office where I worked to pay the short court visit that was all time allowed.

In the course of it, Dorothy suggested that I should put my young child up for adoption—I'd have a better chance of making an advantageous marriage. Considering the way I lived, in what amounted to a tenement, it was the kindest sacrifice a mother could make.

Did he agree with this advice? I asked Cy, who was roaming the room, gathering up notes and getting ready for the evening performance. We locked eyes for a long time. Of course he did, Cy said finally.

I walked out of his hotel room, determined never to see him again. And for years, when the rodeo was in town, I told my second husband that I was going to a movie and drove out to listen to my father's baritone voice rolling out in the darkness of the Cow Palace, setting off seismographs.

What a cornball the man is, I thought, what an insufferable strutting rooster, what a showboat. Then I'd think, you've got to hand it to him, though, he can sure as hell work a crowd.

FOURTEEN

Until Cy's offer to let me apologize arrived, after all those years of silence on both sides, my only contact with the immediate family was with Dorothy. Shortly after I marched out of that San Francisco hotel room, she wrote me a letter she must have been composing as long as we had known each other. Its expressed intention was to make a better woman of me.

Again, she charged me with being an unfit mother, one who lived in an unfit apartment. She complained about the large sums of money Cy had given me, pointing out that when I lived with them in Oakland, she "went without to see you had decent clothes to go to school." The neon-green sweater and plaid skirt haunted her as much as they haunted me.

Most recently, they had invited me to Denver, where my time "was spent mostly in the company of that professor from Boulder. Who had quite a reputation as we bothered to find out."

Cy made no child support payments after the first years of his legal obligation, and few of them then. The professor was a seventy-year-old expert on George Bernard Shaw, with whom I'd had dinner once during my stay. If he had vices other than compulsive reading—bizarre sexual practices or heroin, say—he chose not to share them with me.

Dorothy's indictment ran on for two pages, unanswerable because her anger was irrational and bottomless. My former husband had not beaten me, she wrote. I must have divorced him because he did not make enough money "to give you the life you wanted." I had left my marriage because I was miserable in it, the reason most people leave marriages. My Catholic stepmother seemed to think the only grounds for divorce were compound fractures.

I knew Cy had read this outburst because Dorothy made no move without consulting him, not even planning the dinner menu. He added no postscript reading: "Disregard the foregoing." From that point on, Dorothy's resentment sat in the road leading to reconciliation between us like a heavily armored tank. I think we had equal respect for its fighting capabilities.

For Cy, Terry and Tommy, my stepmother's love was inexhaustible as the life force. By serving as my father's handmaiden, as well as his wife, she made Cy possible; her faith in him and her devotion to his career allowed him to become the man he became.

For her sons, she would have swum oceans or got between them and a hand grenade. Their joys were Dorothy's joys, their setbacks her heavy blows, felt more profoundly than her children felt them.

But I was another woman's child, Cy's role in my existence irrelevant. He had "his own children" to consider, Dorothy told me once, when I asked him for a loan. It was a small loan. I needed it badly. Instead I got a forthright spelling-out that there was no room in my stepmother for what was not hers. Any defection from this view of things, on my father's part, would be seen as betrayal, parceling out his affections rather than delivering them whole.

What prompted Cy to write to me anyway, after nearly a decade, was learning that he had cancer. "This CA thing," as he called it, frightened my father and set him conducting a retrospective on his life, including the part of it he had banished from his résumé. From me, as well as from my brothers and Dorothy, he needed comfort, and moral support, and affirmation of his worth. The worst of his medical problems had been occasional laryngitis. Now he had cancer of the prostate; was ordered to quit smoking after forty years; had to endure treatments that he found painful and humiliating.

Other signs of physical failure assailed him, the loss of sight in his right eye for a few days and what sounds, in his highly circumspect description of it, like a stroke. He rolled a sheet of his letter-head into his portable typewriter and sent me a stiff-necked but unmistakable appeal for help, in toughing out the rest of his life and in mending his broken fences.

I wanted them mended as much as he did, though there was one section I was unwilling to prop up. "Life is too short to go on nursing old grievances," my father wrote me, meaning my grievances against Dorothy. "My own version of 'life is too short,' " I wrote back, "is that it's too short to keep beating one's head against the same stone wall." I could not forgive my stepmother her mean-spiritedness any more than Cy could forgive me for what he perceived as not loving him enough.

To his wife and sons, and to his fans, he had no flaws. To me, he had the usual number. Shaken by his illness, my father began to entertain the notion that while this was extremely unlikely, it was possible.

For the first time since I was a child, he wrote me personal letters instead of sending me carbons, telling me about money worries and disappointments. A rodeo he'd worked for thirty years had not renewed his contract for the following season. "Some of the younger announcers have greatly exaggerated my condition, and taken advantage of it."

Terry was wounded in Vietnam. Tommy was badly hurt in a bull-riding accident. My brothers made impulsive young marriages, as I had, and both were divorced. Cy told me how much anguish these events caused him, both on paper and on the phone, his voice querulous with complaint. "Cyra, old age is hell," he blurted in one conversation. My father was then in his early sixties.

Equally startling to me, because it was uncharacteristic, was his speculation in a letter that "perhaps I am now being punished for things I have done in the past." I replied that cancer was as arbitrary as a roll of the dice and that if there was a God, he hired no goons and kneecapped no one for being fallible. "Your ability to write is certainly reflected in your last long letter of November 2nd," Cy told me, moved by my mixed metaphors. I could recall no previous compliment from him, ever, and joked to my husband about hiring a stone carver.

somber Cy in his early sixties

Slowly, my father and I undertook the task of getting to know each other again, the most important in a long history of such efforts. Because I had not been around to see the process under way, I found it hard to grasp that Cy was as old as he was. My image of him was frozen in his early fifties, when I had last seen him, and even then I had not seen him realistically. Superimposed, always, on Cy in the flesh was the image of himself he'd invented and lived, the dashing cowboy celebrity. I had not seen him on the screen, doubling for Robert Taylor. One more ticket buyer, I had sat in the uppermost reaches of the Cow Palace, watching and listening to Cy a quarter mile away in the announcer's booth. On such occasions, the man for whom I was named was as unreal as an actor in a Western movie, and as inaccessible.

Nor had he any sense of me, living in the suburbs, remarried for ten years, going to school as a "re-entry woman." He did not know if there were "any little McFaddens," misspelled my daughter's name and could not remember how old she was, and politely asked after friends I had not seen since I was seventeen years old. Did I still keep up with my music? he inquired. I had no music to keep up with, as Cy damned well knew; listening to me attempt the national anthem with the rest of the crowd at rodeo openings, he'd shaken his head often enough and told anyone around it was a shame I was tone deaf.

I worked as a secretary for the San Francisco Opera for a few years, and must have told him about it. My job description underwent a transformation when he got hold of it and came back to me later, from someone he knew, as "I hear you sing with the opera company out there in San Francisco." "No," I said, and then, furious with Cy, added, "that was my mother."

It would have bewildered my father, with his P. T. Barnum approach to press agentry, that I did not appreciate his promotional efforts on my behalf. In wanting him to recognize that mine was a reasonable sort of life as it actually was, I was expecting a sculptor to put down his chisel and leave a block of marble intact. For Cy, the showman, one started with fact and took it from there, as far as invention would go.

A crowd at a rodeo was never a few hundred shivering souls, it was a thousand people cheering their lungs out. The hotel and dance-hall bands he had led, in his pre-rodeo days, became the Benny Goodman band and Cy the xylophone soloist. The radio program that featured my mother, in St. Louis, was the most popular program in the country and Pat competition for Sophie Tucker.

I was used to this facet of my father's character, and amused by it, but when it extended to me, I felt compromised. I was in my thirties, with children of my own, and Cy still hadn't acknowledged that he was stuck with the person I was, who would go to my grave with the same straight hair, would never be named Miss Rodeo America and was unlikely to shrink much.

Our letters were affectionate, when they began to travel back and forth every month or so. Cy congratulated me when I got my bachelor's degree. I congratulated him when he got favorable medical reports. Neither of us suggested meeting. We knew that we had best conduct our new accord at a distance, one at which we could sustain it. Had we risked getting together, other than on paper, we would have debated the shape of the conference table, my stepmother's motives and which station to listen to on the car radio.

Parents generally try to dominate their children. Children struggle to break free of them. My father's and my variation on this theme was that neither of us would yield a millimeter of ground, ever. Civilized in our relations with other people, we squared off at each other like a pair of pit bulls.

After twenty-five years of avoiding the mention of her name, Cy asked about Pat. He wanted to know about the state of her health, and whether she was any happier these days, and confessed to an uneasy conscience about her. "In retrospect, I cannot help but believe that much of the difficulty between your mother and me was my own fault—much of it resulting from my immoderate drinking." As if this admission were disloyal, he followed with a paragraph about what good care Dorothy took of the house and of him, despite "a problem involving the nerve endings." Either he was being circumspect again or the problem had not yet been named to them. My father's much-loved wife and my old nemesis was in the early stages of Lou Gehrig's disease.

Pat and Roy in their late years

Pat and Ila Mae in Lincoln, Montana, in the early 1970's

At a twelve-hundred-mile remove from them all, I began to realize, through their letters and calls, that my parents' lives, my stepparents' lives, Aunt Ila Mae's and Wiley's were winding down, trailing off into an accumulation of illnesses and disappointments. Like Cy, all seemed to feel obscurely betrayed, only Pat incapable of surprise.

She wrote of breaking her leg in a sand trap while playing golf. Roy had taught her the game, the one form of recreation they shared. Fearful of telling him that she had been so clumsy, after she fell she played on until the leg was swollen and painful.

Pat's account of this accident is almost jaunty; it restored a little drama to her life. "I have to wear a cast!" she says, sounding pleased, and then pulls herself up short and adds a rote, Ila Mae–like pietism: "However, with God's help I will golf again."

From Roy, not long afterward, I heard of a more serious event in her life, a radical mastectomy. I'd fly home, I told him. Roy was mysterious about the reasons, on his end of the phone, but made it plain that he did not want me there. The house was too small. The trip would be a waste of good money. In the summer, he said, he'd bring my mother to California to visit my family instead.

Although I could have pointed out that I'd been home many times before, and the house had held us all then, I didn't argue. For years Pat had not been more than a few miles from the block on which they lived. Such a journey, for her, would be on a scale with Lindbergh's in "The Spirit of St. Louis." My less altruistic motive was that I hated the Missoula bungalow, with its storm windows in place the year round, so that the air inside was stale and oppressive, and its peculiar smell of vitamin capsules and the sprouted wheat Roy grew in the bathtub.

His health-food preoccupation had become a passion. We started the mornings there with the viscous brew he whipped up for breakfast in his indispensable blender, blackstrap molasses and twenty-one other ingredients outside any normal definition of food. By now, my stepfather's theory was that if it tasted good, it was trying to kill you. Behind his back, Pat and I made terrible faces over our khaki-colored health shakes. Roy left for the candy company. We poured them down the toilet in the bathroom, making our way around the amber waves of grain.

The Ila Mae Chronicles escalated my mother's loss of a breast to both breasts and stated darkly that her doctors weren't telling her the whole truth. "Once It get started it go right thru you, they can cut It out but It pop out somewhere else, Susie her Days Are Numbered. I can't do anything for her only Pray, that I do for the whole world."

She moved on to world affairs:

> Our town is full of Rape stabbings and dope. Last night 12 year old girl was stabbed six times in her home. He tried to Rape her. Didn't make it, he was just out of prison. Few weeks ago 9 year old girl was Raped all most died they haven't caught the man yet. The police said no woman should be out after dark.
>
> So have good day for I love you all.

The blow dealt Wiley worried me more than the latest crime wave in Great Falls. For thirty years, he worked for the same downtown department store, selling suits, ties and what he considered the height of elegance for men, white-on-white shirts. The store was a genteel anachronism, with a cafeteria in the basement that offered weary shoppers chicken salad and angel food cake, and a staff of Wiley-like employees, old family retainers who'd spent their adult lives behind its counters writing up sales of Ladies Necessaries and Better Chocolates.

In the seventies, the store was sold to a large chain. The chain fired Wiley a few weeks before he would have been entitled to retirement benefits. He got a job at J. C. Penney's after a few anxious months, but at Penney's he was no longer "our Mr. Gosney." Ila Mae wrote that he had developed a bleeding ulcer and that the piped-in music in the menswear department made his ears ring.

My mother and father had been adventurers, performers who wrote their own scripts, starring themselves, and expected even the people they loved best to function as the supporting cast. Dorothy played her own fulfilling role as wife of the great man. Wiley plodded along, not thinking very deeply about where a day led. Ila Mae saw the world through her kitchen window but took her limited raw material and wrote it large, interpreting life for the rest of us in its rich, rape-and-murder-ridden variety. Roy made a vocation of injured merit. Now, with the exception of Pat, who accepted broken legs, mastectomies and wheat in the bathtub with the same passivity, they all seemed to feel they were the victims of injustice, in the form of mortality.

At Christmas, Roy sent me a gift subscription to *Prevention*, a magazine that reflected his views about diet and health maintenance. "Your health is all you have got," his card read. Pat's motto had been "Your looks are all you've got." Ila Mae lived for Judgment Day, when God would reward the good and punish the sinners. My father wanted above all to be Somebody. With the end of his rodeo days in sight, he felt the way he must have felt without his cowboy boots on, insubstantial and reduced to ordinariness.

Through their letters ran a strain of melancholy: where had their lives gone? Even Ila Mae, awaiting vindication beyond earthly glory, had doubts about her belief system. God would pin a good conduct medal on her for the suffering she'd endured, she knew, but he was unaccountably taking His own sweet time about it.

FIFTEEN

Wiley was the first to die. He left the world without a fuss after an illness of a week, a workhorse dropping in his traces. My aunt mourned him so deeply we all worried about her. Their marriage, to outsiders, resembled a Punch-and-Judy show. Mysteriously, it was a close marriage all the same, Ila Mae's nagging and Wiley's automatic "Aaa, shut up" their own form of intimate communication.

Cy was on the road when Wiley was buried, but he called on Ila Mae when he was back in Great Falls, the first visit he had paid in years. Time was tearing down barriers between my father and the people he cared about when he was young, or who cared about him; he was seeing his life whole now, rather than in installments. Coming full cycle, he and Dorothy had sold the Denver house and moved back to Great Falls, a few blocks from the house in which Dorothy grew up.

Roy was next. The oldest, he was also the sturdiest, because of his health regimes or in spite of them, and at seventy-eight was still working part-time at the candy company. No longer on the payroll, he helped out at inventory time, in the warehouse, and spent the day he died shifting packing cases. Neighbors called me late the following night to tell me about his death. My mother, they said, had just remembered she had a daughter in California.

At the airport in Missoula, where they drove her out to meet my plane, Pat waited behind the barrier, wearing a cheap platinum-blond wig, slightly askew, and her sweet, vague smile. "Why, hello, dear," she said, surprised. If she knew why I was there, the information was tucked somewhere back in the reaches of her mind. Behind her, the husband of the neighbor couple tapped the side of his head significantly and rolled his eyes

My stepfather died of a sudden heart attack. Pat called 911, rehearsed by him in how to pick up the receiver and dial the three numbers, but he was dead when the ambulance arrived a few moments later. She told the story while I helped her get ready for bed, anxious about getting the details right but dry-eyed. Roy seemed to be vanishing from her memory as quickly and painlessly as he had died in his easy chair, still wearing his hat and overcoat. In his musty room, with its lonely double bed, I lay awake chain-smoking and thought how quickly the house would burn if I were careless. The rugs were thick with dust, the windows hermetically sealed and hung with moldering curtains, the room strung with a maze of frayed electrical cords. Health-food books, piled up on the bureau, on Pat's long-unused vanity table and along the walls, made the passage to the bed a narrow tunnel. I knew why Roy had fended off visitors.

The man who'd had the terrible nightmares in that room lay in a local funeral home, which had left several urgent telephone messages. The gist of these was that the deceased aren't good keepers. I knew Roy wanted his body flown home to Wisconsin, because Pat had come out of her stupor long enough to tell me so, and I got out of bed to look for his address book. For most of the night I went through drawers stuffed full of paper, finding only old order pads, yellowing junk mail and on a closet shelf a paper bag criss-crossed with Scotch tape. On it, Roy had written: "LAETRILE. *Illegal.* Pat, do not tell anyone, in the event of my death, destroy." The contents looked like fine brown dust.

My stepfather and mother, Ila Mae and Wiley had come to see me and my family two summers ago, as Roy had promised. They made a slow trip in the Dodge Dart Roy bought when the station wagon began to send up clouds of smoke, stuck close to my suburban house for a week and then set off for home and safe haven again. I made them promise not to continue a practice that terrified me when I rode with them on their lone excursion into San Francisco, stopping in the middle of the freeway to look around. Cars skidded and blared around them. Roy studied the map unhurriedly and honked back at them.

The Dart had less than a thousand miles on it. Like Roy's bedroom, it smelled musty, and it started hard because it was driven so little. Stalling at every intersection, it made my mother and me late for Roy's funeral two days after I arrived.

In the interest of saving money, I had picked out the cheapest coffin in the funeral home. I regretted it when I saw my stepfather laid out in what looked like a Styrofoam picnic chest. The undertaker had rouged Roy's cheeks and made his mouth rosy with lipstick. I felt an acute pang of sympathy for him, looking androgynous, and mortified about it, beneath his layer of makeup.

Another pang seized me when the few mourners arrived, members of Roy's Masonic lodge alerted by the notice in the newspaper. The lodge brothers did not know him. The older he grew, the more reclusive Roy became, imprisoning himself and Pat in the airless house, venturing out to buy more lecithin capsules and the sacks of worm-infested grains that filled the kitchen cupboards. Equipped with his blender and a few pots and pans, he had taken over the cooking. At the all-you-can-eat smorgasbord where I took Pat for our meals, I watched her pile her tray with plates of cream pie.

Although she cried at the funeral, her tears were perfunctory, as if she sensed that tears were expected of her. She and I were to fly Roy's casket home, to be buried in the family plot, the following day. That night I began clearing out the refrigerator, empty except for the ranks of brown bottles full of vitamin capsules. Pat was asleep. I worked quietly so that she would not see me performing this task and be upset by it.

My mother appeared in the kitchen doorway, in her nightgown. She saw the trash bag at my feet and reached into the open refrigerator, picked up a bottle and slammed it into the bag, with the speed and coordination of a major-league pitcher. Before she went back to bed, she joined me in a beer and a cigarette. I spent a macabre morning filling out shipping orders for Roy's remains, referred to by the airline personnel as Mr. Qualley and "it." Pat sat in the waiting room, her suitcase at her feet, restless with anticipation. On the plane, she sat pressed to the window, looking out into the cloud banks, until the stewardess brought lunch. "This is on me," she told me graciously. "I insist." In Roy's sister's house in Oconto, over and over, she told the assembled family about the manner of Roy's death.

"He said to me, 'Dear, I'm tired. I think I just want to sit here and rest.' Then he said, 'Sweetheart, I've got a bad pain in my chest, call the ambulance.'" Each time Pat told the story, enjoying being the focus of attention, she incorporated more endearments into it, loving pet names Roy had never spoken. She was describing their marriage, for posterity, not as it was but as she wanted it to be. In the coquettish blond wig, from which she refused to be parted, she put on a last performance, transforming life into art.

The Wisconsin relatives, kind people who liked "Patty," listened and nodded and wept with her. I went into my Aunt Babe's kitchen and drank with Uncle Norman, Roy's oldest brother.

Norman preferred bourbon to the hot dishes and sheet cakes neighbors brought to the front door all that week. In the pocket of his plaid wool jacket, food-stained and tobacco-smelling, he had a pint flask, from which he poured an inch into a cheese glass for me. In silent complicity, we bolted the bourbon down, then stood leaning against the counter. "Poor old son of a bitch," Norman said gravely. He had pronounced his brother's most eloquent eulogy.

A young Lutheran minister delivered the more formal eulogy at the graveyard, where I was shamed again by my taste in coffins. In late October, in Wisconsin, snow lay on the ground. A gray sky sent down a drizzle, and Aunt Babe passed around umbrellas to the dozen of us present. Pat cried once more, tears that stopped almost as soon as they started, but seemed more bewildered than grieving. Among her clothes, I'd had trouble finding a dark dress that fit her and a warm coat. The garments I had finally packed were so old they gave her that look, again, of a woman in a period movie.

Now that the week of sorting out Roy's affairs was behind me, it struck me with full force that my mother was helpless, a woman who had not driven a car for twenty years, could not write a check and responded to my "It's Cyra, Mother" on the phone with a thoughtful pause followed by "Who?" Back in Missoula, I began the paperwork for putting her house on the market and found a convalescent home for her.

The day I took her there, my stomach churned with guilt. I was the parent now, and she was the child, and I was abandoning her.

Pat bounced on her bed, testing the mattress, put her clothes in the bureau and the closet and in a cracked mirror applied lipstick to her mouth with her little finger, peering closely at her reflection. She was in some small town in the Midwest, forty years ago, getting ready to play the provinces.

After the long, stifling captivity of her marriage, my mother found the convalescent home stimulating and wrote me cheerful letters about small events in her day. To make the letter writing easier, I sent her stamped envelopes with printed return-address stickers on them. She crossed out "Mrs. Roy Qualley" above her address and painstakingly lettered in "Patricia."

Cy asked me to convey his sympathy, when I told him about her new circumstances, and wrote that he would contact her "at the first opportunity." That he never did had nothing to do with insincerity but with his wariness of the past, and the pain that confronting it held for him. Everyone who knew the ruinous rakehell in the old photographs had forgiven him except for Cy himself.

"Don't come to see him Susie," Ila Mae wrote. "You wouldn't recognize him & he wouldn't want you to see him This way." Cy was a walking skeleton. Dorothy wasn't much better. "She have some terrible disease, some famous baseball player got it. It incurable." Terrible diseases being no excuse for letting oneself go, she noted that Dorothy had gained more weight. "Also, she *huge*."

My aunt sounded the death knell for Cy prematurely. Though he pared down his schedule to a dozen rodeos a year, he kept on working, telling people that he was retiring and would spend his time writing and trout fishing. In 1977, taking note that he was not appearing at the Cow Palace as usual, a writer for the San Francisco *Examiner* referred to him as "slick Cy Taillon . . . a legend who looked like Spade Cooley and sounded like the Reverend Billy Graham."

In Lewiston, Idaho, a reporter wrote of "a voice that rose and fell with each passing crisis on the arena floor below, investing even the prosaic with an element of excitement." By then Cy had announced the Lewiston Roundup for twenty-nine years.

Thirty-one years at the National Western in Denver. Thirty-eight at the Western Washington State Fair, where, for a decade, photographed as a six-year-old in cowgirl regalia, I had been a poster girl. These rodeos were constants in my father's life, and he kept presiding over them despite depression, trouble breathing and "the increasing pain and distress . . . of this cancer thing." Part of the Western ethic was that cowboys die with their boots on. Reading me the latest tribute over the phone, marking his farewell appearance one place or another, he told me irritably, "They're lining up behind the bone wagon, and I'm not even dead yet."

In 1979, a package arrived from him. He was going through memorabilia and thought I might like to have my baby pictures.

I knew that if I didn't see my father soon, I wouldn't see him alive again. I stayed home in California. By the time Cy was hospitalized for what was to be the last time, in 1980, my husband had borne out my theory of the randomness of the lightning bolt. He also had terminal cancer.

Don't come, Terry said on the phone when I made a halfhearted offer. Remember him the way he was. My brothers and I had not seen each other for ten years either, but out of empathy for me, as we watched the people we loved best dying, Terry let me off one more emotional hook. So did Cy. "It wouldn't do me any good," he said the last time we talked on the phone, and seeing him could only cause me pain. At least, he assumed it would cause me pain.

"You know it would," I snapped.

"Well, I certainly hope so," my father snapped back. For us, this exchange was an unprecedented admission of love.

My brother Terry has a growly, good-old-boy Western voice. "We lost him," it told me when he called in mid-April of 1980. Agonizing as it was to see him go, he went on, it was a mercy. Cy had been in terrible pain for days, and so heavily drugged he wasn't anyone we both knew. "Cyra," Terry said through tears, "he was as spaced out as a soup sandwich."

I said I'd lost Cy a long time ago. My brother took exception. "He always loved you."

I wanted to believe this. I also wanted the impossible: to live my life over again, with Cy remaining present in it, not as the parent I could not please but as the father I remembered from my childhood, dangerous but dashing, who'd taught me the words to "San Antonio Rose." Into my scrapbook, Cy Taillon's daughter in spite of him and myself, I pasted the newspaper editorials that people I barely knew sent me from all over the West.

Dorothy followed Cy a few months later, and in some unfathomable scheme of things, it was her deathbed that found me in attendance. Pat had suffered a series of strokes. I went to Missoula to move her into a nursing home. Before I turned around and went back to California, I drove to Great Falls to see my brothers, as adults. With my family "passing away," in the gentle euphemism, one after another, I felt the need to hang on to the relatives I had left.

I stayed at the Cosgriff house with Dorothy's sisters, in the bedroom I used to stay in all those lifetimes ago. We went out to dinner at the same steak house across the Misssouri River where we all used to go when Cy was in town, and where he'd once exasperated me by sending a bottle of wine back. He claimed it was "off."

As is usually the case in Montana, the wine was chilled just short of being frozen solid. Alexis Lichine couldn't have pronounced on its merits or said, for sure, whether it was red or white. Cy still got a stricken apology from the waiter, who brought him another bottle, or possibly the same one, bowing from the waist.

"Much better," my father said regally, without tasting it.

Dorothy was in a nursing home too. She had asked urgently that I come to see her, her sisters said. I went, reluctant but deeply curious; what did she want from me, near the end of her life, and what could we find to say to each other? The nursing home turned out to be the hospital in which I was born, fallen on hard times. My stepmother had done her nurse's training there, under the watchful eye of the nuns. It was hard to imagine the young, auburn-haired Dorothy, in her starched white cap, as the same woman who lay in bed, almost immobilized, no longer my antagonist or anyone's.

Her eyes were as extraordinary as I remembered, large and brilliant, with the familiar wistful expression. They locked on me as I stood beside her and listened to her tell me about her marriage to my father, "the greatest love story ever told." Their ashes would be mingled, she said, so that the two of them would be together in death as they were in life.

While she spoke, I looked at the picture of Cy on the wall of her room, an enormous blowup of a black-and-white photo. In it, he accepted one more award, a plaque or a silver and gold belt buckle, a compellingly handsome man in a Western suit and cowboy hat photographed from somewhere down around his knees, so that he looked tall as a tree.

He not only loomed above me, he loomed above Dorothy. Of all the people who had loved him and lived in the shadow he cast, I thought, only my stepmother had never felt diminished or chilled by it. With an exhausting effort of will, she was serving the legend still, testifying to her part in it to me, the only unexplained interruption of the tale of the schoolgirl and the piano player. I needn't have worried about what to say. I had been summoned there to listen.

SIXTEEN

Cy said that Bennett Cerf urged him to write his autobiography; his was a singularly colorful American life. I began my version the year before he died, intending it to be a journalistic account of his career. The book refused to remain the one I set out to write, the one Cy himself might have written. It wasn't Cy Taillon the celebrity that I needed to make sense of but my onetime polestar, and Roy's obsession, and the hell-for-leather cowboy my mother had sung about loving come rain or shine.

Two years after our father's death, I asked Terry to take me to Miles City, where he had announced his last rodeo. Cy's ghost would be there. I thought it would be pleased to know his adult children, strangers for so long, had reclaimed each other as family, and that I was in the process of reclaiming him.

My brother and I traveled the same route that Cy took out of Great Falls, across eastern Montana and vast expanses of sagebrush, sand cliffs and emptiness. The landscape is dun-colored except for white spots on the horizon, the tails of grazing antelope. Alongside streams, cabins with no roofs stand abandoned, swallows their tenants. The cold winters, or the loneliness, proved too much for the homesteaders who built them. Said Terry, pointing to one of them, "Somebody's dream . . ."

With years as a bronc rider and a rodeo judge behind him, Terry had begun announcing. He was not appearing at Miles City. Though he is following in Cy's bootsteps, he is reluctant to step in them. "Those boots left holes too big for me to put my feet in."

The Western songs he played on his tape deck were the old songs. The bars we stopped at were the same bars, timeless, preserved in their amber light. When we pulled into Miles City on Friday night, the town was unchanged to my eyes although I had not been there for twenty-five years. The false-front one-story buildings on Main Street still looked like the set for a Western movie. Had I leaned against one of them, I would have expected to plunge through a plywood façade. The sale started on Saturday, but Miles City was already full of horse trailers and pickup trucks, the Olive Hotel bar full of stock contractors.

Solidly muscled men, nicknamed Red and Scrapiron, the contractors "signify" because they have earned respect on the backs of broncs or in brawls, the kind Miles City talks about the way veterans talk about the Normandy landing. Shoulder to shoulder in the bar, with its low-lying pall of cigarette smoke, they traded jokes and set up drinks for each other and for us.

Though the Bucking Horse Sale is a relatively small rodeo, it is famous in the West because producers come there to bid on the horses that may make them rich. Cy announced it one last time, on a rainy weekend, when he was easily exhausted and in pain. If it's not hot in Miles City in May, it's so cold that after a few hours at the fairgrounds on the outskirts of town, slogging through icy mud, you keep looking down, making sure your feet have not been amputated. The cold must have penetrated Cy's bones.

The traditional Friday-night itinerary is to go from one of the bars that line Main Street to the next. The Bucking Horse Sale is a notoriously rowdy event that turns Miles City inside out once a year, to the collective civic pride of the place, and alcohol fuels the good fellowship and the fights. Until recently, the city aided and abetted the drinking by closing off several blocks to truck and car traffic, so that celebrants could go from one bar to the other with drinks in hand. The sale was a drunken orgy, local clergy and an out-of-state newspaper complained, telling Miles City what it already knew, and finally, the city sighed and passed an open-container law. Now the contractors, the cowboys and the crowd that comes simply to whoop and holler have to stand packed together inside the bars and relay drinks over each other's heads.

At the Bison, where Terry and I dug in for the evening, the passing of drinks resulted in frequent deluges down the backs of our necks. Conversation blurred into an amorphous roar. Somewhere in the back, a Western trio played to nobody in particular, the lot of musicians in bars the world over. Brusque and efficient, the bartenders wore Gay Nineties dress. They darted back and forth like water bugs while I knocked back whiskey ditches with Terry, calculating his body weight as opposed to mine and wondering if we'd eaten dinner that night. Approximately 960,000 people live in Montana. Most of them seemed to be in the Bison, pleased to see Terry and deaf to my pleas of "Oh no, thanks a lot, but really, I've had enough." His eyes hidden behind black sunglasses, Terry grinned down at me. One of my brother's favorite sayings is: "If you can't run with the dogs, don't piss with the puppies."

So I drank with him, and the rest of the crowd, and tried to catch the punch lines of the stories that all begin, a popular joke has it, "This ain't no bullshit . . ." The press of other bodies, and pride, kept me upright. Around midnight, beside me in the crush, a young cowboy tapped me on the shoulder. "I must be taken into consideration," he said.

Echoes of Willy Loman and "attention must be paid." "How come?" I asked.

"Because I lost my hat. Somebody done took it."

"You can get another one."

"I can't, neither. That was the Beethoven's Ninth of hats."

This exchange seemed hallucinatory, but so did being back in my father's world. I had walked away from it. There it was, tapping me on the shoulder and insisting on being taken into consideration. I knew that to Terry, and to the genial crowd at this bar, Cy had epitomized the last line of defense in a country gone to the dogs, the liberals and Gloria Steinem.

The Western wives I remembered were present too, handsome women who sat a barstool as stylishly as they sat a horse and who told the same breathtakingly sexist and racist jokes their husbands told. "This is a good one, honey," they said, launching into them, friendly and welcoming. They reminded me that the West is still a male world, one in which women are admired for how well they imitate men. On the ranches, these women did the same hard work, taking the pickup out in blizzards to hay the horses; shearing the sheep on sheep ranches and putting up with the smell that permeates clothing with a foul lanolin reek; sharing the driving on the rodeo circuit, with the kids, the blue heeler dog and a horse trailer in tow. I decided not to lobby for the ERA that night.

These women enjoy the lives they have chosen, thank you, and if I saw them as patronized, they didn't. Nor did they mind the affectionate references to "the ball and chain here," perhaps because they knew that if they got fed up with his chippying around, they could bring their man back into the corral like any experienced pickup rider. Lecturing a Montana ranch wife about women's lot at the hands of the male oppressor is asking to get your face rearranged.

The Bison closed at three in the morning. Terry and I were propelled out into the street by a flying wedge of merrymakers behind us. We stood swaying on the sidewalk, confronted with a line of helmeted policemen fingering riot clubs.

Miles City brings in police from Billings to maintain order for the Bucking Horse Sale, a hopeless undertaking. In the afternoon, they had patrolled in pairs, checking out the bars and making themselves visible. By seven o'clock, they traveled in fours. At bar-closing time, they were deployed eight strong, figuring that their small margin of strength lay in numbers. The Billings police are deeply resented, by the rodeo crowd, as foreign mercenaries. For some atavistic reason they were resented that night by me. "I hate those old boys," my brother said. His arm, draped over my shoulder, felt weighty as a redwood log. The two of us fixed the police between us and Terry's car in a hostile gaze.

"Hell," I heard myself saying. "They're not so big, let's take 'em." I had picked out my four, and Terry's, and this idea seemed entirely reasonable.

My brother wrestled me to the car and drove back to my motel. Before he said good night, he told me I was showing signs of turning into trouble.

Saturday morning, badly hung over, we drank Bloody Marys and pushed around eggs in the motel coffee shop, where the breakfast special was twelve-ounce buffalo steaks. More friends of Terry's, and Cy's, stopped by our table to say hello. "Cy's daughter," they said to me. "Well, I'll be damned, where you been?" They were open, and sociable, and I still found them unnerving, these men whose gaze was skilled at appraising horseflesh.

By the time we got out to the fairgrounds, Miles City was running true to form for the Bucking Horse Sale weekend. The rain fell steadily, wetter than other rain, and in the arena, gumbo mud turned the rider who got bucked off his horse into a human Fudgsicle. Gumbo is slick and black, with enough suction to swallow a three-year-old child. You can't walk in it without using both hands to pull one foot clear, and then the other, and if you drive through it, it becomes part of your car. In a reaction to the rhinestone cowboy syndrome that brings out the Taillon in me, I had worn shoes to Miles City instead of boots. I own cowboy boots, but so do computer programmers, hairdressers, rock stars and buyers for Macy's. They belong on cowboys.

The result of this principled choice was that I sank into the freezing gumbo up to my ankles. It climbed my pants legs and oozed over my shoe tops. Said Terry, looking at my feet with compassion and scorn, "You forgot. Never go to a rodeo unless you don't care what you step in."

The only events at the rodeo were bareback and saddle-bronc riding, intended to show off the horses rather than the riders, some of whom were weekend cowboys and young kids from the surrounding ranches. Since 1951, the contractors who supply rodeo stock have come to the Miles City sale to buy bucking horses at auction. Immediately after each ride, the auctioneer starts the bidding. While sellers bring in horses from all over the West, many are local. A rancher finds he has a horse that bucks, a trait that cannot be bred into an animal and makes him useless as a working ranch horse. He brings him to Miles City and hopes he'll show what he's made of, thereby entering the ranks of the elite in the rodeo world. Highly prized, bucking horses have careers that outlast those of the cowboys who ride them and who get to know every horse on the circuit—their cranky personalities, their bone-shattering moves. As catered to as coloraturas, these horses become legends in their own right.

The sale published a Collector s Edition program that year, one with a moving tribute to Cy in it. It contained a lengthier tribute to a horse named Skyrocket. "There were many other great horses, like Limber Jim, Bovee Grey, Flying Devil and the Spinner, but Skyrocket captured the heart of Montana." Six men managed to ride him before he died, after twenty years of putting cowboys in full-body casts.

Terry explained the scoring to me as the first rider shot out of the chute, to be bucked off, hard, when the horse nearly lost its footing. Both rider and horse are judged; the scoring is 1–25 for the rider, 1–25 for the horse. There are two judges, for a total of 100 possible points.

The horses are judged on how high they buck and how powerfully. "Look for the extension of the back legs in the kick, and at the withers. That's where the power is in a bucking horse."

Riders are judged on how securely they sit, on how far forward they keep their feet and on their spur stroke. The rider should spur the horse from shoulder to rump with smooth strokes of blunted spurs, which agitate but don't hurt the horse. Though the spurs will sometimes draw blood on a thin-skinned thoroughbred, bucking-horse stock is too highly valued to be abused. Over the afternoon, at the end of the auctioneer's glossolalia, sales prices ranged from one hundred thirty to twelve hundred dollars, for a black horse that tried to dismantle the bleachers and the cowboy on his back. In previous years, horses have sold for as much as the compact cars most cowboys still wouldn't be caught dead in.

The metal grandstands were open to the weather. I had not brought enough warm clothes with me to Miles City, and the rain drilled through my city slicker. My head throbbed from the bourbon I had drunk the night before. My throat closed on the hot dogs I tried to put down it, the only fare at the concession stand besides beer. Amazed at how much, I missed Cy's voice over the p.a. system; the pilgrimage I had insisted upon struck me as a mistake, a trip back to a world in which I did not belong, and hadn't for most of a lifetime.

Beside me sat the brother I scarcely knew, his cowboy hat soaked through despite its plastic cover, immune to the cold. Terry worked the chutes when he wasn't dutifully keeping me company. He wished he were riding again, he told me, and I wanted to shake him; hadn't he broken enough bones yet? What he replied paraphrases loosely as "A man's gotta do what a man's gotta do."

Tommy, too, was waiting to turn forty so he could ride Brahma bulls in "old-timers" rodeo, held together though he was with steel pins and Superglue. Tending bar in Colorado once, my younger brother had been shot in a fight he was trying to break up. In Great Falls, before Terry and I left, I asked him for particulars. Tom said it was no big deal, the gunshot missed all of his vital organs and the helicopter that evacuated him to the nearest hospital got there right away.

Our father had spent his life promoting this chest-beating ethic. I realized that I'd found it more comprehensible as a child than I now found it as an adult, and as the rodeo and the rain continued, worked myself into a fouler and fouler mood.

Terry, Cyra and Tommy together in 1982

Interspersed with the bareback and saddle-bronc riding at the Bucking Horse Sale are quarter-horse races. It was already dark, at midday, when the track announcer took over for the rodeo announcer, who, at the beginning of the day, had called for a moment of silence in memory of Cy Taillon.

The track announcer asked us to put money in a hat over at the beer stand, a collection for "a cowboy who planned to be here today but didn't make it. He was in a car crash, and had an ear tore off and other minor injuries." This appeal sank in slowly. When it did, the crowd burst into mighty guffaws.

"What do you suppose a major injury is?" my brother asked, laughing so hard himself that his eyes were watering. I didn't know, and couldn't have answered through my own laughter, but I didn't care: that only-at-a-rodeo announcement had replaced my feeling of strangeness with familiar affection, for Miles City, for the sport my father loved, and for Cy.

Even when he was close to dying, he would have been in his element here. He would have made us forget the cold, by stamping our feet and cheering the riders on; pulled out the organ stops until the hat at the beer stand overflowed with money; forgotten his own discomfort, and all else, as long as he had a microphone in his hand.

I thought, with no irony at all, that it wasn't cancer that had killed my father, it was being unplugged.

CODA

Here are some excerpts from the yellowing pages I carry around from one side of the country to the other, in old hatboxes that once belonged to Roy.

Ila Mae to Pat, sometime in the spring of 1982:

Dear Pat, It has been such long time since I have had any news from you you are all ways on my mind cause I love you . . . Please dear let me hear from you. Some one will read this for you Some one will write note for you. I worry about you . . .

Roy to me, undated:

I know you have to consume spirits at all the partys you attend and possibly more than is good for you. If such is the case, you should eat a lot of asparagus, that cleans out all the ammonia in your system. The least harmful of all liquors is vodka made from potatoes; and be sure you get a lot of B-vitamins in your diet. I hope you have a nice exmas and take care of your health. As ever.

Cy to me, 1975:

I must tell you how proud I am of you in your pursuit of an education and in the reaping of the fruits of your efforts now. The important thing now is for you to realize happiness in the short life span allotted to all of us . . .

Ila Mae to me, undated:

Well Dear Keep up the good work just remember that John comes First. This clipping was in our paper the Great Falls Tribune, isn't this terrible? . . .

Each time I move, I ask myself why I keep this accumulation of letters. The writers are all dead; throwing away their correspondence could offend none of their sensibilities. Yet I preserve all these thousands of words, Roy-like, as if they were encoded and someday I will crack the cipher, understand the nature of my family's affections and jealousies. I will learn to see them all through their own eyes, instead of imperfectly through mine.

Ila Mae tyrannized Baby Sister from their days in Paragould, chastising her for everything from marrying Cy, to leaving Roy, to crooked seams up the backs of her stockings. In the months before she died, she wrote Pat almost daily, telling her how much she loved her, and instead of newspaper photos of child polio victims, enclosed dime-store valentines. Their mottoes read: "You're sweet as honey" and "You're very special, be mine," and they are meant for small children.

Roy named me his heir, after my mother. The language of his will says he does so "because I look upon her as my own flesh and blood."

When we drew close again, at our cautious remove, Cy wrote often about how proud he was of me for getting a book published. All the praise he had withheld for a lifetime, he heaped on me then, sending me interviews in which he mentioned me as "the other writer in the Taillon family." A sentence in his will excluded me. I wanted nothing from him, and expected nothing, but found it painful to be struck once again from the rolls of his children. He had acknowledged my existence intermittently. It made me smile a peculiar smile that my copy of the will, mailed to me by a North Dakota law office, arrived with fourteen cents postage due.

My mother, the one who had the greatest capacity to surprise, gave me the most unassimilable proof that I had not really known her. Soon after my husband died, I drove to Montana again to visit her. We sat on the porch of the nursing home, in a thin winter sun, and I told Pat that Ila Mae had died a few months earlier, news I had withheld because I wanted to tell it to her in person. She received it calmly, the way she had accepted Roy's death and my phone call telling her that we were both widows now.

Her most recent stroke had taken away her ability to speak clearly. She communicated with smiles, or arranged her face in a frown, but neither smiles nor frowns had much to do with what anyone said to her.

The nursing home staff was fond of her because Pat was the only patient who never complained.

She seemed pleased to see me, if not entirely sure who I was. A radio played somewhere inside, and she hummed tunelessly along with the music and moved her swollen, slippered feet, a seventy-two-year-old former dancer, who in some core of herself was still a dancer. "I guess I ought to tell you that Cy died too," I said. I thought Pat was entitled to know, and that this knowledge could not touch her because nothing could. As we sat together, her glance had flicked off me and the cars in the parking lot with equal disinterest.

She turned and stared at me, through glasses smeary with thumbprints, and made a sound I interpreted as "What?" "He died, Mother," I said again. "He'd been sick for a long time. It's sad, isn't it? I'm sorry too."

The noise that ripped out of her throat froze me. "No!" My mother's hands jerked up from the arms of her chair and struck at me, catching a finger in one of my hoop earrings, and the keening sound poured out of her as I took the earring off and reached over to comfort her. Her face contorted, she batted my hands away.

"What *on earth* did you say to her?" asked the nurse who came running out to us, alarmed. I let her lead Pat inside and went and sat in my car, too shaken to start it and drive away.

I thought I had guessed correctly at what Pat had forgotten. I'd been massively wrong about what she remembered.

"She couldn't adjust to that life back on the road, with you," Ila Mae had told me, talking about her sister's early life. "Maybe Cy wouldn't come home all night, and that left her in some little room alone with you. She called me and said 'I don't know where Cy is and I haven't known for two days. Can you come over?' I came and got you, and we didn't see anything of him for two or three days. He'd been gambling in a crap game."

The Cy my mother mourned was not the man who parked her in motel rooms and disappeared, not the man who had blackened her eyes more than once, nor the man Cy became, the senior statesman of rodeo. Like me, she mourned another Cy entirely, the husband who had picked her up and carried her, when they danced the night away, because out of vanity she insisted on wearing shoes a size and a half too small. Nothing—not time, not Roy, not other losses—had erased that memory for her, any more than time had erased it for me.

I put this book aside finally, wondering if anyone ever makes sense of fathers, or families, and whether their daughters perceive all fathers as part men, part myth. Whoever the man with the golden voice was when he took his high-heeled boots off, and his tall hat, and the diamond horseshoe stickpin, and the pearl buttons marching up to his elbows, I missed him when he unhitched our trailer in Billings decades ago. I missed him as a child and as an adult, every time I saw him and then didn't see him. And I go right on missing him, even as he eludes me again.

I tell myself that I would be less Cy-like if I had the chance to grow up all over again, less stubborn and more forgiving; that I'd judge Roy and Dorothy less harshly; that I'd understand my mother fully and tend the spark that remained in her, underneath the ashes. I'd do a better job of loving this time, and so would they, and we'd be that domestic group in the *Saturday Evening Post* covers, strangers to both reality and regret.

Then I realize there are no rodeo announcers in those illustrations, no soubrettes, no auburn-haired nurses and no earnest Old Honest Faces—also no daughters with the temperament of bulldogs. I accept the lot of us, at last, as who and what we were: just one more group of people joined together as that mysterious and complicated thing, a family.

When the Drumming Stops

a novel

Steven Wishnia

Manic D Press
San Francisco

When I was younger I used to sing for revolution.
I have kept sacred my beliefs, but I have lost my illusions.
—Linton Kwesi Johnson

Dedicated to the city of New York, where a black man in a Ramones t-shirt can compliment a Jew on his Sun Ra Arkestra number at a $3 outdoor concert by a Venezuelan funk band; my friends from the Lower East Side diaspora and related tribes: we rock together when times are good, we help each other when they're not; and the extended Wishnia family from New York in the north to Cuenca in the south, from Paris in the east to San Francisco in the west, *que viva la mishpocheh!*

This is a work of fiction. Any similarities to real people are purely coincidental. On the other hand, I really did once see a cat knock the needle off a Von Lmo record, and in a more perfect universe, the Bobby Kane Syndrome would have had a hit record.

When the Drumming Stops ©2012 by Steven Wishnia. All rights reserved. Published by Manic D Press. For information, contact Manic D Press, PO Box 410804, San Francisco CA 94141   www.manicdpress.com
ISBN 978-1-933149-66-0   printed in the USA

Chapter 1
The '00s / July

"Kryptonite? Where ya at?"

"Twenty-fifth and Park."

"All right. Come on back to me."

The other phone popped.

"Headcheese. One-forty Liberty."

"All right. Pick-up at Emerson, Lake, Fifty-five Water, twenty-third floor. You're going to Nine West 42nd. It's a rush."

Underend Vicodini needed a cigarette. Three in the afternoon, lunch two hours gone and quitting time at least two and a half away, and his eyelids drooping like he was back on dope. He slumped sideways in the chair, caressing the pack of Newports in his vest pocket. The summer's second big heat wave wasn't helping either. His black t-shirt was stained with sweat from the last time he stepped out. The pores of his nose oozed with grease from the mushroom pizza he'd had for lunch.

The phone popped again, beeping him out of his lead-headedness.

"Zap Messenger," he rasped.

"Rayo."

"Donde estás, papi?"

"Feefty-nine y Lexington."

Underend riffled through the stack of quadruplicate tickets on the fake-wood desk, glanced at the computer monitor. "Okay. Pickup at Sony/BMG Records, Fifty-fifth and Madison. You got two packages, one for Rolling Stone at 745 Fifth; one for Spin, 205 Lex."

Sony/BMG. They owned the rights to the third and fourth albums by Underend's old band, the Gutter Astronomers, which had come out on Permanent Records, a short-lived boutique subsidiary of RCA back before RCA got swallowed by BMG and BMG got swallowed by Sony. Underend hadn't played much on the fourth album. The memory of the A&R man's voice stabbed. "You don't count for shit." He didn't remember much else about that record, part from liquor and drugs, part from whatever brain-chemical miracle cauterizes bad memories.

The phone beeped again. Mobile at 46th and Madison. Black Dave at 75 Varick. Checked the e-mail, see what runs were coming in, filled out tickets. Headcheese again, at 30 Rock, send him to 1290 Sixth. Critical at 19th and Fifth. Wipeout at Citicorp. Terry T at ABC on West 67th.

Five-fifteen finally rolled around. The phones slowed except for a few last-minute runs. The messengers drifted in, sweaty, drained, animated, cell phones clipped to their waists, handing decks of tickets to Underend. Headcheese, a hillbilly anarchist with long brown dreadlocks tied back over baggy rags of indeterminate gray/black/green, his voice an East Tennessee twang seasoned with hip-hop Brooklynese. Kryptonite, from the Bronx River projects, dressed in serious cycle-geek gear, padded spandex shorts and a skintight, lurid yellow, round-collared top with a Pirelli Tires logo. His white counterpart, Critical, who'd argue vehemently about toe-clips and Bush's role in the 9/11 plot. Reek, a crusty punk in a skull-graphic t-shirt and duct-taped boots, from the same Brooklyn loft as Headcheese. He'd gotten his name after a woman at an ad agency sent over an e-mail complaining about having to share an elevator with a messenger who "had an aroma of personal hygiene inappropriate for a place of business." Billy Zap the owner couldn't keep from laughing when he read it to Reek, even as he suggested that he "take a shower at least enough so ya don't bother my customers." Black Dave and White Dave. Mobile, a big hip-hop dude with baby dreads in a Miami Dolphins jersey. In last after catching a run to 110 Wall was Rayo, a short, wispy-mustachioed Mexican cat the color of an upright bass, sweating through a burnt-orange ING Financial Services t-shirt.

Underend separated the tickets—one copy for the messenger, one for billing—and handed them back, clipping them into individual piles for Billy to give to the accountant. Shut down the computer, the screen going black with relief.

He stepped out of the storefront and lit a cigarette. The menthol cooled his mouth; the nicotine cooled his nerves. Down the block he walked past three homeless men dozing on piles of dirty bedding under a construction scaffold. He headed for the subway, joining a river of office workers, women in long rippling skirts and upscale flip-flops, women in thin white pants outlining their asses. The Stones played in his head, his mood dripping matte black as he watched the girls in their summer clothes. He flowed downstairs to the L train, into the harsh oven air on the narrow, crowded platform. Five minutes later there was light at the end of the tunnel. A Brooklyn-bound L. It was already too crowded to get a seat.

Four! Stops! Till Brooklyn! Good old Beastie Boys, I don't need an iPod, I got a jukebox in my brain.

Underend edged into the car's aisle, grabbed a spot on one of the sidebars, stared up at the ads. DON'T LET IMPOTENCE RUIN YOUR SEX LIFE … GIVE YOUR FOOT A BREAK FROM PAIN … 212-MARGARITA … LOS ABOGADOS NUMERO UNO PARA LOS HISPANOS HERIDOS EN ACIDENTES … MINIMALLY INVASIVE BUNION SURGERY.

The window was riddled with scratches that vaguely formed a name, a pathetic echo of old-school graffiti. He missed the old days of graffiti, not the black marker inside-the-car scribbles, but the murals that covered the train sides, big eye-popping balloon and slanted-block letters in ghetto-floral shades of purple and yellow and red and green. The other side of the car had a greenish strip of posters for Mitchum Anti-Perspirant. An old Velvet Underground song clicked on in his inner iPod, about an aging actress once in a movie with Robert Mitchum and now forgotten by everyone except an obsessed fanboy.

Yeah, I'm over the hill, too, but not looking for love. Not with any effort anyway. Too hard to find and too much melodrama when you do, quickly succumbing to boredom or civil war.

He got off at Lorimer, debated whether to walk or wait to take the G one stop. Laziness won. He was tired. Eyeing his reflection in the window as he got up, a hangdog-looking dude with thinning, close-cropped gray-black hair, olive skin, a gray pinstriped vest over a black t-shirt looked back at him.

He lived just north of the Brooklyn-Queens Expressway on a block of old brick tenements and hospital-green frame houses. He didn't feel like cooking so he just copped a pastrami sandwich and a quart of orange juice from the corner bodega. The Mets game was on at seven. St. Louis. In the street a bunch of girls jumped rope and chanted to a boombox blasting "Hollaback Girl." He'd never seen much in No Doubt—weak pop-ska-punk band, why listen to them when there were the Specials and the Skatalites?—but this Gwen Stefani tune was catchy as fuck, like an '80s hip-hop jam. And no woman wants to be a guy's second choice.

He unlocked the red door to the building, climbed the last few steps of his journey to the third floor. The pills clanked in his pockets. He'd found out he had hepatitis C back in '98, three months after he'd finally gotten seriously clean.

Yeah, they got me on all this pharmaceutical shit now. No more dope, not one speck of China white or Afghani brown. No more booze, wine, beer, Jack, tequila, vodka. Not a drop. No more coke. No more reefer—well, that one wasn't as strict, but it was still a slip. My liver can't take any more. Well, thank whatever higher power there is that I didn't get the HIV.

It's Paxil and Klonopin time now. That shit can knock you out as much as dope, especially the Klonopin suppositories they prescribed for severe anxiety attacks. "You won't panic, you'll just… sleep." And coffee and cigarettes at the meetings. Weeknights weren't bad. He was usually too tired to be bored. It's the weekends when there's two days to fill. That's when he usually went to meetings, getting jacked up on burnt-tasting coffee, stepping out for cigarettes.

The apartment was peacefully sunny. The fire escape window looked west from the back of the building onto a courtyard of weed trees and an old Polish woman gardening. Underend twisted the chair so it faced the TV, moved the table closer so he could have the food within reach, unwrapped the sandwich and opened the juice. When he was finished he collected the garbage and threw it out, washed his hands, and got out his bass, a sixties-vintage black hollow-body. He strummed idly while watching the game.

"Two and two to Pujols. Curve ball—just misses. Three and two. Martinez's got good velocity tonight but he's a little wild. Here's the payoff—Line drive hit to third! Wright's got it."

The screen faded to a Cadillac Escalade commercial. Led Zeppelin's "Rock and Roll." The drumbeat they stole from Little Richard. Zeppelin were shameless thieves, nicking licks from anyone from Muddy Waters to an obscure Bleecker Street singer-songwriter named Jake Holmes. Now here they were shilling one of their best songs for luxury SUVs. Underend hammered out the bassline. The hollow-body sounded thin unplugged, but what did he need more for? Music really sucked these days. It was boring. The last time he'd felt any excitement was around Nirvana but that was ancient history and the hype around them was fuckin' annoying. No wonder the kid offed himself. That other band, the Slip Kids, the one everyone said was the best band to come out of New York since the '70s—they sounded like an '80s Bowie rip-off, not even one of his good albums. No energy and lots of attitude.

What was the point? It was like when you're fourteen and everything about girls, about sex, is this magical mystery. You wonder what a pussy feels like, what a nipple feels like, just what do girls think about and what do they feel? Rock'n'roll was like that, too. You'd hear somebody playing guitar and you'd wonder how they got that sound. You'd have no fuckin' clue, like a little kid looking at a computer. It was magic and you wanted it. Like when your girlfriend slipped her tongue into your mouth, you wanted it to go on forever. When you heard Mott or Lou Reed or the Stones and you wondered what made it move like that, what made it wail like that, what made it bite like that. Now you're just a played-out old hooker; it's all transactions, A to B to C. Ho hum, another squelch session.

It *was* magic. Like what was it that made "Pretty Vacant" sound like all the fury in your brain boiled down to sound, *way* more than just a couple of A octaves thumped out on a P-Bass and a Les Paul, and it still made you want to live? It's all product now, like that fuckin' billboard with the guy who looks like Joe Strummer at "PrettyVacant834@ aol.com." Hey, if they wanna be really bad-ass, they could have made it "666." Yeah, then they'd get accused of encouraging Satanism, and Hillary Clinton starts a Congressional investigation.

God grant me the serenity to accept the things that I cannot change. Well, the reality is that I can't change shit. Stinking thinking. Stop it.

He was better off than Rayo, who had a wife and two kids in Oaxaca he hadn't seen in a year and a half, sent them whatever money he saved by sharing a room with three other guys in Sunset Park. Underend had to be grateful to Billy Zap for hooking him up with the job. Billy knew him from back in the day when Underend was in the Gutter Astronomers and Billy was drummer in the Flaming Roaches, doubling on guitar. Billy hadn't been much of a user, just a little coke, but everybody else in his band got high. Unlike most people who didn't use, he had some compassion for the ones who did. Or at least he could sense that Underend was serious about getting his life back, not just trying to conjure up some juice from a sucked-out well of trust.

Bottom of the fourth. Vizcaino dives to his right to stop a shot by Endy Chavez, then flips to second for the force. Top of the fifth. Pujols hits a solo homer. St. Louis up 1-0.

We really need punk rock now, he thought. All the apocalyptic shit we were singing about back then is true. War all over the world. Religious fanatics crashing planes into buildings. Soldiers with machine guns in the subways. Media made for morons, propaganda brainwashing and celebrity spew. No future. No future for you. Underend played a verse and a half of "God Save the Queen," then flopped his hand away. "We need it, maaaan."

Billy Zap still played around, doing gigs with jazz and rockabilly bands, occasionally a recording session with a singer-songwriter. There wasn't any real money in it—these days, you couldn't even get a gig in a pass-the-bucket bar-blues band—but he liked to keep his hand in. Wipeout did, too—well, Wipeout would play any gig anywhere. He used to be the couch-surfing embodiment of the "What do you call a guitar player without a girlfriend? Homeless!" joke. He'd even been gigging five weeks after the accident that got him his name. A woman from Cresskill, New Jersey, panicky about piloting 5,500 pounds of Chevy Tahoe up Sixth Avenue in light snow, had bulled into a right turn. She'd stopped short in time to avoid obliterating Wipeout, but knocked him skidding onto a patch of ice, breaking his left arm in two places. "It was like, 'Bwa-ha-ha-ha-ha—wipeout, baby!' " he'd recounted at the office later.

Underend didn't want to play like that. Too much hassle for a few crumbs. It was dark outside. Martinez went to 3-and-2 on Rolen, then got him to fly out to right. Underend lit another cigarette. Encarnación struck out.

Yeah, Step Nine. They say you're supposed to apologize to everyone you fucked over while you were using. I wasn't a thief so I didn't rob my friends… well, no one I cared about anyway. The only one I really owe it to is Tina, and that wasn't drugs, or at least it wasn't because she was in between me and getting high. It was because I didn't have the guts to leave too after the rest of them drove her out of the band. What good would it do now, other than make me feel like I tried? The damage is long since done and it ain't getting undone.

Bottom of the fifth. José Reyes hit one up the middle for a single. Underend bent some high notes on the G-string. Lo Duca up. Takes two balls, fouls one back, and then rips one into the gap for a double. Second and third, none out, all right! The crowd at Shea is getting into it. The Cards gather on the mound. They walk Beltran to load the bases for Carlos Delgado.

Underend slid up to the D a few times, twanged the "Spoonful" F-D riff, then hit a low F as Beltran trotted to first and Delgado trudged to the plate. C'mon, ya fuckin' has-been. Who you calling a has-been? Look in the fuckin' mirror. The first pitch was a ball. Delgado fouled the next one off, high back of first. Another ball, low and away. Reyes led off third, leaning toward home.

The phone beeped. Fuck. Let the machine see who it is. "This is Underend. You're rolling after the beep."

"Hey, Underend, how you doin'. This is Mickey. I'm out in L.A." Jesus fuckin' Christ. The lead singer from the Gutter Astronomers. The fuck he want?

Underend picked up midstream. A cold shell instantly surrounded him. "Hi," he said from deep within it. He knew he sounded really sullen. Delgado swung and missed. Underend took a swing at being sociable while protecting the plate. "What's up?"

"I got an offer for us to do a reunion tour."

"You what?"

Mick jumped into full-on spiel. "Yeah, I was in the club a couple nights ago, and I ran into Alan Bryson. He's been in the business since way back, he used to work for Lizard Records back in the day. He used to book Pulaski Hall before he moved out here, and he remembers us. He said we were one of the most underappreciated bands of the '80s, said the time is ripe. And you *know* we were. You hear people say the Slip Kids and the Strokes are the best bands to come out of New York since the '70s. Well, what about us? He told me, 'I could name a whole bunch of great bands that never got what they deserved, but you guys stand out. You were really unique, people should totally give you your props, and the time is now.'"

Fuckin' Mick. Always gotta give you the sales pitch before he tells you what's going on.

"…And he's got a new label. He said, 'Every band from back then is doing reunions. There's a whole new generation of kids who are hungry for it. Why don't you get the guys back together?' He said they'd love to reissue the old stuff and hook us up with a tour this fall. I already talked to Scott, and he's down."

"I can't really quit my job. I'm fucked without one. My rent's $950."

"You still working for Billy Zap? He's a musician, he'd understand. He'd be glad to let you go out for a bit."

"I can't just leave it to go sleep on people's floors again."

"Alan's got connections up the ass. We're not going to be playing holes in the wall. People out here, people who come in the club, they remember us all the time. We could get hall shows, not little dive bars. College gigs, too, they pay really well. Anyway, what are you doing now that's better?"

"I don't even have gear anymore. All I've got's an old Hagstrom hollow-body bass, and a little 10-watt Peavey practice amp. My old amp's busted."

"What happened to that old Epiphone you used to have? The red one? That was a fuckin' awesome-sounding bass."

"I sold it for 250 bucks."

"Aw, maaan! You know how much those are worth now? Easy a grand. I heard one went for three grand on eBay."

"Well, I was in a bad way. And I got it for $125—remember when I found it in the pawnshop on Atlantic and Fourth? So I came out ahead."

"What about the other one? The black one?"

"The Tele? I sold that first. I got six bills. I wasn't so bad off then."

Mickey Sapirstein couldn't understand. From his lead-singer perspective, these guys treated their instruments like a cross between their cocks and their cars. They'd spend hours nattering about arcane details of gear—split-coil pickups! chickenhead knobs!—and if you asked them to turn down so you wouldn't blow your throat out screaming by the third song, they'd act like you wanted them to cut their balls off with a broken bottle and auction them off to raise money for the PMRC censorship campaign. And then they'd let them go for next to nothing. For what? Two weeks' worth of pizza and beer and dope money?

Don't be too hard on him, Mickey thought, I need this, too. His own luck hadn't been so spectacular either since the band broke up. One solo EP that got a few decent reviews but didn't sell much, some acting gigs, another band that gigged around L.A. in the '90s, getting signed and doing an album but never hitting the "alternative" jackpot, and now this bartending gig at the Moto Lounge in Silverlake. It paid well, better than music had most of the time. He could make $300 in tips on a good night. And lots of people—some pretty big—remembered him and the Gutter Astronomers. But nobody was going to immortalize him for mixing Cosmopolitans and Dirty Martinis.

"Well, you can get a decent bass cheap now, right? And it's not like it used to be, when we had to hump gear all over the country. A lot of the clubs and venues rent backline now, they get a couple Marshalls and an SVT and a drum kit."

"Who're we going to get for a guitar player? Tina's not going to want to do it, and I don't want to play with Jen or Jack."

That was the tough one. Getting Scott Crowley the drummer to re-up was easy, Mickey thought, he'd never quit playing. That Underend had asked who we *are* going to get and not who *would* we get was telling— he was in, he wanted it even though he wouldn't admit it yet, he'd say no if you asked him flat out. Tina had barely spoken to either him or Underend since she quit the band—the acrimony possibly stemmed from Mickey calling her "an incompetent slut." And Underend had never really gotten along with Jack, the guitarist who'd superseded Tina during the sessions for their fourth album, or Jen, the keyboard player they added around the same time.

"Listen, this is about the future, not the past. We need to move on. We don't want to spend our whole lives wallowing in bitterness, stabbing ourselves to death with old grudges. This is about whether we're going to play the music for a new generation of people, whether we're going to get the Gutter Astronomers the place we deserve instead of being in the dustbin of rock'n'roll history. So I'm not gonna ask you to say yes or no right now. But think about how we can make this happen in a way that's best for all of us. Okay?"

"I guess so," Underend strained out.

"All right, cool. I'll give ya a call soon."

Underend dropped the phone, missing the cradle. He bent over to pick it up, an awkward stretch, cursing. His heart was hammering like a death-metal kick drum. What the fuck did I get myself into? It was like when you had an ex you swore you'd never speak to again, out of revenge or self-preservation. She'd fucked around on you, cut you down in the way that only somebody really close can, and now she's back and you ease into it like it's the most comfortable thing in the world. Even though the senior voices in your head are intoning DON'T TRUST THIS DON'T TRUST THIS, there's other voices, clear strands of infatuation filament wrapped around you and pulling back in. You remember what it was like when it was good and you haven't been that far above the ground since. There was a magnet sucking him in, like the tattoo on the left side of Amanda's chest that started in the hollow below her collarbone and inexorably led down into the whirlpool around her nipple. And he was getting hard thinking about it. It's like hepatitis. Once it gets in your blood you're never the same.

On the TV it was the bottom of the seventh, the Mets down 5 to 2.

He shoved a Klonopin up his ass and went to sleep.

Chapter 2
1979

On the day in 1979 when he rode a Long Island Railroad train from Ronkonkoma to Brooklyn, Underend had felt like he was Muddy Waters arriving in Chicago. Leaving the boredom of suburbia as the train coursed through Bed-Stuy, clicking past blocks and blocks of abandoned buildings, the burnt-beamed ruins of an African-themed bar, and the station platform where B.T. Express posed for their *Do It Till You're Satisfied* album cover. The city was a walking disaster and a wonderland. It was a place that teemed with life, not like the Island where everybody was locked up in their cars and televisions. He remembered waiting for a subway on the way home from CBGB one night and there were three black kids dancing on the platform to Chic's "Ahh—Freak out!" song on a boombox the size of a Fender Twin Reverb amp. Block parties popped with conga drums. And coming out of the crumbling tenements of the Lower East Side was the most exciting rock'n'roll ever, music that shook the rails like the West Side IRT express train, and he was going to be part of it.

He sat by a window, clutching his blue-sparkle Univox bass—a cheap knockoff of the Mosrite Ventures guitar Johnny Ramone played—and keeping an eye on his other possessions, a frayed green backpack and a small Fender amp. The city wasn't like people on the Island said it was, but you still had to watch your back. People on the Island bragged about how long it had been since they'd been to the city. They acted like if you rode the subways you'd never be seen again, that your charred bones would be found at the bottom of an iron pot in a rubble-strewn vacant lot where they cooked honky chitlins and arroz con blanquito. But you still had to be careful. The lowlifes could smell when you were from out of town, when you were spacy or lost, when you had something to take off. Like the scene in *The Harder They Come* when Ivan comes to Kingston and the guy runs off with his stuff. Underend had the bass, the amp, $300 in cash, and a check from his mother for $500 more. That was supposed to be his apartment money when he got a job.

He got off at Atlantic Avenue and trucked underground to the subway, heading out to his grandmother's apartment on Avenue P. The plan was that he would sleep on her foldout couch until he got an apartment. He hoped that was soon. There was no privacy, it was an hour from the city at night, and she nagged him all the time.

"Why do you have to wear black all the time? It's summer, it's so hot."

"I'm not that hot. It doesn't bother me."

"When are you going back to school?" she demanded. "You don't want to be a nothing all your life."

"Grandma, I'm going to establish residency in the city," he said back, tinged with exasperated whine. "Then I can go to Hunter or City or Brooklyn."

That was the cover story at least. His real plans had more to do with CBGB than with CUNY. The Long Island music scene was a wasteland. There were only three people he knew at Suffolk Community College who were remotely into punk, or even Lou Reed or the Dolls. He'd hooked up with a singer named Jeff and they'd done a handful of shows under the name Nova Express, but they'd never been able to find a solid guitarist or drummer. Guitar players on Long Island were either hippies or metalheads, and in both cases that meant one thing: long solos, guys more into playing solos than songs. They'd used a longhaired Zappa fan named Mike for their two paying gigs—opening for a parody act called the Transsexual Toads at an ice-skating rink in Ridge, and a Thursday night at the Rock Shack in Rocky Point—but he'd quit after they'd almost got booed off the stage at the Rock Shack, the crowd calling for Skynyrd and Foreigner covers. For Underend and Jeff, the Ramones had been a revelation. For Mike, they were a lame joke. "You really want me to sound like that?" he'd sneered. "My five-year-old sister could play better."

The best times they'd had were at parties at Crazy John's house in Ronkonkoma, where Jeff sang through a Fender Twin. Crazy John was an older dude, a good guitar player who got what they were trying to do. He was a big Velvet Underground fan, but he was so agoraphobic he never went out of the house. The story was that he'd done thirty-one tabs of Orange Sunshine in an LSD-eating contest in 1970. He'd won, but the prize was an eleven-month stay in the Central Islip bin and fragile sanity ever since.

His garndmother broke into his thoughts. "Richard, why do you want to be in the city with all the animals out there? It's not safe. You, a nice boy, walking around with that guitar. They'll hit you on the head and take it."

"Grandma, there's nothing for me on Long Island."

Her calling him "Richard" grated on his nerves. That name had pinned him as the target of dick jokes and Nixon gibes all through junior high. He'd dubbed himself "Underend" almost as soon as he'd picked up the bass, part because he loved the feeling of driving the music from below, part because of Overend Watts, the silver-maned bass player in Mott the Hoople.

I know she loves me, but I wish she'd stop fucking nagging me. He didn't have much family left. Most of them grated on his nerves, the women always whining about their weight, his Uncle Tony asking him, "Your sister still seein' that yom?" every time they saw each other after the Thanksgiving when Cheryl came home from SUNY New Paltz with an eggplant-colored boyfriend named Raphael Ashford. He hadn't been close to his father's side, the Italian side, since long before his father died, killed in a head-on collision on September 29, 1977. They said he'd been drinking a little. The guy who hit him had been drinking a lot. Screaming careening into the wrong lane on Route 25 in Selden.

His parents had split up three years before the crash when his mother realized that she was really a lesbian. He could see where that came from. Women in the '50s weren't supposed to like sex. They were supposed to close their eyes and think of a gleaming new refrigerator and electric range. Then in the '60s if they weren't into it, they were frigid, repressed. So they went through twenty years with that corroding their marriage, accumulated resentments eating away until there was nothing left but a band of crumbling rust, and then—"Eureka! I'm a DYKE! No wonder!"

He'd gotten into playing bass then, his father taking him to Huntington one visitation weekend to buy the blue Univox. He could get lost in it, scorch out his frustrations on it when he was pissed off, space out on it when he was high. His father, an engineer at the Grumman aircraft plant, hated rock'n'roll, the disorder and noise of it—"Turn that shit down!"—but he seemed at home in the world of electronic circuits, asking the sales guy at the Sam Ash music store about amp specs. It was like he was making an awkward effort to get into Underend's world instead of just demanding that he live up to his expectations.

Bass looked easy. It only had four strings. And you could always find people to jam with because nobody wanted to do the grunt work of pumping out the groove. Everybody wanted to be the lead singer or the guitar hero. That suited Underend fine. He didn't want to be the one going, "Look at me, here I am." He wanted to be cool, shadowy, like only the ones who really understood would know how essential he was. Like Keith Richards instead of Mick Jagger.

He trudged the hot pavement of midtown Manhattan looking for work. There wasn't much an A.A. degree from Suffolk Community qualified you for, especially in the middle of a recession when it was obvious your head was elsewhere. Messenger, retail, low-level office jobs like stuffing envelopes for $3 an hour, an endless week of folding bank brochures and filling gray plastic bins with the product. Being a messenger got you out on the street, but it only paid minimum wage, and people looked at you like you were a trained dog coming in with their envelope in your mouth. He needed his vinyl records. Then at least he could come home and blast.

The chance to blast came Saturday night. Joey Rush and the Users were playing Max's Kansas City. They were a spin-off from the Speed Queens, second only to the New York Dolls as local glam-rock legends. Underend copped a loose joint for a buck from a black guy outside the club—"loose joints, six for five, try 'em before you buy 'em"—and a couple ups for another from a white guy inside, washing one down with a beer.

The club upstairs was packed, about a hundred people. The speed kicked in just as Jackie Ryan whacked the snare for the Users' opener, "Mexican Brown." Underend was in the front lines immediately, dancing his ass off to the wall of sound, twin guitars exploding raw and naked through Fender Twins turned all out, Jackie making the onslaught snap and throb. Some people shoved the tables aside so they could dance, others posed back on the sidelines.

"I want everybody out there to eat organic vegetables," Joey intoned in a thick Bronx drawl, " 'cause if you got bad habits, you gotta compensate… This one's called 'I Don't Know Where the Fuck I'm Goin' … One-Two-Three-Four!"

Underend was dancing with a split brain, half on the band, trying to soak up every detail—Joey Rush in a t-shirt, black spandex sleeves over his elbows, playing feedbacky high notes, power chords, and corkscrew hammer-ons on a gold Les Paul. He was the star, but the rest of the band was what made it move. Lenny Lust, the other guitarist, in a pink suit jacket, ripping out amphetamine Chuck Berry licks on a red SG; Hiroshi the bass player, a pinstriped movie gangster thundering a sunburst Fender Precision; and Jackie driving the lot. This was it. This was what he had come to the city to feel. The other half of his brain was checking the crowd, the spandexed blondes, the Brooklyn guys in Ramones t-shirts, trying to catch the eye of the short girl with curly black hair and a plaid skirt dancing a few rows away. She was oblivious so he got lost in the music.

Underend was still revved up when the band ended after an encore of "Village of Love," an obscure R&B tune from 1962. He heard people talking about an after-hours club called the Boxx on 14th Street, a few blocks away, and followed the crowd over. He'd already spent eleven bucks but fuck it. The Boxx was on the corner of Third Avenue, on the third floor upstairs from a coffeeshop called Disco Donut inhabited mainly by low-budget pimps and junkie hookers with faded skin.

At the door were a small woman in red lipstick and a big guy who looked like New Wave Mafia—black collarless suit jacket over an immaculate black t-shirt and monster muscles. David Johansen's "Funky But Chic" pumped out from inside. People filed in, the woman putting their fives and tens in a gray metal box.

"Private party tonight," she said when Underend stepped up.

"You just let all those other people in," Underend said, almost stuttering.

The bouncer stepped out. "Where you from, New Jersey?" Underend's eyes came up to his Adam's apple.

"No, Brooklyn."

"Too many bridge-and-tunnels coming here," the woman snipped.

Fuckin' Studio 54 assholes. Underend stalked back down 14th Street, the Dead Boys going off in his head. "Sonic Reducer." Sonic revenge. You think I'm nobody, but wait till I blast you.

"Ts and Vs. Tooies and Valium," an emaciated junkie muttered at him. At Union Square the number 6 subway train came mercifully quickly. The F train at Broadway-Lafayette took forever. Underend dripped sweat. The light at the end of the tunnel was a garbage train, dirty golden gondolas transporting rows of reeking dumpsters.

A black woman, head shaved except for a quarter-inch of bleached-blonde nap, came down the stairs. She handed him a flyer. "Hey, come see my band at CBs on Wednesday." In sparkly 1950s motel-sign lettering next to a Barbie doll holding a martini glass with a brain in it, the flyer billed The Universals over Galactic Trash and the Accidents.

"Yeah, I just saw Joey Rush and the Users at Max's. Fuckin' great."

"The Users? I love them!" She introduced herself as Queenie, and paused before asking, "Got any pot?"

Underend still had the loose joint. "Yeah, you want us to smoke it here?"

"We can go down to the end of the platform, and if you see a cop coming throw it in the tunnel. They don't want to go down there with the rats. It's cool."

They finished it just as the train pulled in, talked music to Brooklyn. Queenie got off at Fourth Avenue. Underend got home at 5:30. The weed had calmed him from the speed, but his head was still spinning, churning. He was too tired to fold the couch out, and the plastic covers on the cushions were crunchy and uncomfortable even through a sheet. He finally drifted off around 6:30, just as it was getting fully light out. At 8:30 his grandmother was up with a glass of tea.

Wednesdays he got the *Voice* and called any band ads that looked promising. There was one who said no when he said he didn't use a pick, another who hung up when he said he lived in Brooklyn. The one that claimed they sounded like the Ramones and the Damned turned out to be a joke band whose drummer had a groove like turds plopping into a toilet.

Saturday afternoon he lugged his bass and amp up to a white-brick highrise on the Upper East Side, for a singer/songwriter who'd advertised "Infls: Patti Smith, Blondie." She was kind of cute, with shoulder-length brown hair, a striped top, and a Les Paul. "This is my song," she said, and launched into, "I don't want to take a man to wed, I want to take my money to bed. "

After a couple minutes of silence, she asked, "Are you stoned?" It's okay if you don't like it. It's about how I'm disappointed in men, so I just want to fuck my money."

Underend didn't know what to say. Great, I schlep all my gear all the way up to fucking 90th Street and First Avenue to hear this woman who wants to sit on Benjamin Franklin's crinkly paper face.

Tuesday night he was standing outside a basement rehearsal space on Second Avenue and Fifth Street, going to check out a surf/art-noise band called the Brainwaves that said they shared the studio with Joey Rush and the Users. He was drinking a bottle of grapefruit juice in the heat, waiting for the guy auditioning before him to finish, when a taxi pulled up. A skinny, pissed-off guy with black hair and glasses busted by, followed by the cabbie, who was taller. "You motherfuckers want to audition guys to replace me and use my fuckin' amp?" he was screaming. "I don't fuckin' think so!" The skinny guy and the cabbie hustled the amp up the stairs, the shorter dude fuming, "Behind my fuckin' back … I don't believe the fuckin' nerve, the chutzpah."

When Underend walked in, he was greeted by two art-geek types, one wearing big plastic glasses and an olive button-down shirt. "We're sorry you came down here but we don't have an amp for you to play on. If you're still interested, call me tomorrow."

Underend didn't think so. As he turned to leave, in the far corner behind a trap case sat Jackie Ryan, a thin pink silk tie wrapped around his bicep, quietly probing his forearm veins with an eyedropper needle.

At CBGB the next night, the Universals had just come on when he walked into the long subway-like room, a thin pathway of booze-soaked wood under the glow of dirty neon beer signs with the stage at the far end,. They had a great sound system. Queenie sang in a Poly Styrene screech over a lurchy Talking Heads mutant-disco beat created by a hippie bass player who played lots of notes and a hard-hitting greasy-haired drummer with teeth like one of the worse blocks in the

South Bronx. Queenie exclaimed, "Hi-and-thanks-for-coming," when he went backstage but was preoccupied with holding court. Galactic Trash was an extremely loud band with a Japanese metalhead guitarist, a screeching, dissonant sax, and a silver-suited, silver-faced lead singer with a German-android voice. The Accidents, on last, played speeded up, punked out rockabilly. They were a three-piece band with a lead singer who looked like a model and a bass player who looked bored. The drummer—a thin, muscular redhead with half a quiff and an anarchy tattoo on his arm—impressed Underend. He was fast but chunky, defying the law of rock'n'roll physics that the faster you play the thinner you sound, the heavier you get the sludgier you sound… you've got to break it enough to find the right communion. Speed + weight = power. Underend was up front dancing. Other than "Be-Bop-A-Lula" he didn't know the songs, but they plyed mostly covers. Two songs before the end of the set the lead singer announced that they needed a bass player. Underend went backstage and signed on for an audition.

Three practices later—it was blues-based stuff, easy to pick up on—they were playing a Tuesday night at a club in the West 20s called Turquoise. It was almost empty, black walls and thin carpet on the floor, strangely bland like a cokehead's unlived-in apartment. It was exciting to be onstage in New York City at last but Underend expected more. The club's booker was playing pinball while they sweated away. Friday night they opened for the Brainwaves, who'd presumably found a bass player. It was a small, arty, brick-walled room called X79 on a back street south of Canal.

The place was packed and the crowd popping. It would've been great except Rob the guitarist and frontman was pissed off. Pissed that most of the people there were the Brainwaves' friends and didn't pay him much attention. Pissed when Underend and Scott the drummer sped up the train-track rhythms he wanted to hold back. Pissed at Underend because his equipment wasn't cutting it, his bass sounding thin and his undersized amp straining and distorting at live volume. Pissed that Underend kept running out into the crowd, dancing with people, settling on the woman who danced back, a round, brassy brunette in a semi-psychedelic pink and black dress and Converse high-tops. Her name was Laura, she was in from Chicago.

In between sets the DJ played deep reggae, bass-and-echo dub, mixing it up with Johnny Cash and Joy Division, plus some English band that sounded like a cross between the Sex Pistols and Chic, singing about "at home he feels like a tourist" over jagged guitar and ripped-up disco bass. Laura leaned close into him when they went to get a drink. He could smell her sweet-wine breath, feel her lips on his ear, her breasts against his elbow. By the Brainwaves' second set they were rubbing up against each other while dancing, kissing in between songs.

"This ain't amateur hour," Rob snarled at Underend when they loaded out. "You don't play with me unless you have decent equipment, not those piece-of-shit toys you got. And this is my band, not yours. You don't go running out in the crowd when I'm singing or playing."

Underend ignored him, concentrating on Laura. Fuckin' jealous creep. Doesn't know how to have a good time. He collected his gear and left, vaguely hearing Scott shouting at Rob, "How many more guys are you gonna run off?" Laura took him back to her friend's railroad flat on the Lower East Side. "We've gotta be quiet," she warned him. When she came she was like a quivering mountain of flesh.

Underend resolved to get more serious about it. Find something that's solid, what you really want, not just any mediocre egomaniac who puts an ad in the *Voice*. There was a lot of mediocrity out there. The bland, polished kind, like most of the stuff on the radio, music that felt like a gray Tuesday afternoon in pre-rush-hour traffic. The people who had good ideas but not the chops, intensity, or inspiration to pull them off. He put himself in that category for now, at least as far as chops went.

All right, you know what you *don't* want, now what do you *want*? Well, since he didn't sing or write lyrics, he had to hitch himself to a singer and lyricist worth riding with. Somebody who had the intensity he loved in punk, but wasn't just going to follow the formula, afraid to break loose from the crowd of clones. Somebody who had brains but could write simple, and could be transcendently stupid instead of pompously stupid or just plain stupid. Somebody committed to being in a band and making it happen, but who really feels it, not one of these "I just want to make it, I don't give a fuck how" assholes.

And he also had to get better gear, a better bass and a real amp. That was the one thing Rob was right about. He skipped lunches for a week to save money. On Friday he cashed his paycheck and walked up Eighth Avenue. It was another Midtown heat wave day, the air, your sweat, and car exhaust particles forming a toxic ooze on your skin. Women in hot pants and thigh-high vinyl boots lined Eighth Avenue. "Want a date?" called a pale, wobbly redhead. "Goin' out?" inquired a black woman in a wig that looked like it had been ironed straight. White women in new-wave office clothes, angular haircuts, and turquoise blouses rattled by, nervously rushing for the safety and air-conditioning of the buses to New Jersey. A scar-faced Puerto Rican with a scraggly beard blasted distorted disco from a boombox on his shoulder, amplifying it through a bullhorn with "Fuck You" scrawled inside the bell.

He turned right onto 48th Street and headed for the row of instrument stores between Sixth and Seventh: Manny's, Sam Ash, Alex, Terminal, Silver & Horland, We Buy. A cornucopia of guitars and basses. Racks of them hanging in the windows, pasteboard price tags jammed through the strings, yellow and purple Stratocasters, thicker Telecasters, black and gold Les Pauls, a thousand-dollar aluminum Veleno whose neck ended in a V-shaped headstock. A venerably worn slab-bodied Fender Precision, touted as " '51 P-Bass #0005. If you have to ask, you can't afford it."

"You tryin' or buyin'?" a sales guy with a shag haircut demanded. Underend tried a couple, a Gibson and an Ibanez, but nothing really excited him, and most of the Fenders were out of reach, more than the $272 he had. Then he saw a '72 Telecaster for $200. It had a thicker, slabbier body than a Precision, black with a badly fucked-up finish, patches of the glaze scraped off down to the wood. He checked it out. It was love at first pluck. The humbucking pickup gave it a fuller, deeper sound than a regular P-Bass. And even after buying a case and paying the sales tax he still had $18 left.

That meant he couldn't go out that weekend, but he didn't feel like going home. Not to sit in the too-bright old-people light and play unplugged. He took the subway down to the Village. Maybe sit in Washington Square and check out the new baby.

On West Third and Macdougal a bearded old hippie strummed the well-worn changes of "All Along the Watchtower," scat-singing the Jimi Hendrix guitar solo. Macdougal Mike, the greasy-haired record store potentate, berated a departing customer, shouting, "You're banned from the scene for life!" On the corner by the park, Underend got hit by the sound. A girl with dyed black hair, sort of a shag, a hooked Italian nose, and an ash-blond Telecaster, playing "Will You Still Love Me Tomorrow?" She couldn't sing that well, but she could play, pummeling bar chords on the verses like a Troggs-troglodyte version of its Brazilian rhythm, blossoming into shimmering fireworks for the open minor-key pre-chorus, flowing into the hook. And she was getting a whole Phil Spector wall of sound from a Pignose battery amp and a couple of effects boxes. He could almost hear drums and backing vocals in the waves. He stopped to listen, leaning on his bass case.

"Hey—you sound great. You looking for a bass player?"

"I might be," she said, launching into the Runaways' "Cherry Bomb" straight through to the distorted intro of Patti Smith's "Ask the Angels." Three songs in a row he liked. They couldn't talk much because she had to work the crowd, making eye contact with passersby to entice them to pause, singing to the ones who stayed to encourage them to drop quarters onto the blue lining of her Tele case. Underend stood a step off to the side, out of her way, but by the time he split east, they'd exchanged names—she was Tina Toxic—numbers, and brief bios. She was from Glendale, "a redneck neighborhood" in Queens, and had escaped to the East Village three months ago.

On to St. Marks Place. He got a slice of pizza on the corner, stopped outside a clothing store called Creative Destruction. In the window a mannequin with black lipstick and nail polish flaunted a t-shirt that read "DESTROY" over a shattering swastika. Inside were racks of leather jackets, black and red jeans, t-shirts with half-inch stripes—red and black or black and white—and more conventional used clothing, rumpled button-down shirts dyed fuchsia, turquoise, and black. A tall fashion punk presided over the lot from behind the counter, over a glass case of studded wristbands, striding around on the floor in a tight black synthetic t-shirt with a zipper across the front, his immaculately spiked hair bright green, the color of Jello or Prell shampoo.

"Yo, what you got in there?"

"Telecaster bass. Just got it."

"You in a band?"

"No, but I'm lookin'."

"What are you into?"

"Punk, but something more. Not Ramones clones. I don't know," Underend explained.

"I'm trying to, too. I'm Mick Septic, I used to be in the Droogs," he introduced himself. "You got a minute? I gotta close up the store, but you wanna go get a beer, we can talk?"

They went across the street to a bar, the crowd a mix of punks, generic singles, old hippies, and Ukrainians. Mick got two beers while Underend scoured the jukebox for something good amidst radio hits by Dire Straits, Fleetwood Mac, and disco. Looking for something that might represent his taste to Mick, at least within the limited selection, he settled on Bob Marley's "Sun Is Shining," the Stones' "Everything Turning to Gold," and Blondie's "Heart of Glass."

"A taste of the old moloko," Mick toasted. They settled in to talk. Mick was from Flatbush. His first band was Captain Pissgums and the Pervert Pirates. His parents had moved to Jersey six years ago when the neighborhood turned black, but he'd stayed on in the city, got a place in the Village, and started the Droogs after he saw the Dolls. The Droogs had straddled the cusp of glam and punk, like red leather and lipstick, but went sour on the lower rungs of the club circuit and broke up.

"Yeah, so I'm tryin' to start something new. Now that I know what the fuck I'm doing. I don't want any egos, any bullshit. It's gotta be real. I don't want people just to say, 'Hey, man, nice set,' and then go back to their boring lives. I want to shake people out of it, shock them up. I want them to be totally possessed, taken somewhere else by it, and then bring it back. Like an ancient shaman, you know, the guy the Indians had, they had them in Siberia too, the guy who'd absorb all the pain of the tribe, be the psychic adventurer for them, do mushrooms and see visions for them, dance out to the edge and bring it back for the people, tell 'em what they'd seen."

It was not so much the words he was saying that drew Underend in, but the force of his conviction. The architecture of a dream. A dream he wanted in on, too.

"I got the connections now. We can get gigs no problem," Mick went on.

"Heart of Glass" came on, the synthesizer pulsating.

"Fuckin' disco sellout," Mick muttered. "Bland, complacent, robot music." Underend looked shaken. "What, you put this on?"

"It's a good song," Underend defended, his voice thinner. "I like dance music. Not disco, but like funk and soul. Rock'n'roll's supposed to make people dance. Like, I did a gig at X79 a couple weeks ago, and the DJ was playin' some song that had sort of a disco bass line but really noisy guitar, and I was dancing my ass off. I don't know what it was, something like 'at home he feels like a tourist.' "

"Gang of Four. New English band. I saw them open for the Buzzcocks at Irving Plaza, and the Buzzcocks were great, I love the Buzzcocks, but Gang of Four blew them away."

"The thing I hate about disco isn't the music. It's that fuckin' Studio 54 shit. They got some fuckin' gorilla outside tellin' people, '*You* can come in, but *you* can't, you're not cool enough.' And it's coming into punk now, like at the Mudd Club and Boxx. Like I went to Boxx after the Joey Rush show at Max's, they were letting all these fuckin' posers in, but they wouldn't let me in."

"Ya know something? Fuck 'em," Mick explained. "I'm from Brooklyn. The Ramones are all from Queens. The Dolls were from Queens, except David Jo's from Staten Island. Lou Reed's from Long Island. Joey Rush is from the Bronx. Patti Smith and Debbie Harry are from Jersey. Same thing in London. The guys in the bands there are from Shepherd's Bush, Finsbury Park, Bromley, same kind of places. I was there in '75, just when the whole thing was bubbling under." That had been where he acquired his stage sobriquet, his birth name of Michael Owen Sapirstein fortuitously coinciding with "Septic Tank," the rhyming epithet for "Yank."

"So who are the really cool people, the ones that built the scene?" he went on. "Who are the ones out there being creative? The bridge-and-tunnel kids. Not the fuckin' Manhattan snobs. The misfits, the kids who feel like there's nobody in the world like them till they come down here. We gotta escape from where we came from and we bring that energy, that desire."

"I just met this guitar player on the street, she's really good," Underend said. "And we might be able to get this drummer I played with in a rockabilly band. He's still in the band, but the lead singer's an asshole, it's not gonna last."

A round robin of phone calls set up a session at the Trisonic rehearsal studio in the West Twenties: Mick, Underend, Tina Toxic, and Scott from the Accidents. It was a windowless room with fluorescent lights and a muddy-tan rug with dull-red diamonds. Underend checked out the gear: an Acoustic bass amp, a pale blue face with flat aluminum knobs atop a five-foot speaker cabinet; two Fender Twin guitar amps with cigarette burns on the top, their silver-gray grille cloths tattered; a black drum kit with pockmarked heads and a cracked crash cymbal; and three Shure vocal mics, their round balls dented and misshapen. But for ten bucks an hour, it was a place to play where the neighbors wouldn't be pounding on the door with hammers.

They introduced themselves, turned the amps on, tuned up, plugged in. Tina opened with the two-chord riff of X-Ray Spex's "Let's Submerge"—"we're going down to the underground"—and it was an instant explosion. She and Mick raced up to the mic to sing the tagline—"If you've got the urge/C'mon, let's submerge"—clicking in like they were born to do it. Nobody spoke for a half minute when it ended. Awkward what-next.

"Ya know 'What Goes On' by the Velvets?" Underend ventured.

"Yeah," said Mick.

"Sort of," Tina said.

"It's easy, D-C-G on the verse, A-G-D on the change," Underend explained. They'd clicked in by the end of the first chorus, Scott rocking up a cradle of rhythm for Underend to push and pull, easy yet driving, Tina clattering the rhythm chords and then dropping into long, liquid tones, thirteen perfect notes in four bars. Mick wailing the chorus like a prayer. They jammed on it for seven minutes.

They messed around with a few more simple covers, a couple Ramones and Sex Pistols songs, the Dolls' "Chatterbox," the Shangri-Las' "Great Big Kiss," jammed on a couple riffs from Tina and Underend, a two-chord drone, a Bo Diddley beat. Underend's head swam like sex and violent rage. It was fun.

Tina turned the tremolo and reverb on her amp all the way up, creating a helicopter-in-a-cave buzz, and played the Electric Prunes' "I Had Too Much to Dream Last Night." Mick flung himself into the vortex, screaming it into a whole. Scott powered it with a frenetic roll and Underend struggled to keep up, playing a burbling one-five lick with his thumb and forefinger, swept away with psychedelic mind overload and punk rock fury. You know when it's happening, when it's right. It had the raw power and garage soul of punk, but was something more, was breathing in the other music out there.

They convened at a pizza place on Seventh Avenue after they finished. "Well, are we a band?" Mick proclaimed. Everybody said, "Yeah." They gobbled slices. The radio played some jazz-fusion thing, a busy, jivey guitar solo over a too-fast-to-be-funky rhythm.

"I fuckin' hate guitar solos," Mick spat. "I wanna play songs."

"Yeah, I used to live on the Island and I jammed with a lot of guys who are like that," Underend echoed. "They're just goin' on and on, *di-di-di-di di-di-di-di* for like ten minutes, and you're just playin' some blues riff over and over, and it's like getting stuck in traffic behind a really stinkin' garbage truck." They all laughed. "But there are some good ones."

"Lou Reed on the Velvets' 'Rock'n'Roll,'" Tina jumped in.

"Steve Hunter and Dick Wagner on *Rock'n'Roll Animal*." Mick immediately contradicted himself.

"Brian Jones on 'Heart of Stone." Underend. "And the second one on 'Anarchy in the U.K.' The one that goes *"Dot-dot dah-dahh."*

"Paul Burlison on 'Train Kept A-Rollin.'" Scott.

"Who's Paul Burlison?" Underend asked. "That's a Yardbirds song."

"No, it's a rockabilly song. Johnny Burnette did it. On Sun. That's the original," Scott corrected. "Did you ever hear the story about Sonny Boy Williamson and the Yardbirds? They backed him up when he toured England, and he went back to Arkansas and told one of the guys in The Band, 'Those English boys want to play the blues so bad, and they play them *so bad*.' I'm into white funk."

"Play that funky music, white boy," Mick sang, giving his voice a wah-wah inflection.

"No." Scott cut him off, like a rap on the snare. "That's *not* what I mean. The Dolls had it. The Ramones had it. Rockabilly wasn't just 'white guys playing the blues.' It had its own rawness, its own wildness. You should dig the blues, not try to play them. You're never gonna be Elmore James or Howlin' Wolf, so do something original with it."

"I don't like playing lead that much anyway," Tina reassured them. "I like playing rhythm. That's what makes a band rock. A lot of these guys who play a lot of lead… they remind me of guys who are always telling you what great fucks they are, like 'I'm the best, baby!' "

"Why the fuck would you fuck somebody like that?" Mick inquired.

"You ever buy an album and it sucks?" She was answering Mick, but she seemed to be talking to Underend. "It's like you see an album, it's got a really cool cover, and you heard the band was great, so you buy it. And then you take it home and play it and it's totally lame? It's like that. You don't know what's inside till you take it home and play it."

The four of them cemented the bond by going to see the Clash at the Palladium. They already felt like a band strutting down 14th Street to the show, Mick and Scott the tall ones, Christina and Underend the short ones, gang hair colors of red, black, and green. The Clash blew them all away, the balcony shaking under the weight of the rocking bodies.

"That was fuckin' intense, man," Scott gasped. "It was like getting beaten up and getting laid at the same time." We're gonna be up there soon, and we're gonna be just as good, they were thinking. Joe Strummer came out for the encore with a torch of rolled-up tabloids, waving it through the slow reggae throb of "Amagideon Time." The set finished in a blaze of spotlights with "White Riot," Paul Simonon smashing his Fender bass on the stage, the image that would be the cover of *London Calling* a few months later.

"Motherfucker shoulda given it to me, I just spent 250 bucks on a bass," Underend muttered.

At the end of the month Mick hooked him up with a two-room apartment upstairs in his building, on East Fourth Street between A and B for $166.43 a month. A fifth-floor walkup, bathtub in the kitchen, plaster falling off the walls, and less than half a block from a busy dope spot—but it was home. A mattress on the floor, a turntable, and two orange crates of vinyl records. He also got a decent amp, a used Acoustic head and a Kustom cabinet with black tuck-and-roll covering.

After a few practices at rehearsal studios—the last one at Galactic Trash's drummer's place, a basement on Forsyth Street that reeked of mass quantities of cat piss, the unchanged litterbox sat right by the studio door—Scott hooked them up with a space in the basement of the carpentry shop where he worked. It was in the meat district on the West Side. Racks of hooks hung over the darkened loading docks, the sidewalks slippery with grit and offal, patrolled by spandex drag-queen hookers topping six feet in spike heels, traversed by armies of flannel-shirted, mustachioed men headed for the trysting grounds of the Anvil, the Spike, and the trucks on the waterfront.

They practiced five nights a week, retreating into the womb, gestating songs and a sound. Sawdust on the floor rose into a cloud when Scott hit the kick drum, the piles of lumber rattled when Underend hit the low E.

"You wanna get to Carnegie Hall, man, you gotta practice," Mick would lecture. "That's what my mom used to tell me. We don't want to be just good enough to do Wednesday nights at Max's."

Scott routinely sent his flimsy crash-cymbal stand flying to the floor. "That's how I know when I'm playing hard," he'd say. One time the edge of the cymbal bisected Underend's guitar cord. And guitar cables, unlike certain species of worms, do not regenerate when cut in half.

Underend stopped going to shows; all his money went to rent and studio time. He couldn't really afford to buy records either, and that sucked. The Village record stores teased him with an unattainable abundance of music—English punk 45s in day-glo pink and green vinyl, bootleg live LPs of Patti Smith and the Stones, the three-record set by Public Image Ltd, Johnny Rotten's new band, with Jah Wobble doing dub-punk bass lines that sounded like pools of molten lava deep under a volcano, encased in a metal can and costing $25 on import. He hardly got high anymore, too. He'd been a serious stoner in high school, dipping deep into the smorgasbord of antidotes to suburban teenage boredom. Cocaine was too expensive and heroin largely taboo, but everything else was wide open: ups, downs, acid, nitrous oxide, cheap booze, and boatloads of weed. He had no memory of the Aerosmith show at Nassau Coliseum in 1976 beyond waking up in the back seat of his friend's car somewhere around Exit 60 on the Long Island

Expressway. They said they'd found him in the bathroom puking up Quaaludes and blackberry brandy.

This was way better. It wasn't sitting around watching shit happen and going, "Wow, man, that's cool." It was making shit happen. Doing it yourself, not waiting for it to come out in a package. Now the band barely even drank; sometimes they'd pass around a joint at the end of practice when they stopped working and started messing around. Even then they hit on ideas and grabbed them, like the time Underend found a deep reggae groove, Scott played light thunder on the tom-toms, and Tina hung long, shimmering chords in the air. They worked it into a song called "Urban Babylon."

"We're not going out till we're ready, till we're really on," Mick insisted. "You only get one chance to make a first impression. If we're lame or mediocre, word gets around fast, and then we're goin' nowhere."

The nights got darker and colder. November and December descended on the city, the wind the winos called "the Hawk" savaging the streets, the geriatric tenement boilers sputtering out of heat and hot water. In the outside world the Russians were invading Afghanistan, irate Iranians were taking the staff of the American Embassy hostage as revenge for their torture-happy dictator getting asylum in New York. The Pittsburgh Pirates had beaten Baltimore in the World Series, the players' wives dancing on the dugout roof to "We Are Family." The band spent nights huddled in each other's apartments, spinning records. Christina had the *Nuggets* double album of '60s garage bands. She loved it even though she complained about its lack of women. Mick had hordes of obscure punk 45s, the Dils from L.A., the Pagans from Cleveland, the Lurkers from London. Underend realized what he'd felt was missing but couldn't name, discovered why all the parking-lot car-radio rock he'd grown up with never excited him. This was the real thing. It wasn't hyper-complicated, over-produced. It was music that went straight for the gut, for the heart, for the ass, brutal and simple, the pure garage spirit. Like the movie of some show in the '60s when James Brown went on before the Stones and danced his soul out, then Mick Jagger did weak imitations of the moves he'd just seen, but the band saved the day from embarrassment, just pounding out three-note riffs.

They developed their own slang. Dealing with the outside world, running errands, paying bills, moving gear, and the like, was "logistics," hustling and trying to book shows was "pimpery." An off night or an uninspiring band was "slug." A track that moved, that drove, that made you want to dance and kick down walls, was "on." They took that for a name. The ON. But it lasted only a few days. Mick thought it was "too power-pop-sounding." He suggested the Gutter Astronomers. Why? "Because we're in the gutter, but some of us are seeking the ancient heavenly connection to the starry dynamo in the machinery of night." It felt like a South Bronx DJ cutting up 12-inches by Oscar Wilde and Allen Ginsberg. The name stuck.

They did one pre-debut gig the Friday before New Year's, a party in a rehearsal studio on West 27th Street that was about to be evicted. The owners didn't care if the place got trashed; it was revenge on the landlord who wouldn't renew their lease. Drunk punks, kids in spiked hair and 'Sid Vicious Dead at 21' t-shirts, milled in the studio and the hall outside, piling up empty beers and vodka bottles, punching holes in the sheetrock. They played five songs in between an Italian punk band from Bensonhurst called the Razors and a black band called the Klanflakes. A pudgy kid in a motorcycle jacket staggered up to Underend, putting an arm around his shoulder, breathing booze in his face. "Great set, man, you guys were original," he slurred. Then he blundered to the corner and puked. Kenny Kwell from the Lice, who'd broken up in the summer after two albums, wobbled in late, ripped to the tits on dope, crashing out ragged fiery licks on guitar, jamming with Underend, Scott, the Razors lead singer, and the Klanflakes guitarist on sloppy versions of "God Save the Queen" and "Personality Crisis" and a spacy noise jam that turned into Pere Ubu's "Real World."

Sunday they practiced again, the last one before their so-called official debut on New Year's Eve at a Soho loft party. They had Tuesday the 8th at Max's and Wednesday the 16th at CBGB. Mick had hooked the party up; he was doing the hostess. The $300 they made went straight to a PA system for the gig. They loaded in through the freight elevator. Lila, the hostess, was a 31-year-old with short blonde hair and a little black dress from one of the minimalist shops with one rack of clothes and a thousand square feet of polished wood floor. The loft was minimalist, too, a huge white room with black-and-white paintings on the wall.

They opened with "Let's Submerge" and it was perfect. Nervous, but the adrenaline rushes drove them deeper into the channels of energy instead of jittering them off the track. Scott hunched over the drums, his red-quiffed head looming between the rack tom and the crash cymbal, hammering the snare with his left hand, smashing the crash with his right, dropping into dub style for "Urban Babylon." Midnight came and they did a Ramones-style version of "Auld Lang Syne."

In between sets the crowd—about 150 people—danced in the loft's open space to Motown, Elvis Costello, and Blondie's "Heart of Glass." They were mostly older, arty but moneyed, at least moneyed to the Gutter Astronomers' minimum-wage eyes. A lot of guys dressed like David Byrne, in floppy geek-chic shirts and pants.

"Ready for the '80s?" people asked. Lila ushered the band into the bedroom and laid out lines of coke, which made them feel like they were rock stars, albeit rock stars with dental-tasting snot dripping down their throats. "Downtown is so exciting now, there's this amazing synthesis of art and music and film and fashion," she reveled.

During the second set, a vision flashed through Underend's head. Rows and rows of identically suited men seated at computer terminals, fading off into infinity. Staring at green numbers on the screens. The '60s was the decade of the rebels. The '70s was the decade of the pleasure seekers. The '80s was going to be the decade of the moneymen.

It wasn't a pleasant thought, but he kept on playing. They blazed through the rest of the set, and the crowd danced on.

Chapter 3
The '00s / August

Saturday morning boiled harsh over Brooklyn, sticky with omens of thunderstorm. Underend lit a cigarette, creaked to the kitchen, put on water for coffee. Took a piss. It took eons to start coming out. He was woozy as fuck from the Klonopin. It wasn't as mean as a booze hangover, but it was worse. More head-slapped sluggish than a dope morning-after which, when you weren't sick, was kind of warm and sloppy like a drunk woman's kiss.

Acid twinged his stomach. There wasn't much food in the house—the dry end of a loaf of Italian bread. He swallowed the stale bread and his morning meds, a pink Paxil oblong and a milk-thistle capsule, and washed them down with the coffee.

He flipped through his CDs, trying to find something he wanted to listen to. Something fast, to get him going. All the rock'n'roll he had was old and stale, like the leftover bread he had for breakfast. Kinks to Ramones to Social Distortion, it seemed like he'd played them all a million times. Maybe jazz. An old Miles track. No, the bebop speed grated on his nerves. Made him queasy and twitchy. Fast-forward to the next tune, a ballad. Still not working. He took it off. Maybe slow down more. Lucinda Williams, *Essence*. No, it was like drowning in her loneliness, oppressive and depressing. And the last thing he needed was a gorgeous pinpoint-eyed blonde begging him to "help me get fucked up." Howlin' Wolf. The Sun sessions. Distorted guitar, trashcan drumming, and the dirt farmer's lupine growl. You always come back to the blues, hoary as it is. And Wolf was older than he was when he cut his biggest hits.

Fuckin' hell. Can't believe that fuckin' Mick called me last night. Memory surged back. I was a useless piece of shit who couldn't play, that's what he said last time I played with him. Can't believe he wants us all to get back together. How many more years am I gonna let you dog me around?

Well, I was a bit of a fuckup. Gotta admit that.

Temptation. Yeah. Up on stage at CBGB under the lights and the archaeological layers of graffiti and stickers on the wall. Pumping out the underdrive, the crowd pushing and pulsing in, girls and guys and couples, their waists pressed against the lip of the stage. Strutting up to them, eyeing their Elvis-on-*Ed Sullivan* upper-half bodies and receive-me faces, pouring out the sound. Would be good.

Yeah, a shot of Jack and a cold, cold beer on top of the amp. And a couple quick lines of dope in the dressing room. CB's didn't have enough privacy for drug use that required more technology, no doors on the dressing room and no toilet stall, only the most desperately diarrheated had ever dared to shit in the bathroom there. Put a nice glaze on everything, smooth and warm, no fear.

The fuck. You can't think like that. Couldn't think of going out in public without it. A shield. For his insecure arrogance, the classic rock-star personality type, impossible to sustain sober for long unless you were really deluded.

He lit another cigarette. Time to get out of the house. He walked south towards the meeting, through McCarren Park. A bunch of stubby Latino guys were playing soccer, a boombox blasting weird reggaeish music with a driving accordion. It sounded good, whatever it was. He stopped to watch and listen.

The meeting was in a senior citizens' center full of false cheeriness. Fingerpainting by seventy-year-olds on the walls, an excuse for something to do. The lights bugged him. Overbright fluorescents, not warm but dreary, like a hospital waiting room or a junior high school classroom on a rainy winter morning. Harsh and unforgiving, providing an unsparing inventory of everyone's physical flaws and manneristic quirks. Unlike the soft brown glow of barrooms, these were lights to focus on your problems and those of everyone else around, not forgive and forget them. Well, if you could open up here you could do it anywhere.

He was still nervous. Confessing in a dim booth to an unseen priest was one thing, confessing in the bright light to a whole bunch of strangers and acquaintances was another. He'd never gotten used to it. Who knows what the fuck they were thinking? They tell us not to judge but who could stop people from judging? Like, this dude's really fucked up, man! Even worse than me. Or, is that all? That's all the problem you had? That's nothin'. That's pathetic.

And getting up in front of people when he didn't have a bass in his hands AND wasn't too fucked up to give a shit what happened was another ordeal. That was what he was supposed to be learning how to do but it made him shiver.

People filed in, got coffee, chatted, sat down. Vodka-soaked Polish construction workers. Puerto Rican ex-junkies, former hookers and hustlers withered and wizened in their forties, a smattering of Williamsburg hipsters. A fat black woman in a pink Rocawear sweatshirt talking about how she used to buy vodka with food stamps. "Now you know they not supposed to do that, but where there's a dollar, there's a way. And my little girl, she wants a bag of potato chips, and she say, 'Mommy, how come you can get that, but you don't have money to get me potato chips? It's only a quarter.' And I said, 'Shut the fuck up, bitch.' Now can you imagine how much this drug had me in its power, for me to talk to my precious little girl like that? I should have seen it. But I was blind."

This was not making him want to stay sober. Talking about drugs bored him, except when it amplified the story. Like going on stage with a brainload of liquor, till the music ripped as hard as your head was torn up. Dope letting loose tendrils of sweetness to decorate the spiked iron gates of reality. Okay, this was a community of people trying to keep each other from fucking themselves up any more, which he liked and needed, but the constant talk about drinking and drugs grated. A mirror image of junkie talk, like old quinine-shuffle jocks reminiscing about the great scores of the past and man-I-was-fucked-up epics, but all the experiences were negative, dwelling on the degradation like football players lamenting their shredded knee ligaments and how steroids shrank their balls to peanuts.

The hardest thing about not getting high any more was going through every day feeling permanently unsettled, tense, mentally queasy, and knowing that there was something out there that could make you feel right—but the price of doing it was too high. The antidepressants helped a little. Shit that should have really enraged him didn't bother him that much, but it was more about quieting the extremes than about giving him the core of positive energy everybody else seemed to have. It took the edge off, but left everything dulled.

In the end, getting high was a cold-blooded chemical shortcut. If happiness or at least the absence of pain was neurochemical, then why bother with friends, creativity, community, whatever? The simplest and shortest route from Point A to Point B is a straight line. Of course, they were now adjusting his brain chemistry with more legally and medically approved substances.

He needed to go out tonight. Staying in the house staring at the walls would be far too depressing. But there weren't many options for nightlife anymore. The music scene was arid, anybody he'd ever heard of was thirty-five bucks, and the newer bands were strangely bland and passionless. "Indie" seemed like it had become code for an inbred in-group of white hipsters, all about the niche marketing. Bands that would spell out the name of their website after every song, w-w-w-payattentiontome-dot-com. And the alternative was watching people half his age and twice his income get drunk and stupid. In either case, trying to talk to people felt like reaching through bank-teller glass.

He needed to talk to somebody. Angeline. Yeah, Angeline Zonik. I should call her. He'd known her back in the day but not well; her boyfriends were one echelon above him, one generation older. They'd met again at a show at the Continental around ten years ago, the Carburetors or Craterface or the Convent Strippers. She was drunk and falling on him. They'd spent the rest of the night telling bad jokes and dishing the bands and the scenesters, flirted a lot but hadn't fucked, became good friends.

She used to be a photographer. Now she didn't go out much, stayed home with a hellbroth of diseases. Yeah, she'd be someone I could talk to about all this old band bullshit.

On St. Marks Place, half the people pictured on the t-shirts being sold were dead. Almost all of the rest were for bands that broke up or peaked twenty or twenty-five years ago. Nostalgia and archaeology. Coney Island High was boarded up and the place the Velvet Underground played was a mini-mall. What was the point of being geeked on bands these days, like, of knowing who was in the Faces and who was in the

Small Faces, or feeling like you were Overend Watts with a Thunderbird or Arthur Kane because he had a Telecaster? It was just another form of celebrity-sucking now.

The sidewalks were packed with legions of the rich and clueless, people who would have been scared shitless to come east of First Avenue even ten years ago. Shiny, waxy young women gabbling and chirping on cellphones, filing toward the hundreds of bars. They all reeked of money. Ten bucks a drink or more, it'd cost you thirty bucks just to get a mild buzz on. When he was their age, he was working for minimum wage. These days that would be two hours' pay for one cocktail.

"Excuse me," asked a black guy with smooth dreads, "which way is Alphabet City?" No one who actually lived there ever called it Alphabet City. It was the Lower East Side to the Jews and leftists, the East Village to the arty, Loisaida to the Puerto Ricans, the Lower to the B-boys, or Letterland, as one campy young queen put it, back in the days when it was A you're adventurous, B you're brave, C you're crazy, D you're dead, and FDR you're face down in the river. It was like seeing the corpse of an old friend who they hadn't had the fucking decency to give a proper burial.

The walls used to blossom with homemade flyers for bands, plays, art galleries, and politics, with weird graffiti and murals: there was one guy who did metal-paint stuff that looked like silver rake handles; another who stenciled THE WORLD IS BEING RIPPED—two giant sets of incisors crunching into the globe—BY MEN WHO TRADE IN HUMAN BLOOD; that Missing Foundation upside-down martini-glass thing; some band called Health Hen that spray-painted stencils of chicken tracks and old-style black dial telephones. The former bush telegraph of the underground, messages and directions and cryptic symbols, now it was all posters for cellphone companies and prison-rape reality shows, big, full-color glossy ones for breath mints, blockbuster movies, and hip-hop albums by some wanker in a chauffeured Hummer. It was illegal to put up flyers but that law only went for the little guys. He vaguely remembered some zine editor getting busted for it, fighting it and losing; CBGB getting fined six hundred dollars for some band putting flyers for their show there on lampposts.

"Move it, pops," someone interrupted. Who the fuck? Two guys around six inches bigger than him. He edged aside, lit a cigarette. He headed east, passing by the bars he'd spent a thousand nights in. Pluto, the Lizard Lounge, the Snakepit, Gloria's. Passing by the new bars he'd never been in, scores of them, upscale lounges with glass windows, theme-park dives, faux-French bistros. Picking his way through more hordes of the young and rich, gaggles and clusters smoking outside the bars. Snatches of conversation: "That's one of the benefits of alcohol." "For $300,000 all you can get is a hovel." Where the fuck do all these people come from? He crossed Avenue A to the power-station side where the crowd was thinner.

"Yo, Underend! Bassman!" called a voice from the shadows by the wall. Part Spanglish, part Brooklynese spit and glee, a bit of dying-chainsaw junkie grind, from a short dude in a ragged camo jacket, spectral and chunky, steward of a spread of used books and magazines on the sidewalk.

"How's it goin', man?" A generic greeting while Underend's brain fumbled to remember who the geezer was.

"Tato bien, man, can't complain."

Oh yeah, Tato, an old scenester long gone from the world of bands and clubs and into that of dope and memory. Tato was of uncertain ethnicity, somewhere between Italian and Puerto Rican. He'd grown up on the Lower East Side, drugs his bridge between the ghetto street and the neighborhood's countercultures, between the pleasure-seeking utopians and the looking-out-for-number-one hustle. Acid, weed, and pills in the Santana hippie days, dope moving up in the urban crisis and when punk came in, then taking over, taking him back to the street. He'd gotten his name from "tato bien," the olly-olly-oxen-free of the Loisaida junkie world, called by lookouts when the cops were gone and picked up by Tato as his mantra of positive thinking.

"How you doin'?" Tato clapped and clasped his hand.

"Not bad. What's up?"

"The Gutters, man... when you gonna get back together? How's Mickey?"

"You know, he called me a couple nights ago. But I don't know."

"You should, man. You and Mickey and that girl Trisha."

"Tina."

"Whatever the fuck her name was. Tanya. Patty Hearst. Tammy Faye Bakker. You oughta do it. Why dontcha?"

"I don't know. There's a lot of issues, you know." Underend wasn't into expounding on the reasons for the band divorce, the petty and the real.

"Nah, fuck that, it's all old stuff. Forget all that old bullshit. Youse should do it. Fuckin' rock out, there ain't no real music any more. You hear CB's is closing?"

"Yeah, that's fucked up."

"And Coney Island, too? They're sellin' it to Disney World."

"So we couldn't do 'Cyclone,' it'd be a Disney commercial?"

"Cyclone" was a Gutter Astronomers instrumental, the B-side of their last indie 45. Scott started it out with a hip-hop beat while Underend did scratches, scraping his roundwound strings with a pick and running it into a wah-wah pedal. Then Tina hung a chord, Scott detonated a surf roll, and Tina raced into some double-picked clockwork palpitations over Underend's Ramones rumble, then the three of them traded riffs and rolls, breaking down back to the scratches again and roaring back. Underend had brought the basics in, and the band fleshed it out and fertilized it. He liked it, felt he'd captured the spirit of Coney Island in 2 minutes 49, and that they'd also done something original, doing a loud-fast tune that wasn't a punk cliché, copped a hip-hop flavor without doing lamo imitation rap. But it had been gone from the set the minute Tina was gone from the band. Mick couldn't stand to shut up for three minutes, and he wouldn't condescend to be a lowly tambourine or maracas player.

" 'Cyclone.' That was a great tune, man!"

"Yeah, thanks." Well, if Tato knows that one, he's a hardcore Gutter Astronomers fan, not just some old burnout trying to suck up to a faded star. "No, seriously, it's fucked up, what's happening in the city."

"You know it, man." Tato dropped to a whisper. "You need anything?"

"No, I got six years in the program now."

"That's good. You doin' the right thing." A weird bit of junkie psychology, admiring those who left the life they were unwilling to quit.

Underend walked on. If they close CBGB's and Coney Island, they cut the soul out of New York, like the Aztecs cutting out the heart of a sacrificial victim. Only it's not a Jimi-Hendrix-at-Monterey "I'm gonna sacrifice something that I really love" immolation, not an offering to the gods of Newyorktitlan so the streets of Sunset Park may ring with corrido accordions, that Roosevelt Avenue may pulse to cumbia, for the Bronx to boom and bump with reggaeton. Just the routine carnage of the market, the ruthless god that chews up everything in its path and shits it out as product. Cut the heart out and sell it to a dog food company. Replace it with a logo, a theme park bar where it costs five bucks to breathe and $12 for a drink of water. And you will buy the product because it is the closest you can get to the original, the thing you want.

He turned onto Angeline's block, East Second between A and B. It was darker and quieter. He rang the buzzer, walked down the narrow hall; first-floor back, a dim two-room apartment. She had dyed black hair and pale, almost dead-white skin. That and the sickness gave her a wrinkled, ghostly effect accentuated by her red lipstick, which was gone by the time she finished vomiting into the bucket by the side of her bed.

"I hate for you to see me this way," she apologized.

She used to look good, and still did, even in the sickbed fashions of a ragged Ramones t-shirt, sweatpants, and fishnet house slippers.

"I can't drink any more tonight," she said, putting her beer down. She had a vicious migraine. She got them four days a week. This was on top of surviving ovarian cancer two years ago and having some weird brain syndrome that fucked up her sense of balance. She shook an oxycontin out of a pill vial on the night table, washed it down with water. Picked up a half-smoked joint and relit it.

The last thing she should be doing is drinking. But if she's getting fucked up, that's her path. He didn't have to be on it. Not good, sometimes annoying, but she does what she has to do.

It wasn't for him. He'd been down that road before. And with all the meds he was on, if he started drinking again he'd probably end up like Hank Williams, except he'd be expiring alone and forsaken in a Brooklyn tenement, without the ghost-rider legend of the corpse leaving Knoxville at midnight, stiffening on the lost mountain highways on the way to a gig he would never make.

"Walk me to the living room, okay?"

He helped her up, put his arm around her. She felt wispy, fragile, brittle, like a 5'4" sparrow. She hung onto him and wobbled to the couch.

Angeline put on Duke Ellington, "Harlem Air Shaft" and more, Jimmy Blanton walking the bass. She finished the joint and riffed on the '30s. Said it shouldn't have been that bad back then, they had music like this—she stood up and did a tottering jitterbug, then fell back on the couch—and legal pot. And everybody was poor but they stuck together. Voice coarse and raspy from smoke, pain, drugs.

"Not like today," she finished, segueing into one of her usual rants. "Fuck Bush. I hate him. I hate all of them. Bush makes Reagan look good. That stupid old fuck with a face like a cancerous prune, so fuckin' senile he probably couldn't find his wife's pussy. That's why they hated Clinton. Clinton ate pussy. That's what Gennifer Flowers said, she said, 'He ate pussy like a champ.' Reagan, he'd have been like, 'Mommy, where is it? Mommy, where is it?' And everybody acted like he was fuckin' God, like he was such a nice guy because he told some lame jokes at a press conference. He fucking killed people, the bastard.

"I hate Bush more. Every time I see that stupid smug asshole on TV I want to smash the screen in. He thinks he's so tough. He's a fuckin' pussy. He never went to Vietnam, he was drinkin' in some bar in Alabama on his rich daddy's money but he talks like he's fuckin' Dirty Harry. 'Bring it on.' Fuck him, he's a pussy. It's all advertising. You tell people shit often enough and they're too fuckin' stupid not to believe it."

When Angeline was drunk and on a roll you didn't talk to her, you temporarily interrupted her monologue. Now she was into her life story, telling about her father yelling at her after she went to an antiwar protest with her boyfriend when she was fourteen, waving the *Daily News* editorial and hollering, "Just who do these unpatriotic garbageheads think they are?" She'd been raised Brooklyn provincial in the southwest corner of Park Slope, the daughter of a Polish plumbing contractor. "And then when I started hanging out with Fernando Luna, they freaked. Our daughter bringing home a Puerto Rican—and he's a fag. I don't know which they thought was worse. We used to go dancing in the gay clubs. It was so much fun, they had all these underground discos before it was 'disco.' "

Her parents had moved to New Jersey to escape "the element," and she'd escaped to the city. "I'm lucky I got out. I'm lucky I never got it." She's switched subjects from Brooklyn to AIDS, then about how some of her gay friends get curious about heterosexuality once they've had a few drinks or some Ecstasy. "They tell me, 'You know, I haven't been with a woman since I was in high school. I wonder…' But I'm so sick now I don't feel like sex. Not even if Joey Ramone came back to life and was singin' 'Be My Baby' on his knees by my bed." She coughed out a bitter chuckle.

Underend was jonesing for a cigarette. "Mind if I smoke in here?"

"You mind doing it by the window?"

"No. My lungs probably look like the inside of the Con Ed stacks."

"You remember the Newport ads in the subway? The ones that had a guy sticking a garden hose in a woman's mouth? And they said 'Alive With Pleasure.' "

"Yeah," Underend laughed. "And then there was the one for Midnight Dragon Malt Liquor they used to have in the bodegas. They had this woman in a red nightie drinking a 40 through a straw, and it said 'I could SUCK! on this all night.' They had another one, 'The Most Expensive Taste,' and it was like 89 cents for a 40."

"You remember Sid Berkowitz? Used to be the bass player in the Bad Words? He did a story for the *Outsider* once that said, 'Ounce for ounce, say the homeless of Tompkins Square Park, Midnight Dragon is the most cost-effective way of getting alcohol into their bodies.' "

"That shit's nasty. Instant hangover." Pause. "So… you know, Mick called me last night?"

"No."

"Yeah, he wants us to do a reunion tour."

"Well, why not?

"Well… I put eight years of my life into that fuckin' band."

"That's not a reason. Don't you want to get something back for that?"

"It's like this. You know how the crusty punks are always going on about 'creative destruction'? Like when Broken Glass opened for us at Y DIY and we couldn't play because their lead singer smashed up the monitors with the mic stand? We were all really pissed off, and then this fuckin' idiot says, 'The urge to destroy is a creative urge.' Like fucking up a DIY space is real anarchy, man. Then there was this pompous ass in, what's that paper? *The Column*, saying it was good that CB's was closing, going on about 'the creative destruction of the market,' like everything gotten rid of was old horse-and-buggy shit.

"Fuck that, I want to build something. But you know, you put so much work into building something, and then people just come along and fuck it up. Like, I wrote a lot of the music and nobody appreciates that. People always focus on the singer. They don't know how much it takes to create a perfect song. You know Thee Midnighters?"

"Hank Ballard and the Midniters? 'Work With Me Annie'? Yeah."

"No, Thee Midnighters from L.A., a Chicano garage band from the '60s. They had one absolutely fuckin' perfect song, 'Whittier Boulevard.' Nobody appreciates that, how hard it is to get the right hook and the right riff and the right structure for a song. Nobody gives a fuck. So I never got credit for what I did, they just pissed on me."

"Well, don't be mad at me for saying this, but you were fucking up, too. Like the Stones fucked over Brian Jones, he was the leader of the band when they started and Mick and Keith just pushed him out. I used to go out with a guy who was an engineer for the Stones, he said they'd have Brian do overdubs and they wouldn't even roll tape. And he was so talented, he was the one who did the sitar on 'Paint it Black.' But he was so out of it, he could have been playing air guitar and thought he was Segovia. What else were they supposed to do?"

"Yeah, like Florence Ballard in the Supremes. She was their original lead singer but they pushed her back for Diana Ross, and then she got into drinking, and the more she drank, the more she fucked up onstage, so they'd push her back more, and then she'd drink more. And then they kicked her out, and she died on welfare."

"I know. So don't get mad at me, they did fuck you over, but you gave them an excuse to do it."

"I fucked Tina over," he says. "We all did. But I shoulda stuck up for her more. Instead I was like, keep the band going at all costs."

"Yeah, you did. So apologize. Sometimes you just have to let that shit go. You're the one who's supposed to be all twelve-steps now. Aren't you supposed to make up for things?"

"I guess so. I'd like to do it, but I don't want to get burned. Like when

I did a show with Joey Rush at Pulaski Hall, I really wanted to do it. I loved him and the Users and the Speed Queens. He said he was gonna pay me five hundred bucks, he was gettin' two grand for it, and then after the show his fuckin' manager gives me fifty. I spent that much just goin' to practice. I got really pissed off so he gave me a hundred, but then he starts running all this 'you'll never work in this town' bullshit."

"Frankie asked me to do the last tour with him, but I turned it down. I didn't want to get beat again. It's good I didn't do it because I would have been on the road when the squat got evicted, but maybe I could have done something to save him."

"Joey was a junkie, whaddaya expect? No, you couldn't stop him. Not unless you stole his stash, and then he would have gone out and found some anyway. But I loved him. He had this real sweet, damaged side. He was like a wounded kitten. So, like every other woman on the scene, I wanted to heal him. And he played so hard, it was sexy, the two together… You know he dedicated 'Angeline' to me once? 'This one's for sweet Angeline,' he said. I'll never forget that, it was so nice."

"Oh yeah, Mott. They were the ones who made me want to play, you know. When my parents split up, my sister and her boyfriend were going to the Mott and the Dolls show at the Felt Forum. So my mom told her, 'If you want to go, you have to take your brother.' So they had to drag me along. And Mott did 'All the Young Dudes,' 'Sweet Jane,' 'Rock and Roll Queen.' It was like Saul on the road to Damascus. Then for the encore everybody was yelling out 'Angeline!' so they did that. And the Dolls were even better. That's when I knew I HAD to be in a band. So my mom can blame herself."

"One of the Boys" had been the one, the song where his desire clicked in, Mick Ralphs playing a few keening notes before crunching in hard, then Overend Watts doing the underdrive. That was what he wanted. Mott was a cult band before then, nobody he knew was into them until "All the Young Dudes." He'd found *Brain Capers* in the $1.99 bins at the mall record store the year before.

That's what he should have listened to this morning. "Your Own Back Yard." And "The Moon Upstairs." Except he didn't have it any more. His vinyl was gone. First the rare stuff, then everything, dumped in the used-record stores or flogged on the street for spare change.

Borrowed a gypsy Gibson just to show them. Now I'm a rock'n'roll bum nobody wants to know me.

"When the fuck did it all turn into pimpery?" Underend groused. "I don't know what the point is any more. Like rock'n'roll is the music of the establishment now. How can you give a shit about the Beatles when Paul McCartney's doing bank commercials? Like he didn't sell enough records?"

"Well, what else are you doing now? Are you bored at work?" Nod. "Of course you are. You thought you were bored when you were young? You didn't know what boredom is. Doing the same thing every day and the only way out is when you're too old and sick to do it any more. And you've got it good," Angeline reminded him, "you're not on your back wondering when you're going to stop wanting to puke, stop feeling like there's a hot railroad spike in your head."

"I don't know if I could do it and not start using again. You know, like it would feel really weird going up there without a beer on the amp, a couple lines before, a beer and a couple lines after, you know…"

"I know. We all grew up on that. 'Ozzy's stoned tonight, ain't he?' Jimi and Janis and Johnny and Keith, Kurt and Courtney and Bird and Lady Day. Well, look at me saying this, fucked up like I am, but don't you like to play? Isn't that enough? Can't you do it for itself, not just for being high while you're doing it?"

She was a fuckin' mess but he could talk to her, feel something with her. He admired her. She was drooping. The cable box glowed 2:39.

"I gotta kick you out." She needed sleep. They kissed goodbye, lingering a bit.

Underend walked up Avenue B, back to the L. The bars were already almost empty. He smelled pot. Then three plainclothes cops jumped to jack up a black guy, barking commands at him. "Where's the bag?" a white guy in a Yankees hat shouted, grabbing at the victim's pockets. "Hands on the car! Don't fuckin' move!" Underend's heart dropped, his stomach queased. The cops had the dude with the dreads who'd asked him how to get to "Alphabet City."

Mick stood behind the bar at the Moto, a long gray, black, and white swirl of mother-of-toilet-seat pearloid. It was a sunny day in L.A., but dark inside, half pit, half oasis. Opening time. Slow in the bar, a couple unemployed actors and procrastinating screenwriters. He could concentrate on formulating what he wanted to say to Tina: what to say if she answered, what message to leave on her machine if she didn't. He dialed the number he'd gotten from Scott. She probably wasn't home from work yet, he figured. She wasn't. Good. Let her digest the idea a bit, don't just spring it on her.

Into his periphery stepped Morena, the actress he'd been sort of seeing. She sat down. He hadn't called her in two weeks. Exes, he thought as he clicked his cell off. I'm surrounded by a constellation of exes. But out of many she was the hottest prospect. She had the warm maple-syrup skin and tangled hair of Hollywood exotica erotica. You could easily imagine her in one of the soft-core lad mags, posed nude on a beach with oozy lips, glycerin droplets, and strategic camera angles. But that would have been in 1998 or 2000. She wasn't feeling like the hottest prospect now. Everyone was abandoning her. She was pushing thrity and not an up-and-coming starlet any more. And why hadn't he called?

Mick stashed the phone by the cash register, strolled over to the jukebox. Punched in 6513. The Detroit Cobras doing "Let's Forget About the Past," an old Clyde McPhatter song, a slow '50s blues waltz.

"Let's dance," he murmured. And they clutched and glided, hanging on to each other. Forgetting about the past was the best they could hope for. It couldn't be undone.

Tina'd been massaging all day. Monday. It was slow, only three clients. Mondays weren't that bad normally, people were recovering from weekend sports strains and bruises or wanted to do it before they got too stressed out from the week, but it was summer, a lot were out of town. And she couldn't do the evening shift, she had to pick up Damian at day camp.

She liked it. Liked touching people, feeling their muscles relax and release, the smell of the oils and lotions. She could pick the music, too; she liked giving a massage to dub, Jah Wobble, and Bill Laswell. She hated the New Age muzak most therapists used. Wanted something peaceful, but with soul and a groove, some body in it.

She'd been a secretary after the band broke up. Hated it. Hated the corporate world, the management-speak about "core values" and "branding mission" and "win-win situations going forward." The bland, always-upbeat politeness masking icy greed. "We had to let her go," they'd said when they dumped Rosemary the office manager, who'd been there for fifteen years and was about to have surgery for breast cancer. They wouldn't even cover her health insurance; she had to pay the five hundred bucks a month out of her unemployment. And they acted like that was unfortunate when they did it to replace her with someone half her age and half her salary. But if you criticized them in the slightest, then you were being "negative" and "disruptive." And at her last job, at a dot-com, they'd all acted like the Internet was going to make everyone in the world billionaires.

Never trust anyone who uses the word "right-size" unless they're being sarcastic, like "Lorena Bobbitt right-sized her husband's penis." The axe had fallen on her when she'd gotten tendonitis. She couldn't do anything with her hands without stabbing pains shooting up her forearms. Couldn't play, couldn't open a jar, could barely turn the knobs on the stove. And they'd fought her about paying for her health insurance, fought her about getting on disability, fought her about workers' comp. All that stuff the company said about "respect" and "integrity" and "excellence." Somebody e-mailed her Enron's ethics code as a joke and it had been the exact same phrases. She wasn't kidding. It was good to be out of there. She got healed, got into massage. It was less stable but it was real.

Now she was crammed into a Q train along with almost a thousand other Brooklynese. Inching over the Manhattan Bridge, diving under downtown Brooklyn, then laying in the cut in Flatbush, the crush easing a bit at every stop after DeKalb. She hung on the overhead bar, checking her cellphone the minute the train poked out of the tunnel. A voicemail from Janis, her seventeen-year-old: she'd be home from work late, probably around 9:30.

She got off at Cortelyou Road, squeezed up the narrow subway exit stairs behind two men in black suits, a skinny Haitian and a portly Hasid. She picked up onions, green peppers, mushrooms, plum tomatoes, spinach, and two boxes of blueberries on sale at the fruit stand, lugged her bags over to the schoolyard that was Damian's day camp. Through the chain-link fence she could see him bouncing a basketball on the blacktop with Igor and Qabir. She could see him, a lithe, coffee-colored kid with a rat's nest of black hair. The most beautiful boy in the world. Igor was a tall, pale kid in a yellow short-sleeve shirt, with a bit of a Russian accent; he'd come here in second grade. Qabir was the littlest, in a blue and orange Knicks jersey with the number 3 on the back.

He ran up to her. "Ma, can Igor and Qabir come over?"

"I don't feel like cooking for five people."

"We can get pizza or Mexican food."

"Do I look like I'm made of money? Do I look like an ATM machine?" Damian started pushing imaginary buttons on her stomach. She ruffled his hair. "I only had three clients today. Remember how I told you if I don't have clients I don't get paid? I can't spend twenty dollars every time you want me to."

"I know. The rent's $1,050 a month. You told me it's like every four times you pass 'Go,' you land on Indiana Avenue with a hotel. But, c'moooooon! Please?" The three boys surrounded her, jumping up and down. "Please? Please?"

"Oh, all right."

"YAYYY!" they exploded. "Mushrooms!" "Pepperoni!"

"We gotta get vegetables on it. You know Janis and I don't eat meat, and Qabir can't eat anything with pork in it. So no pepperoni."

They walked the remaining blocks home, over to Ocean Parkway. Streets of low brick buildings, old beauty-salon storefronts, bodegas with their windows papered with international phone cards. Past women in gold saris and homeboys in overgrown-graphic t-shirts, signs in Russian, Spanish, and Urdu, groceries selling okra and sacks of onions. The boys were chattering about video games and slinging insults at each other.

"U-G-L-Y, you ain't got no alibi," Qabir chanted.

Igor stared at him.

"What are you looking at?" Damian demanded.

"I have fascination with hideous things," Igor growled, draculizing his accent.

The sky was clouding up, looked like rain, but the benches on the parkway were still full, old people gossiping, reminiscing, kvetching, a Hasidic man in a shiny black overcoat reading, a slick-haired young guy jabbering on a cellphone in Russian, a bag lady resting her overloaded shopping cart.

The parkway was flooded with cars. Damian edged over the curb, leaning out to look for a gap in the traffic. She grabbed his arm, pulled him back.

"Watch out. I don't want you getting run over."

"I know. I wasn't going."

They turned into the courtyard of the Spanish-castle building, the boys bounding ahead. Tina trudged up to the stoop, unlocked the front door, into the sudden darkness of the lobby. The old tiles echoed the boys' noises like an out-of-tune piano with the pedal down. A wigged Hasidic woman with a double stroller was waiting by the elevator. They said hello, but no more. The woman stared at her. Tina wondered what kind of religion makes women wear such ugly wigs. And that drab long-sleeved dress. In summer. It's like they're trying to be unattractive and uncomfortable. And she's probably looking at me, thinking there's the one with no husband and a half-schvartzer son.

Damian's father had been the bass player in a reggae band called RRT, the Righteous Riddim Tribe. Should have been called BDD, the Bumbaclot Deadbeat Daddies.

"Damian, can you feed the cats?" Pretender, the gray one, and Cow, a white one with large black spots, weaved underfoot. The boys clambered into Damian's room, turned on the PlayStation. Murmur-argued about Final Fantasy and Grand Theft Auto. Tina flipped through the junk mail and bills, called the pizzeria and ordered. Emptied the grocery bag. One box of blueberries popped open, scattering across the kitchen floor like asteroids. Most in a predictable belt between Mars and Jupiter, a few further afield, one out by Neptune under the table. She needed a toke and a shower. She went to give Damian a $20 bill to pay the pizza guy.

"Yeah, you can pick up a hooker and have sex with her, and then you can throw her out of the car, beat her up, and take your money back."

That was Damian saying that? She shot into his room. "I DON'T WANT TO HEAR ONE MORE WORD OF THAT MISOGYNIST

BULLSHIT OUT OF YOUR MOUTH! I DIDN'T RAISE YOU LIKE THAT! NOW TURN THAT FUCKING GAME OFF!" She ripped the plug out of the wall. The kids protested meekly. "Ma, we'll lose our data."

Ten years old and they're talking like that, she fumed. She slipped into the bathroom. Pink and black tiles like a Brooklyn-Jewish anticipation of Elvis, she'd loved them when she first saw the place. Now it was cluttered. Shampoo, conditioner, lotions, Tampax boxes, her Clairol Herbal Essence 70 Sapphire Black hair dye. Her makeup, Janis's makeup. Damian's boy stuff, garish and cartoony, superhero toothbrush. It will never be austere and minimal in this small space. She turned on the shower, pointing the spray away so she could spark up the pipe, hunching over by the window to blow the smoke out. She tried to be discreet about herb around Damian, especially when he had friends over. Janis knew. In fact, once when she'd laid off weed for a month, Janis had told her, "Ma, you need to start getting high again. You're such a bitch when you're out of pot."

She finished the bowl and got in, letting the hot water work the stress out of her neck and shoulders, breathing in the steam. Yawned, spat out the tar from the pot. Stop your gobbing, she thought. Laughed, sang a couple verses of "Stop Your Sobbing." Her voice full, enhanced by the shower-tile reverb. It felt good.

She got out, put on a clean black tank top. Smiled at herself in the mirror, the high settling in. Being mad at the kids makes you look too sour, you don't want to end up a pickle-faced hag. She giggled a bit. Checked herself out. Who is this aging crone staring back at me? Lines forming on her face, fat hips and thighs, loose, puckered baby-belly flesh between the stretch marks on her sides. She braked that train. Looked again. Yeah, not bad for my age. I've been through a lot of weather and miles. A few lines and a bit of extra flesh but still pretty good. A rose tattoo on her left arm, an ouroboros snake around her right.

How long has it been since I had sex? she wondered. Two years? In the old days two weeks would have been a long time. Well, there wasn't much out there. The rockers her age were dissipated wastes or irresponsible egomaniacs, the family guys who'd be into taking on a woman with two kids were mostly boring or had kids of their own, and even if the kids got along with their sudden siblings, where would you put a Brady Bunch in New York, the most expensive city in the Western Hemisphere? Move to the Poconos or the far reaches of Suffolk County? Not in a million years. And she wasn't into a one-night stand. It wasn't worth dumping Damian at her mother's house for half a weekend so she could have a quick one with some schmuck she picked up on the Internet or in a bar. Not having her own room also complicated things—Damian and Janis got the two bedrooms, so she had the couch, sharing dresser space with Janis.

She'd had no one since she ended her brief ride on the Bipolar Express, aka Andrew Goldman, the Lower East Side poet. It had been good for a bit, he'd gotten her back out in public when they'd done a couple Patti-and-Lenny things with her backing him on guitar at the Church of Howl, the Centro Rivas-Pinero. But she'd tired of his late-night phone calls, waking her up at 1:30 in the morning to brag about his latest revelation or enlist her in his scheme for artistic world conquest, then flipping into a pissed-off abyss when she'd say, "I have to get the kids to school in the morning." He'd berate, "You have no artistic commitment. You're holding me back with your mundanities and earthbound trivialities."

She walked out of the bathroom. The answering machine blinked 04. She pushed the button. "Hello, C Sedici, this is Kathy McCarthy from Debt Consolidation and you've been selected for our special..." Beep. Delete. A client. Save and skip. "Don't hang up. You're paying too much for auto insurance." I don't have a car. "Hi, Tina, this is Mickey..." Jesus fucking Christ. "I know we've got a lot of baggage, but please hear me out on this." He's fucking begging me? What's he want? Lost in a red mist of recrimination, she missed the rest of the message, had to play it back. "I've got a serious offer for us to play again, it's real, we're not going to be playing holes in the wall. Scott's definitely into it, Underend's down, too, and you'd make it complete. It's time to put the past behind us so we can play the music for a new generation of people. So, can you at least think about it?" After all these years? But then the phone rang again. The pizza was here.

She apologized to the kids as they ate. "I'm sorry I yelled at you like that, but it got me really mad to hear you talking about women like that."

"Ma, it's a computer character. It's a game."

"She's still a person. I raised you to respect women. And your mothers did, too, Igor and Qabir. And you're gonna be teenagers soon, you're going to start liking girls, and you're not going to get women acting like that."

Janis being out gave her a couple hours to herself. She lay on the couch, strumming her old Telecaster unplugged. She wished she could play more but she was always tired. She loved packing a bowl and playing after Damian was asleep, but she'd almost always pass out within ten minutes. It's a good thing Teles are indestructible, she thought, because otherwise the neck would warp from neglect. Janis was learning a bit; she'd inherited Tina's acoustic guitar, and liked Johnny Cash.

Janis occasionally bugged her to play more. "It'd make you happier, Ma, and you're so good, why waste it?" She tried to explain without dumping too much on her. Sometimes they sang together. Once they'd done a perfect, beautiful version of "Bring It on Home" just sitting around the living room on a Sunday night, Janis on acoustic strumming the basics, Tina on electric, framing it with twangy low notes and blue-light soul inversions, their voices blending like an organ chord. We could be the Brooklyn Judds, Tina thought. But let the girl find her own path. I don't want to be a stage mom. Encourage her, but don't push her. And Janis could be so aggravating sometimes, talking to her in that obnoxious you-utterly-hopeless-old-retard tone. C'mon. I'm cooler than my parents were, I let her be what she wants to be, I don't call her a slut, all I want is respect, and this is the thanks I get?

She was too old to do open mikes, though she'd been urging Janis to do them. But was she going to rip up her life for a week or six on the road? Where would the kids go? And any time she'd gotten back together with an ex the old problems had quickly come out again. Doing the Gutter Astronomers again was tempting, even discounting Mick's normal dose of exaggeration they'd be sure to get some good shows, but she could also see herself wanting to stake a broken guitar neck either through his heart or up his ass. And what state was Underend in?

Mick called back the next night. Straightaway he went into the pitch: "I got kids coming up to me all the time—kids? what am I saying? they're in their thirties now—and they tell me, 'You guys kept me sane when I was a teenager.' I get women telling me all the time that you were the one who inspired them to start playing, like Sarah from the OxyKittens. When they asked her, 'Who are your influences?', she said 'Tina Toxic from the Gutter Astronomers.' And there's kids now who weren't around back then getting into us. It's cause we were something real and they're looking for it. So whaddaya think?"

Tina was thinking, it's amazing how much some things can piss you off twenty years after they happened. "What am I supposed to think? The last time I wasn't good enough for you. Now you want me to just drop everything and run off? I've got kids, I've got work. I can't just leave them."

Hold it in, hold it in, Mick thought. Don't snap. If there was one thing he had learned about women, it was that one wrong word could blow it with them for a lifetime. Diplomatic, my son, diplomatic. "You know, Joe Strummer said the worst thing he ever did was fire Mick Jones. He said he didn't know how much it would fuck things up, how irreplaceable he was to the band."

Half an apology, she thought.

"You hear CBGB's is closing?" he probed.

"Yeah. It's fucked up. I haven't been there in years. Everything's closing. You wouldn't even recognize the neighborhood now. It's all yuppie bars and condos."

Well, she's talking to me at least, Mick thought. Good. Keep her on, keep her on. "We gotta do CBGB's before they close. We had something really of value, you know?"

"A lot of the scene was just gross and negative. I looked around after a while and I was thinking, what the fuck am I doing? There's nothing for me here. It was ugly. It wasn't like it used to be."

"Yeah, but we needed negativity, we needed to reject all the garbage that was around. That's the only way you keep from getting swallowed up in it. Look, what does any politician or corporate asshole say any time someone criticizes them? 'They're being negative.' Sometimes the healthiest thing you can say is 'Fuck no.' And we did do something positive, we built a band and a scene."

"And then it turned into the same star-tripping shit as everything else."

"You think I'm just about being a star. But I'm actually making an idiot of myself when I'm up there onstage. I'm making a fool of myself. I know there were people out there going 'Look at that schmuck, look at that fuckin' stupid jerk.' I'm not afraid of that. It's the risk you have to take. It's what you have to give up to gain power. I guess I was such a fuckin' oddball when I was a kid that I thought the only way to stay out of the insane asylum was to be a star. You know, if you're poor and weird, you're a fucked-up nutjob, and if you're successful and weird, you're eccentric and quirky." He shifted gears. "I need it. I need to do it. And I need you. I need the real band."

Tina was shocked by his pleading. She'd never seen him open up like this. Gone was the people-come-to-see-me arrogance and bluster, though part of her suspected it was shtick, like an I'm-down-on-my-knees plea circus from a boyfriend who'd frayed her tolerance far longer than she should have let him. "Teatro de amor," like the old tango song her mom liked.

"I can't leave my kids."

"Can they stay with your parents?"

"No, I CAN'T just dump my kids on my mother for a month. They've got lives. I've got a life. I have to be with them. Somebody's gotta be the responsible one, because their fathers are fuckin' useless bastards."

Hold on, you almost blew it, Mickey thought. He'd never liked Tina's ex, Ricky from Black Steam. But if he told her "I told you so," the great Gutter Astronomers reunion was gonna be missing the original guitar player. On the other hand, she was objecting to the practicalities, not the concept.

"If we kept it local, just did CB's or Pulaski Hall, something like that, maybe somewhere in Brooklyn, would you be able to do it then? And maybe if you can get out for a weekend, we could do Boston, Philly, D.C. Because we gotta do something, it'd be a waste not to."

"If we keep it local," Tina hesitated, "maybe I could."

"That might be a problem for me. I can't come out just to do two shows. I need to make some money doing this, because I gotta cover my plane fare."

"Well, I can't afford to take six weeks off work. I don't think Scott can, either."

"Tell ya what. I gotta come East anyway to see my folks, my dad just got out of the hospital. We'll do some rehearsals and see how it goes. And if you're into it, give me a call and I'll start booking."

Lunchtime. Underend walked down the block to the deli. He was thirsty, slurping water like a cat with failing kidneys. Women passed by with their electronic work ID cards hanging from their necks, the traveling passes of the 21st century. But it was still disco time on the radios of lunch-hour Manhattan, still 1978 and Boogie Oogie Oogie and Turn the Beat Around. Party-down divas over the wall of Lucky Dog and Amazing 8s and Set4Life lottery tickets, the Mexican countermen and Korean cashiers doling out sandwiches and ringing up soda and coffee.

Stuck on line, coffee spilling onto the back of his hand, behind a black woman with pencil braids buying a wad of lottery tickets. "I want 4610, 7519… no, 7518… give me 1123, that's my daughter's birthday… and 3425." Donna Summer's "I Feel Love" on the radio. He felt impatience. Hurry the fuck up. Pissing away her dollars on a dubious dream. Well, it was a better retirement plan than he had, which was getting a cat so they could share dinner.

Construction hammers pounded. The little Puerto Rican lunch counter he liked was desaparecido, nothing left inside but an abandoned steam table, a Retail Space for Lease sign in the window. New highrises grew all around him, concrete weeds adding new floors every day, then plated with a platinum aura of polished stone and glass. Billboards blared their luxurious lures: Dream it. Envision it. Build it. Well, if you're a fuckin' billionaire, you can buy anything. The rest of us are more fucked than we've ever been. "What's in it for *you*?" Sweet fuck-all. Good God, y'all, absolutely nothing. Who the fuck lives in these places? Nobody with a real job can afford to. He wanted to get high. Let the warm-bath bliss wash all the golden scum off the streets. No. You can't. Remember how you fucked up after 9/11? He stepped into Billy's office just before closing.

"Can I talk to you for a minute?" Hesitant, almost quavering.

"Yeah."

"Listen, Billy... I don't wanna leave you dry or anything... but Mick called me the other night. He's talkin' about getting the band back together. I don't know if I'm gonna do it, but..."

"You want time off if you go on tour."

"Well... yeah... if it happens. Like I said, I don't wanna leave you dry here."

"Listen. Don't tell anybody this because I'm not sure it's gonna happen, nothing's definite, but we might be fucked on renewing the lease. They haven't told me anything solid yet, but they're talking like they want to put the rent up to $18,000."

"What are you gonna do?"

"I can't pay that much, that's for sure. We might be all collecting unemployment come November so you do what you want to do. You should be playin' anyway, you're just wasting yourself sitting around the house all the time. Just give me notice. I can get Black Dave or somebody to cover."

Underend carried that news onto the subway home. Coming up the stairs at Union Square he heard a fiendish James Brown groove. Live at the Apollo, Brown ad-libbing, "Everybody relax... and watch me work." Six breakdancers working to the beat, five scrawny, wiry kids in doo-rags and t-shirts almost long enough to be nightgowns, spinning and bumping with pyrotechnic grace, one pudgy, clumsy one for comic relief. Yeah, it was great, funk and flash and pleasure and pride, not a drop of guns or bling. But it was ancient history: the record around forty years old, the dance around twenty-five. He hung out for two songs, headed down to the L train.

At Lorimer, four Mexican guys in black cowboy hats and maroon vests got on. One with an accordion in red, white, and green sparkles, one with a 12-string guitar with bizarrely thick strings, one, the youngest, the only one without a mustache, playing a small nylon string acoustic, and the capper, one wheeling an upright bass onto the train. This I have to see, he thought. I can walk home from Graham. They swung into an odd two-step beat, the accordionist singing something about contrabando and traicion, then the young one collected donations in his hat.

I still love New York, he thought.

Tuesday night Underend was restless, couldn't stay in. His brain was ranting. I hate it when the only thing you get from a band onstage is "We want to be rich and famous." That's the most boring cliché ambition in the world. It means they're giving the audience nothing. They don't have to be making a serious political statement but get the people off, entertain them, do something to move them. Give something back. Give something more than, "C'mere, people, throw us your lovely money." More than the placebo syndrome. Parasites. Beat as a bag of quinine and baking soda. But you gotta want something more. I don't know.

He walked south of the highway, turned into a club. A shoebox-shaped room with a band on in the back. They sound like the Ramones and Link Wray. Two guys up front around my age, I should know them from somewhere. Lead singer with fucked-up teeth and a Mother To Be t-shirt over his beergut. Guitar player in a black fedora and shades, a red hollow-body, he looks really familiar, he can play pretty good but he can't sing for shit. The drummer's a younger woman, bleached blonde, around seven months pregnant. Bass player's tall, quiet, looks wasted.

They're pretty good… Got energy and drive and a couple decent tunes. And they're playing to maybe twenty people: the ten friends they managed to drag out on a work night, five regulars propping up the bar, and five unknown stragglers like me. There are more than twenty people in the city with rare tropical diseases. And you know this band's not going anywhere. You wonder why the fuck they still do it.

There's one guy at the bar, the milky skin of a drained-out alky, looks like he's getting off on it, like it's speaking to his soul. And a few people are dancing, one guy and two women. The rest are just sitting there with their drinks or Coke or club soda for the wagon-bound like me.

They encore with what the guitar player calls "an old Irish folk song from 1979. And these are middle-age kicks, too." The Undertones' "Teenage Kicks." Underend's mind went off. These guys could've been a hit twenty-five years ago. They're good enough. But people like us haven't won anything in twenty-five years. They're chasing a ghost. A beautiful ghost, but still a ghost. You can't put your arms around a memory.

Underend was in a good mood at the end of the set, ordered a nonalcoholic Beck's, put two bucks in the jukebox for five songs. Holy shit, they've got *Brain Capers* on here. Sat at the bar rocking to the screaming distorted organ in "The Moon Upstairs." Slowed down for "Your Own Back Yard." A Dion tune about recovery, Ian Hunter Dylan-whining about staying crazy without being fucked up all the time. Yeah, Angeline was right. The trick was to get pleasure out of the act of doing it. The jukebox died, cutting off the intro to "Angeline." Another band took the stage. The club suddenly filled.

Bad from the first note. Imitation hair metal, probably supposed to be ironic from the way they were camping it up, the shirtless singer grabbing his crotch and throwing every pose, pout, and sneer in the book of 1980s rock video. Not a lick of originality, reveling in clichés. Reveling in clichés while mocking them. They wanted the cliché, the Marshall stacks of cocaine and pussy and arenas galaxies of flashing lighters. We all wanted it a little bit, even the most ascetic straight-edge fiends and the schlumpiest indie-rockers taking the stage in the height of laundry-day fashion, but were too cool to admit it. And there was nothing else there. Because showing passion would make you look stupid, so you had to make fun of anyone who did. You wanted what they had but you didn't want to do the legwork.

These dudes took themselves way too seriously to boot. The guitar player had a mesh trucker hat and a vintage REO Speedwagon t-shirt he'd probably paid eighty bucks for. And the fuckin' guys in the club were lapping it up, crowding the stage like it was the long lost Spirit of Rock'n'Roll Past come back to life; Elvis and Jimi jamming on a purple hunk of burning love. Hunka hunka burning shit. New Jersey refinery fart gas. The Jamaica Bay garbage dumps with Charles Manson crooning over them. Somewhere out there, the rock'n'roll world was awaiting a new Aristotle or Nietzsche who could exposit the complete aesthetics of musical suckdom, and they probably had something to do with arrogant pretentiousness amplified by comical incompetence. Underend's memory swirled with the worst bands he'd ever seen: the last-minute replacements at his ninth-grade school dance, the 45-minute mystical-hippie guitar solos, the clunky white-funk band whose squeaky-voiced and graceless lead singer thought he was James

Brown for a day, the punk band at C-Section who couldn't even manage the changes to "Roadrunner" and "Louie Louie," the arty math-rock ensemble whose singer had denounced the audience as "mindless bacteria" over electronic wind noises and then they collapsed in an out-of-time trainwreck ninety seconds into the second song. The same emotion he'd had seeing all of them came back. I could do way better than this. I should be up there.

He left a buck on the bar, went home, and called Mick. It was still early in California.

Chapter 4
The '80s

Sunday morning on the Lower East Side was cold and overcast, the sky an opaque pale grey, an overwhelming dome of ashes and oil-burner smoke above the sooty maroon tenements. "Bajando!" cried the drug dealers' lookouts in droning-siren geshrei, thug muezzins warning the junkie umma that infidels were afoot.

Tina awoke musing on music, half-dreaming about the sounds she liked. She was butch like that, most of the women musicians she knew were too folky or punky to care about their equipment. All they knew about their guitar strings was that they came in a little plastic bag. She used 11s, strings where the high E was eleven-thousandths of an inch thick. They were harder to play, but they gave a fuller tone than the wimpy 9s most people used. Setting up her gear was her private ritual. Blocking out the world. Tuning her guitars, dialing in a sound on her amp. Duct-taping her three effects pedals to the stage: a taxi-yellow overdrive with two knobs, adding just enough distortion to make her licks sing and sting; a flanger of States Avenue purple, four knobs for whooshing and swirling; and a big sheet-metal analog delay, for slapback space or cascading-repeat dub madness. Then she was ready. A raw and spacy, sensual, burning wall of sound. Her Telecaster's neck smooth and silky, like a man, full of barbed-wire scratch and twang. The Melody Maker, her backup, warmer and more resonant.

She turned to the guy sleeping next to her, felt his warmth, stroked him. Mmmm. He grunted semiconsciously, rising to half-awake as she climbed on top of him. Patrick from Pittsburgh, her boyfriend of the moment, a tall, mussed-haired art-wreck type, a painter and junk-metal sculptor who favored flannel shirts, a long herringbone thrift-shop overcoat, and half-pints of Scotch carried in the dappled, concave metal of a 1920s-vintage hip flask. She rode him in the soft smoky light of the tenement morning. She looked down to admire her lover. Fuck him, he's bored.

Underend woke up cold. There was still no heat. Fingers stiff. Huddled under the blankets, not wanting to get out and face a world as frigid as the toilet seat. Lisa, the scrawny, near-anorexic, black-haired acquaintance he'd gone home with last night, slept beside him. He knew her from Open Wound, the short-lived group she'd played with last fall. They were sort of a low-budget Velvets. She'd plucked steady, deadpan dissonance, two-note tritones and half-step drones on the bass while the singer who called herself Obnoxious Cunt screeched despair and defiance, and a bookish violinist made tortured-cat noises. Perfect music for a near-empty slum club on a cold, bleak night. On this one, the lack of heat had stifled most of their hopes for sex. She'd said it was too cold to take her clothes off, joking that she should order crotchless longjohns from Frederick's of Anchorage. She'd given him a blowjob and he'd brought her off with his fingers, his right hand constricted inside her pants.

They'd slept in their clothes. His were waxing crusty from last night's show. No heat meant no hot water, too. He shuddered under the blankets for long minutes, trying to suppress the itching pressure inching up from the end of his dick, the dull-pain drumbeat from his distended bladder. Eventually, letting go and pissing the bed loomed as the inevitable alternative to getting up. He stumbled to the bathroom, blowing out clouds of frost. He had a cigarette, made coffee, put on Joy Division. Lisa slumbered on.

In the East Broadway loft that was the band's rehearsal space, Scott hunched over the turntable and cassette deck, making a mix tape of jump blues, the jivey postwar boogie that bridged big-band swing and early rock'n'roll. He'd scored a stack of ancient 45s from an old black woman at a yard sale in West Philly the morning after their gig at the East Side Club. His girlfriend, a big blonde named Rebecca, was in the kitchen they'd painted yellow, making some noise with the pots and pans, frying eggs and brewing coffee. He tugged her away from the stove to twirl-dance to "Shake, Rattle & Roll," Big Joe Turner and the gloriously fat baritone-sax solo.

Mick got up last but was on instantly, prancing around his apartment wearing nothing but a pair of Union Jack boxer shorts on his head, riffing and ranting about Larry McDonald, the Georgia congressman whose wife divorced him because he told her he wouldn't fuck her again until Communism fell. All this was for the entertainment of his date from last night, a girl with melted-trapezoid eye makeup and a spiky bird's nest of black-dyed hair who called herself Deadly Diane.

The band was rolling this month. Last night at CBGB. Friday at Rude Rockers, a Jamaican punk club in Flatbush, just off the avenue on Martense Street, called "Tense Street" by the locals for its highly touchy rude-boy cocaine dealers. They'd expected the music there to be new wave, the light dancey side of punk, but the sound system slammed with the Dead Boys and the Bad Brains, mixed in with deep-space dub and rockers riddims.

They had to be at the Brooklyn Academy of Noise studio at 2 pm to finish mixing two more tracks—if needed, do a couple minor overdubs—and then their first 12-inch record, a seven-song EP, would be done. The studio was in an old loft building in a desolate industrial area near the Gowanus Canal, the wind blowing litter and the aroma of kerosene. The band drifted in, copping half-burnt coffee in the empty-shelved bodega on the corner, taking up seats in the control room. Lenny the engineer, a longhaired geezer in a black t-shirt advertising some kind of studio gear, was already at the board, sitting in a captain's chair of frayed brown leather, rolling the tape and setting up the basic drum sounds.

They were producing the record themselves. The studio wasn't that big a mystery. People said the mixing board looked like a jet plane's control panel but it wasn't that complicated. It was just volume, bass, midrange, treble, and reverb repeated twelve or twenty-four or thirty-two times over. The art was in the alchemy: placing the mics to capture the sounds perfectly, tweaking the knobs of the outboard gear stacked in its 19-1/2 inch rack, the parametric EQ, the digital delay and reverb, the compressors with their red-green-red meter bulbs blinking in line. Making the tones clear without being too clean, dirty without being murky. They had ears, and they relied on Lenny for the heavier tech stuff.

"We don't want anybody fucking around with our sound" was the mantra. The vines of oral history dripped with tales of records fatally enervated by somebody trying to polish a band's sound, twist it into their idea of what would sell. A bad producer is like an incompetent pediatrician. He'll make your baby sound like crap: the bass strings like rubber bands, the guitars cheap and boxy, the drums a jumble of ringy overtones or a flimsy edifice of reverb cardboard. Or worse, he's like one who fronts for an S&M child-porn ring, one who has his own agenda of dominance and exploitation and doesn't care if it destroys you and your kid.

Sometimes the producer needs to push the band, to tell them one more and they'll get it, and sometimes the best thing they can do is say stop being such a neurotic perfectionist, you got it… when "no, you can't do it any better" is a compliment, not an insult. Like Ben Bart told James Brown, "If I'm paying for this, I don't want to cut any more. This is it." "Papa's Got a Brand New Bag" was a first take.

But they'd done it themselves. When you're on, you know when a take is good. You feel it in the first thirty seconds, and then all you have to do is keep riding it and not screw it up. "You can save *all* of that."—Lazy Lester. "That's a take."—Joe Strummer. "That's it, we done cut a good record."—Elmore James.

All that was almost over now. "Scratch and Claw" was first up. A rocker, with a jagged, feral guitar kind of like Richard Hell and the Voidoids' "Love Comes in Spurts." Lenny set the levels, brought the vocal a hair down on the verses to blend with the track, pushed it a hair up to stand out on the chorus. Isolated the snare, put a bit of gated reverb on it.

"It's too pristine," Scott interrupted. "It sounds like a new-wave record. It needs more of a wall-of-sound feel."

"Well, it doesn't have a wall-of-sound guitar." Lenny. "Tina doesn't have a Ramones sound; it's thinner, more jagged. I gotta work with what I have."

"Yeah, but it's like you can hear, Here's Every Instrument In Its Proper Place. Here's the vocal. Here's the snare. Here's the hi-hat. Here's the bass. It needs to be darker, murkier."

"More fucked up," added Mick.

"I don't have a button on the board for 'more fucked up.' They haven't invented it yet. They're still working on the 'SUCK' button for live bands that piss off the soundman." But he decreased the stereo separation so the mix sounded more like mono, thickened the bass, and brought up Tina's broken-bottle rhythm chords, then made the guitar break pop out like a yowling cat. It buried the vocal a bit, but it worked.

"Urban Babylon," the album's closing track, fared better. Lenny had done a rock-dub mix on it, echoing the toms so they sounded like a subway train looping around the dark side of the moon, the overdubbed tambourine and scratchy cabasa crackling like rhythmic snakes, the guitar shimmering like a silvery moon over the jungle night beat of the bass. The band was thrilled.

"I did a rough mix and tried it out on my boombox first," a proud Lenny explained.

Mick broke out a bottle of cheap champagne to celebrate while they listened to the final playback, Lenny dubbing cassettes for the band. They detoured for beers on the way to the subway and the celebration continued. The train pulled in right away and they dived on, quaffing and toasting before they realized it was a G, the wrong line. They got off at the next stop, Smith-Ninth Street, and raced around the platform shouting, "It's finished! It's fuckin' done! We did it!" from eight stories over the factory rooftops, the red-giant KenTile Floors sign, the fetid waters of the Gowanus Canal. Mick clambered up the crumbling cement wall, grabbed the chain-link fence, screaming, "Mickey Septic Sapirstein! Top of the fuckin' world! The Gutter Astronomers!"

The F train came, curved down over the canal, above the industrial sand pits. "They got skeletons wearing concrete Converses down at the bottom," Mick the tour guide related. "The Mob boys who tried to go to the mattress with the Godfather's mistress. Or the entrepreneurial visionaries who thought there was room in Brooklyn for an independent garbage-collection company. And on your left is the foulest garbage dump north of the Belt Parkway."

"Oh, garbage dump, my garbage dump, why do you call it a garbage dump?" the rest of the band sang, in harmony that would have got them bottled off most stages. That was the only good song on the Charles Manson and the Family album Underend had bought off some old hippie in Cooper Square for a quarter.

Late the next night was postering time. They would debut the album Thursday night at the Emerald Palace on 44th Street. Mick tried to beg out, but they guilt-tripped him into going. They gathered at his apartment clad in dark coats, pouring wheat-paste into a plastic bucket, filling it with water from the kitchen sink, stirring it with a paintbrush. Elmer's Glue was more discreet, you could slip the bottle into your pockets if the cops or an irate property owner happened by, but it was expensive. A $1.99 squeeze bottle was good for only about fifty flyers. A bucket-and-brush apparatus was a lot harder to explain.

Mick's friend, Berlin, had designed the album-cover graphic used on the flyer, a broken lightbulb glowing with pachuco-cross rays. The album cover was yellow and purple on black, but the flyers were black and white. They started flyering on Avenue A, hitting the wall outside the A7 Club, the lampposts by the bar across the street. Mick pasted one on the base of a lamppost on the corner of St. Marks.

"You're fuckin' wasting them," Scott remonstrated. "No one's gonna see it."

"I'm thinking about the long run. No one's gonna cover it up down there, it'll still be up in six months. Keep our name out there."

"C'mon, c'mon, I'm freezing my clit off out here." Tina. The temperature was in the low twenties, and the hawkwind wasn't just whistling "Silver Machine."

The wall of the abandoned brownstone at St. Marks and First was a prize postering spot. Everybody on the scene passed by there, and you could put a whole block on the wooden fence there. The rough etiquette was that you weren't supposed to poster over another band's flyers if their show hadn't happened yet but major-label acts were fair game, as was any local band who covered up your flyers or hogged the space. Mick and Underend pasted up an X-shaped array, Tina brushing, and Scott keeping lookout. The wind blew drops of goo onto her coat. She cursed. They passed down the block between Second and Third, hitting the lampposts, the empty walls, the black metal staircase outside Trash & Vaudeville.

"Let's do the cube," Mick urged. The cube was a local landmark, a black metal sculpture across from the subway entrance in the Astor Place plaza, gateway to St. Marks Place and the East Village. It was tilted up on one corner, and it could be rotated if you pushed hard enough.

"Nah, leave it alone," Scott cut him off. The unwritten etiquette said pasting flyers on the cube was tacky. They turned south on the Bowery, toward CBGB. Another wood wall beckoned. Mick stopped to talk to a girl he knew from Creative Destruction. Tina and Underend pasted while Scott brushed. Then a cop popped up.

"Pull 'em off, or you get a summons," he commanded.

Underend complied. A hooker in spike heels and a ragged fake-fur collar stumbled up. "Fuckin' cops, they suck shit," she growled sympathetically. Her jowls were slathered in pancake makeup. It didn't conceal the beard hairs poking through.

The Emerald Palace was a former hotel basement ballroom, a velvet-rope disco in the Studio 54 era but now a venue for the bigger semi-underground rock bands. To get in you passed down a short hall and a stairway colored by emerald-green lights. The club was silently owned by mobster Vito "The Ugly One" Virupa, who'd once shot out the lights in a bar rather than pay his tab. There was a story that when Richard and Linda Thompson played there, somebody told them to dedicate "Shoot Out the Lights" to Vito, and before they got paid, they got surrounded by several of the larger bouncers while the night manager dropped hints about how Richard was supposed to be the best guitar player in England, but finger bones were extremely delicate.

Mick had stepped into punk rock legend with the Gutter Astronomers' first show there, the previous March. They'd opened for an English band called the Electric Slags. The vibes had gone sour immediately. They'd rushed to load in to make soundcheck, only to be told by the Slags' road manager that they weren't getting one. His voice a precise modulation of posh snob and pub bully, "You're the support band. Get it?" The Slags had taken almost three hours to do their soundcheck, adjusting the tones on their double-bass drum set, taking half-hour beer breaks, guitarist Gaz Hinton spending another half-hour tweaking the knobs on his orange half-stack, and the Gutter Astronomers were steaming. "What's his fuckin' problem?" Scott fumed.

"He thinks if he diddles with his amp long enough, he's gonna learn how to play," Tina cracked.

Then the Slags wouldn't move their drums off the riser, forcing Scott into a corner on the right, Underend and Tina on the left wedged in by the Slags' refrigerator-size SVT bass amp, and Mick trapped on a two-foot strip in the middle, two steps away from a six-foot drop off the stage. The only consolation was that the club gave them a case of Heineken.

The minute they got on stage, there was a cretin down front heckling them, barraging Mick, "You SUCK!" That was the problem with the bigger, more disco-style clubs. In the small ones you got assholes but at least they were part of the scene, they weren't gonna hate you for what you were. "Fuck you, ya faggot," resounded over Tina's tuning between songs. Why someone would pay eight bucks to see something they hated was a mystery, but it happened pretty often. "Fuck you, ya green-haired freak!" Mick took a swig of beer, stalked over to stare him down. The guy flung his beer. Missed. It landed harmlessly on the Slags' drums. He spun around and stumbled. Mick whipped it out and drenched him with a high-pressure golden shower. Right down the back of his neck, then a direct hit on his face when he turned back around. He screamed curses and death threats and tried to climb up on stage but it was six feet high. The crowd laughed and cheered.

The Electric Slags got their comeuppance two nights later at the Warehouse in Boston. Packed into the sixth row was a Southie named Sean Hill who, including the pre-show bar stop with his mates, had consumed seven Budweisers and five shots of Seagram's. He was working on his eighth beer when he suddenly noticed the color of Gaz Hinton's amp: orange. And then he noticed the logo on the crossbar between the four speakers: ORANGE with some kind of knights-and-heralds logo. It blinked on and off in his brain. A fuckin' insult… and it was almost Saint Fuckin' Paddy's Day.

"Fuckin' Orange bastard!" he screamed, spitting a mouthful of beer. Gaz shot him two fingers.

Sean's mates joined in. "Fuckin' Brits! You suck! Go back to fuckin' England!"

"Wot's all this?" inquired Waddy, the lead singer.

Jonesy the bass player intervened. "Thick Micks with little pricks."

A northeaster of beer, spit, and cans inundated the stage. The bouncers rushed out front, but the band had to retreat after two more songs.

"Fuck me, that wasn't half as bad as the time Jonesy wore a West Ham top in fuckin' Manchester," Waddy observed later.

But tonight belonged to the Gutter Astronomers. Their first headlining gig there. They drew about two hundred people, not enough to pack the room but enough to fill it. And the crowd was into it from the first lick, knowing all the songs, shouting the lyrics back when Mick stuck the mic out, the kids in the front row peering up and smiling whenever somebody in the band looked down to see them dancing.

Shows came and went, growing slowly, not fast enough. CBGBs. The A7 and C-Section. Rascals way out in Brooklyn. The Rock Lobster, a converted Top 40 club on Long Island. Another one at the Emerald Palace, opening for Joey Rush and the Users. To do a weekend in Wilkes-Barre, Pennsylvania, and Binghamton upstate, they rented a van. The only place they could get one without a credit card required a $200 cash deposit and was in Maspeth, Queens, a half-hour bus ride beyond the end of the subway. In Wilkes-Barre, guys with mustaches shouting for "Free Bird" booed them off the stage. One woman up front, a chunky, feathered-haired blonde in a tie-dyed t-shirt, shook her finger at Tina while screaming, "I hate you! I hate you!" The only people into them were three punks who'd driven all the way from Lewisburg for the show. The club stiffed them for half the $300 they were supposed to get. They piled into the van and slept four in a cheap motel room somewhere in northern Pennsylvania.

Binghamton scorched. They burned it out for two sets under a green neon Genesee Beer sign in a small club called Lou's. Four inches of snow were falling, but the twenty-five or thirty people who turned up loved it. The adversity made it intimate, special, a hearth of outsiders who had endured it. They had discovered a secret ritual bonfire from the Gambian forest, amped up with pyrotechnics and transported to this cold city of faded shoe factories, wood three-deckers, and a concrete-block college for smart kids whose families didn't have the money or pedigree to get them into a big-name school. No one else knew, and the band fed on it, the energy feeding back like Tina's amp until she hit a power chord and roared into the next one. Almost everyone was up dancing, and the band played off the rhythms of the dancers, pushing or teasing or driving the beat to match their moves. They did every song they knew and stretched out on covers of "What Goes On" and "Pressure Drop." Tina hit a singing-chainsaw D chord, spinning it with industrial blues licks, and they jammed on it for a few minutes. For an encore they took requests, the crowd shouting along with garageland versions of Ramones and Patti Smith faves.

Mick and Scott went to get the money. The club manager apologized for paying them only $100 and invited them back. Tina and Underend were both in promising flirtations—him with a SUNY Binghamton student, her with the guitarist in the opening band—when the order came to load out. They had to get the van back by 1 that afternoon or they'd have to pay for another day. Hunched over the dashboard to see through the frosty windshield, Scott swerved along the deserted highway, a color-drained strip of blue-white snow, black road, and dark, looming mountain walls, creeping at barely 20 mph past unseen villages called Occanum and Deposit and Fishs Eddy.

"Can't you go any faster?" Mick nagged. "There's no cops around. We're out in the sticks."

"Get off my fuckin' back. Ya see how fuckin' icy it is out there?" Scott snapped back. "If I go any faster, we're going over a fuckin' cliff. You don't drive, don't complain."

Underend, the only other licensed driver in the band, was curled up on the drum rug, sleeping off four beers and two shots of whiskey. Tina slept next to him, both covered by their coats, using the bass head for a pillow. They got back to the city just in time to hit the morning rush hour, bickery and bleary. After gas, tolls, food, and the van rental they came home clearing $5 each.

After that Scott copped a coppery rustbucket van for $500, and it took them to Philly and D.C. and Baltimore, Boston and Providence and a basement in Stamford, Connecticut, back to Lou's in Binghamton and then to a student-lounge DIY show at SUNY Albany. The out-of-town gigs got their name out there, the record on college radio, and blurbs in the zines, but often didn't pay much more than gas money. Sometimes they'd hit a new town where nobody had heard of them and play to twelve people, but overall the crowds were growing.

They were beginning to worry about where they fit in the scene. The overground was getting blander, the doors in to commercial success narrowing, and the music in the underground around them was getting harder, more violent, less sexy. Reflecting the new reality in the streets, the winter of Reaganomics. Wall Street was spewing flumes of cash at the yuppies. The ghetto was scratching for nickels and bitter as fuck. Bands from D.C. and L.A. playing shorter, harsher, faster. "Hardcore" the word and stance on everyone's lips. "We should have gotten the album out six months ago," Mick fretted.

Tina loved the raw power of punk, but the changes alienated her. She desired rhythm, melody, texture, dynamics. The music was like sex. There were times when she was screaming "Fuck me hard! Fuck me hard!" and she couldn't imagine life without that, but she also needed to be held, caressed. Two sides to every story, and if you didn't have both, you were useless or annoying, a limp wimp or a dull and dangerous brute. She needed someone with enough drive so she could give herself up to his maelstrom, but one cold look or insensitive dickhead remark could turn him into a worm in an instant. Or turn her into a worm in her eyes.

Not much rock outside punk made her feel anything but bored, but the new hardcore stuff felt like a gay porn movie of a Marine barracks gang-bang, camo pants around combat-booted ankles on concrete floors. The dance they did to it—all guys, big shaved-head fuckers strutting in a circle, slinging their fists like spiked maces and smashing into anyone at the edge or the pit—looked like a cross between Jamaican skanking and Nazi goose-stepping. We're bigger than you and we'll fuck you up.

She hated it more when nobody was slamming, because it meant playing to a U-shaped empty space, everyone too cowed to come near the stage. Like the last time they'd done C-Section, they'd played to a vast expanse of red concrete floor.

Money was tight. They were playing too much to get or keep full-time jobs. Underend was collecting unemployment. Tina did office-temp work, but often got 86ed for a bad attitude, wearing non-designer jeans, not being properly submissive to the boss. Scott cobbled together occasional construction or housepainting gigs, occasionally using the band PA to do sound at a DIY show. Dinner was often macaroni and cheese à la Reagan, generic elbows with cheese from the five-pound blocks of government handouts that were easily available on the street, with ketchup as the vegetable.

Mick was bartending at Delirium, a three-story club in the lower garment district that tried to collect credibility from the Lower East Side art-freak world and cash from the newly flush yuppies. They hired him for his looks and minor star status. He knew he was being exploited for it, but he could make decent money and work flexible enough hours for practices and shows.

He shared the second-floor bar, the lounge between the main dance floor and the VIP room, with an aspiring actress named Yvonne, a bronze-skinned woman with orange curls. It was a French-curved island with a veined mirror top, a mirror that served perfectly for other purposes. Like here came the guy in a slightly disheveled pinstripe, collar open and the yellow-and-small-red-diamond power tie pocketed, who ordered a Heineken and laid out four lines for him on the bar top, the bar's black leather lip concealing them only to the most oblivious. Mick bent over and snorted them, the guy tipping him $10 and asking if there were "any hot chicks looking for blow."

Mick picked up the bill. The guy was a fuckin' moneyed loser. He'd steer the club's coke B-girls his way, not that he needed to, they had a nose and a grapevine for who had it, and they'd caress the vialed one with seductive hints, flirt with him, as long as he kept the powder fountain flowing.

Underend walked around a lot on the Lower East Side. Low-grade depression clenched his eyes. There was a lot to do but he didn't have money to do it with. None to drink, buy records, or see shows other than the ones they were playing or at the clubs where they could get in free. He hung out a lot at Yerba, a coffeehouse run by Liza Reilly, the wife of a poet named Papo Quintero. You could get a cup of coffee for 50 cents or a bowl of rice and beans for $1.25 and nurse it all afternoon or all evening, conversating with the regulars. On the far side of the heroin district's main strip, it was out of the tourist ambit—on the east-of-First-Avenue travel scale, it fell beyond brave and closer to crazy. So it drew mainly neighborhood regulars, poets, art wrecks, free-jazz players, the more intellectual punk rockers, hangers-on from all of the above, and the occasional dopefiend. They started keeping the bathroom key behind the counter after a flame-haired drag queen named Cherry Bombalurina left a freshly used Blue Tip point impaling the roll of toilet paper.

Underend got the Gutter Astronomers on the bill for the first-anniversary party. The band enlisted a gaggle of friends, roadies, and lovers to convoy the gear through the pirate-infested waters of the Avenue B dope zone, everybody carrying one piece—a guitar, a tom-tom—or rolling the heavier bits on speaker cabinets, trying to keep Scott's kick drum from teetering off the trap case when it lurched into a crevasse in the sidewalk.

They cleared out the back room for the musicians and a dance floor. The DJ mixed up reggae, funk, rap, Latin, a bit of punk. The punks and white art-types didn't dance to the salsa, only the older Nuyorican hipsters did. The Nuyoricans didn't cross over to the punks the way they had with hippies. They'd mixed hippie aesthetics with ghetto toughness, the soul-searching Hendrix-Clapton-Santana trip on top of a hard core. If they hadn't done time in Rikers, the Tombs, upstate—like Santos Soto, who'd written his first book of poems in Coxsackie—they could walk with dudes who had. They had to, even if their own path was more positive, raising kids and raising the community. They shared the same streets, schools, tenement halls, and project elevators. The punks were a bunch of scrawny, arty runts pretending to be way more bad-ass than they were, and they rejected the reverence and flowery virtuosity of the old scene, its sense of beauty. "We got enough ugliness in this world, man," Papo would philosophize. "Look around, all the basura, all the abandoned buildings and broken glass and shit. It's ugly, man. We gotta create something that will take us out of all that. Like the line in Santos's poem, 'a flute playing in D yard.' "

Soto was reading with Maurice Jonas, an old Beat with gray streaks threading his hair and beard. Underend knew Maurice from the coffeehouse. He'd asked him to back them up, along with a conga player named Alfredo, one of the Tompkins Square Park drummers who came out every spring with the crocuses. Maurice talked as if he were lifting weights with his tongue, every word a barbell that had to be strained up and out but on the mic, he flowed.

"Play free until I nod, then give me a Bo Diddley beat." Alfredo and

Underend rolled and rippled low. Maurice turned to the audience.

This is the story of the first Black superhero.

He crossed the frigid watery grave depths of the North Atlantic Ocean
on the back of a baleen whale.

He dodged ship-rippin' icebergs.

Sharks with fearsome jaws.

Prehistoric Precambrian sea monsters.

And then he landed… in Harlem.

Maurice nodded. Alfredo thumped the intro.

The eighth of May was a hell of a day

The day the Titanic sunk…

It was an old epic poem, the legend of Shine, the black boiler room stoker on the Titanic. Maurice had recited it as a teenager on the doo-wop corners of 142nd Street, Santos in the gray-barred cellblocks of the Tombs. Now they traded lines and phrases, sharp as two young rappers, as they spun the tale of the white folks sneering at Shine's warnings and then begging him to save them.

Alfredo did a set with a Philly-born free-jazz violist named Juan Callison, who alternated between lyrical Beethoven-blues passages and paroxysms of screeching dissonance. The Gutter Astronomers played last. Most people stayed in the back, drinking and talking, or slipping outside to smoke a bit of mota.

Practice the next Monday night went well. Mick was in a good mood because one of his girlfriends had just gotten a VCR, and they'd watched *Pink Flamingos* the night before. They worked on a new fast punk tune, "Radioactive Jellybeans," spinning off a bassline Underend had brought in, about what Mick wanted to force-feed Ronald Reagan or maybe the toxic trick-or-treat candy he was feeding the people. They ran through the set a couple times. Afterwards they were messing around, Tina passing a joint, Underend and Scott with beers, and Mick started warbling, "How much is that doggie in the window?" camping up the stiff time-clock rhythm. Tina hit the singing-chainsaw lick she'd done in Binghamton, and the others joined in, hitting a driving, hypnotic groove somewhere between AC/DC, the Stooges, and Suicide, repeating and building up power as Mick riffed on the word "filth." "Remember that one," he said. "It's a hit."

Underend left his bass in the studio. Lisa from Open Wound was off work and had invited him to come over. He trudged up Avenue B, weary and wary. Cat-like, an eye out for the predators. Tina had gotten her purse snatched by a kid in Tompkins Square two months ago, and all 6'2" of Scott hadn't been enough to scare off the guy who'd caught him in a phonebooth and poked a gun in his back.

Lisa was another suburban refugee. Her family had moved from the Bronx to Jersey when she was eight. Her apartment was small and sparse, a mattress on the floor, a bookcase, and some records in milk crates. It was neat, the floorboards painted battleship gray, except for piles of books and papers by the bed. She had a half-finished novel and had put out three issues of a zine called Rants in a Void. The stuffed animals on the bed—a gray seal, a plush regal-red pig—contrasted with the black and white on the walls, photos of a woman in bondage and a rubble-filled lot in Berlin or Bed-Stuy, flyers for bands, and pages of cryptic messages in marker or typeface, collages of apocalyptic and sleazy tabloid headlines, DOCTORS WARNING DEADLY DISEASE, SEVEN HOURS OF TERROR, FACE OF A SEX BEAST.

Anticipation mixed with doubt. She wasn't stunning-looking, but there was something intensely sexy about her. She was little with dark curly hair, scrawny but for a perfectly curvaceous ass, and when she climbed on top of him in nothing but a G-string his cock got harder than a maple bass neck. He would come with jolts of tantric electricity zigzagging up his back, his brain bursting with scarlet and lavender clouds. But she was getting on his nerves. She was too jealous, constantly accusing him of fooling around when the band was out of town. She alternated between waitressing and stripping at Broadway Rose, a Midtown topless bar. It was a champagne-hustle club. The game was to lure the horny customer into the back room, where "the lady is drinking champagne," and he'd shell out two portraits of Benjamin Franklin for a split of white wine mixed with seltzer and the false promise of sex. At least that's what she told him. She swore up and down she didn't do anything with them. And her dope use was inching up. "Get off my back, I don't do it every day," she'd whine. Her nihilistic silences had gotten longer and deeper. Once he'd asked her if she wanted some food, and she'd answered, "It'll just turn into shit and fat." She hadn't put out her zine in six months, and her bass leaned unplayed in a corner by the radiator, its neck slowly warping from the heat.

She'd turned him on to dope for the first time. "C'mon," she'd said, cajoling him out of his reluctance. "It's not like you think it is. It's really sweet." It had been. They'd spent the night in bed, cuddling and floating away on salmon clouds of dub, then into the languid electronic worlds of Bowie's *Low* and *Heroes*, two of her favorite albums.

They'd done dope again occasionally, but it unsettled him. Like getting pulled back up to reality by the sound of the needle knocking against the final groove. It filled the void between shows, but he felt his time eroding, drifting away. Not enough was happening. You could only practice so much before it got frustrating. The days between shows felt like filler, mediocre tracks just taking up space on the album.

He turned right on Tenth Street. It was wider and better lit than the block of 11th between B and C. There was no line at the dope spot mid-block, a few night-shift workers coming home, a stray drunk, a woman pushing a little kid in a stroller. He turned left up C, crossed over to Lisa's building on 11th. I hope she doesn't start in on me tonight.

An arm snapped around his neck, a blade edged his cheek. A coldly calm voice. "Give it up, nice and easy, and you'll be all right." No choice. He had two dollars and 49 cents in his pocket, twitched it out and handed it over. "That's all you got? Fuck you, honky maricon!" the one behind him spat, shoving him. The one with the blade made some chill-out noises. They ran off.

Underend staggered a bit, steadied himself on the wall. It was painted bright green, with the lyrics to John Lennon's "Imagine" hand-lettered in gold. He rang the bell. She came down, kissed him. He sputtered the story.

"You wanna get high?" she inquired, untaping a small glassine postage-stamp bag stamped D.O.A. The receptor-binding molecules soothed him as the bitter taste oozed down his throat.

Two weeks later he went over her house again late one night after practice and after she'd gotten off work. She was high as fuck, her eyelids hanging cartoonishly low and distended.

"I got a present for you," she slurred. She handed over a dark-green metal box. It was the echo unit he'd been coveting, the used one they had at Eddie's Guitars on St. Marks.

"Thanks. Ya didn't have to, but I really wanted it," he said. They embraced and oozed into bed. He slipped her G-string down her thighs, kissed her pussy, ate it until long after the album side had run out. She couldn't come. He eased on top of her, pushed a shaky-tree hard-on fast, came with a ripple instead of a wave.

"You're not mad at me?" she asked.

"No. Why?"

"A guy at the club gave me $200 for a blowjob."

"The fuck? What'd you do that for?"

"Two hundred dollars. And he was so drunk he couldn't come. It was easy."

He jammed his clothes back on, stalked out. Took the echo unit. She dragged herself up to lean out the door and yell at him. "I bought you a present with it, you fucking useless, selfish pimp bastard," she called down the hall.

On the way home he stopped at the all-night bodega for two half-pints of under-the-counter Bacardi. Then he drank until his teeth were so numb he wouldn't have felt them being kicked in.

June waxed better. The band got a couple good shows. Underend's unemployment benefits got extended, and Tina started collecting, too. At least Reagan was good for something, he'd fucked up the economy enough so it was easier to collect.

They hooked up a basement rent party on Rivington Street. It belonged to a guy named Aaron who was around the scene, who fancied himself a metal sculptor and poet but was more of a rich-kid scenester, prating grandiose artistic theories and schemes that never seemed to pan out. He lived in the small storefront, and a corkscrew staircase led down to the much bigger basement where there was a makeshift bar and a DJ with two turntables plugged into the Gutter Astronomers' PA. Somebody collected $2 at the door, and the room filled with a hundred people drinking and talking and warming up to dance. The DJ spun a mix of hip-hop, reggae, and punk, the room churning to the Ruts' "In a Rut," bouncing to the rubbery disco-funk of Fonda Rae's "Over

Like a Fat Rat," and chanting righteously to Grandmaster Flash and the Furious Five's "The Message," the summer's urban-jungle anthem, everybody knew the words and the feelings, about being pushed close to the edge and trying not to lose it or go under. He followed it up with the Anti-Nowhere League's "So What," the crowd answering the singer's biker boasts about drugs, venereal disease, and goat-shagging with "SO WHAT? SO WHAT?"

The band went on after midnight, the crowd oiled and ready. So was the band and they locked in right away. All the wood was resonating right, the sounds juicy. Underend playing as if the guitar cord was his 18-feet, 6-inches umbilical to sanity. Tina was in the same mood, they both felt it, skittering around the small bit of space between the gear and the leaning faces, the crowd pushing up against them. They fed off each other in instinctive microrhythms, Underend pushing harder and faster, Tina torching out sheets of sound, grape bunches of high notes, then letting the sound swirl down, letting the riddim ride through. Scott was the most solid, pounding the beat like a piledriver, dust blew up every time he hit the kick drum. Mick threw himself around, raced out into the room, twisted and shouted on the floor like an electroshocked worm in the beer and broken glass.

The DJ came back raucous, the Ruts' "Babylon's Burning" into the Clash's "The Magnificent Seven." A big-haired woman, masses of crimped and teased dyed-black locks, came up to Underend, offered him a beer as he was putting his bass in the case. She had a '70s-rock vibe, more glam than gutter. Her name was Amanda. He'd noticed her before the set, knew who she was vaguely. Someone had whispered that she'd gone out with one of the Speed Queens and one of the guys in Aerosmith back in the day. She was now going out with a neo-rockabilly phenom named Jimmy Lee Hudson. But he was on tour in L.A.

"You remind me of a young Johnny Thunders, the way you move," she told him, brushing closer. The records cooled down to a sensual groove with the Wailing Souls' "Jah Give Us Life," the long dub version. They danced, swathed in the song and sound, the vocals sweet, the bassline warm and thick and hypnotic, the guitar chinking and twanging in the spaces between. Someone passed them a joint, and then they were rubbing up against each other as the echoed-out percussion percolated and burst, dropping petals all over their brains. They eased into a corner to the sound of "Love Will Tear Us Apart."

Klangenmuzic of feedback and thrash interrupted. Some new band was on stage and using the Gutter Astronomers' gear. Then Scott was raging. "Who the fuck said you could use my drums?" They were called Nuclear Waste. The little fuckers had been sniping at the Gutter Astronomers behind their backs, calling them soft and sellouts and rock stars. Trying to imply we thought we were too good for everyone else on the scene. Not that they had a problem with borrowing our gear without asking.

"Aaron said we could," one of them said. Scott found one of his cymbals keyholed and went off, smashing empty bottles into splattering shards, a red-faced bull raging after Nuclear Waste's drummer with a cymbal stand, intending to inflict grievous cranial harm. His first overhead swing welted off a ducking shoulder, then three guys nelsoned him, straining him back while he spattered letmeatthefuckinasshole, fuckinpieceofshit fuckedupmydrums.

Aaron had discreetly invited Mick upstairs for lines and flattery. Amanda spirited Underend away. She had a tattoo of a flowery vine that started near her right shoulder and curled saucily downwards. He traced it with his tongue.

Time slipped on. New Year's Eve 1984 they rented a vacant loft on Chrystie Street, put on a show with four bands. For an encore they brought out the violinist from Open Wound—she was now in a performance-art thing called Yes No What—to do the disco-string licks of Bowie's "1984," then crunched into "God Save the Queen," which at the end imploded into a rubble pile of feedback.

Yes, 1984 was finally here, so there were lots of jokes about Room 101 and Big Brother and telescreens. No joke: Room 101 was in the basement of an army barracks in El Salvador, Big Brother was in the fuckin' White House, and the telescreens were telling us it was Morning in America. Our real mornings had us with no heat, trying to make the rent, yuppies trying to drive us out, dope dealers on the corner with a baseball bat. The cops began pushing the dopefiends off Avenue B and the joke was that the landlords must have outbid the drug dealers for protective services. C-Section closed after a police raid while Social Distress was on stage. The sergeant leading it smacked the lead singer in the mouth and told him, "It's scumbags like you in the way of progress in this neighborhood."

Terminal Records, the local label that had put out the Gutter Astronomers' first record, got stiffed by DEA, its main distributor, and went under owing the band royalties on the about 3,000 records it was supposed to have sold. The band organized a mission to the company, on the third floor of an old cast-iron building on Broadway in Soho. They bum-rushed the office and liberated as many armloads of their album as they could, grabbing cartons of 25 and hustling them down the stairs. They got sixteen boxes, enough to cover about two-thirds of what the company owed them if they could sell them all at gigs.

That convinced them they needed a manager, somebody other than themselves to take care of business. Gerard Antonelli, the elfin booker at the Emerald Palace, had been touting them to the label people who came by but wasn't interested in taking them on. They got a high school friend of Mick's named Rob Byrd, a short and pudgy hustler full of grandiose half-ideological schemes. "We're going to play the White House lawn," he postulated.

"There's gates," Tina pointed out.

"And it'd be pretty fuckin' ignominious to get popped before we could even set up," Underend piled on.

"But that's it! Barbarians at the gate! The uncivilized hordes storm the portals of tyranny!"

That idea didn't fly, but Rob hooked them up with a Boston label called V2, and they recorded their first full-length album, *The Liberating Power of Filth*. The cover shot had the four of them lying in the street, heads pillowed on the curb and pointing cardboard-tube telescopes at the sky. "Filth" was a minor hit off the album, as was another anthemic track, "We Will If We Have To." "God Made Me Shit," which Mick described as "a gospel song of intestinal praise," got college radio airplay back-to-back with the Butthole Surfers' "The Shah Sleeps in Lee Harvey's Grave."

A new venue called Rat City opened in the far west Village, in a converted meat locker near the waterfront. Mick went over to see the Aggro Boys from London, with locals Combat—riding their first album, *Crush the Weak*—opening. Up front it was almost wall-to-wall skinheads. In front of him were about ten, all wearing matching boots and cutoff denim jackets with "Blüt ünd Eisen" stenciled on the back over Iron Crosses. Blood and iron. It set off obvious ancestral memories. His parents' aunts and uncles and cousins shuffled off cattle cars in a gray Polish railyard, punched and barked and clubbed into two lines, a short one to slavery and a long one to lice extermination.

Not an exact match, but close, very, very close. The Nazi white-power thing wasn't big with the New York skins. They hated fags and peace punks more, probably because it was a lot safer to beat the fuck out of lone queers coming out of Baghdad on Avenue A than it was to mess with Puerto Ricans from the Avenue D projects. But the power-worship, the brute-force fetish, was dangerously near.

The Aggro Boys banged out their first hit, its chorus a football chant based on the Ventures' "Let's Go"… "A! G! A-G-R! A-G-R-O! AGGRO!" Up front was a maelstrom of moshing skins. Mick fought off the 11,000-volt urge to rage on them. One-on-ten suicide.

He walked out of the show, stalked the blocks by the waterfront. Gangs of meathooks hung over loading docks. The cobblestoned streets reeked of rotting suet. The other meat business in the neighborhood, the wholesale sharing of cut and uncut pork swords and tubesteaks, had been fading under the rising plague. Three newbie-punk kids with a paper-bagged quart of beer hassled a black tranny hooker in a long curly wig and pink Spandex tights. They looked about 14. Little suburban boys who thought it was punk to come to the city and act like redneck bullies. "Leave her the fuck alone, she's a freak like us," Mick shouted. They slunk away, catcalling, "Fuck you, faggot" from a safe distance.

What the fuck hath we wrought? Mick thought, as the queen called out "Freak? Honey, I could tell you freak stories that would curl your pubes." We were tough because we were city kids. We were from the streets. We had to deal with reality and not some it's-all-good hippie nonsense. But we were fuckin' outcasts and freaks together. Gabba gabba we accept you. It wasn't about ganging up on whoever was weaker or weirder than us. These are the people who used to fuck with us for being odd. That's what the scene's turned into.

They were fucking up the scene bad, but they weren't the real danger. Fascism in America wasn't gonna be street thugs and the guttural hate growls of Adolf Hitler. It was gonna be the smiling, grandfatherly visage of Ronald Reagan, genially reassuring the nation that we stand firm against the evil hordes. The dirty work would be elsewhere, a place they didn't show on the ads.

He stalked the streets back to the East Side, a new song forming in his head. A Joy Divisionish groove, electronic, doomy, and danceable. Reciting the Birkenau images from before. A one-word chorus: "Selektion." Then a bridge—"Six million and one/I'm the one that got away/Six million and one/I'm the one you couldn't kill"—leading into a chant, "Alive is my revenge, alive is my revenge. I'm alive, I'm alive."

The next day he went to a tattoo artist named Goat who operated clandestinely in a tenement on the side streets between CBGB and the Hell's Angels. He got "6,000,001!" inked on his right forearm. Goat, an old bikerish hippie with a shaved head, long ZZ Top beard, and full-sleeve art galleries on his arms, worked quickly with the whirring needle, then painted the skin with soothing collodion.

But things were looking up for the band. Antonelli was touting them to labels. They did a 12-inch of "Selektion," with a dub mix and an instrumental called "Cyclone" on the B-side, and it got some radio and club play. Rob was hustling, working the phones, lining up press, setting up their first national tour for the fall. They got ready to do another album when they got back. Rob said a deal with possible major label distro was in the offing, maybe with Permanent Records.

They headed out on the road, got up far too early in the morning to load up the van and cruise off through the Holland Tunnel. They looped over the Jersey City ridge and west towards Allentown and the Alleghenies. The Mellow Yellow in Pittsburgh was an inauspicious beginning. When Mick and Rob went into the office to get paid, the club owner pulled a gun and told them, "You guys sucked. Get lost." Buffalo. Cleveland. Detroit, where Michigan's broad, smooth freeways turned to crumbled rubble the minute they crossed the city line. Flint was the first really smoking show. Four hundred people packed into a rented VFW hall, the crowd berserk, bodies flying off the rickety stage.

Michigan rock'n'roll boys in black t-shirts and blue jeans, lank brown hair and eighth-generation WASP faces six cousins away from the social register, fresh faces not yet ground weary by the assembly line or its disappearance.

The band relaxed. "Selektion" waxed less automatic and more organic, Tina riffing off Underend's stream of bass power chords and ominous minor sixths, the surging voice evoking doom and getting away from it.

They drove four hours to another city in the Midwest. Scott at the wheel of the van, inching and cutting through rush-hour traffic, Tina reading the directions off a sheet of paper transcribed in a phonebooth. They pulled up behind a warehouse near the river, backed up to the concrete-slab loading dock padded with tire rubber. It was just before six. These streets, a few blocks from downtown, were empty. Old brick factories with the windows knocked out, grassy weeds growing in the cracked sidewalks. A few 7-to-3-shift luncheonettes locked and gated. The other open business was a sports bar, once an after-work shot-and-beer joint, now offering buffalo wings, mozzarella sticks, and large-screen TVs with the Reds or Indians or Bengals games.

In a few hours there would be three hundred people lining up and packing in. They passed the gear up onto the dock, lugged it into the club. Products of the rock-industrial complex, battered black boxes filled with circuitry and tubes, projecting sound through black paper cones on metal frames, bolting together the drum hardware of steel and brass. Connected through microphone and wire to yet more black boxes, these sleeker, more minimalist, less mythical. This was the prep work, slicing and dicing the ingredients of their sonic stew.

What we do is abstract. The product of our physical labor is just ripples in the air. What we do is loud as fuck. Those ripples strike the eardrum like sticks slamming a snare, hard and sweet. What we do is food for the damaged soul, efflorescent detox like bamboo trees sprouting amok in a defoliated jungle. The Agent Orange poisons us all. We spit it out. On the beat, like bullets. We take the damage and we rock with it.

Chicago, second on the bill at a North Side ballroom of red-velvet curtains and gold-painted bas-reliefs of the nine Muses. Down to St.

Louis, a DIY show in a warehouse south of downtown, the opening band an art-noise outfit with homemade guitars and crudely buzzing electronics. Omaha. Minneapolis, another good one, where they encored with a camped-up two minutes of "Purple Rain" exploding into Husker Du's "Pink Turns to Blue." Then west across the prairie, a one-night stop in Rapid City for a punk hall show attended by twenty-seven underage kids and three middle-aged drunks; they made $81. A two-day drive to Seattle, Montana flat and endless miles of browning prairie, then up into the copper-mine slag piles and mountain forests. Then down the West Coast, Portland marred by skinheads fighting outside, Eugene a good one, Sacramento, two shows and a day off in San Francisco.

Tina was lonely. Walking around in a shell, an emotional shell within the metal shell of the van. Separate from the boys in the band, they were her brothers sometimes, but it wasn't enough. Longing for skin on skin, soul on soul, connection, communion, contact. Something as hard to articulate as it was to describe music in words, the vocabulary was inadequate the way "red" couldn't come close to capturing the whole pulsing, vulnerable, life-giving ventricular mess of the human heart. For intimacy, the normal barriers, distances, and reservations falling away as she ascended into a sphere of devouring desire, conversational exploratorium, extrapolating wordplay and thought like bebop vines in a fertile bed.

So as the band touched down, alighting from the van and going through the rites of loading in and setting up, the crowd beginning to filter in, she began searching. Antennae attuned. It was too much to put it all out for the people and have nothing to love her back but a blanket, the four walls of the van. The void. "Onstage I make love to 25,000 people, then I go home alone." She knew what Janis Joplin had been talking about.

Playing with people was intimate, too. You had to listen to them, feel them, excite them, respond to them, drive them on. Which just made it more painful when they were cold-blooded assholes. Most of the boys coming to their shows were younger now. So were the ones in the bands that opened for them. Sometimes they were childishly rude, overgrown pubescent bad boys; sometimes they were awed and reverent. It was different from when they'd opened for bigger bands, the established ones, who came on interested but condescending. And the women looked up to her, she the goddess who did what they wished they would, alchemizing estrogen and tech power and audacious strut. The wild one pulling sound from the air and screaming it out through a Fender Telecaster, reclaiming the hard rock maple neck for womankind. She'd gone off with a few of them, too. Lana, a college radio DJ in Madison. Corinne, a zaftig, curly-haired zine editor in St. Louis who lived in a rickety, semi-collective house papered with feminist posters and punk rock flyers. Nikki, the guitarist for the opening band in Seattle, a bony girl in a denim jacket with black bangs and stars tattooed on her shoulder. They'd jammed a bit, talked about doing a record together someday.

They came into L.A. on 101, following the long trail of taillights over the mountains, along the San Fernando Valley, and into Hollywood. It felt like a strange but banal world—not so much a city as a hyper-dense suburb, an agglomeration of strip malls packed so tightly there wasn't room for a sprig of grass in between. Smog hung over the basin like pot smoke at a Pink Floyd concert in 1974.

The show here was another big one, in an old ballroom in a Mexican neighborhood west of downtown. They were nervous. No one here really knew them. They opened with "Scratch and Claw" to get them moving, followed it with "Radioactive Jellybeans," and then skittered into "Cyclone." That got them going. A massive pit broke out. They brought it down to a groove mid-set for "Urban Babylon" and "Selektion" and knew they had the crowd. Then they turned it back up, closing with "Filth" and the fury of bodies flying off the stage, the kids scrabbling up and diving off, leaping and plummeting like crazed seagulls.

Then they turned back east, into the desert. They rolled on through the anomic boom towns of the Sunbelt. San Diego, Phoenix, Tucson, Denver. Endless stretches of arid strip malls, tract houses, and mini-mansions sprawling over the desert, gridding it with miles upon miles of new yellow franchises, a sea of brand names: McDonald's KFC Exxon Burger King Walmart Applebee's Shell. Not towns, just strings and patches of suburbia, one cluster the same as the other, new traffic lights shining under desiccated sky, sandstone-colored furniture showrooms, theme restaurants with balloon-lettering funtime logos. Miles upon miles of parking lots and car dealerships.

The kids there were desperate and the band played some of its best shows ever. Tina's guitar strings pinging out burning, keening melodies, driving the music higher and higher while leaving plenty of room for Underend and Scott's subway-train groove to roar through, and Mick dancing on top of it all, prancing to the lip of the stage, diving into the crowd, declaiming like a mad prophet chanting down Babylon, making the walls shudder and crack. And the kids loved it. It gave them meaning in a life amid the undifferentiated-tissue landscape, lives of moving from one fast-food town to another, houses on the last block before the desert began again, awkward dinners with their mom's new boyfriend, the only constant the color TV irradiating away. The kids drinking, dancing, moshing, fucked up on speed or pills or raving on straight-edge testosterone and adrenaline, fucking in the bathrooms, puking in the garbage cans, passing out in the parking lot. Kids in full punk regalia, kids in back-to-school clothes, kids in their first rough attempts at punk regalia—their father's white shirt with band names inked on it. Shouting along with Mick on "Filth" as he wallowed in the stage sludge, rolling in the sticky schmutz of shoe grime and spilled beer, "I'm filth! We're filth! Free as dirt!"

The kids burning for something to hold onto, in this rootless vaporous world that was smacking them around. They came backstage, told tales. Armed security guards and drug dogs sniffing lockers in their schools. One suspended for wearing a blue bandanna because it was "gang attire." Fundamentalist parents, divorced parents, cool parents, occasionally hushed confessions about abusive parents. Kids just discovering that what they'd been taught was a lot of lies. The band was a window into a different adult world. Kids enthralled by the band vibe, family and gang and tribe, a renegade collective roaming from town to town spreading the spirit. Enthralled by the power of the music, what made them move, get out of their seats, cast off the chains of order. What they'd been itching to do while strapped down at school, work, home. The Dionysian energy the whole human race had in them, but this world was scared of it. Scared of freedom, love, risk. Terrified of what might be cut loose.

Because once it cracked you'd never go back. Once you'd kicked it out you never wanted to be jammed down again. It was more than a temporary escape. It was a taste of something better, a window into a whole different way to be. Something you might have to pay for but couldn't buy. It was beyond money and couldn't be sold, no matter how hard they tried to package it.

Because there were two sides to every story, and once you opened the door, some strange shit flew in. When it was good, it was ecstasy, great pulses of joy rocketing around the church of the collective unconscious, flashing and flowing back and forth. You could look at someone for an instant and feel the connection, like you were all part of the same incredible thing. When it was bad, it was a nightmare beset by raging specters, voracious vultures, warplanes and fists. You never knew when you'd be the victim of someone else's demon.

Up to Denver from Tucson. It was way out of the way, looping up there and then to Oklahoma City, then south to Texas for shows in Dallas, Austin, and Houston. Almost nine hundred miles to Denver, 670 to OKC, and a mere four hours more to Dallas. The band's nerves were fried, and Mick insisted on taking the van through downtown so they could make the 120-degree turn onto Elm Street and pass by the Texas School Book Depository and the grassy knoll. He steered with one hand while he spieled about the single-bullet theory, the man with the umbrella, and the Watergate burglars disguised as bums.

Tina got ominous vibes the minute the club started filling. There were a couple dozen skinheads, crazy baldheads in suspenders, bleached jeans, and oxblood-red Doc Marten boots with dead-white laces. Crude spiderweb tattoos on their elbows, one bare-chested with Texas White Pride on his stomach in Gothic script. Ugly fuckers, she thought. They're about as sexy as a cinderblock. Deliberately repulsive and reveling in it, that was their power. You don't want to fuck us because we're ugly? We'll make you, and there's nothing you can do to stop it unless you want to get your face smashed in, turned into a bloody mess of mutilated monkey meat. And the bouncers looked similar, although they sported the venue's black t-shirts instead of white ones advertising the English Nazi band Skrewdriver.

Nobody danced during the set. The floor was empty. Cowed punk rockers rimmed the edges, with a handful of college students giggling by the bar. They looked far too preppie to be punks or hippies, too mysteriously happy to be yuppies or anything near sober. The front line was a row of skins. Predictably, they yelled "Show your tits" at Tina, called the rest of the band fags. Mick rushed the band through the show and got off.

They filed into the dressing room. The world closed down to a cell, a low-ceilinged rectangle with institution-bright fluorescent lights and piss-yellow cinderblock walls barnacled with band stickers and red and black graffiti. Tina blew up. "You're all mouth all the time, where the fuck were you when we needed it?"

"What did you want me to do, get us all killed? You think the bouncers woulda had our backs? You're fuckin' crazy if you do."

The air in the van the next day was a tense miasma as they rolled south across the prairie on I-35. Silently. Nobody could agree on music. Scott put on a Minutemen tape. "Get that shit off, it jangles my nerves," snapped Mick. "Then just don't play nothing," Scott growled. And another downsmack was awaiting them in Austin, where they were scheduled to open for Hollis Stone, lead singer of '60s psychedelic-garage legends the 709th Mushroom. Stone had just suffered another psychiatric relapse and been admitted to Austin State Hospital. They played to twenty people in a club that held 350. They had a $600 guarantee and got paid $100.

The way home ran from Houston northeast through provincial border-state cities. Shreveport, Memphis, where they made the obligatory visit to Graceland, much to the disdain of their native tour guides. Louisville, Charleston, Charlottesville. Morgantown, West Virginia, where the club was a former Underground Railroad stop. Rob had decided it wasn't worth having them drive out of the way to Athens, Georgia and the Raleigh-Chapel Hill area, the only places in the South where they had much of a following. So these were mainly gas money gigs, filling the gaps on the drive home. A long asphalt string beaded with isolated bumfuck towns, the service roads lined with gun and souvenir and construction supply shops. But the band eased back into a groove. The crowds were small but intense, the kids starving for music, bubbling in the front lines like molecules of boiling water.

They weren't making enough to stay in motels so they usually slept on people's couches. Mick stayed up late, holding court—it was what his role demanded—but the others would chill with a cold beer and a joint, winding down pleasantly burnt from a job well done. Sometime they'd play slow or minimal jams, punk or rock'n'roll oldies, on unplugged electrics or borrowed acoustics, Scott essaying guitar or drumming on a wood Fender case, somebody from the house or a local band sitting in, too.

The wee-hours drive from Morgantown after their last show landed them in Jersey City at rush hour, home and their own beds tantalizingly close, the tunnel entrance only a few hundred yards away, the only way in clogged with hundreds of cars and buses and trucks. A cloud of exhaust and impatience welcomed their sore eyeballs.

Back home and back into the swirl. They started work on their third record, to be called *Tribal Eyeballs*. It came out on Permanent, distributed by RCA. "Selektion" was the hit, but people also picked up on "I'm Sick of This," a medium-fast Velvetoid rocker—"I'm sick of greed. Take me to the living"—and two groove tunes, "5:55 Babylon to Brooklyn," a Clashoid dub, and "Arctic Avenue," a cold chill-out. It got a good bit of college radio airplay, blurbs in *Rolling Stone* and *Spin*, and a B plus from Robert Christgau in the *Voice*.

It hadn't come easy. The crop of songs that had filled the first two records, the ones they'd worked out live, had run out. And Mick wanted the new material to be instant crowd-pleasers, muscular, arena-big numbers. He didn't want to go out there with anything less than full power. "People come to see ME," he told the band.

Scott was irked by the "disco" direction. Tina sort of agreed. Mick dismissed them. The record's DJ play and success were opening doors for him in clubland: scenesters and hustlers inducing him to the men's room to inhale rails off mirrors perched on the toilet tank; the women he dated evolving to fashionoids in little black dresses and fingerless fishnet gloves supplanting the high-style punkettes with immaculately lurid hair, lemon and raven and candy-apple red, never mind the raggedy combat-boot girls with ridged thermal underwear peeking through the ripped knees of their jeans. And Underend caught the flak when he brought in a two-chord groove, a 1969 soul-funk bassline.

"Disco!" Scott lambasted.

"It's like James Brown," Underend defended.

Mick piled on. "He's so fuckin' boring. Same riff over and over. It's music to keep people asleep and mindless."

Amanda ditched Underend right before they left on the tour. It shouldn't have been a surprise, Tina had warned him about the perils of porking the attached. "They always go back to whoever they're with. You shouldn't expect anything but a fling," she'd told him. But it knocked him into a downward spiral of depression. He needed a drink before every show, a tall double vodka and orange juice on his amp during it.

This tour was bigger and smoother than the last one. They weren't doing DIY shows, where you didn't know what would happen, any more. The aroma of spilled beer and smoke still lingered in the afternoons when they arrived for soundcheck, but the clubs they played had grey-black carpet walls backstage instead of cigarette burns on linoleum. It was more secure, the crowds steadier. The big stages felt good, a base for the roar of electromechanical power. Scott's drums miked up to gunshot volume, Tina's Fender Twin loud and juicy, Underend with a brainload of vodka, slinging his long-necked Embassy around, 300 watts of power thumping and throbbing into two 15-inch speakers. And they were more consistent; they rarely wavered live now. They burned pretty often, too, and the kids ate them up either way.

Still, it felt oddly distant. Routine. Doing the same set every night. Big gestures drawing hoots and applause instead of give-and-take, the audiences more worshipful than wiseass. They didn't hang out as much either. Sometimes they stayed sequestered backstage until they went on, the gates guarded by bouncers. The people who came in afterwards all had passes, music-biz types and groupies and fanboys with connections, liggers and scenesters and hangers-on. Most of them wanted to get next to Mick. The ones who talked to Tina or Scott or Underend were the leftovers and they'd be constantly turning their heads, looking to see if someone bigger was in the room. When they did go out, people seemed awed by them. Or that the first ones who'd come near were the lead singers of local bands who'd jam demo tapes into their hands, persistently insisting that they had to open for you next time you came to town, and you couldn't brush them off to talk to anyone else without being rude enough to piss them off.

They were getting interviewed a lot, radio and alternative weeklies instead of little photocopied 75-circulation zines, but Mick usually hogged the mic, blathering away in run-on typewriter-throat chatter. That was when Rob hadn't set it up so that it would be Mick exclusively. And the photos that ran were often of him instead of the whole band.

Things were happening too fast, spinning beyond their control. Scott played harder, angrier, paradoxically making the band more intense. "C'mon, fucker, faster," he'd growl at Underend like he was an engine bolt resisting the wrench, inaudible under the volume, but you could lip-read his mind. He didn't want to live like this, his hopes of success—hell, his hopes of just making a living—dependent on and torn between greedy egomaniacs and messed-up burnouts. He liked to get fucked up, too, but he was disciplined about it. He'd hold himself to one beer before the show to ease his nerves and loosen his muscles, and maybe one or two tokes if they were doing a smaller gig where he could stretch out, or an up or a couple lines of coke if he was really fried and needed energy that coffee couldn't do. Afterwards he'd get razrezzed. But onstage the rhythm section drives the band, and the drummer can't sputter and lag.

Tina withdrew, didn't talk much. And Underend sought solace in old soul music, broken love meeting transmuted longing for Jesus. James Brown singing "I Lost Someone." "Wish Someone Would Care," by Irma Thomas from New Orleans. The Four Tops' "Standing in the Shadows of Love," with one of James Jamerson's best basslines ever. Jamerson, the Motown house bassist who'd given the groove to a quarter-billion records, got ditched by the label, and died an alcoholic death in L.A. a few years back, a couple months after Michael Jackson moonwalked into megastardom on the Motown TV special.

Underend needed to get fucked up on something more than liquor. Dope was hard for him to find outside the city but pills weren't. As they headed back home through the upper Midwest he got deeper into it. The set list was so regular he could play it in his sleep. In Detroit somebody gave him a 60-milligram vial of liquid methadone after the show. He was woozy as fuck the next night in Cleveland, but it gave him a nice sleazy-grind rhythm. Mick, hyper, pushed straight ahead, turned and glared back whenever he wasn't singing. Backstage he blew up.

"You fuckin' play the way you're supposed to play, the way the songs are supposed to go. You don't change the beat. That leaves me hanging. People come to see me. And if I fuck up, I'm the one who hears it. Not you. You don't have to answer for nothing."

They drove east for an hour, stopped in a cheap motel outside Youngstown. Underend got a half-pint of vodka. Tina grabbed him into her room. He needed comfort. She needed him to keep it together. They drank and vented. "I'm sick of this," he told her.

"Yeah, I'm not happy about it either. But fucking yourself up isn't going to make it any better," she said. "The more you mess up, the more excuse they have to dump on you. If you're fucked up, make music out of it. That's why we got into this music, right? We were fucked-up kids who needed an outlet or we'd go batty. So put it into the music."

She was right. No one wants to see listless nihilism, apathetic, pointless schlumpery. So burn or get off the stage. Put the pain into aching slow jams—you feel it, you know it, you show it. And let the rockers roar with rage and escape. For one moment you've flapped out of the morass, skybound with muddy ankles.

She was wrong. "It's hard when we're just a fuckin' machine, same set every night. I don't wanna be some egomaniac's boring backing band. He's pissed at me for getting high? What about him, with half the Bolivian army marching up his nose? And the other half going up Rob's deviated septum? I need something more. I'm sick of this."

"Yeah, take me to the living," Tina half-sang at him. "Seriously. You can't afford to sabotage yourself when the world is against you. And if they think you're a liability, they're ambitious enough now to cut you off."

"I don't get fucked up to go on stage," he said. "I get fucked up to deal with all the bullshit you have to go through to get on stage."

Stretched out on the bedspread, a scarf over the lamp to soften the light, they passed a joint. It smoldered down to the roach. They held each other. Then the caresses of comfort slipped into sensuality. Their lips met, then their tongues.

They shared an awkwardly quiet breakfast the next morning. Neither one wanted to delve into the murk of motivations, of stonedness, affection and need, to stir the subterranean snakes of what-next, of implied commitments, and violating the band's incest taboo.

Tina caught a riff in her apartment late at night while they were coining songs for the next record. Playing by herself on headphones, a one-chord groove off B and a repeating echo. She had to hit the strings just right to get the riddim to click, then keep at it for the echoes to build up and the intensity to grow. It was one of those really simple things that you had to get perfectly for it to work, if you didn't it would be "ah, what's the big deal," but once it got going it was infectious and insatiable. Like Keith Richards with an electronic pulse, a hypnotic repeating cyberheartbeat with a sexy sway and grind, tomcat growl and blues-crow caw.

She and Underend jammed on it, and he loved it. Only one chord but so much groove, you could play all night with the texture and dynamics. They did a seven-minute demo of it, flying full out, dropping down to muted punk, dubbing out the second half. All organic, nothing static, never losing the drive. It felt like a hit.

This album needed to have a hit, Rob had lectured. They'd been one of the few acts kept on when RCA acquired Permanent outright, he reminded them. That meant they were now on a real major label, which would want to sell 100,000 units minimum, if not 300,000. The 50,000 copies that would be a huge hit for an indie label would be a disastrous stiff to them.

"We'd be dropped like a leaky rubber," Rob warned. "They're going to invest a lot of money in us, and we've got to give them a record that makes them their money back. That means we've gotta be open to making some accommodations. We've gotta work with them."

They did the album at a studio in Midtown, produced by Dick Z, whose aviator glasses and suit jacket over black t-shirt bespoke an aging rocker's attempt to persuade himself that he still looked cool and persuade the boardroom that he was modern, burying any traces of a slovenly, decadent hippie past. The accommodations he wanted translated as a more mainstream rock sound.

Scott was the first one to chafe. The beats they wanted from him—a precise 120 or 132 per minute, hit the snare evenly on the two and four—constricted his style. "You could get anyone to play this. A machine could do it. Get a fuckin' Linn drum." He wanted the chaos and drive of rockabilly and punk, the oddities of the Minutemen, not taking dictation from a click track. And he also objected to the pieces of towel duct-taped to his drums. "If my drums sounded any fuckin' deader, you could lay them out and wake them. They sound like I'm hitting the phonebook. Like I'm using fuckin' pizza boxes for heads."

"The tape is there so we can get a professional drum sound. No ring," Dick said coldly. "We'll put reverb on in the mix."

They were also pressuring Tina to play more conventional rock guitar, more traditional leads. Solos weren't her style, especially not obvious guitar heroics. She was a rhythm player, seasoning it with fills and textures. She could play as hard and driving as anyone, but when she did single notes, it was a different world, like black-and-white psychedelia from a bleak city. They wanted something she couldn't deliver and didn't want to.

So they brought in Jack Axe to overdub some leads. They knew him from the scene. He was a minor Lower East Side guitar hero; he'd been in a band called the Operators that had one good single in 1980, a Max's Kansas City jukebox hit. Now he preferred the demo shuffle, forming bands and rehearsing in private, trying to develop a package to get signed, instead of the public grind of building a following on the club circuit. He was a nondescript except for narrow eyes that gave him a perpetual sneer. But he could definitely play. Maybe too well, ripping off barrages of even-fire sixteenth notes.

Tina brought in a cassette of her tune. Dick heard it, said he heard a hit—if it was altered. "It needs a more modern sound."

She said no. "What's not modern about it?" she asked, suspecting a euphemism for "make it fit a commercial formula." Underend agreed with her, Scott less emphatically.

Mick said, "Let's try it." He argued about broadening and reaching bigger audiences. "Do you want to play kiddie shows with seventy-five people, or do you want to be big? What else is out there? I'm not Madonna, I can't blow the DJ at Danceteria to get my record played."

"That was her boyfriend," Tina slapped, "and if your girlfriend gave you a blowjob in the DJ booth, we'd be hearing you brag about it for weeks."

Mick ignored her line. "We can't be a punk band any more and make money. We're not hardcore, we're definitely not metal. You wanna play to a bunch of ugly fuckers fighting each other, or you wanna make an impact? Where's our niche? Where's our place? We have to find one."

"I just want to play music that sounds good," Tina pleaded.

"So do I. But we have to get it out there. And it's the message that's important. We can dress it up a little differently if we have to. It's about being open to new ideas."

"Not if they're wack," Scott interjected.

"It's time to push it," said Rob. "This is our break, this is our chance at the big bucks. We don't want to blow all the work we put in to get this far. We don't want to blow it for some juvenile ideas about purity." He held the word off his tongue as if it was a shitty diaper.

They remixed the track behind Tina's back. Her guitar was almost inaudible in the final version. Jack did a cocaine-tone solo, lots of top-of-the-neck pyrotechnics and Van Halen finger-tapping. And they brought in a keyboard player, Jen, a friend of his, a bleached blonde with a Yamaha DX7. She overdubbed an electronic pulse, complete with the DX7's preset fake-horn and synth-strings sounds.

Tina flipped out when she heard it. "It's a piece of shit," she screamed. "I don't even recognize it. It's got the same cliché sounds as every shit slug record on the radio."

"It wouldn't have happened if you could play better lead," Mick said. The argument escalated until he called her an "incompetent slut."

She quit. So did Scott. Underend hung on. He wasn't ready to jump into the void.

That left them with half a band and a half-finished album. Finding a new drummer was easy. Ray Riot called the next day. He'd run into Scott on the street and gotten the news, along with a blessing to go for it and a warning about what he was getting into. Underend liked him. He was a veteran of a chain of punk and club bands, with a constant skein of wisecracks delivered in a thick Brooklyn accent and semi-shag black hair not that far from a '70s hard-rock band. They'd jammed after-hours back in the day.

Mick and Rob wanted to have Jack play guitar, "at least for the tour." Underend wanted to find someone different. "C'mon, he knows the songs, we've gotta get out on the road, we can't waste time teaching someone," Mick argued. But they agreed to put an ad in the *Voice* for a new guitarist. It drew a lot of phone calls, but they were almost all chaff. You could tell what they were going to sound like before they even plugged in. The guy with the tweed jacket and a Strat played slightly stilted intellectual funk, like a bad Talking Heads/Gang of Four mix. The one with the hollow-body and the chain of effects played jazz-fusion; why Rob had even booked him was a mystery, unless he was trying to sabotage the search. The woman with the big burnt-sienna hair and the Japanese Strat copy with a Floyd Rose whammy bar talked a good game but played wanky leads with no sense of rhythm or dynamics. One guy could play competent punk rhythm and some lead but was so bland they didn't want to bother. Another had good drive but his distortion box and flanger produced grating, metallic out-of-tune overtones, and he refused to turn them off.

"It's my sound," he insisted.

"Like someone pissing on tin," Mick observed after he left.

The young cat with the Mick Jones quiff and a red shirt with the collar turned up played Clashabilly… badly. Lots of energy but so green and shaky that he bobbled a simple blues progression. Mick dismissed him as "a grimpler," Yiddish for "someone who insists on playing even though they have no talent."

"Yeah, he can't play," Underend retorted, "but at least he's fuckin' interesting, not like these other jokers."

Finally they settled on Jack by default. He knew the songs and could get through them on stage. Underend had misgivings but didn't make much of an effort. In his heart he knew it was over, but his brain wasn't going to accept that, and the only alternatives were all scary failure.

He was in a haze while they completed the album. They stuffed a few extra tracks on so it would make it up to the 35-minute mark, and finished the overdubs on the ones they'd done with the old band. Dick and Rob and Mick handled the mixing, shutting him out. "It's not your decision," Dick told him when he tried to get an idea in. "You don't count for shit."

They rushed back out on the road, doing a quick week in New England, Buffalo, and the Midwest before heading south on the first leg of a national tour, bringing Jen along as keyboardist. Underend and Ray quickly discovered shared drug tastes. They stocked up on dope before they left but burned through it by the time they hit North Carolina.

Raleigh at sunset, a low sprawling city of small hills and dumpsters. They played an old brick mill and drove out the next morning through miles of suburban construction. In Charlotte, Ray and Underend, hungover as fuck, had breakfast in a shoebox ghetto café where bearded black men in worn coveralls copped coffee while walking to work. Underend had eggs, hash browns, and sausage lolling in grease. Ray ordered livermush, a square, undersized patty like a White Castle burger, " 'cause we're mushing our livers." Boxes of paper towels and cans of shortening narrowed the hall to the bathroom. The opioids leaving their systems had their guts perched precariously between locked-up icecap and septic tank explosion.

The road was a blur of vodka and Valium, Pernod and Percoset. Stopping for gas on the way to Atlanta, self-serve pumps under a dazing rectangle of police-bright lights, the onramp hillside covered with clumps of dead kudzu, brown and matted like a wino's hair. They traveled in factions. Mick, off in his star cocoon, ignored Underend. Jen and Jack jumped on him after every show, nailing every little mistake he'd made and some that he hadn't. "That's really unprofessional," seemed like her mantra. Well, maybe he was, but the music was meaningless now. Same set every night, every tune Just Like the Record. It was like a totally different band and he didn't recognize any of the people they played to.

In Pensacola a half-dozen fundamentalists picketed them. They should be picketing us because we're an abortion of what we used to be. They got to New Orleans early. He walked over to Bourbon Street. The music coming out of the bars was lame. He dreamed of catching unsung piano professors, old geezers playing tailgate jazz, voodoo-child funkateers. What he got was generic bar blues and Top 40 cover bands. One was doing Jefferson Starship's "We Built This City." One of the worst songs ever, and from a band that used to be good. Well, he was never heavy into them, he was too young, but he remembered his big sister getting pumped up for antiwar protests by listening to "Volunteers." Now they had maybe one original member left but the brand name was a cash cow if you obeyed the right formulas. That's what they want to turn us into. That's why they're trying to drive me out. He decided to stay straight for the show, in a club over a bowling alley on a wide boulevard. He played solidly, moved around a bit. That didn't change anything. They were still pecking away at him.

"You speeded up 'Filth,'" Jack started in.

"It's supposed to be fast. It's a fuckin' punk rock song," he shot back.

"It's not that fast on the record. That's what people want to hear."

"And you're playing too loud," Jen joined in. "That's really unprofessional."

"What, because you can hear me? because I haven't fuckin' disappeared? Who the fuck are you to talk to me like that?" he demanded. "You've been in the band, what? A whole two weeks now?"

"This band was nowhere before we joined," Jen shot back. "Now we're on a major label."

"Yeah, you were playing shitholes on Avenue C," Jack piled on.

That's more than you were doing, but it's not worth fighting for. He left with the guitar player in the opening band. They had pharmaceutical radar. The guy invited him to jam, but first they rode deep into the Ninth Ward to cop, to a rutted street of shotgun houses. They picked up from a heavy bearded dealer, a voodoo-looking dude with one missing and one silver front tooth, while two little kids on the couch watched a scratchy video of *Return of the Jedi*. Then back to a club on Decatur, on a red-lit block under wrought iron balconies, where they jammed for two hours, the drummer playing funky second-line beats, the crowd drinking and wining up against each other.

In the morning someone banged on his door. Underend took a long time to stir. "C'mon, time to go, you're late," the voice shouted.

"Fuck off, I'm not going anywhere," he shouted back.

"We're leaving without you."

"Go ahead. I don't give a fuck."

They banged some more. He heard Mick calling, "C'mon, don't do anything stupid," and Jen saying, "Fuck him, we can leave without him.

I can do the basslines on my keyboard."

Underend went back to sleep, woke up at four, went out for breakfast. It started to sink in. The rest of the band was headed for Houston. He left enough money for a train ticket in his room, then headed back to the French Quarter to start drinking.

Mist hung over the far end of the Quarter. Dank, dense, and glowing in the desolate streetlight. A blank brick wall. No one was out on this block. Mist was in his brain, too. Hurricanes on Bourbon, tequila sunrises on Frenchmen, shots of Jack in some worn-wood dive on Decatur. The smoky night colors of a boozeria, half open to the street weather. After the rain and covered with lizards. Houseplants above. Purple, gold, and green target bunting. The sidewalks a shining drab. Seasick slopes in the concrete, a warp and woof of seismically shifted squares. His teeth were so numb they could have been broken.

Memory drifted by like a plastic bag on a slow wind. Pump and pulse of the bass and drum, sheets of organ and measured crackle on guitar. A skinny night creature, dyed black hair, red lipstick, and a broken tooth. In his face with sweet liquor bouquet on her breath, a maroon scrape-scab on her right cheekbone. Where did she disappear to?

He got a slushy Hurricane on the way to the train. It was a long ride home, thirty-two hours from Union Passenger Terminal to Penn Station. He slept through most of the low woods of Mississippi, Meridian the singing brakeman's home, Birmingham the vulcan city of steel and bombs and the magic city of Sun Ra. Woke up near Atlanta, dozed through Toccoa where James Brown went to reform school. Midnight in Spartanburg, wee-hour layovers in North Carolina for cigarettes on the dark platform, morning in the Virginia foothills, then D.C. and the homestretch in the red-brick jumble of the Northeastern megalopolis, past crumbling rowhouses in Baltimore, the ruins of factories in Philadelphia, abandoned warehouses in Trenton and Newark. He'd brought plenty of provisions for the ride: two pocketable vodka bottles, two bags of dope left from the other night, three Percosets, and four Valiums. And his Walkman with a tape of Aaron Neville singing songs of true love that would never be.

Chapter 5
The '00s / September

Mick stood by the long steel table leading to the X-ray machine at LAX, taking off his boots, rings (cow skull, onyx, and eyeball on his left hand; threaded copper, pentagram, and Celtic-filigree poison on his right), bracelets (spiked leather on his left arm, silver and turquoise on his right), and necklaces (a small padlock on a chain, a Star of David, a forest-green dagger), and dumping the lot in the grey plastic bin, a five-minute process. Even so, his piercings set off the metal detector so they pulled him out of line and wanded him down, the wand beeping when it passed his eyebrows, ears, nipples, and nose.

The businessman behind him was staring contemptuously. Mick returned the venom. First-class fuckhead shit in a suit even if he's casual Friday today in a polo shirt and khakis. Fingering his BlackBerry like a crack fiend combing the rug hairs for the rock that got away. Can't be out of touch with the office for two fuckin' minutes. Republican creep.

At O'Hare there was a layover. He paid six bucks for a stiff, sugary "Chicago style" pizza. The PA intruded, "The Department of Homeland Security has raised the threat level to Orange. Please be advised that any unattended luggage or packages will be confiscated." A whiff of totalitarianism in the consumer-logo muzak tourist-trap fiesta of McDonalds gold and Starbucks green.

The air on the plane was dry and chemically sweet. Mick felt a tickle in his throat, a red and raspy patch. Six hours of this is really gonna fuck up my voice. It was gonna be hard enough singing with a band for the first time in who-knows-how-long. He needed a continuous flow of tea with lemon and honey. The girl across the aisle was reading a celebrity magazine. EXCLUSIVE! BRITNEY'S KIDS SUFFER. LINDSAY IN REHAB. JESSICA DANGEROUSLY THIN. CATFIGHT OF THE YEAR: OCTOMOM SLAMS KATE. We're back in the era of prepackaged idols again. Only they're not squeaky-clean anymore, they're fucking up in public. Royally. And that's what makes them big. The media builds them up and then cannibalizes them. Obsesses and sanctimoniously reviles them. And people lap it up. What makes me any different from them? If I'm big, I'm gonna be part of the same shit. So what am I doing this for, besides my ego, besides living out some middle-aged personality crisis in a pathetic last-ditch bid for celebrity. What's the point? Well, I've got a calling. I've got a gift. If that makes me better than other people, so fuckin' what?

Okay, so performing separates you from the crowd, especially if you're any good, if you have better technical and emotional skills than other people. But there's a difference between being like a griot, a shaman, somebody who expresses the feelings of a community, the one who brings themselves out so people can see what they didn't know before, and being in a spectacle where the only thing that flows back to the stage is celebrity adulation. It's more complicated than that: it's like a yin-yang thing, it's got both sides embedded in it. But you know, some music is universal, like Muddy Waters and Bob Marley move people who've never been anywhere near Trenchtown or the South Side of Chicago. And some is imperial, all over the world like Nike and Pepsi. Like, if I went into a little one-room grocery store way up in the mountains in Mexico or in a shantytown in Calcutta, they'd probably have a fuckin' *American Idol* poster on the wall.

No future in anything else for me. I've had a good run but it ain't got much longer to go. I'm making it now as a character but sooner or later I'm gonna get old and sick and start missing days, or they'll get sick of my stories and ditch me for some flavor of the month. I gotta do something. What can I do to make it new?

It wasn't just like he was getting old and out of touch. Music seemed really dull these days. He remembered one night out where each club felt like walking into a different time capsule. In the 1974 Room, we've got four longhaired guys who sound stoned and sludgy like Black Sabbath. In the 1992 Room, we've got four longhaired tattooed guys who sound stoned and sludgy and choppy like Alice in Chains. In the 1977 Room, of course, we have punk, an eighth-generation Ramones knock-off. And in the 1965 Room, we've got four guys and a woman with pudding-bowl haircuts, polka-dot shirts, and a Farfisa organ, cloning the classic garage-band sound. All the neo-rockabillies who hung out at the Moto, the dudes with greasy hair, sideburns, and sleeve tats, the women in fluffy party dresses, bad-girl tight pants, or the '40s pin-up girl look with Japanese-rose lipstick and heavy tattoos… it was a museum culture. Fifties rock'n'roll was great, there were some things about it that nobody was ever going to do better so you tried to catch the spirit of it. But it came from one time and that was never going to happen again. Same thing with punk, and now you could buy all the accessories at the mall or on the Internet instead of having to seek them out or make them up yourself.

The public is fuckin' stupid. They're still worshipping at the altar of Sid Vicious as the spirit of punk, all the brains and rebel heart and twisted humor of it stripped away to one easily digestible myth: get fucked up and die young. What was it the guy from RCA had told him, one coked-out afterparty night? "There is a market for music that sucks, and we have a fiduciary duty to our stockholders." Yeah, but rock'n'roll lived off the myth as much as the reality, and that's what made you larger than life, more than just a bar band playing for wobble-dancing drunks shouting, "Wooo!"

Tina, Scott, and Underend had never understood that, how much you had to create a persona and keep it up, otherwise you'd be just one of many. Despite all the punk rhetoric against rock stars, the scene craved icons just as much as anyone else. Still, you couldn't forget the reality. You had to bring it on stage to live up to the myth, and what gave it the power was the boys—and girl—down in the boiler room stoking the groove. It was gonna be good getting back with the originals, after all these years of missteps.

The whole culture was boring now. Everyone was either a sales pitch or was cowed. No passion. Except for the ones who took their love for themselves, their beautiful selves, their obsession with riding the accelerator to stardom, and transmuted it into intensity. You could look in the mirror and have yourself one hell of a wank. This is the cum shot, the money shot. Some minimum-wage janitor would be in later to wipe up the simulated splooge of baby oil and yogurt.

Some of the kids were encouraging. Todd and Ramon from the Lewd Boys, a neo-glam group thinner than anyone over thirty could ever hope to be outside of methamphetamine addiction or anorexia, cute guys in wide-striped suits, scraggly pudding-bowl haircuts, and black-velvet shoes. They kept hocking him, "When are you going to get something new together? Why don't you get the Gutter Astronomers back together?" They were good, energetic and catchy, but it was a buzz, not a revelation. Sarah from the OxyKittens, a girl with straight brown hair and glasses who looked far too studious to play as hard as she did, who probed him for stories about Tina.

"You need to," Ramon told him one night. "You were made for more than this bar. You got talent. Dude, you oughta be out there doing it."

But what could you do new that wasn't some cheesy flavor-of-the-month shit? Fucked if I have a clue. Keep going and make it real, or more than real. Go for the raw barbed-wire power. Leaven it with sensuality. There's a moment when you catch it, when you're part of something bigger than yourself, and you pump its heartbeat. Maybe it's once in a lifetime, and then it's gone. Without it, you're just a high-class bar band. Or maybe you're just digging away in some obscure vineyard, cultivating a local vintage known but to a few. Maybe you, or they, have inflated notions. Or maybe you don't realize how special it is.

Scott took a break from taping sheetrock, wiped the sweat off his brow with a navy-blue bandanna, tapped on the wall to check the soundproofing. Clapped his hands to check the echo, the liveness of the room. Four o'clock, a half-hour to go before they packed up the tools and loaded up the van. Him and Gene, his son; Hutton, a friend of Gene's from Fort Greene; Quint, a quiet singer-songwriter in his early thirties; and Enrique, an old Lower East Side squatter. Enrique was usually neutral in the disputes over what music to play on the plaster-spattered boombox. They'd either alternate between rock and hip-hop or compromise on '70s soul.

This job was building a recording studio in an industrial area on the border between Bed-Stuy and Hasidic Williamsburg. It was a hip-hop/R&B/house music studio, the main room smaller than what they'd build for a live band, just space for congas and bass, and two vocal booths, one live with tiled surfaces, one warmer and deader with wood and rugs. Most of the work would be done in the control room, on synthesizers and samplers, and that one was plush, with walnut paneling on the walls to match the kidney-bean-shaped wood around the board.

The owners were a pair of Bed-Stuy rappers called A-Train: Big Balla, obese and freckled, and Peace, a minuscule guy thinner than an old-school dollar joint. They'd broken through last year with a track that was big locally and a moderate hit nationally, and had decided to put the profits into producing.

"Money, power, respect, that's where it is," Big Balla averred. "You gotta be in command of your business."

"That's one thing we fucked up on, that's for sure," Scott had told him.

"You gotta be higher up on the food chain. If you ain't, it's like 'that nigga's food.' I ain't in the game to be eaten. And we ain't the only ones who can make records. It's a creative process."

Peace had nicknamed Scott "Elvis," and it stuck. Well, he cultivated a rockabilly elder-statesman look, with a full gray-tinged quiff and sleeve tattoos flashing flames, fish, and dames, an ace of hearts with Too Fast To Live, Too Young To Die on his left forearm and an ace of spades with Born To Lose, Live To Win on his right. And he'd definitely acquired a beer gut, though it fell far short of Presleyan proportions. It didn't affect his playing. There'd been plenty of pot-bellied drummers who could hit as hard and fast as any young stickboy.

The two showed up around 4:30 with a friend called Wayne. Gene greeted them with a flourish of "A'ights" and "Wassup, dawgs." Scott gave them a quick tour of what they'd done that day, and then the UPS guy showed up with boxes from Roland and E-mu, samplers and sound modules. The almost-finished control room was stacked full of unopened cardboard. An Akai MPC. A long synthesizer box leaned against the wall, a large cube containing a computer monitor sat in a corner.

Peace, wearing a Remember the Day-Give Something Back t-shirt with a picture of a food stamp on it, said he wanted to make "conscious" records, but "People want the hustler thing. They wanna be the king. It's good to be the king. They want 'the world is yours.' The ride with the spinning wheels, goin' out to the clubs. What else is out there? Crawling for pennies? They called it Money-Makin' Manhattan back in the day, but you look in one of them offices now and they ain't got but one brother there, some Cosby-show mothafucka."

Big Balla sat on a folding chair, breaking up a Phillies cigar and crumbling green buds on top of the boxes, wrapping the lot into a blunt, expounding tour stories. "Philly's rough. They got MCs with records out and they're scufflin' over a fifty-dollar bag of trees. Baltimore was savage, man, it was ill. Houston, they was all fucked up. They all drinkin' codeine cough-syrup iceys, everybody's... s-l-o-o-o-w."

"DJ Screw," Gene chimed in. "That shit is twisted. It's like walkin' in Jello."

Gene, short for Gene Vincent Crowley, was twenty, a big, husky kid, wearing a size XXL t-shirt, voluminous silvery-gray jeans, and a red Yankees cap with around forty little NYs and the gold size tag still on the flat brim. He's more at home in this world than I'll ever be, Scott thought.

Tina got on the 7 train at 82nd Street after shepherding Janis and Damian through the crowds on Roosevelt Avenue, threading past women peddling plastic bags of mango slices, more record stores per block than in the Village, and longhaired Latino boys in Nirvana "Flower Sniffin', Kitty Pettin', Baby Kissin' Corporate Rock Whores" t-shirts, sierra faces the color of granadillo wood. Cars oozed by booming bachata music, soft bass clave and guitar lines sprinkling like rain.

It was hot, yet another five-day heat wave. They'd gone to visit her Aunt Rose, the last gringo on her block in Jackson Heights. The kids were pissed they'd had to spend a Saturday afternoon being dragged out there. Janis railed against the old woman's anti-immigrant rants while Damian petulantly puttered with the PlayStation Portable, sweaty crankiness tainting his baby-bull joy.

"We don't have a country any more," Rose had spieled. "I go on Roosevelt Avenue, there's no more signs in English. Everything in Spanish, except the pizza place. What is this, Colombia? You can't tell what anyone's saying, they could be plotting to cut your throat. And the Spanish isn't the worst, at least they use our alphabet. You can't read the scribblings they have up on 74th Street. It's probably terrorist messages from the Muslims in Pakistan."

When Janis had asked, "Didn't your parents speak Italian when they came over here?", Rose snapped back, "That was different. We were here legally. We didn't break the law."

"What a hypocrite," Janis was now complaining. "She's always telling us about how her mother came to Ellis Island, and what it was like for them, living in the tenements on Elizabeth Street, blah blah blah."

"I know," Tina said. "You don't know how much shit they gave me when I was your age. And not all of our relatives were completely legal when they came here. But she's family, we have to live with it." It was safer to talk about how the kids had grown, she thought. Janis was now four inches taller than she was. They both had the same black hair. Damian would pass her in a couple years.

The train stopped for a red light. "Ma, what time is it?"

Tina checked her cellphone. "Five after seven."

"I wish this train would hurry up. I have to get ready." Janis was supposed to meet her boyfriend for a ten o'clock movie in the Village.

The train rolled into the sunset. It was dark when they reached Long Island City, anonymous skyscrapers checkerboarded with light lining the once-industrial neighborhood where the tracks curved down into the tunnel. It looked like science fiction, Tina thought. Well, it was. A satellite neuron of glowing towers, cogs in the global machine, humming with computers zinging messages and images around the world at the speed of light. Life was like science fiction now, too. You could click on a mouse and get scenes from Brazil or Bangladesh on a screen in your bedroom. Everyone walking around with mobile phones. The iPod, holding a wall's worth of weighty vinyl in a box the size of a cassette tape.

But there was a dark side. Dystopia, like a science fiction nightmare, a future of techno-dictatorship where everyone lived in identical highrise pods and had electronic implants for the state to track them. Whatever happened to the idea that in the future we'd have so much technology that we'd barely have to work, the machines would do it all? Everybody Tina knew was just working, working, working. She never had time to hang out any more. She felt like she was endlessly swimming through life, and for every moment where she got a bit of respite, where the waves lulled, there was one where they were slapping her in the face, splashing over her head, filling her nose with sputtering water. And eventually she'd wear out and go under. Submission. Like the heat, the unnatural heat, global warming turning the air into sandpaper, slowly and inexorably baking us all. The pressure was dropping on Tina, and she could feel it.

The world was at once more futuristic than she'd ever thought she'd see and more medieval than she'd ever believed it could go back to. People using technology that wasn't even imagined when she was a kid… to post screeds arguing that evolution was a myth, to argue that the sun revolved around the Earth, to argue for holy war and torturing the enemy sluts, perverts, and infidels to death. A high-tech Burning Times. And the worst thing was that these people had *power*. More power than she'd ever have.

Sometimes she felt like she'd committed a grievous sin against her children by bringing them into this world. Forgive me, God. She'd stopped going to church at fourteen. That was yet another cause of friction with her family. It was the story of Abraham and Isaac. God wanted to test Abraham's faith, the nun explained, and his faith was so strong that he was willing to sacrifice what he loved most. That didn't make sense to her, even though the nun said God wasn't really going to go through with it, it was only a test.

If God really loved you, He wouldn't ask you to kill your kid. That belief got more solid as she lived. Nothing comes between me and my kids. I'm Mama Lion, expecting anything else was an abusive loyalty test. Barrington had gotten severely Rasta on her after she got pregnant with Damian. Told her to stop wearing revealing clothes, to stay home with the baby, "That is your proper role." Get fucked, she'd told him. Who do you think you are? You sound like a schoolmaster. I was wearing a short skirt when you met me. You called me "one sexy dawta." And now you just want me to stay out of sight so you can chase other women.

Underend stayed in that night. The four walls were depressing, but going out alienated him. Watching rich kids get drunk, there was no one even close to his age in the clubs, and everyone looked well scrubbed. Even the half-scruffy ones looked like they'd never been an outsider, never stepped off the school-office track.

He felt less alone at home, though not by much. He turned the amp on low and practiced a bit, playing along with the old record. He wasn't on, he was clumsy, struggling to keep his fingers rocking steady, but the riffs were starting to slip into place.

The phone rang. Tina.

"Hi, how ya doin'?"

"Okay, I guess. I took the kids to my aunt in Queens. I just got back."

Awkward small talk before they got into the deeper issues. "So you coming to practice tomorrow?" she asked.

"Yeah, it's at Scott's at four. You know how to get there?"

"It's by the J train, right? That's not too bad from here." Then she dropped the question. "Why didn't you quit when I did?"

"I should have. Jack and Jen were pissing on me from day one, like they already knew which way the power lines were running. I knew it was over in my heart but I wasn't ready to deal with it. I couldn't leave. What else did I have besides the band? So I just got deeper into getting fucked up. I was running away from a lot of things."

"I felt like you betrayed me. We were tight. You didn't back me up. Why didn't you stick up for me?"

Silence. Fraught with danger. Underend could feel his shoulders shrinking into a turtle shell. He tried to figure a way to crawl out without saying something that would terminally piss her off.

Tina filled the vacuum. "It was like you were out there pretending, promoting a phony version of our band. We were supposed to stand for something real. And the music sucked. That last record was so lame I can't stand to listen to it. And you were so out of it, you were in such a cloud, nobody could talk to you, you didn't care you were ruining our reputation."

"I can't disagree with ya. It did suck. And I really did care, I just couldn't deal with it. I can't remember makin' that record, except in my daymares." He lit a cigarette, exhaled long and slow. "Look, I was fucked up back then. I can't make excuses. I've been sober for eight years now. I'm trying. I'm still fucked up, but I'm tryin.'"

She laughed.

"Y'know, all I wanted was to crawl into a shell. When I was a teenager I had a fantasy that the perfect life would be lying in a hospital bed getting a blowjob while on a morphine drip. The perfect continuous pleasure, and I wouldn't have to do anything."

"Life isn't like that. You wanna fuck, you gotta engage with the world."

"Yeah, music got me outta being like that, but then I had to crawl back in." He toked the cigarette a couple times. "That's why I wanna do this. What else we got going on in our lives? I got nothin'. I just don't want any bullshit."

"So do you think we can all deal with this like adults? Not like a bunch of little kids fighting nuclear ego wars?"

"I sure as fuck hope so."

Sunday afternoon Underend rode the G train down to practice, staring at the dermatologist ad—"CHEMICAL PEELS: The New Exciting Way to Improve Your Looks"—where the Before picture looked like serial killer Aileen Wuornos' mugshot with a few more zits.

He walked over to Scott's, a block off the Broadway El. Past an old woman with a tray of sugary churros, a street-worn man hawking cigarettes—"Newport, Newport"—like the loose joints of yore. Past a fat kid about 17 sitting on a stoop chanting rhymes, "I got a thing/ Hangin' under my shirt/And when I pull the trigger/Some bitch get hurt." Wearing a Mets cap embroidered with multiple images of denimed booty, he sounded like he was looking for approval from his friend but the other kid was oblivious, lost in the jumping pixels of a Nintendo DS.

Scott had a loft on the third floor of an old thread factory, with a sealed, soundproofed studio in one corner just big enough for his drums and a couple small amps. Tina walked in, put her guitar down. "I remember when you couldn't walk around this neighborhood if you were white," she said. "Squawk used to have a place out here, and Ariel said once you were in, you were in for the night. You didn't even go out for orange juice."

"Wasn't just whites," Scott said. "Winston Smith got robbed for a custom-made guitar—you remember that weird metal one he had? It had no neck, just an aluminum bar and metal tubes instead of frets, I think it was made in Israel. They had a studio in the same building."

"Oh, yeah, Confluence. They were rockin'," Underend contributed. Smith had had a five-piece band that had been the great black-rock hope of Brooklyn back in the day, they had opened for P-Funk and Talking Heads. But when they got signed and their first album didn't crack six figures, the label insisted that the only way to sell a hot black guitar player to the rock audience was in a Hendrixoid power trio. They indicated that no second album would come unless the rhythm guitarist and percussionist departed. The band called the record *Three Fifths*, and the company bought Smith's mystical babble that the title signified a trinity of archetypes and symmetries in the cycle of fifths. But he was severely pissed about having to ditch his friends and lose the polyrhythms, and an A&R guy had overheard him ranting about "we're three-fifths of a band. Like the Constitution said a nigga is three-fifths of a person." The office grapevine soon pegged him "too militant."

"So where are we gonna play?" Underend asked.

"Mick said he could hook up a show at the Arcadia." Tina.

"Fuck the Arcadia," Scott said. "Fuckin' yuppie shithole. I played there last summer, it's like 99 degrees in there, I'm sweatin' bullets, and they wouldn't even give me a beer. I'm like, 'I'm in the band,' and they're like, 'Eight dollars.' Most places you play you're the star but there they treat you like a servant."

Mick showed up late, as ever. "Oh, man, the trains are all fucked up today. The A's running local, then the F's running on the A, then the J's out of service in Manhattan. It took me two hours to get here. I had to go all the way out to fuckin' Eastern Parkway/Broadway Junction and come back in."

"They always are on weekends," Tina sympathized. "And for two dollars? It costs me twelve bucks to take the kids anywhere."

Mick had toned down some of his fashionista side. It's hard to have green hair or a Mohawk without calling attention to your receding hairline but he'd adapted. In the late-summer heat, he was wearing a blood-red Chinese suit jacket with embroidered dragons. He checked Tina out. "Put on a little weight, did you?" he asked. She stapled him with her eyes.

"How long have you been going out with women?" she asked coldly.

Mick did the math. "Almost forty years now. Damn, that's a long time."

"And you haven't learned that you NEVER say anything to a woman that even hints she's the slightest bit fat? Even if her ass is bigger than the planet Uranus, you don't say it."

"Sorry, I was just making an observation. The ravages of time."

"I know. And I don't need you to remind me."

Scott rapped the snare three times. Testing the tone, tightening the lugs, but also a not very subliminal shut-up, don't-start-with-this-bullshit-now message. Underend plugged his bass in, hit a note. It was too thin. Turned up the low end on the amp. Better. It fed back a bit, so he turned away from the speaker.

He rolled into the intro to "Radioactive Jellybeans." A simple, trashy punk tune, a classic Class of '81 I-III-VII riff, hanging and whirring on one chord and then crashing through two quick, choppy changes to spin it back to the top. It fuckin' exploded. Tina jumped into "Let's Submerge" and it was rocky, their fingers were rusty, stumbling off the traintrack pace but it felt good. A recording would have been embarrassing but the spirit was there.

They missed the sensations like an old lover. Hands and wrists smacking sticks on cast bronze, the drab brown rug under the kit scented with beer. Bass fingers driving like a subway train. The exorcism of screaming out your pain and rage, and the adolescent pleasure in rude and cool noises. This guitar sound is like a semi downshifting on a mountain road in Pennsylvania; this one like a chainsaw cutting through fallen tree trunks; this one like a cat having its tail pulled by a psychotic three-year-old. Speed and ecstasy and getting possessed. You needed it. You forgot how much you needed it until you got it.

"We gotta practice all out," Mick said. "Do it like we're on stage. Don't stop, don't slack off. We gotta work at playing at that level of intensity. Stamina."

They ran through a set and took a break. Mick gulped water and spieled about business. "You remember Rob? He's gonna be booking us. Alan said he'd help us out whatever way he could but it's better to have someone on the East Coast doing it, someone on the ground here. He's working at a music-licensing agency now—they find songs for movies and video games and put them in—but he's got enough connections to do us on the side. I can talk to some of the people in the clubs who remember us, they like the personal touch but Rob can take care of the details and close the deal."

No one noticed the evaporation of Alan and his promised powerhouse. The substitution seemed reasonable. Underend had deeper worries anyway.

"So who's gonna come see us? Who's left? Who gives a shit about rock'n'roll now?" he asked.

"You do." Tina.

"Yeah, it's coming out of your pores." Scott.

"Rock'n'roll's like Martin Luther King. He was a James Brown fan." Mick.

"Really?"

"Yeah, Brown did a benefit for the civil rights movement in Mississippi, and King and Stokely Carmichael skipped out on a meeting to go. But like I was saying, now that he's safely dead, all the people who hated his guts when he was alive, who called him a troublemaker and an agitator and wanted to kill him, now they make him a plaster saint."

Yeah, Mick was right. Music that was once sexy and rebellious was now a ritual for the stolid and conservative, muzak to suck people into buying rebellious cars and sexy detergent. A cliché. A museum piece, venerated by the people who wanted to squash it when it was real. Even politicians liked it.

"I mean, some senator, he says he's a Doors fan. A fuckin' Republican anti-abortion Doors fan, what's wrong with this picture? Can you imagine that stiff motherfucker getting up in front of a $2,000-a-plate fundraiser, in front of all those fat-cat lawyers and lobbyists and stockbrokers, and going 'Father? Yes, son. I want to kill you'? Or 'You wanna see my cock? How fuckin' bad?' What do you do to make it real? And fresh?"

"But there's still something real about it," interrupted Scott.

Yeah, thought Underend, the wailing guitars and the crash of the drums, the moment when everything clicks in and makes you want to kick out the jams.

"Yeah, like sex sells everything from beer to foot doctors," Mick continued.

Underend flashed back to last night. Sitting in front of the TV watching a porn DVD and trying to jack off. He couldn't. His dick didn't get beyond half-mast. Well, the disc wasn't too inspiring. Artificial women with razor-burned pubes and twats like open wounds. Even the scene with the punk girl didn't do it—the one with black lipstick and spiky, pouffed-out hair, unsnapping her bustier on the staircase of a San Fernando Valley McMansion. She was fucking some guy with a Mohawk and a make-the-poseur-bitch-suffer attitude. Underend's dick felt like overcooked ziti. Or maybe it was all the drugs he was on. Or maybe just the fuckin' light's gone out. Period. There were next to no romantic or sexual possibilities in his life. Maybe Angeline, but she was far too much of a mess.

What people want from porn is vicarious ecstasy, he thought. Same thing they want from rock'n'roll. His ex, Amanda, had once told him that the expression on his face when he was fucking her was the same one he had when he was really getting into it onstage. But they can't imagine the ecstasy without seeing the performers race through permutations. Maybe that's what people really want: whatever they're told is cool, whatever is flashed before their eyes to play on their reptilian brain strings. They like the imitation better than the real thing, more than being alive in places the dollar couldn't reach.

"It's for sale everywhere," Mick went on. "They got the billboard with the chick's purple ass hangin' out over Houston Street but that ain't gonna make people stop fucking, stop them from bumping and humping and pumping."

"You sound like Andre Williams," Scott interjected.

"Yeah, we got his album on the jukebox in the bar. The one with 'Pussy Stank'—"

"Like good marijuana," Scott finished the riff. The two giggled and high-fived.

"What are you, in eighth grade?" Tina remonstrated.

"No, it's not like that." Scott. "It's like they say it smells but we love it. Shit, Tina, with all the weed you smoke, if we went by a dead skunk on the highway, you'd probably go, 'Smells like good herb.' "

"Seriously," Mick tried to put his message back on track. "You know how when you were young and you got a job and you saw the old people there, the middle-aged lifers, and you thought, fuck, I am NEVER going to get trapped like this, in this dead-end life where the most exciting thing in your day is getting pizza or a burger for lunch and figuring out what you're going to watch on TV at night? We're them now. People are looking at us like that, at me pouring drinks or Underend answering phones, that's all they see of us. But fuck that, I'm not just anyone, I am somebody."

He was making sense, channeling the spirits of Jesse Jackson and Stiv Bators. Us middle-aged motherfuckers are struggling, squirming, screaming, writhing against the tightening bonds of nine-to-five work and bodily decrepitude. How do people too rebellious or dysfunctional to fit in the corporate world, the ones who didn't want to fit in that world anyway, the ones who found a place for their spirits going against that world, manage when the dream is over? What do they do with their revolutionary zeal and missionary egomania?

"So we're gonna come back from the dead and make some noise, stir some shit up, and in the process we're going to get some props for ourselves that we never got and we deserve."

"So where we gonna play?" Scott put in.

"We're gonna tour, man, we're gonna go all over the fuckin' country and show 'em who we are." Mick was flying like a bipolar bear over the Arctic icecap.

"Wait a minute. I told you I can't leave my kids." Tina tried to keep it grounded.

"What about the mission? We've got a mission to make our mark, to change the world. Not some small-time shit to distract people for a few seconds before they go back to work on Monday morning… Before we go back to work on Monday morning. Are you admitting defeat?"

"Yes, I am." Underend interposed. "If I jump out the fuckin' window because I think I should be able to fly and that gravity is just one of society's stupid rules, I'm gonna end up impaled on a fence with a wrought-iron spike up my ass. And I gotta watch myself. I can't be somewhere where I'm gonna start using, getting fucked up again. So let's do something where we're not gonna crash and burn, okay?"

"You think all of society's shit—all the stupid music biz you-gotta-be-this-to-be-commercial crap, you're a useless eater if you're not working all the time—is as much a law as gravity? That's weak. That's fuckin' chickenshit. You can't just submit to that," Mick argued.

"I've got kids." Tina. "And you might not understand it, but I'm the only parent they've got. I wanna do this again but they need a mom. Around."

Mick suppressed the urge to say something snotty about her past taste in men. What she had seen in Ricky Steam was beyond him—he'd been one of the trainload of Johnny Thunders wannabes on the scene, didn't care about anything beyond the mirror, if he'd been in L.A. he would have been in a hair-metal band. Anyway, he was dead of an overdose of Jack Daniel's and dope sometime in the mid-'90s.

"C'mon." Scott. "It would be nice if we could all do this and pay our rent but that's like hittin' the lottery. I'm not gonna go sleep on people's couches for two months and come back to find the landlord's padlocked my place and put all my tools for sale up on Craigslist. I thought we said we were just gonna do local shows, maybe go out for a couple weekends. I mean, I can't piss off work and cancel all my jobs. Tina's gotta get her kids to school, Underend's workin', too. Yeah, I wanna do this, but we can't act like a fuckin' stupid hippie blowing pot smoke in a cop's face 'cause he thinks weed should be legal."

Underend stepped out of the office for a cigarette. It was around 3:30 Tuesday, a lull in the calls. The air was heavy and polluted. It was like the entire city had been sealed into a miasma chamber of concrete, car exhaust, and heat-blast. Breathing felt like lifting weights. Here I am adding to it with my little baby cancer stick.

Gino, the new guy, was outside too, a short, skinny pale-olive Puerto Rican with scraggly fragments of beard and black eyes like orbs of wrath under his backwards BRONX baseball cap. He leaned on his bike with an unlit Kool in his hand. Underend offered him a light.

"Bitch wanted my fingerprints," he started in.

"What?"

"I had a job in the mailroom, J.M. Young, you know them? Twelve bucks an hour and benefits. And this bitch from Human Resources comes in, tells us all they're gonna—what's that word?—outsource us, they're turning the department over to a private contractor and they'll hire us all back at nine bucks. I said, 'What the fuck? I got a wife and baby,' and she says, 'The company has very generously recommended that you all be rehired by the new contractor. We're protecting your job for you. That's more than fair.' Fuckin' robot bitch.

"And then she says we all have to get fingerprinted, and I ask why, and she says, 'It's part of the procedure. Because you're employees of an outside contractor who will be handling sensitive company correspondence, and we need to verify your identities.' The fuck? I been workin' there eight months, you know who I am. And then she puts her hand on my arm and says, 'C'mon, You-jean-ee-oh. It only takes a minute. It doesn't hurt.'

"Fuck that! I say, 'I'm a working man. I don't steal, I don't rob, I don't sell drugs. I'm a working man,' and she waves to this faggot rent-a-cop, and he says, 'You're trespassing. You have five minutes to get your stuff and leave or you'll be arrested.'

"I'm a go back there. I'm a go back there with my boxcutter and put it up that bitch's throat. 'It's 9/11, mothafucka, I'm flyin' this plane!' I'm a chop that rent-a-cop's faggot ass into hamburger. Cuidado con esa hacha, Eugenio!"

Underend sympathized, but the dude's fury unsettled him, had a psycho edge that could lash out and slash anyone within range on any imagined provocation, a streetwalking creature with a squirt gun full of nitroglycerin. "Hey, if you're gonna go out like that, do it to the CEO. He's the head asshole in charge. The others are just stooges."

"Fuck them. They're the ones in my face talkin' bullshit. But if it makes ya happy, I'm a go back there with a motherfuckin' bat and pound that chump's bald head like I'm Carlos Beltran."

"Yeah, but the way the Mets are goin' these days, you'd probably swing and miss."

"Ha ha, that's funny, man." Gino slapped him five. They finished their cigarettes and went back in.

Underend felt the same way a lot. A lot of rage in the city. Pressure building on him and everyone he knew, like a steaming ghetto block five minutes before the clouds go off and the sky goes black and the rain blasts down like a Birmingham firehose. Every bang of a construction crane, pounding together yet another yuppie habitat, Titanium Towers or HedgeFund Heaven, felt like it was hammering into his head. Hammering in a message: *You don't belong here anymore. You can't afford it. We've taken over.*

Fuck you. This is my city. I was born here. But the pressure was dropping on him. All around. Helter Skelter coming down. Getting back with the band had awakened something. He was practicing again, feeling it. When he was a kid, he was painfully shy. Getting fucked up was the only way he could talk to people, when he didn't give a shit because nothing could hurt him. The band brought him out of that. Then it got fucked up and he had to black it out. Then that didn't work any more. It had been a moment rare and fleeting, when they all seemed to flow in tune and in time, each lick and action generating more, growing and proliferating. He should have appreciated it more. He'd been settled into a depressive rut, living on a narrow plane, passively accepting a dull isolation. He needed to crack the barriers. Break through the terminal stasis. That meant love, too. The ecstasy of sex, getting into a different state of matter, burning green plasmatic fire, then cooling down to a slow-glowing intimacy, like someone to cuddle up and watch movies and drink coffee with in the morning, to be clumsy and spacy together. That looked a long way off.

Tina was going through the same thing. These days she was hesitant to take what Patti Smith called "the big plunge." She wanted to know what lay below: shoals and rocks and shallow stagnant waters, whether she was diving into the Caribbean or the Gowanus Canal. When she was younger it was easier. Pounded by the surf at Rockaway—yeah, the bus ride *was* too slow—luxuriating in a low-tide lull at Coney Island, or braced by the chill of an upstate lake, it was all enticing. Now she remembered the time she took the kids camping upstate and they were all running and jumping across a six-foot-wide ditch. Damian was around six, Janis thirteen. She'd trotted up to the edge, then pulled up and stopped. "Ma, you're chicken," they'd teased. But she'd had visions of sprained ankles in her head, of walking on crutches for weeks.

They practiced again Wednesday night. Tina asked Janis if she'd mind watching Damian. No, she said. "Ma, it's good you're doing this. You've gotta do something for yourself. You need a life."

Alice, Scott's wife, made a pot of coffee while the band trickled in. Tina asked Gene what he'd been listening to. Hip-hop and old soul, he said. "It's the beat we move to on the street, on the subway. It's not something that was old when y'all were my age, but the best stuff is underground."

Mick showed up last. "I stopped off at CB's, and Hilly said he'd definitely give us a show before they close."

"Cool."

"Good."

"What the fuck is going on in the neighborhood? It looks like a fuckin' mall!" Mick had switched modes out of nowhere. "I thought I was lost, with all the highrises around CB's. I didn't recognize it. And I walked all the way down from St. Marks and didn't see one single Puerto Rican till I got half a block from Delancey. They got this blue building full of Wall Street guys in suits having their after-work drinks, it looks like the fuckin' South Street Seaport."

"That's what's happening." Scott. "All over the city."

"Where the fuck do all these people come from?" Mick.

"It's insane." Tina. "I don't know who has that kind of money."

"No, it's not insane. It's just cold." Underend surprised himself with his sternness. "Insane is when you're fucked up, bipolar or depressed or whatever, schizophrenic, and believe the aliens are amplifying your brain and if you think bad thoughts you're gonna send nuclear missiles shaped like dicks to blow up your mother's house in Canarsie. These people know what they're doing. Sociopaths. They got no feeling for people. They saw the territory they wanted and they took it. That's why they kicked us out of the squat, like we were the Indians. There were fuckin' riot cops with serious guns all around the block. We fuckin' fixed that building up from nothing, and they said we were 'nihilistic elements hindering progress in the neighborhood.' Now it's like $3 grand for a place in there, except they got a few token ones they say are 'affordable units.' They aren't crazy. They know exactly what they're doing."

"I'm going to Bushieworld," Mick interjected, stretching his arms out like a wide receiver jubilating out of the end zone. "These fuckin' fascist fuckwits, I couldn't make this shit up, you'd think I was making stuff up that couldn't possibly happen. Giving a gay hooker from hotmilitarystuds-dot-com White House press credentials under his porn name—that's like fuckin' Caligula putting his horse in the Roman Senate. It's like they're deliberately pissing on people and no one's got the guts to say so. It's like they had a state dinner for the president of France and served chou-fleur a la merde."

"What's shoe-floor?"

"Cauliflower a la shit. And then their PR flack would say it was the finest products of the American heartland's animal husbandry."

Fuckin' Mick, you had to love him even when he wouldn't shut up. He was deep into spiel now. "It's how Jews stay fuckin' sane. When a positive attitude would be pathetically naïve, and a negative attitude would be obnoxious and destructive, a sense of humor is a good thing to have. Black people sing the blues; Jews tell sick jokes. 'Judenschwein filth! Get in that shower! Mach schnell!' 'Ah, a little Irish spring. No, I smell almonds, it must be Dr. Bronner's Magic All-One.' But sometimes there's no way out, you just gotta fuckin' scream."

That's what the music was for, the old slogans: *Beauty will be convulsive or not at all. Poetry is puked, not plotted.* Well, we did refine it some, we didn't just get up there and spew. That's what practice was for, to be on instead of wanking, to get solid enough so we could let loose instead of struggling to hang on, to build a launching pad so we could explode and burn, not sputter and squib.

There was more to it than designing a website to sell band t-shirts, linking up on Facebook, putting up video clips on YouTube. That was sophisticated TV, everyone alone in their little rat-cubes tethered to the electronic feeding tube, insulated and isolated. You needed to do it in person. Be with others. See it, feel it. Community. Communion. In a room full of bodies and noise, where you could put it out and get something back, the heathen church of amplifiers and stale beer, magic-marker runes on the walls. When it was good you felt renewed, when it was spectacular you were reborn.

It was happening. They were on. They were getting good again. Back in the bicycle saddle, back in the New York groove. Catching the noise, the rhythms of battery and clattery, the grind and rasp and twang, the distortion and spaces and thumps. It was starting to feel like music, not like them struggling to keep up with what they used to be. They didn't have any new songs but the old ones felt alive.

"Another one like this and we'll be fit for public consumption," Scott cracked, in an I-'ope-we-passed-the-audition voice.

The other three took the train in different directions, Underend north, Mick west, Tina southwest. She was fried but it felt good. It was close to eleven when she got off the train. She lugged her guitar down the long rickety stairs from the El and trudged the six blocks home, past the all-night bagel shop, the Polish and Mexican delis sandwiching a pizzeria, frayed posters in Hebrew, the CVS, and the Russian drugstore advertising orthopedic shoes. There were only a couple people out. She was anticipating curling up on the couch with a bowl of herb and one of the cats purring on her chest, zoning out on some entertainingly inane TV, giggling at the ads' surreal absurdity.

The kids had left the kitchen a mess. The frying pan and pot sat on the stove, caked with drying sauce and calcifying spaghetti, the enamel spattered with oil and burnt onion fragments. Shit. I told Janis to cook dinner for Damian. They knew they were supposed to clean up. I'm not the fuckin' maid here.

"Janis?" she called.

No answer. The door to her room was ajar. Dark but candle-lit. Janis was strumming her guitar and singing, a tune bouncy like Motown, but with a desolate feel, like she was miniscule and abandoned. It sounded familiar, but it took Tina a moment to recognize it. Oh yeah, "Back to Black" from the Amy Winehouse album Janis liked.

She must have broken up with her boyfriend, Tina thought. That kid, Jason, the one who looked like a scrubby little Bob Marley. Janis was bigger than him. Tangled dreadlocks, yellow-olive skin, duct tape covering the logo on his sneakers, always wrapped in an Army jacket with an English Subhumans patch. He wasn't even born when that band was out. He seemed like a nice kid, seemed like he respected Janis, but he also looked depressed with a perpetually pained face, a stray with the agonized dark eyes of Jesus.

Janis felt crushed and insignificant. A tiny penny indeed. A tiny penny on the subway track. I miss him, she was thinking. He'd listened to her, acted like she had ideas worth talking about. She felt smarter around him. When he was wasted, she could tell. He'd deny it, but there was a wall around him and he'd get angry if she asked what was wrong. "Nothing!" he'd snap.

She loved his idealism, his intensity about how the world needed to be changed but it was a dangerous subject. "We're not gonna live to be forty," he'd rant. "None of us. We're gonna be the last generation. The fuckin' glaciers are melting. The fucking polar bears are gonna fall off the ice and drown. The city's gonna be under fifteen feet of water. And nobody's doing anything to stop it. Nobody. They're just going to continue shopping and driving their fuckin' gas-guzzling SUVs and eating their overprocessed lardburgers while we slowly destroy ourselves as a species and the entire fucking planet." When he got into these apocalyptic one-track rants she couldn't stop him. None of her love could distract him, never mind save him. And they inevitably meant he was going for the pills, plunging into a fog of vicodin or xanax or chewing oxycontin.

They were supposed to go out last Saturday night. She'd gone to the Village, waited under the marquee at West Third Street, like a fool. He hadn't showed. The robot-woman's voice kept telling her, "Your call has been forwarded to an automatic voice-messaging system," pause, and then his voice would come on, "Jason Silva," and then the robot-woman, "Is not available." She hadn't wanted to leave too many messages, didn't want to be too possessive like a stalker but she was pissed. He'd called the next day to say he'd fallen asleep with his cellphone turned off. Then Kayla told her she'd seen him in Prospect Park with his ex, Michelle, on Sunday morning. That zitty little bitch who stole her mom's migraine painkillers. *She'd* have something to share with him.

Janis had extracted a confession. The details grossed her out like worms emerging from a sick cat's ass. How he'd run into Michelle, gone over her house, gotten high, and passed out. And… And nothing, he said. No. And… no … that wasn't all. That made two things he loved more than me.

That would make a good song title. She laughed for the first time in days. She noodled at the guitar, playing around with the chords from "Back to Black." Tina came in and Janis told the story.

"Janis, I'm sorry this happened, but it's better you find out now.

Some men just aren't worth you."

"Ma! How can you be so casual! You know how much he hurt me, and you just flip me off like that?"

Tina pondered, trying to phrase what she really meant. She felt a breath of empathy for the men she'd known who'd fumbled in fear of saying a fatally wrong word, like Underend the other night. "I know it's hard, it means a lot to you. I'm not going to deny it means a lot. It doesn't get any easier either when you get older but don't let him ruin your life. His problems aren't your fault. It's not your fault if they're bigger than you."

Mick flew back to L.A., promising to set up six shows for November. That meant Tina and Underend needed amps big enough to gig with. "Go small," Scott told them. "You don't have hundreds of dollars to spend. And get something you can carry. You don't have the back to carry a fuckin' refrigerator, and you don't need one anyway."

Underend checked out Secret Guitars, a few blocks away, on his lunch hour. Mike Segretti, the owner, remembered him but they didn't have much in the way of bass gear. There was a new Ampeg B-15. It was the sweetest amp he'd played on in years and louder than the old ones, but it cost almost $1,700.

He and Billy lingered outside the office at closing time. The sun glowed red in the smoky orange sky to the west, a tinge of fall in the air, the streets choked with cars bound for Jersey and Westchester. Underend toked on a cigarette, trying to keep it going before the wind blew the ash off. A middle-aged black man with baby dreadlocks neared, his army jacket overgrown with Rasta and Vietnam-vet patches, three long feathers rising from his brown fedora.

"Bird lives," Billy called out. The man laughed and slapped him five, then strolled on, squawking at the sparrows, cooing at the pigeons, cawing at the crows. The suited yuppies stared in contempt—weren't all these people supposed to have been locked up, gotten off the streets?— and the Latino construction workers gaped in bemusement. ¡Que loco norteamericano!

"Who the fuck was that?"

"The West Side Birdman. You never saw him? He goes around

talking to the birds. You just gotta talk to him in his own language."

Janis came up, bopping down the straight street to the piano of the Fiery Furnaces, parting the waves of people, swaying crookedly to the song's chorus. A Middle Eastern fruit peddler made her think of Damascus computer cafes, rows of little bearded guys and women in headscarves pecking away at little black monitor screens. She unhooked her earbuds. "Hey," she said to Underend and Billy. "I wanna get my mom an amp. Can you help?" She'd conceived the plot and worked extra shifts at Starbucks to save up for it. Billy said he'd walk her over to Secret Guitars.

They found a used Fender Blues Junior. Billy said it was perfect. And Mike remembered the Gutter Astronomers. "Your mom's Tina? Ya know, it's funny, the bass player—Underend, ya know him?—was just in here before. I'll tell ya what. Pay cash, I'll give it to ya for $250." Janis put down a deposit.

Underend, meanwhile, headed down to the new Music Planet superstore in Union Square. The people at the door, twentyish rocker types, said hi. He couldn't tell if they were being friendly or if they'd been told to, like Walmart greeters in Ramones t-shirts. One wall of Les Pauls, one wall of hollowbody guitars that were either $300 or $3,000, supermarket pyramids of Marshall practice amps. The bass stuff was in the back. Most of it was toys, little sweatshop-manufactured amps for kids banging away in their bedrooms. Nothing there either. Scott said he'd check Craigslist. They found an amp in the neighborhood for $250. Scott came over to help him check it out. The seller lived in one of the new buildings off McCarren Park. Oe building looked like a New Jersey Turnpike chemical refinery crossed with a Florida condo. Another was neoconservative architecture, flat, curvy decorations suggesting the colonial era pasted onto the monolithic concrete surface of a corporate-Stalinist edifice. The large smooth squares were a long way from the urban soul of bricks laid and stone carved by Irish and Italian immigrants one hundred years ago.

"Look at this cheap shit," Scott monologued as they entered the hallway. "They just slapped it together, and these people are paying an arm and a leg for it. This thing's gonna collapse in thirty years."

The guy answering the door was in his mid-twenties and wearing a

Van Halen tour shirt with the baby on it. The apartment was tiny with brightly polyurethaned floors, dominated by a flat-screen TV on one wall and a large computer sound system on the other. "You were in an '80s band?" he asked. "Cool." Underend and Scott flashed disparaging eyerolls at each other.

The amp he was selling was a Gallien-Krueger combo, a classic '80s bass amp, good-sounding but small. They tried to talk him down to $200. He said he'd throw in an extension speaker if they did it for $225. "I don't need it, I don't play out anymore. I just do stuff on the computer."

"Perfect," Scott said. It was loud enough to play with drums and small enough so Underend could carry each part with one hand.

Janis shanghaied Damian into the city on the pretext of taking him to the movies. "We're not going to the movies," she informed him on the way to the train. "We're going to get Ma a present."

"That's lying," Damian protested.

"No, it isn't, it's keeping a secret. Like, if you asked, 'Ma, are you getting me an Xbox?' and she says no, and then she gets you one for Christmas, is she lying to you? No. It's not hurting you. You can't tell someone when you're getting them a present."

She paid off the layaway and got Damian to help her carry it home.

Tina was floored. Her eyes were full. It wasn't the money, the material value. It was like appreciation for all the years of raising the kids and missing out on her own music. And how many extra shifts had Janis worked to do this? They stayed in that night and played, Janis with her acoustic, Tina electric with the new amp, trying different songs. Janis had gotten into Jimmie Rodgers through Johnny Cash, so they sang his version of "Frankie and Johnny," catching each other's eyes on the last verse and laughing emphatically.

This story has no moral
This story has no end
This story just goes to show
There ain't no good in men.

Something banged, out of rhythm. They couldn't tell if it was their imagination, if the neighbors were stomping, or if it was the door. Then the door rapped, clearly. Tina got up. She heard the staticky chatter of a police radio. She checked quickly to see she hadn't left any pot paraphernalia in plain view and opened the door. The young black cop looked mildly surprised to see a middle-aged woman. "Ma'am, we've got a complaint about the loud music."

It always happens like this, she thought. It's not how loud you are. You get the noise complaint when you're really getting into it.

Chapter 6
The '90s

New Year's Eve was bumping as usual. On Avenue B and Bushwick Avenue the liquor stores did rush-hour business, spinning legions of champagne and cognac bottles through the bulletproof glass. In Washington Heights bars named the Quisqueya and the El Mocambo bustled and bailandoed to the palpitating horns of merengue, women in ruffled burgundy dresses percolating to the jukebox. Across the river in the Bronx an eleventh floor apartment in the Highbridge Houses pulsed with hip-hop, the walls rimmed with red and blue Christmas lights, a spirit tensed temporarily by the arrival of eight thugged-out boys in fat down jackets, a posse moving as one sinister unit, until the rising beef got damped by the hostess's uncle passing around a blunt. In a six-room apartment in Flatbush a subway track cleaner and a nurse's aide stuffed the kids into the back bedroom and the coats on the bed in another one, then the front thumped with dancehall, chattering 'pon mic until the mix tape segued down into McFadden and Whitehead's "Ain't No Stoppin' Us Now." In a converted meat locker on the cobblestoned reaches of the far Village waterfront, three hundred hunky young men jacked their bodies to house music, the beat and the lights and the liquor exorcising the weariness of the old year, ringing in hopes for the new one. All over the city people were ten-nine-eighting, couples and acquaintances and strangers exchanging quick pecks and long kisses of drunkenness or love, women in silver shoes wobbling and reveling on the sidewalks despite the cold dust of light rain.

Underend scoured the streets and clubs of the East Village and Lower East Side, bass on his shoulder, looking for a drink, love, someone to kiss, someone to jam with, someone to help him remember who he was. It was the first New Year's Eve he hadn't had a gig since 1979. He felt unmoored. One drink, one more, then another. His eyes soft-focused. In CBGB the only people he knew were on the door or behind the bar. Midnight came in Pluto. A zaftig woman in a fake fur coat kissed him hard, straining the roots of his tongue with her booze-tasty lips. They made out for about five minutes, then she broke it off and went to the bathroom. When she came out she told him to leave her alone.

He wandered more, latching into a basement somewhere south of Houston. Music smoked up from under the sidewalk. He inched down the slippery steps, entered a dank room with picnic benches along the walls and a makeshift bar, three bottles of liquor and a garbage can full of ice and beer. About thirty shadows drinking, talking in each other's ears. He got a drink. Busy, jivey, neo-'70s riff rock hammered, resounding off the concrete. The band was set up at the far end, on the floor. Young dudes, strutting their new tail feathers on this baby-step walk, especially the singer and lead guitarist. Not long off the boat from Minneapolis or Mineola, their mall-rocker roots showing. Underend felt ancient and jaded. He sat in with them on a version of "Whole Lotta Love" that warped into "Whole Lotta Rosie." Emerged into an opaque-orange sky and staggered home.

The year before had been a whirling blur of disasters. The end of the band. He'd celebrated his thirtieth birthday in November by copping two bags of dope and a pint of vodka, shuffled through the back of the Voice looking for a show to go out to... nothing. Decided to take a bath, put a tape on in the boombox on top of the refrigerator, nodded out in the kitchen tub. Woke up with the water cold and the cassette tangled and sputtering. Lou Reed's *Berlin*. The most depressing album ever made. He contemplated how the Gillette Trac II on the edge of the sink would feel biting into his wrist. Were you supposed to cut across the veins or lengthwise? Which way was serious and which way was poseur? That was an untapped market for razor-blade companies. The Bic Fini. The Schick Slitto. They could pitch the smooth painless way it sliced into the median antibrachial veins. The Lady Sylvia. What a thrill, your wrist instead of an onion. Magazine pages of alabaster-pallid Goth chicks with wavy raven hair reposing on porcelain with a delicate crimson web. On the other hand, they probably wouldn't get too many repeat customers.

"Personal and musical differences," the official reason for a million band breakups. What it means is when you're in a room with the people you've played with for years and none of you can stand a single note the other plays, every breath you take is inhaling their exclusive oxygen, every breath they take is exhaling toxic gas. In a bad marriage there's always dirt, and every insult and slight is permanently inscribed in the Book of Memory, ready for recall. Fucking Mick and his fucking lead-singer ego. All about him and his fucking star trip, me-me-me, people come to see me, this band is about me, your job is to showcase my performance. That last album was excruciating even to think about. You guys are my backup band. Fucker actually said that. And fucking Jen and Jack, looking at me like they made the band and I was dead wood, dead weight, old baggage long beyond its six-months-to-be-donated-to-charity date.

Sixteen and trying to cop the riffs to *All the Young Dudes*, *Exile on Main Street*, *Rock'n'Roll Animal* in his room on Long Island with the old blue-sparkle bass, that cheapo Univox. What would he have said to see himself burning it up at CB's, in San Francisco, L.A., Detroit, laying down tracks in the studio womb of headphones, gray carpet baffles, and the mixing board, knobs rowed out like an electronic wheat field? And then doing the last year or two in a total greyout. He'd gotten to live out the dream—and fucked it up in ways he'd never imagined possible. Be careful what you wish for.

The alarm went off. Seven o'clock. Seven sharp swords searing into his skull. Why the fuck is it going off Saturday morning? Oh, yeah, gotta get Gene. Scott had overloaded on the Guinness last night at Rhonda's, played the longest pool game in the history of the bar, losing to a guy who fell on his ass three steps after he finally sank the eight-ball. Now his brain was paying the tab. Okay, gotta get up. Rebecca wanted him to come by early.

He thanked whoever it was who'd invented sunglasses. Gene and his friend Edwin already had their gloves and caps on, jumping and champing to get out and play. He took them to the playground in Tompkins Square, the only open space in the park not closed down and guarded round the clock. He fungoed them flies and grounders. The kids declaimed the Mets batting order like the PA announcer at Shea, "Leading off—the center fielder, number 7, Daryl Boston."

Scott tossed the rubber ball up, swung and missed. "C'mon, Dad, you're supposed to bat lefty," Gene called. Lefty? He swung from the wrong side, nubbed one foul, then tapped a grounder to Edwin. Fortunately, the next one was righty. He hit a one-hopper to Gene.

"Batting third—the left fielder, number 25, Bobby Bonilla." Scott took a hard cut at the ball, missed. The sharp motion jabbed his head with pain. His eyes clenched. He stopped, rubbed his temples. Felt like puking, inhaled, and swallowed to quell it. *Am I a bad father for coming out to play when I'm this fucked up or a good one for doing it anyway?* He tossed the ball up again, was too slow to swing, let it drop.

"C'mon, Dad, get your head in the game!"

The kid was certainly picking up the clichés. It was cute. Once more the spheroid flew. He saw two orbs floating and swung between them. Smacked it with a satisfying sound-of-spring thunk. Well hit to deep right. A high drive over Edwin's head. It rolled under the fence, into the forbidden zone.

"My favorite ball!" Gene cried.

They trekked over to the police mobile command unit, a trailer by the Boys Club on Tenth and A. A sergeant and three officers escorted them to the Ninth Street gate. "You two stay here with them," the sergeant ordered two of the cops, pointing at Scott and Edwin. "You escort the other kid," he told the woman cop. The sergeant unlocked the gate. Gene's ball was under a bush about fifteen feet in.

"Thank you for keeping the park safe from marauding anarchists." Scott turned to see who was talking. An angry black-haired woman pushing a stroller.

"I mean, it could have been a hand grenade." Tina.

"It's always our pleasure to assist the public," the sergeant said. "Have a nice day." He turned his back and left the scene.

"Tina!" They hugged.

"Scott, great to see you. What was that all about?"

"Gene's ball rolled under the fence. They wouldn't let him get it without a police escort."

"Really? He looks like a dangerous criminal. The little thug!" she chuckled. "How old is he now, seven? Wow, he got big."

"Yeah. How old is yours?"

"Janis? She's going to be three in December."

"So how you doin'?" Scott asked. "Are you still with Ricky?"

"No, I broke up with him a long time ago." She turned her head slightly, trying to be halfway discreet in front of Janis. "I got tired of getting stood up every time he was supposed to come over. He'd be like 'ooh, my baby girl' when he did, but most of the time he just wouldn't show. I got sick of it. I told him not to come back if his daughter wasn't important to him. She's his own flesh and blood and he wouldn't make any time for her. He's probably off getting wasted."

"Yeah, I don't wanna say I told you so, but I always thought he was useless. The only thing he loves is the mirror." Scott squeezed his head. The hangover was biting hard. Gene and Edwin were tugging at him, bored. "Ya wanna go get breakfast?"

"We wanna play," the boys whined.

"Yeah, but this is my friend from my old band, and we haven't seen each other in a long time. And I'm tired."

"Why are adults always tired?" Gene wondered.

They went to Odessa, a Ukrainian coffeeshop. Janis banged on the table and spilled the adults' coffee. Gene and Edwin poured sugar into the puddle. "The Okefenokee Swamp!" exclaimed Gene. Edwin stuck a piece of burnt toast into the sludge, calling it "Bayou Billy's house." Tina and Scott got the kids to behave just before Gene added ketchup to the mix. They needed half the napkins in the dispenser to clean up the mess. Still, the coffee and greasy omelet soaked up a good bit of Scott's headache.

Underend bounced around aimlessly, occasionally auditioning for bands, none of which were beyond mediocre. Eventually he latched onto No Name Maddox. They did doomy, dissonant versions of murder ballads, a mix of industrial sludge and country twang. John, the lead singer, was a tall, stringy, sunken-cheeked geezer with dyed-black hair, nubbled charcoal '50s suits, and a rumpled complexion; a Jersey Johnny Cash in the body of a dead and slightly decayed Neil Young. Reed, the guitarist, was a bleached-blonde fireplug, a refugee from a redneck town in northern Pennsylvania.

They boiled up a brew of swamp gunslinger menace, Underend throwing down a four-note bass throb, Reed answering with a one-chord drip and drone. Then a fast one, the drummer pounding a fast piledriver, Reed clatterscratching slide noise. They covered Nick Cave's "Deep in the Woods," slow and grinding—what other way was there?—with Reed sounding like a cross between gale-crashed zinc garbage cans and a pig being slowly strangled, and a fast, sloppy version of "Cocaine Blues." They obeyed neither of that tune's injunctions about what to stay off and what to let be. There was a third intoxicant, one not mentioned in the song, that they shared a taste for, too.

New York is fucked, Mick decided. I'm totally played out here. He put out the tentacles to L.A., got some promises back, and loaded up a red van he bought off an Italian guy in Marine Park. He spun through various bands and projects, getting a nibble here and a nibble there from record companies. There was always "label interest;" it was the fuckin' oxygen any band serious about succeeding breathed out here in smogland. At least he didn't have to do the pay-to-play scene, where bands that coveted the 10:45 slot on a Friday or Saturday on Sunset Boulevard would have to buy a thousand dollars' worth of tickets to guarantee their draw for the showcase. He was too hip for that. So he bounced around the red-upholstered lounges and the little underground shoeboxes and a few of the bigger clubs, writing and rehearsing and trying to pull something together.

He didn't have a problem finding slick musicians. He never had to worry about hearing the snare crack on two and four, a steady stream of notes from the bass, crackling licks from the guitarists, but something about it was off. There was too much sheen and not enough spirit. And the ones with the soul and the sound were either dopefiends or playing in five different bands, especially the bassists and drummers. It was like trying to get with a girl who had five other boyfriends.

He didn't buy the myth that you had to reject commerce to be an artist. That was stupid. There was no other pathway to the public. You had to deal with it if you were serious, but you had to give the people something more than a hustle, had to reach them with something real. You had to forget everything except throwing yourself into it onstage, and then take care of business offstage. That was the beauty and the balance of it that almost nobody seemed to get. Too many guys were all bullshit veneer, like the guitarist who'd given him a spiel about how he wanted to be "alternative."

Alternative? What the fuck was that? Alternative to what? The lamest name for a genre in the entire history of music. New Wave had at least meant something once: it was the artier and poppier bands that came out of the '70s underground and didn't sound like the Dead Boys, before it came to mean "we want the street cred of punk, but we don't want to get their gutter dirt on us." But alternative? That's like Dr. Pepper instead of Coke or Pepsi. Tame and lame.

He couldn't complain that much. He put together a band called Asphalt, slower and doomier than the Gutter Astronomers, a little more Goth and Black Sabbath flavor. He could sing a lot more, stretch his voice high over long, looming notes and pumping fuzz-factory riffs. And after Nirvana blew up in the fall of '91 the record companies were snapping up bands like fat cats let loose in a fish store. Asphalt scored a deal.

They got one album out, did one tour. They fell apart doing demos for the second album. Their first set of songs had come easy but now they couldn't write anything. Whatever grounds they had for collaboration caved in. Mick thought Ron the guitarist's riffs were all infected with cock-rock clichés, and Drew the drummer wanted in, too, strumming rudimentary chords on the guitar to present his mediocre ideas. The musicians were enjoying their bit of success too much, heavy on the booze and coke and light-to-medium on the dope, getting laid a lot and showing up for rehearsals late, hung over, and idealess. I've been down this road before and they haven't, Mick thought. This is when you need to push twice as hard. They don't know what they're in for, how many things you need to go right and how many can go wrong.

He wasn't that far away from forty. He couldn't let this shot get fucked up. But it already was. That's one reason why outcasts made the best rockers, his brain added. Nobody wanted to hang out with them so they had time to practice and they got original because they didn't give a shit about fitting in—they never could.

Asphalt's high point was when Lemmy joined them for an encore of "Killed by Death" at the Roxy. That was beautiful, Mick's sweet-scream tenor weaving over Lemmy's bike-exhaust growl. I got to sing with one of the greats, and I pulled it off.

"We should've done 'Stand By Your Man,'" Lemmy had cracked to him afterward, sharing a drink backstage.

"Yeah, but which one of us woulda been Wendy O?" Mick shot back.

No Name Maddox was playing the Lizard Lounge, a basement on Avenue A. A small catacomb with barrels for barstools and black walls splotched with pink, blue, and green day-glo spots and streaks, it looked like a surfer bar on a beach condemned for toxic waste. They did a sinister version of Jimmie Rodgers' "Gambling Bar Room Blues," a lurchy strut with the guitars crunchy fuzz and screeching slide, harsh and bright like drunk-tank lights. An accidental slayer gets trashed with the cop who should be chasing him, archaic fatalistic for the modern world, John growling the lyrics with a serial killer leer. They had interest from Virtual, so a couple guys from the label came down. The younger one chopped out some lines in the tiny dressing room. He sported a Sonic Youth t-shirt, a black-and-white cartoon of a sunglassed couple with the legend "Within a week, we killed my parents and hit the road."

"Charlie Starkweather," John commented. "America's first rock'n'roll killer. A baby-faced teenager with the look of a demented James Dean. Getting revenge on the world that smacked him down and going out in a bloody blaze of glory. He killed his girlfriend's family and they hung out for a couple days eating potato chips and fucking. Then they stole a car and ran to Wyoming. They put a sign on the door that said, 'Stay A Way Every Body Is Sick with the Flu.' Hey, that would be a good album title, *Stay Away, Every Body Is Sick*."

The deal didn't happen. "I don't know what to do with you," the older one, the A&R man, told John on the phone a couple weeks later. "I don't hear a radio hit and I don't know how to pitch you otherwise."

"An evil twist on Americana? Murder ballads for modern lovers?" John spun for ideas, scratching the wall.

"I'd love to work with you but I have to come up with a hook to get my boss to commit to spending money on the project. And I've been racking my brains trying, but I just can't."

The band didn't believe him. Fuckin' liar. He probably thinks we're too raw, too abrasive. Or too old for teen appeal in the heartland, not like those fucked-up waifs from Seattle, those stoner slobs from SoCal who can't dress for shit but look like Everydude, like they're wearing a bag of dirty laundry. Or as much as they party with us backstage, they're gonna go back to the office the next morning and say we're "too unreliable." With all the fuckin' money they're throwing around. Signing everything in a flannel shirt that ever pissed out a bladderful of Olympia Beer.

Underend went to a bodega near Avenue C to cop. It looked like a bodega, red-and-gold metal awning and windows stacked with soap and olives, candy and beans but when a woman came in with two kids looking to buy bananas and soda, the bananas were rotten and the store didn't have change for a five. Joey Rush was in line ahead of him. Underend nodded hi, not wanting to push it more than that, this wasn't the place for networking. Everyone was on their own private mission.

Joey interrupted. "Yeah, they don't take small bills here, ya know. Hey, you were in what's their names, the Gutter Philosophers? How ya doin'?"

"I'll be good in a couple minutes," Underend answered.

Joey cut to the point. "You were the bass player, right? Hey, do me a solid, okay? I'm doing the Pulaski Hall weekend after next. I need a bass. Buy me a bag and you're on the show. I'll give you five hundred bucks."

Practice was Wednesday but the Lower East Side was dry that day. Joey talked Underend into going up to the Bronx. You can always find something there, he said. They trudged up the hill to Hunts Point, the sidewalk a mosaic of cracked concrete and dog shit, grass and glass punctuated by rusted shopping carts. "The things we do for love," Joey half-sang. "This is where to go when nobody else has anything."

They walked past car carcasses strewn under the Bruckner Expressway, bland beige battered tenements on the far side. Salsa percolated, spiced with horns. Ice cream bells rang, a slow jam version of "Pop Goes the Weasel." White flowers, cake, and tulle announced a baby shower. Teddy bears and glass candles mourned the latest shooting victim. A mother whacked her son upside the head, sending him crashing to the sidewalk. The kid flopped like a basketball player trying to get the referee to call an offensive foul.

Joey knew where to go. An abandoned building, the only one still standing on its block. They paid an extra buck each to get off in a back room, just enough to keep them going for the ride back, saving the big blast for their home turf. They got back forty minutes late for practice, then took another ten to get off.

Backstage. Getting high before the show. The opening band a distant din filtered through the walls. Joey strummed his old Epiphone hollow-body. Played the intro to the Only Ones' "Another Girl, Another Planet" note for note, twangy, restrained, then a buzzy whoosh like a blast of molecules rushing toward the receptors in the brain. Sang about looking sick, flirting with death, and loving being stuck in that extraterrestrial world. "Shit, who does he think he's kidding?" Joey rasped. "It's not a love song to a *girl*, it's a love song to *dope*! But they're all out there. 'Sea of Love.' Nobody over the age of fifteen can fall in love like that. You know what women are like, nobody's a fuckin' perfect love goddess. They're just as fucked up as you and me."

He wasn't telling the whole truth. Half his songs were pining for Maureen Morphine, who'd ditched him for Johnny Thunders in 1977. Sister Morphine, who'd once gone to a show dressed as a nun and carrying a giant syringe. Underend knew it but let the spiel go on.

"But dope, that's another fuckin' story… O.V. Wright, you know him? Fuckin' great soul singer. 'Eight Men, Four Women.' A jury of eight men and four women found me guilty of possession of your love. 'Afflicted.' What do you love so fuckin' much you're afflicted? Yeah, I am, but I don't give a fuck. Nobody's gonna abject themselves and put up with that kind of abuse, you'd ditch the bitch in a minute, but dope? It makes you feel good when nothing else does, and it don't talk back. That's something you'll sacrifice a lot for."

Pierre, Joey's manager, flashed a five-minute sign. He looked sort of like Joey, but where Joey aimed for gutter angel—cultivating what used to be unconscious—Pierre vibed sophisticated creep, like someone who could pour champagne with a courtly flair and an accented compliment and give you a handful of losing lottery tickets for change.

The intro tape rolled. They stumbled out to the stage, cheers rising when the crowd recognized Joey. "How ya doin'," he croaked, then hit the intro to "Smacksie," their speeded-up version of an old New Orleans instrumental by James Booker. Underend was nervous as fuck despite the buzz. They could have used one more practice. He hunched back by Frankie the drummer, concentrating on the beat. They locked in together, driving the sex-train rhythm. It ended in a milk-it-to-the-last-drop puddle of drum rolls and guitar sputter. Joey punctuated it with one loud chord, then rammed into "I Don't Know Where the Fuck I'm Goin.'"

This is who I saw at Max's when I was a kid, Underend marveled. The band wobbled, stumbling uncertainly over the first change, then caught themselves upright and burned into the chorus. It wasn't gonna be a trainwreck. He could breathe. He came out of his hunch, confident enough to step out front and move with it. Raggedy but right, roaring and rattling like an old El train going express, they did eight more tunes and two encores.

Backstage they celebrated. Friends, fanboys, and scenesters came by to congratulate them and drink their beers. Joey held court, half a dozen women arrayed on the couch around him, a dukedom of red cocktails and black stockings. Pierre doled out the money. Two twenties and a ten to each sideman.

"The fuck?" Underend chomped. "Joey promised me five hundred. He's getting two grand."

"Joey doesn't handle ze money. I handle ze money. If I let him do zat, eet would be all gone. So you can take ze fifty, or I can promise you five hundred and give you nothing."

"That's fucked up. He's makin' two grand."

"I give you a choice. Make up your mind. Don't waste my time, which one?"

"Gimme the money, fucker."

"How rude. But here's an extra fifty, because I am nice guy. But don't expect to work for me. Ever again."

Tina was frustrated. Staying home with Janis all the time. Doing phone sex after she was in bed. It was the alternative to moving back with her mom. Her mom took Janis one weekend so she could get out. She went to the clubs and was bored. Nothing happening. She did an open mic on Sunday. She knew it wasn't much but it was a way to play in public without going through all the hustle of booking. Did a couple songs to decent response, a couple compliments but overall it was a drag. Nobody there could play guitar. All they did was strum. None of them knew how to phrase. She'd always been a rocker. Hadn't grown up on the Joni Mitchell school of music. Now she liked it more, but this was bad. The lyrics she could make out were banalities better left in private diaries. What a fucking comedown.

Janis woke up and started to cry when she was in the middle of a work call. Quietly at first. Go to sleep, she thought. Shit, I hope he doesn't hear it. Maybe I can get him off before she gets too loud. "Oooh, I want you to come all over me!" she cooed. "I want you to come on my tits! I want to feel your hot cum all over me!"

"Don't rush me," the guy muttered.

Janis got louder, going into full-on wail. *WAAH-WAAH-WAAH.* Like a siren of baby pain.

"Is that a baby crying?" the guy snarled. It was obvious. "I want my money back, you fuckin' bitch! You're an unfit mother, you fuckin' slut! People like you shouldn't be allowed to have kids!" He hung up.

Tina dragged herself up and over to the bed. Picked Janis up. Checked her diaper. Dry. Offered her a bottle. She turned her head away and kept squalling. Uh-oh. Toddler existential angst. She cradled Janis in her arms. She was probably going to get a complaint from work. Fuck it, what can I do? She murmured to Janis, "Baby, I know you were born into a fucked-up world, but you'll always have a mommy who loves you."

Janis finally calmed down. Tina placed her back in the bed, marveled at her with awe and trepidation. You are so precious. What did I bring you into? The kid slept. Tina was running low on pot. She parceled out a pinch and packed it in the pipe. She exhaled a cloud of smoke. The cat looked up. The light caught its eyes and they flashed eerie green.

Underend had a one-night fling with a woman named Robin he'd met on the street outside CBGB. She was cute but had fucked-up teeth. On the train out to her place in a no-name neighborhood by the subway yards in west Brooklyn she'd perorated about her communications with dead rock stars, the messages she got from Sid and Johnny and Jim.

They were talking to her. They had sacrificed themselves for our sins and failures. They knew she was out there to carry their word on. She had a two-room walkup jammed with junk, five-year-old newspapers piled on the floor, dried black roses wrapped around the bars of her bedstead, photos of her icons covering the walls.

She was on top of him, arching her back, kegeling his cock as he thrust and she bounced, screaming, "oh! Oh! OHHH!" harder, possessed, pushing the extreme, then she threw her arms back as her body exploded in rippling convulsions of pleasure, and she screamed again, "SID!"

The Red Spot was a floating party that ran from midnight to six every few weeks. Red lights gave the club a Martian lascivious glow. Black walls splattered with paint, a smooth, worn concrete floor speckled with sparkles and occasional puddles, small glass candles burning on each table.

"How you doin', baby?" asked the barmaid, a lithe blonde queen in a black bra and fishnet slip. The basement housed a rock'n'roll dance party. Guys from Queens in leather jackets and Ramones t-shirts, pudgy Goth girls from New Jersey on their big night out, laced and glittered to the max. After 4 a.m. they locked the doors and kept it going, rocking with anthems of flash and desperation. Jim Carroll's "People Who Died," everyone silently remembering and dancing to exorcise their own Teddys, Kathys, and Eddies, the ones they could write their own verses about. Joan Jett's "I Hate Myself for Loving You," the women singing along, reliving when they went through that. Underend spotted a likely woman and asked her to dance. She said yeah.

Her name was Arlene. She was curvy and hooknosed with lampblack hair, ugly-beautiful, like a Rolling Stone. They danced, the DJ spinning it back to the '70s with the snake-hipped slink of T. Rex's "Mambo Sun" and the guitar cannonade of Bowie's "Suffragette City," the soundtrack switching to soul and '60s garage bands as dawn neared. Underend got her number before he staggered home and a quick flick of sweet-wine tongue when they kissed goodbye.

They were an item by the next weekend. Neither one was getting much work so they had time. They both liked brainloads of vodka for loud-guitar nights out—her with cranberry, him orange—and a spray of dope for staying in. She liked weed a lot more than he did. It made him paranoid; it put her in a sensual land, a vermilion moon sparkling over a lush and shadowy jungle. One midnight they L-trained it to Brooklyn to a party in an empty warehouse, a giant room filled with electronic beats, bleeps, and blorps, the banging and grinding of a boiler factory on Jupiter, egg-yolk gobbets of blob pulsing in the mucous lower atmosphere. Giant wheels whirled on a movie screen. A little girl with black hair and giant insect glasses spun jungle, drum'n'bass, and bits of playful '60s organ. She dropped it down with dub, then set it off with "Original Nutter" and the floor packed and throbbed. Then some pounding, pulsing, palpitating psychedelic trance, the spring-loaded dancefloor uniting everybody on the same beat, the repeating arpeggios firing in tune with their serotonin-flooded synapses.

Underend and Arlene cuddled on the frayed velvet pillows in the chill-out room, a space delineated by hastily hung sheets. They were both oozy and buzzing from the bag of dope they'd split. She fired up a joint, and they kissed for a long-tongue time. "Fuck Ecstasy, I'll stick with this," she whispered.

Something was up. The music had stopped. A flexicuff of cops had cracked the glass. They were barking about confiscating the DJ gear, lining everyone up and kettling them out. They walked in line to the narrow exit. "Keep moving," cops ordered. One prodded Arlene.

"I remember when it was legal to dance in this fuckin' city," she snapped. They pulled her out of the line, grabbed her wrists. "What the fuck…"

"… are you arresting her for?" Underend finished the sentence. They grabbed him, too, twisting his hands behind his back.

"Disorderly conduct, obstructing governmental administration." The plastic cuffs snapped on, cutting into his wrists. "And being an asshole," one cop muttered. Frenetic hands pinched his pockets, jabbed into them when they felt a soft lump. Oh, shit. He was carrying Arlene's pot. Chivalry has its price.

"And possession of marijuana in public view," the one who'd called him an asshole exulted, holding up the little plastic bag.

Shit. I don't even fuckin' smoke pot and I get fuckin' nailed for it. All the other drugs I did and I get banged up for the one I don't do. They were carted off to the precinct, separated by sex. Arlene and the insect-specs DJ and an incomprehensibly giddy woman, Underend and a few of the crew and two Ecstasy dealers.

Locked in concrete. Boxed up in a place of eternal harsh fluorescent light. Sunday dripped away. A shifting cast of thirty men in one room treading the waters of time, waiting for the slow helicopters of justice to pluck them out of this fetid pool, for the system to squeeze them along through its duly constipated bowels. Crackdealer ruffnecks spitting nigga-nigga-nigga, wizened winos and bottom-end dopefiends begging cigarettes, dreadlocked ganjamen in bondage to Babylon one more time, scared teenagers trying to act tough or invisible. Monday moved like a snail with a cigarette burn on its pseudopod. They made it into court at three in the afternoon. The public defender said he could get off with time served if he pleaded guilty. He got out at five.

He'd missed a day of work. Worse, he hadn't showed up or called in on a day he was scheduled. There went the rent, and the agency was going to be pissed. Tuesday he had to get high before getting it together to call in and try to explain.

Friday morning, knock at the door. Underend jammed on his jeans and peered through the hole. Eurotrash artiste type, leather jacket, shades, expensively tousled hair. The kind of guy who looks like a fashion shoot when he hasn't shaved in five days. Where do I know him from? Oh, shit, it's the landlord. Mr. Greedy Greg Schlang himself in the flesh. The fuckin' snake. Underend tried to talk to him standing in the doorway.

"Can I come in?" the landlord insisted. "Listen, you're behind in the rent and you're always behind in the rent. I got people here paying eleven, twelve, thirteen hundred bucks to live in this building. I got people who want to pay fifteen, seventeen. You can't even make your lousy four hundred, and if I brought the cops up here, who knows what they'd find, right? So, you know, I could be an asshole about this but I'm gonna be a nice guy. I'm gonna give you five thousand bucks to get lost by the end of the month. Fair enough?"

No use arguing. He's got the handle and I've got the blade.

Running into Scott saved his ass. Scott had moved into a squat on Ninth and C. It was the only way he could find a place where his son Gene could have his own room. "They've got a space open. As long as you don't mind pissing in a bucket until you get a toilet put in. All you gotta do is put in your workdays and a hundred bucks a month for the building. And no violence and no hard drugs."

Underend figured that was one rule he could evade as long as he was discreet and kept his shit together. He got a space on the fifth floor, spent a Saturday working with Scott hanging sheetrock in it. They hauled the unwieldy bundles up the stairs, held them up over the crumbling picket fences of lath between the studs, and bolted the sheets on with a cordless screwgun. A guy named Irish Dave followed, taping up the gaps. They called him Irish Dave even though he was from Glasgow. He and Scott both wore plaster-crusted blue jeans, beers ever-present in their hands. Underend limited himself to one. He wasn't experienced enough to mix alcohol and power tools.

"You gotta hear my new band," Scott enthused, popping a cassette into his paint-splattered boombox. "Irish psychobilly." They were called the Black Potatoes. Scott's drumming transformed jigs and reels into psychotic stomps and rave-ups, the fiddle a fever-waltzing banshee on top. They also covered Eddie Cochran.

"Aye, ye should play that fuckin' drum kit with a bleedin' boxcutter," Irish Dave gently mocked. "Stop fuckin' molesting the ears of the good people of the Lower East Side. It would improve your tone a hundred percent. Ye sound like a fuckin' spastic skeleton having a wank on a fuckin' tin roof."

"Listen to this fuck. He couldn't play guitar any worse if you dipped his hands in plaster and let it set."

"Och, better me hands than your nob. The poor wee thing would hardly make an impression. Cynthia Plaster Caster would be disappointed. 'No Jimi Hendrix, that one.'"

No one could beat Irish Dave at the art of the windup, the Anglo-Celtic dozens. Underend was moved by how genial their insults were.

Underend slept for a couple hours after they were done. He woke up around ten and went out to Rhonda's. Scott and Irish Dave were already there, knotted with squatters unwinding the week's construction job. A reclusive older woman with dot patterns tattooed around her eyes sat near them. Underage punks occupied the back, playing the Buzzcocks, Subhumans, and Pogues on the jukebox. The captions on the overhead TV said the Yankees were up by two with Bernie Williams at bat. The bartender hustled like an eight-armed alchemist, plucking rhinestones from the bottom shelf, emeralds from the middle, and diamonds from the top, passing pints of brown and gold elixirs to the forest of outstretched arms. A longhaired rocker guy sat by the beer taps, drinking and spooning with his obviously new girlfriend. A woman with disheveled blonde hair stormed in, picked a full pint off the bar, and dashed Guinness into his face.

"YOU ATE MY PUSSY FOR FIVE YEARS!" she screamed. Heads turned. She stomped out.

"That's not exactly something *I'd* complain about," a woman with a Southern accent cracked.

A few drinks later Frankie from Joey Rush's band dropped by with a girlfriend. He bought Underend a drink. "Joey's supposed to do a tour this fall, fly to L.A. and drive back, do around two, three weeks. Ya interested?"

"Nah," Underend demurred. "It was great playing with you and Joey, but fuck Pierre. He fuckin' stiffed me at Pulaski Hall."

"Suit yourself. Pierre's a cheap fuck but he takes care of business for Joey. I mean, I love Joey, he's my boy from way back but that's not an easy job, keeping his shit together for him. I couldn't do it. He's got his artistic temperament, ya know what I mean?"

"Yeah, but it's like I don't wanna get stranded in Bumfuck, Arkansas."

"We ain't goin' to Arkansas, but I know what you're sayin', it's like one of those old jazz-cat fairy tales, ya know… 'And Bird fired the band in Cleveland, so Philly Joe had to pawn his drums to get trainfare home.'"

The jukebox flipped from Hank Williams' "Lost Highway" to the Chemical Brothers' "Lost in the K-Hole."

Underend woke up in a shitty mood. The sun annoyed him until he got high. He put on his sunglasses and walked down to the far Lower East Side, down by East Broadway far away from the trendy parts, the sun shining brilliantly on old stained-glass synagogues and neon Chinese lights. Worn stone Hebrew lettering and Puerto Rican storefront iglesias. The trees just sprouting with luminous green buds. The dope was singing to his endorphin receptors like Bob Marley on a moonlit beach in Jamaica, three little birds sharing a post-coital spliff. Behold, a place where all the peoples of the world dwell as brethren. It was the first thing that made him believe in God since he was a kid. It made him marvel at the miracles of creation. Fuckin' hell. The hippie kids in high school babbled about dropping acid and seeing God. I snort dope and feel the presence of Jesus.

The hippie god squad annoyed him. They were usually kids brought up strict religious, rebelled just like everybody else, and then went back to what they knew. "For the cosmic energy so loved the world that it gave us its only begotten chemical, to reveal to us the secrets of its existence." And then they joined all those fucked-up cults that were around in the '70s, the Moonies, and the 14-year-old Perfect Master, and the ones that infested the Village with the "Get Smart-Get Saved" badges. This was different. It was more like what Mary Matheson, the single mom who lived on the first floor of the squat, said. The night they had the party in the garden next door, Mama Mary's prematurely lined face illuminated by an oil-can fire, she looked like an ancient witch-goddess, casting spells with red menstrual magic. Irish Dave strumming plaster-stained hands on a cracked acoustic guitar, and the younger kids, the studded-jacket anarcho-crusty punks, clanking rhythm on pieces of scrap metal.

One of them, Spraypaint, was ranting beer-in-hand about religion is the opium of the people, fuckin' brainwashing bullshit, dope to keep their brains shut down, propaganda to keep them locked up in a world of illusion, pie in the sky when you die, while the capitalists hog the food supply for the living. "No," Mary said, calmly, maternally. "He was talking about something deeper. He said it's 'the sigh of the oppressed creature, the heart of a heartless world.' It's a way for people who have no hope to feel like they have something to live for. Something more than drudgery and death. They want to find hope and peace. He understood why people want it. But what he was saying was that it doesn't change anything. The oppressor is still there the next morning."

Then Emma, her eleven-year-old, and Palabra, her six-year-old, started chasing each other and Spraypaint's brindle pit-bull puppy around the fire, threading among the knots of people, and several 16-ounce Budweisers toppled like dominoes, birthing a brief watershed of golden creeks.

Eviction loomed. The City wanted to kick them out, part to crush the rent-refusing rabble and part to give the building to City Councilmember Antonio Asqueroso's housing development group. A lawsuit to stave it off was creeping through the courts. It was a longshot. The lawyer said they had a good case but even if they won, it might get shot down on appeal.

Everybody pondered what they'd do to resist when Giuliani's goon squad showed up. The mayor's underlings were calling them "parasites," and Asqueroso told the press they should be put in a zoo if they wanted to live like animals. Spraypaint and the kids downstairs blasted hardcore. Throat-disease growl, an army of angry skateboards scraping concrete. DEAD CITIES DEAD CITIES. It got on his nerves and he fed on it. Pure venom. Take it and turn it back on the world. I WANNA SMASH YOUR TV IN. Hate music. No detail, no foreplay, no relapse, no remorse. FUCK SHIT UP. Is it loud enough to break the banks of marble? Is it hard enough to crack the concrete walls of the prison?

You wish. And they're all pouring the few quarters they have into the great capitalist arcade of G. Heileman, Miller, and Anheuser-Busch. Revolution brewed in giant silos outside Newark, the proud elixir of frat boys and anarchist punks alike. They sat in the first-floor community room for a meeting. The courts had issued a stay of eviction and it was still in effect, but the city was making noises about declaring the building in "imminent danger of collapse" so it could kick them all out "for their own safety." People filed in. Ray in a surfer t-shirt streaked with day-glo pink, plopping down on a milkcrate and placing a bag of beers next to it. Millie, plump and pregnant, got the best chair, a score from the P.S. 15 dumpster. She sat next to her husband, Ramon, knitting a sweater for the baby. They were united but on edge, chafing each other. "We're gonna get kicked out, and nobody's doing shit to stop it," somebody whined.

"Bricks and bottles, they ain't comin' in without us taking a few of the fuckers out," spit Spraypaint.

"We have to resist nonviolently," counseled Mama Mary, "because we've got kids here. And if anyone gets hurt, they're going to blame it on us, 'those anarchist troublemakers.' "

"Fuck that, that's got no balls. We need a people's revolutionary army to fight back," blasted Blackflag. "Barricades on every street. People's self-defense."

"You talking nonsense, bro," interjected Ramon, his speech reefer-slow, hesitant and measured. "You got an army? They got guns and helicopters, and you've got three of your boys and a couple milkcrates full of empty beer bottles. And you're endangering my family if you go out like that. It's like my five-year-old nephew bringing it to King Kong."

He and Millie turned to each other, shared a private laugh remembering when they'd taken Jovanny to the Museum of Natural History, the kid a flaco little wireball in a Teenage Mutant Ninja Turtles t-shirt, shaking his bantam fists at the fearsome fossil of Tyrannosaurus Rex and shouting, "I ain't scared of you, punk! Come down here, I'll kick your butt!"

"You remember what happened on Eighth Street?" Ray cut in. "They put a scaffold up so they could start to take down 309, and Willie and his boyfriend snuck back into the building and dumped the pissbuckets on the demolition crew. Doused them with fermented squatter pee! Chemical warfare Loisaida stylee! So while those dudes are washing it off, we go out in the street and pull the fucker down. It was like the walls of Jericho tumbling down!"

That was an inspiring tale, a victory story told hundreds of times, but everyone knew the end of it, too. The next week hundreds of cops sealed the block off, the city got a judge to lift the stay of demolition at midnight, and the wrecking ball came in at one in the morning. Emma and Palabra's kitten was still in the building. The cops hadn't let them get it out.

Thursday afternoon Underend's phone tolled with bad news. Joey Rush was dead. An OD, what else? The bells clanged with mourning and details and rumors. Shit, another one gone. In a motel room in Albuquerque, on the old Route 66. One of our patron saints, our homegrown Keith Richards, they found him with the guitar in his hands. The OD story's a cover-up—it was a ripoff by Mexican drug dealers. Well, he outlived Johnny Thunders by a few years.

Underend was guttered by the news. He spun dreams of how it could have been different if he'd done the tour. I could have watched out for him. I could have woken him up, walked him around, gotten him in a bathtub of ice water. He threw on a coat and headed down to the bar.

He wobbled home to find the squat in a state of alert. There was an army of riot cops amassing by the Con Ed plant. Fourteenth Street was blocked off from Avenue B to the river. They rushed around the squat nailing boards up behind the door, dragging cinderblocks and construction debris into the street, piling them up into barricades. A hastily erected Maginot Line of old bedsprings, crumbling sheetrock, and a refrigerator with no door. They flipped over a rusted-out VW Bug carcass and spun it around to the pile. The cops lined up at each end of the block. Crowds of protesters blocked them, dazed and woozy from the early hour but rushed out from the phone-tree warning. Snipers silhouetted on the roofs of the surrounding buildings, helicopters hovered overhead, buzzing like lethal dragonflies.

The Rock Squat people had the east end, the Avenue C end. Most people thought they were strange and cultlike. They weren't a zombie monolith, there were others living there, punk rockers and single moms and alky-loner construction workers, but most of them followed the teachings of Isaiah Ross, an ex-junkie philosopher. Their rap seemed plausible on the surface, the usual railings against war, rape, environmental destruction, toxic food, the fat of poisoned and massacred cows congealing in your arteries, but it took on an obsessive glow when they ranted about "morticulture." That was their catch phrase, repeated with devout intensity. We are life and morticulture is death. They were thirty strong, dreadlocks flying in the wind, chanting over a three-beat rhythm pounded on plaster buckets. *Boom-boom-BAP, boom-boom-BAP.* We're solid as a ROCK. *Boom-boom-BAP.* We're hard as a ROCK. *Boom-boom-BAP.*

The cops moved into the intersection. Helmets, plastic riot shields, and padded uniforms in stormtrooper black. Tense, like at any moment someone would lash out and suckerpunch somebody and then it would go off, explode into a roiling mob of clubs and bottles. They were better trained than that. They formed a wedge, holding out their clubs gut-high and parallel, and plowed forward slowly, a human being lawnmower shoving everyone aside till they reached the barricade. "Big sticks, little dicks," someone catcalled.

The action stalled. Helicopters buzzed overhead. Gun barrels pointed over the parapets of every building on the block, black-clad snipers flickering in and out of sight. A white-shirted lieutenant barked into his radio. The squatters called out more insults, blasted music, Peter Tosh's "Get Up, Stand Up" and the Beatles' "All You Need Is Love" segueing into N.W.A.'s "Fuck tha Police." The lieutenant conferred, then the black swarm parted and a white armored personnel carrier crawled through, pushing through the barricade and crunching the debris under its tracks. The cops poured through in its wake, the first five charging up the stoop.

They smashed the door down with a battering ram, and then the azure mob swarmed up the stairs and bulled their way into the apartments. Underend had just enough time to grab his bass and a bag of clothes. As they marched him downstairs they had to stop while five cops slammed the ever-mouthy Blackflag to the floor, belaboring his head and kidneys as he tried to twist out of the way. "Turn the fuck around and face the wall," a cop snarled, enforcing the order with a spin and a shove.

They escorted Underend down and out and off the block. His amp and all other possessions were now bound for the bowels of the police property unit somewhere in Queens. Irish Dave was in front of him, wrapped up in a wool hat and a green-and-white striped scarf that looked like he'd had it since he was twelve, donkeying a large duffel bag and a red toolbox. The cold bit like a polar bear.

Scott was luckier. He'd been presciently paranoid and a couple days before had moved his drums into El Taller, the studio where the Black Potatoes rehearsed. And he had a place to go. He'd been spending a couple nights a week in Williamsburg with his new girlfriend, Alice, a big, redheaded poet/waitress.

Tina needed to get out of the house. She couldn't remember the last time she'd seen a band. She'd been doing nothing but working or taking care of Janis since who knows when. So when her girlfriend Toni called her up and said the Righteous Riddim Tribe was doing a free show in Prospect Park, she packed Janis off to her mother's house for the night. They plotted their clothes like teenagers. Tina in a short black skirt and green fishnets. Toni looked like a punk rock receptionist, her black bobbed hair flying in five levels of tonsorial architecture. No automatic voices for her, though; she cackled like a manic wiseass pranking the switchboard. They had Chinese food before they went to the park.

Toni had some good herb and they passed it around as the space around the bandshell filled with dreads and yuppies, hippie wannabes in Rasta-color caps, and Jamaicans, men in sharp tan slacks and women in efflorescent tropical dresses, blazes of yellow and red and deep leafy green. Little kids in strollers sucked on juice bottles and pacifiers. Tina missed Janis for a moment, then caught herself, remembering, I need a night out. The trees slipped into shadow as the sun flamed its last pinks and oranges in the west, the air jasmined with ganja and coconut oil.

Then the band was on, the bass fat and pumping, drums and congas flapping and flying. Tina and Toni were up front dancing. She needed this. Yeah, there was a trailerload of them, stepping to the riddim. The bass player, a tall dread, caught her eye, and she danced harder, and he caught her eye again, and Toni—never one to miss a trick—leaned up in her ear and said, "he got a TV Eye on you," and Tina turned back and mouthed "I know" and mimed the Stooges lick on air guitar. The band segued into Bob Marley's "Could You Be Loved" and she and the bassist both looked at each other and mouthed "And by you."

Toni was plotting how to blag their way backstage when the guy came out. Barrington, he introduced himself, and began flying lyrics at her. "It is a most irie pleasure to meet such a fine lady." But there was a subtle irony in the way he said it, like he knew it was a line but still meant it. She liked that. A lot. It didn't take long for them to head back to Ocean Parkway. He got the car service. Inside, he lit up a spliff the size of a small carrot. When he left the next morning she felt lonely, like walking off the beach at sundown on the last Sunday in September.

She loved the way he touched her. Reverent and rutting. Like he was worshipping at the altar of her flesh, savoring it slowly, then devouring it like a starving child, like he couldn't get enough of her deliciousness. She couldn't get enough of him either. Even thinking about it had her horny. Love or desire? It had been a long time.

Things moved fast. They spent the next Saturday night together. He stayed over Sunday and they took Janis to Prospect Park. He bought her a coconut icey from the old pushcart man. She liked that. Pretty soon he was spending most of his extra time over. He only sort of had his own place—he lived in the basement of his parents' two-family house in Crown Heights. It gave him the security of depending on their permanence and the freedom of having separate walls.

They went to visit his family one Sunday afternoon. The block was a low-rise oasis in the shadow of the towers that buried Ebbets Field. The nearby supermarket advertised cow feet for 59 cents a pound. The faint smell of rancid beef made Tina queasy. She liked Barrington's father. He was a short, oval-faced man with glasses and a trim white beard. He was really nice to Janis, telling her about his job as a subway electrician.

"I help the subways run. They work on electricity, just like your lights or your television, you understand that?" he told Janis in soft, kalimba-lilting tones. Tina could almost hear him carpentering his phrases, measuring twice and cutting once. "And there's a third rail next to the ones the train runs on that's full of electricity, and all the cars on the train have a little metal shoe that takes up the power from it. But you have to take very good care around that third rail, because it's very dangerous. If you step wrong, it will shock you." Janis was captivated by his knowledge and grandfatherly attention.

Tina wasn't so sure about Barrington's mom. She was polite but Tina didn't feel a whole lot of warmth, for her or Janis. Her staid, solid clothes vibed hardcore church lady, despite being enlivened by a bright purple hat. When she spieled about the wickedness of the neighborhood crack kids, she sounded like an island version of one of Tina's relatives in Queens going off on "we need the death penalty for these animals." And she told Janis "mind your manners" at least three times. Tina sensed disapproval. Janis was just being a kid. Not disrespectful, just bouncy and chatty. Some people couldn't handle that. They wanted kids to be little statues. Frozen stiff with fear of punishment.

Still, she couldn't get enough of Barrington. A sinuous gypsy man with cigarette-thick dreads, curved sunglasses, and traces of beard, radiating cool and intelligence. She wanted him wrapped around her.

Scott kept on working and playing. Days with the whine of a bandsaw and the smell of sawdust, a couple nights a week practicing, occasional shows. The place in Brooklyn was a find. Once he fixed it up, he had a space to set up his drums. Gene lived with Rebecca most of the time because the ghetto schools in Brooklyn sucked, especially for middle school. Gene would have been one of the few kids who hadn't been left back by fifth grade, and they were on the Bed-Stuy side of Broadway, so Gene likely would have been the only white kid in any school there. They didn't want him going where every pissed-off little thug would single him out and claim his lunch money or his winter coat for reparations.

Alice agreed. She was going back to school to be a teacher. "I can't be a waitress all my life and live for five minutes at open mikes and a twenty-minute feature every couple months," she decided.

Gene was a great kid. Even though he was pushing puberty and getting bratty—he knew everything, you couldn't tell him even the most common-sense things without getting on his nerves, he was like a five-foot two-year-old screaming "I KNOW HOW TO DO IT MYSELF!"—it was still a joy to watch him exist (when you didn't want to throttle him). Edwin came out from the city and the two of them were trying to be rappers, cocking their baseball caps sideways, sagging their jeans low, and making up rhymes. *I survive nuclear wars and crawl through the rubble/I go places in the universe you can't see with the Hubble.* It harked Scott back to when he was a kid, the way he loved noise and sound, banging on his mom's pots and pans with knitting needles and wooden spoons until they finally gave in and tried to make the racket coherent, got him a teacher who put him through the rudiments and the exercises in *Stick Control* and *Syncopation for the Modern Drummer*. Running around in the street whacking garbage can lids with a stick, the rich clang of a freshly minted zinc one and the duller bong of a squashed and corroded one.

People used to do shows with that kind of shit on the Lower East

Side back in the day, like what's-her-name—Rebecca's friend, Sarah—who opened for us at some avant-garde hole in the wall with a sprawling mongrel of a kit, a basic set augmented with dog-bitten cymbals, oil drums, and car springs. She was good but her band was pretentious as fuck. All that we're-all-fucked, it's-all-futile shit. It seemed like an annoyingly precious pose, working your ass off to maintain your existential misery.

Maybe it was all hopeless in the end but you couldn't be nihilistic like that and have a kid. What were you going to tell him, Hey, there's some fresh drain cleaner under the sink, wanna taste? How about some iodine? See that truck coming? I bet you could make a big red splat! I'm ashamed of you, that was a pathetically wimpy tantrum. If you'd put any effort into banging your head on the wall, you would have given yourself a concussion but you didn't even draw blood.

Scott didn't feel tapped into the veins of world rock'n'roll history, but things were happening. So what if he wasn't playing Pulaski Hall or CBGB any more, he was doing erstwhile Polish bars on Bedford Avenue and beer-soaked DIY outdoor shows among the abandoned warehouses on the waterfront, a generator spewing diesel smoke behind the makeshift stage. He'd helped build that stage. He was still doing stuff, he wasn't broke or dealing with a mountain of band melodrama, and he had time to hang out with Alice and Gene. The past was receding.

Fuck it, Scott thought, I'm a lifer. Who said I had to stop when I turned thirty? Who made it a rule?

Underend spent days raging at the ruthless real estate scum who ruled the city. Stalked past some kid with a boombox blasting pissed-off hip-hop, the beats hammering under an MC spitting homicidal fury, simmering on the fumes from a 40 and a blunt. He could understand. He was living in a single-room hotel called the La Scala, a name intended to evoke the opulent pageantry of Milanese opera, not the pitter-patter of rodent feet in the walls and halls, the squabbles of crackheads, the crabby whine of the crazy old woman next door.

All your life culminated inside four small walls. $440 a month. Cheap. Cooking canned ravioli, beans, and ramen on a hot plate. Drinking vodka on Monday nights in front of an undersized TV. Creaking down the hall with a towel in the morning. Pissing in the room's sink when you weren't up to dealing with the outside world.

He worked temp jobs, tried to lay off dope, drank way too much. It wasn't easy not to. He was playing the bar-blues circuit, four sets a night to people who looked like a beer commercial, yuppies and tourists raising their bottles to the spirit of Jake and Elwood. Backing up a singer he'd met at a Sunday afternoon jam named Pancakes Taylor, a crease-faced old geezer from Macon, Georgia, full of stories about how he was supposed to play with Otis Redding before he got sent to Nam and how when Little Richard worked in a restaurant, he'd whip out his dick in the back of the kitchen and pretend to swab dishes with it. Who knew what was true.

Four sets a night of blues and soul covers. Booze tunes went over well, like "Drinkin' Wine Spo-Dee-O-Dee." They tried to do something different than the same twenty songs everybody else did, but they couldn't avoid being asked for "Mustang Sally." Pancakes would turn to the band and quickly suck his teeth, then spin back and announce, "By special request." The dance floor would fill, and they'd pass around an ice bucket for tips.

"I bet none of these motherfuckers ever rode in a Ford Mustang. Ever seen one. But if the man puts twenty in the bucket, you play what the man wants to hear," Pancakes would philosophize. "That's what she said. He's buyin' your drinks; Alvin's, too. What's that Viking cough syrup shit he likes, Jaggerskeister? Hey, that's why I like you, man. You a functioning alcoholic. Like me."

Fourth set when the crowd had thinned, they'd stretch out, all of them by then well charged. A blue-flame jam, a slow-burning Memphis soul groove. Bringing it down way low, setting it up for Pancakes to testify. "And I come home late… I'm a workin' man, you know what I'm talkin' about… I put my key in the lock… And I open up the door… I get a bad, bad feelin'… And you know what I see? You know what I see? Nothin'. The house is *empty*. She's *gone*." Then they'd slam into the song, Johnnie Taylor's "Jody's Got Your Girl and Gone."

They'd follow it with a slide-guitar scorcher. Or sometimes Pancakes would just sit down with a sullen drink and let Alvin, the lead guitarist, take a long solo. Those nights were touchy; he'd be testy about paying the band.

Mick considered getting off the freeway at Crenshaw but then traffic opened up. It seized up again the second he passed the exit. He switched the CD player off, aborting the onslaught of L7's "Fast and Frightening," and jabbed the buttons on the radio. A swatch of Mexican accordion, a creepy-crawling whine of gangsta synth, a traffic report. *The 405 heavy but moving in both directions, the Santa Monica westbound backed up from La Brea, accident there.* Shit, shoulda gotten off. He sat and waited under the palm trees and smog, in the stilled stream of painted metal and burning oil.

He still couldn't get used to the amount of time he spent in the car, even after the years he'd been out here. Well, this was a cherry one, a black mini-hearse with blood-red racing stripes and a grinning demon on the back door that looked like a cross between Bela Lugosi and Gene Simmons. "The Drac-mobile," some kid in South Central had called it. He'd been on the set there all day, playing Drug Buyer #3, a guilty bystander to the main action of gun-toting homies and cops kicking in doors, another one-word part. It was still a good gig, one he'd lucked into by being one of the punk-zombie extras in the *Living Dead* series. His biggest role had been playing butler to a pot-smoking vampire in *Vlad the Inhaler,* suave but a little perverted and not too bright. Cult crowds cackled when Vlad berated him, "Radu, you haf spilled ze bongvater." The vampire-mobile had been Vlad's vehicle.

Music? He was living without it. Well, he'd taught himself a bit of guitar and keyboards, had a cheap '50s jazzbox-wannabe acoustic and a Casio. There was nothing like having a whole crowd in the palm of your hand, squeezing them, stroking them, making them scream with adulation. That was certainly a long way from being eighth fiddle on a movie set, a big step above the extras but a lot more disposable than the focus puller, but he didn't need the melodrama, betting his life on longshots that would flame out and crumple from other people being failure cocks.

The sprinkle of screen dust stoked his sex life. He was getting older but he hadn't lost his moves, might have refined them, even. Just the right notes of pursuit, courtliness, and mystery, a whiff of sinister ministry. They worked smoothly, lubricated by his minor celebrity. He weaved through the whirl of bars and party scenes, art openings and poetry readings, a groovy ghoulie with elder statesman rock cred. His nights were a symphony of panties slipping down. Blonde bombshells, brunette Bettie Page pinups, and Gothettes cloaked in Regency vampirella maquillage, the latter two with enough black hair dye to paint a stripe down the freeway from San Pedro to Ventura. Anglos and Chicanas and half-Japanese hapas, women in party dresses and tight black jeans, black underwear, red underwear, no underwear. Arms and shoulders inked with green snakes and Celtic spirals, butterflies on ankles, tribal heraldry on lower backs over the portals. Wet satin lips lasciviating his cock. Oh yeah, back in the saddle again. Underneath the red and blue lights blending on his bed, in a two-and-a-half-room bungalow, a quiet place down a thin path behind someone else's house on a side street in southern Hollywood.

Barrington was gigging every weekend now and Tina couldn't get out of the house for most of them. She got the feeling he was fine with that. The eternal musician's-girlfriend dilemma: if you met him at a show, there were plenty more like you out there. He definitely wasn't going out of his way to invite her. When she could come out, he'd harangue her about the proper mode of dressing in public. Rastawoman wear, orthodox roots-daughter outfits, head covered and long dresses, never pants. The complete opposite of most guys in bands who wanted you to dress like a rock'n'roll sexbomb, wearing flesh-flashing clothes that fit the style they played. She'd never wanted to look like a Sunset Strip bimbo, a punk/metal/hard-rock/whatever version of collagen lips curled in a cowlike come-hither look, but this vexed her, too.

"Why can't you want me like I am?" she'd ask, with a razor-sharp undertone.

"It's not proper," he said coldly.

"Proper?" She blew up. "Who the fuck are you to tell me to look 'proper'? Where are we, in Afghanistan?! You want me to wear a burqa?"

"It is an abomination for a woman to wear the clothing of a man. And you are a mother. You must respect yourself. It's not dignified for you to look like a Babylon porn star."

"I'll get a fucking burqa. In red, gold, and green. Just for you."

"I'm getting vexed," he said, a long, slow German-shepherd growl.

She was pregnant. They both wanted the kid but the relationship was careening. He didn't come over after shows much anymore, and then he'd accuse her of stepping out on him. And his mother didn't take well to the news of her impending grandchild. She called Tina "that Jezebel."

Tina called Toni for advice. Toni came over and they cooked spaghetti. Toni brewed tea and rolled a joint while Tina put Janis to bed and read her *The Cat in the Hat Comes Back*. Tina and Toni sat in the living room on the brown leather couch and two bucket seats, all salvaged from the ruins of a minivan discovered under the Brooklyn-Queens Expressway. Janis's toys littered the room, an old Cabbage Patch doll, a Barbie missing a leg, some sparkly princesses in purple tulle.

"I need something called VOOM to clean up the mess of my life," Tina sighed.

Toni cracked up like a machine gun. "Sorry, I shouldn't laugh at you like that."

"That's okay." They sipped the tea and passed the spliff.

"So why do you put up with it?" Toni asked. "Do you need a man that bad?"

"Well, it sucks being alone. He's the first one who made me feel like he loved me in a long time. But I'm getting to feel like it was a performance for him, part of his game. I mean, he loved being with me, he meant it while he was there… but it was like playing a gig. He was gonna be doing the same set somewhere else tomorrow night, you know what I mean?"

Toni nodded. She laid back, let Tina vent and muse.

"I like his calmness, his spirituality. But I'm feeling there's something cold under it, like a fanatic. He wasn't like that when I met him. I met his mom, I see where he gets it from. She's always talking about 'wickedness.' And he's rebelled against that, but it's just to claim his male privileges. He can fuck around all he wants but I've got to look like a Mormon housewife."

"Our friend, the madonna-whore complex."

"Exactly. And I can't win. If I'm a madonna, he's gonna want to fuck other women instead of me, and if I'm not, I'm the whore of Babylon.

He's telling me he wants me to cover my head when I go out. Why does women's hair get men so bent out of shape? Are they going to be overcome with lust if they see a few stray locks? Or is it just a power trip?"

"It's a power trip," Toni told her, "and you're better off being alone. Go on welfare for a year or two if you have to. But dump the bum, okay?"

Fourteen weeks before her due date, she did.

The Pancakes gigs were drying up. McSweeney's, the bar that was their best-paying one, lost its lease and got replaced by a yuppie lounge. They had a Saturday night show somewhere down by the World Trade Center, a couple dozen people sprinkled about. Underend, nursing his fourth drink in the second set, felt like he was going to piss himself. Lose control like a baby. He held it in to the end of the song, whispered for a drum solo, ran off to the urinal. Nothing came out.

The next morning his ass blew out a geyser of liquid that reeked like burnt rotted chicken. His stomach was next. He doubled over. His black underpants lacked the catching powers of an air-sickness bag. It felt like his entire body ecosystem had broken down. This was too much.

He knew why he liked to get fucked up. Liquor could flip the world to a better place. "Good, Good Whiskey," like the Amos Milburn tune they covered. It helped with romance. Only by blotting out the distracting negativities could this world look enticing, benevolent, mysterious. Turn the lights down low and the echoes sparkle. Listen to some wasted woman rant and you think she's an epic poem, in heroic struggle against the demons.

Dope helped with music. It blotted out everything else until it was just you and the sound. It relieved the pain enough so you could abstract it and play with it. Alcohol was cruder, stripping the sound down to the raw emotions, the phrases down to country or blues or punk. But then the wheel flips again and it's joyless. She's just a crazy drunk repeating herself. It's like going to a job, a slow grey day in the office or the factory, squeezing rivets to squash your liver, punching computer keys to obliterate brain cells, the quinine shuffle as dull a routine as cramming into the 8 a.m. subway, pouring drinks down like sitting in a cubicle at 3:30 wishing you had some energy, waiting for the five o'clock bell.

You could achieve neither oblivion nor flight, never mind the emerald-dragon combination of both, and you didn't want to be just another sad old man pissing his life away at the bar or in front of the TV, or a raggedy-ass dopefiend in filthed-out jeans and sneakers spending the night in the bowels of the Tombs trying to get some rest on the gray concrete floor, grateful for the manna when they handed out oranges along with the stale baloney and cheese sandwiches.

He headed down to 14th Street. Residents of the Former Heroin Republic of Methadonia and those still domiciled in the old country consorted on the corner, scuffling for a way to get through the day. Jimi Gimmix, a wizened old punk rocker of thiry-five going on sixty, nodded hi. His babyfat girlfriend, Tiffani, wobbled up from the 11th Street stroll on crutches, her right ankle in a Bellevue cast, fixing her makeup in a parked car's side-view mirror. Jimi himself wobbled in a crooked-back walk, as if the drugs made his spinal muscles fire in a funky sine-wave spasm, like a broken spring setting itself free. "William Burroughs copped here" was part of the block's local mythology. In the '70s and '80s it was a pill bazaar—Placidyls, Valiums, Elavils, Tuinals—the downers-to-meds spectrum handed out to what the social workers called MICAs, mentally ill chemical abusers.

Underend turned into an office building hallway painted peeling brown, and edged his way around rickety ladders and old paint cans. The few remaining occupants were dubious business enterprises like a Filipino psychic surgeon, an Asian happy-ending massage parlor, and a real-estate office run by Serbian gangsters. Climbed the stairs to the fourth floor, turned into a room with school-bright fluorescent lights and two metal urns of coffee with styrofoam cups in the back. "My name is Underend and I'm an alcoholic dopefiend."

Underend got a job and found an apartment in Greenpoint. He hadn't played out in three years when he ran into John from No Name Maddox. John was sober now, too. They lined up a couple shows as a minimal three-piece, them and a new drummer. The first one was a Monday night at the Red Hat, a basement on Ludlow Street. And this Monday-night bottom-rung venue, a harbinger of future stardom to the kids in the other bands reveling on the cusp of man and teenager—

actually playing a rock'n'roll club in the city! With their names in an ad in the *Village Voice*! (even if it was in eight-point type in a third of a column at the bottom of the page)—felt like Palookaville to Underend. Four bands with next to nothing in common with each other; the doorman checking off which one each customer was here to see: less than ten and the band didn't get paid, more than ten and they got $2 for each one. As the second band played mediocre post-grunge on cheap guitars heavily processed by distortion and flange, the first NYU-student emo band was shouldering their guitars and cymbal bags out of the club, their friends finishing their drinks and leaving.

A couple of dozen Middle Eastern-looking metalheads with long black hair, studded denim, and jagged/Gothic/skull t-shirts and regalia, filtered in. Their band was Jaharram from Queens: an Afghani lead singer and a Pakistani guitarist and bassist from Jackson Heights, an Iranian lead guitarist and an Uzbek drummer from Rego Park. They played in front of a green backdrop with "Jaharram" in Arabic-style lettering above a long scimitar. Below it read "Islamic Death Metal" in Teutonic script.

"I'm Syed. If I was still in Afghanistan, I'd be fuckin' crushed to death with stones for doing this. This one's called 'Holy War.' " Double kick drums sprayed machine-gun clatter, the bass and rhythm guitar pummeled and crunched, the lead guitar keened in Marshall modal maqam mayhem. Syed squalled and growled of apocalypse, "Purify yourself for the crusade / Holy war burns through the world / Teenage soldiers march through minefields / Blown-off legs fly straight to Allah. Eternal submission!" And the Muslim metalheads loved it, moshing in the small space by the stage, flashing fists in the slow part and chanting "DIE! INFIDELS! DIE!" Jaharram got an encore. They deserved it. They did Slayer's "Skeletons of Society," an apocalyptic world where death runs wild.

Underend wasn't nervous before going on—cocky even, we're gonna rock this dive—but the minute he hit the stage paranoia struck. He missed a change going into the first chorus and cursed. The demons of nervousness flew in and attacked like a flock of amphetamined woodpeckers. His hands felt arthritic, his forearm cramped, his nerves clogged. And the house amp was clacky, amplifying the creaks of his fingers sliding along the strings.

John had matured a lot as a singer, he noticed. They did an ancient murder ballad, "Banks of the Ohio," that sounded like it was from 1803. Before John would have camped it up, dragging the song through the morbid swamps of serial-killer chic. Now he crooned it with a tenderness that belied the teller's evil deed, fingerpicking an electric 12-string to create a Byrdsy drone. But Underend's nerves broke the flow, fractured the mood.

Getting wasted had given Underend the audacity to come out on stage, even though it had ultimately cost him. Being sober meant no shield against the fear of fucking up. Imagination fled his brain, leaving him clinging to getting the notes right. He'd settled down a bit after four songs, but by then, there were eight people left, not counting Jaharram, the sound guy, and the woman behind the bar. Three had come to see No Name Maddox, one of them the drummer's girlfriend. And they were the "headliner." Palookaville.

It looks magical when you're young, but it turns out to be tinsel and cheap plastic imported from a no-name sweatshop. The purveyors aren't supernatural, they're schmucks. The barroom of transubstantiation of light and sound is just a palace of small-time hustles, stale beer, and music-biz calculations, a back room of cocaine and logistics. The one thing you can't fake is passion, but I don't have it anymore. Those kids were having fun, being heroes to all their friends. But what do you do when that all falls away? Do you have it in you to go on?

The next morning he woke up late. He was walking to the subway just as the first plane made its Nike just-do-it swoosh into the north tower of the World Trade Center. He knew what he was going to do that night. Drinking. Locally, because you couldn't get below 14th Street without ID. Vodka flowing like the Volga. Wound up going home with an obliterated woman in a gray t-shirt dress and Spice Girls platform flip-flops, a flying fish tattoo on her ankle. Yuppie-hipster, worked in an ad agency. "Fuck me before it's the end of the world," she told him. He lost his hard-on after two minutes, limpening inside the condom. Couldn't feel a thing. They lit cigarettes. "Why do they hate us so much?" she asked.

"Because they're fuckin' religious-fanatic assholes. And because we're arrogant rich fucks who want to rule the world."

She blew up. "They killed innocent people! THOUSANDS OF THEM! GET OUT!" she screamed. She grabbed her panties and threw them in his face, knocking the ash off his cigarette.

He stumbled up Bedford Avenue, groping his way along the storefront gates, puking into a sewer grate. The next morning he had the mother of all hangovers. It felt like a railroad spike impaling his left temple while CIA-trained acupuncture torturers probed the pressure points along his cranial nerves with barbed dental picks. And he couldn't keep anything down, not even a piece of bread. Never again. This time I mean it.

Chapter 7
The '00s / November

ROCK'N'TERROR screamed the red headline in the *Post*. The *Daily News* front page blared QAEDA ROCK. "So where the fuck is Tina?" wondered Scott, opening the paper to page 4.

The Afghanistan-born singer for a self-styled "Islamic death metal" rock band was arrested in Queens yesterday on terrorism charges.

Syed Hassan Habibi, 26, of Jackson Heights, is tied to a plot by five New Jersey men to blow up chemical plants along the New Jersey Turnpike, said Justice Department spokesperson Magdalena Quant. Federal agents nabbed the five in Jersey City last week, based on tips from a confidential informant who had infiltrated the group.

"We've pulled the plug on this jihad rocker," Quant said. "He openly advocated terrorism and murder, and now we have evidence that he was part of a criminal conspiracy to create an unspeakable disaster that would have killed thousands of people and crippled the economy of the region."

One of the five suspects was listed as a friend on Habibi's MySpace web page, she added.

Habibi's MySpace page features MP3 sound clips by his band, Jaharram, and photos of him in front of a banner reading "Islamic Death Metal." The songs posted include "Suicide Bomber," "Holy War," and "Avengers," and one has a chorus of "Die, infidels, die." Another song, "Commuting to Death," depicts a terrorist attack on a commuter train similar to the recent bombings in London and Spain.

The Taliban tunesmith, who immigrated to the

United States from Afghanistan with his family as a child, is being held at the Metropolitan Correctional Center in Manhattan.

"Holy shit," muttered Underend. "They were on the bill with my band the night before 9/11. At the Red Hat."

"So were they any good?" Mick asked.

"Yeah. I'm not much of a metalhead, but they were. Better than we were that night."

"You think he was hooked up with those guys?" questioned Scott.

"All these plots are fuckin' overhyped," Mick ranted. "Some schmuck named Abdullah cuts a nasty baba-ghanouj fart and they accuse him of plotting to poison half the population with biochemical warfare. 'TERROR GAS PLOT! SILENT BUT DEADLY!' "

"The fucked-up thing is, he said he was a refugee from Afghanistan," Underend answered.

"So they can't torture him by blasting Metallica," Mick interrupted.

Scott jumped in on the riff. "At least not with the old stuff. 'Waterboard me! Pull my fingernails out! Just take off that St. Anger shit! Gimme something with Cliff Burton! BAT-TER-REE!'"

"The Taliban banned music," Underend stressed, trying to turn the conversation back to his original lick. "Kite-flying and soccer, too. The only entertainment they allowed was public executions. He told me 'Jaharram' means 'unclean' in Arabic."

"Sorry I'm late," interrupted the arriving Tina. "I had to drop Damian off."

"C'mon, we gotta move," interceded Scott, the clock superego. "It's gonna be rush hour by the time we get to the tunnel. There's gonna be bad fuckin' traffic." They were headed for an all-ages show in Montclair, New Jersey. Scott was prophetic. Traffic was molasses on the Williamsburg Bridge, glacial going crosstown, gridlocked getting into the Holland Tunnel. Rain dripped from a grim sky.

Music comes from motion, Underend thought. Music of the city, subway rhythms, like when you were high as fuck on an IRT express train, tagged wall to wall with STITCH I and STAY HIGH 149, and your brain was trying to find a pattern in the clatter, a groove in the swoosh of acceleration, feedback screeching around a curve, the call and response of the wheels.

Rock'n'roll comes from train tracks, 1928 railcamp piano boogie, left hand a steady-rolling eight to the bar, right hand plinking the dozens, Chuck Berry hitting the sixth with his little finger, rocking like the rhythms that the drivers made. Cars, too, roadrunners in the modern moonlight with the radio on; Harleys heading out on the highway. This wasn't it. It wasn't supposed to be the grooveless stop-and-go of bumper-to-bumper traffic, inching through urban capillaries, stuttering past stripmalls, crawling through the endless sprawl ten feet at a time.

"You think people are going to come out for us in the rain?" Tina wondered.

"Nah, it's not gonna hurt. Not for an all-ages show," Scott answered. "People our age stay home in bad weather, if it's cold or if it's raining. But the kids, they'll come out in whatever."

"We gotta make every one of these the fuckin' show of our lifetimes," Mick preached.

"It's good we got this one as a warm-up before the bigger ones." Scott. "But don't delude yourself. One great show isn't gonna make you a rock star, unless you're Santana at Woodstock or the Ramones at the Roundhouse. But we better not suck, because one shitty gig can ruin your reputation. Especially now, with the Internet. They'll blog you to death, and ten people will link to it."

"Whadda we got calendared, anyway?" Underend rose out of his reverie shell, moved to head off an argument.

"Three shows this weekend, local, and three next, out of town," Mick listed. "The one tonight, a place called the Submarine. Pulaski Hall tomorrow, we're opening for 900 Dead Cretins. And CB's on Sunday."

"Aren't 9DC touring without Napalm?" Tina asked.

"Yeah, they are," said Scott. "That's gotta be a fuckin' joke." The reformed version of the band was doing shows with a new lead singer, a hearty nasty-divorce fuck-you to their original frontman, Napalm McDonald.

"It might be, but it's what we got," Mick said. "Goodness had nothing to do with it. We're not gonna pack out Pulaski Hall by ourselves, that's for sure. And we got a mini-tour next weekend—Friday in Philly, Saturday in D.C., then Sunday in Springfield or Holyoke, Massachusetts.

It's one of those art-building shows like we used to do, when they have a whole building with bands and installations. Rob's still trying to nail down D.C."

"What kind of show is D.C.?" Scott.

"Anarchist collective," Mick.

"Ah, fuck. It's gonna be a mess." Scott. "Every time I've done a show organized by anarchists, it's been a fuckin' disaster. Those people couldn't organize wiping their asses, and they got an ideology about it."

"C'mon, we gotta do it for the people. It's a grassroots thing, not a corporate rock star show. We wanna support that, right? Philly's a DIY show, too, and Rob says they're totally solid."

"Well, how together is it?"

"As together as three anarchists can get it."

"Yeah? Tina, you better bring your own toilet paper if you wanna pee. Unless you want somebody lecturing you about you 'obeying authoritarian ideas about feminine hygiene.' "

They snailed through the strip of cheap gas stations in Jersey City leading to the Turnpike, then crossed the swamps on I-280. Past truck terminals and wetlands stuffed with thickets of brown cattail weeds, rusty gas tanks and an old warehouse, a fucked-up checkerboard of broken and mismatched windows. Through Newark the traffic began to move, then up the Garden State Parkway to Exit 148.

Stressed about being late, they eased down a long avenue of swooping slopes, past Shell and Exxon stations and convenience stores. It unreeled into a real city, with urban church daycare centers and a downtown with old brick office buildings. It was dark by the time they got there. The show was on a side street, in a bunker-like one-story building between old mini-mansions converted to dentists' offices. The Submarine occupied the basement, a converted meat locker. The opening band was already setting up as they loaded the gear downstairs. Too late to soundcheck, the place was beginning to fill.

They wandered the room checking it out. The younger bands were stocking their merch tables, unloading gray plastic tubs full of t-shirts, stickers, and CDs, and taping samples to the table. Tina and Scott watched with a mix of admiration, jealousy, and cynicism.

"We never had any of this shit back in the day," Scott muttered. "Not until we got signed." Left unsaid: They've got it a lot more together than we ever did, but are they making music or marketing t-shirts?

The show was all ages. That meant mostly high school kids and only a few people over the age of twenty. Some were nondescript, some punk rockers wearing t-shirts and patches of bands from before they were born. Only three people here with any kind of style, Mick thought. A fat Bettie Page girl and her two gay-looking boy friends, one in an Oscar Wilde cape and the other a blonde in a black velvet Cossack coat with scarlet embroidery. He's far too young to pull off the dash needed to rock it right, he looks like he hasn't even started shaving, but points for trying. Not like these fuckin' ordinaries in dull-colored hoodies and logo t-shirts.

Underend paced, nerved out. Mick went up to him. "You nervous? Just think about everyone out there taking a shit. They're all full of it, they're not any better than us."

"That's a weird fuckin' perverted pedophile fetish. Girls half your age sitting on the toilet. You want me to get one of those subharmonic processors, play notes lower than anyone can hear, and make them let loose like a flock of fuckin' pigeons?"

Mick laughed. As long as you kept Underend sick and amused, he'd be okay. If he thought about the show, he was gonna get obsessed with what was gonna go wrong.

"Yo, it's great to have you guys playin' here," Jake the promoter told Mick. He was a wiry, dark-haired guy with long, narrow features and a patchy beard. "It's like having a piece of history. You were the ones that got it going back in the day."

"Well, thanks, but I'm not ready to be in the fuckin' wax museum yet," Mick answered, half laugh, half growl.

The club slowly filled as the opening band played. Six or seven hippieish kids clustered at the side, blond girls in peasant blouses; longhaired boys, one with baobab-topknot dreadlocks; a brown-skinned boy with a big Afro; and a girl with two-tone hair, shoulder-length crimson and black. The first band, After You Move, was pretty generic pop-punk mixed with slower emo tunes. Underend scanned the crowd. The only people remotely close to his age were two women, one semi-derelict in an old Molly Hatchet t-shirt, massive tits and missing teeth, and the other obviously a band member's mom. Dressed in an After You Move t-shirt and sensible jeans and sneakers, she was shooting Hail Mary digital photos, holding her camera an arm over the crowd and hoping for the best.

Mick collected the band to write a set list. "This is the Submarine, we gotta open with 'Let's Submerge.'" No one disagreed. They'd pretty much worked it out in practice. The only dispute was over the slower songs. Tina wanted to do two.

"One," Mick insisted. "We can't have too many, they'll drag us down."

"What, you're afraid they'll think we're not hard enough?"

"The kids wanna dance. We don't wanna lose them."

Tina's train kept rolling. "Look at us! We're harder than you! I got tired of that shit years ago."

"C'mon, give me a fuckin' break. I'm up front, I'm right in the middle of everything. I can't hide behind a guitar like you. When they're not into it, I'm dying up there. Minute by minute. Like a comedian playing to Mount Rushmore."

"I know, but I don't wanna go *bang-bang-bang* just like everybody else. We're better than that."

"All right, which two, then? Arctic Avenue?" Mick shot back.

Scott groaned. "Let's just be who we are. We're too fuckin' old to pretend. If we're good they'll be into it. If we suck, pandering ain't gonna help."

They compromised on the two Babylon songs, "Urban" and "5:55." Underend wrote the lists out, four copies with shorthand titles in black marker on the back of flyers. Traditional, even Luddite, next to the computer printouts the younger bands used.

SUBMERGE
SCRATCH
JELLYBEANS
URBAN B.
SHIT
5:55
SELEKTION
SICK
WE WILL
FILTH

Lucyfer was up next. Two girls and two boys, all really young, around fifteen or sixteen. The singer was kind of punkish in a nuts-and-bolts necklace, the drummer fast and sloppy like Rat Scabies, a fat girl with her belly spilling out of her t-shirt. A dark-haired, intense Latina zoned into simple, repeating basslines and shot dagger eyes at the guitarist whenever he played too-many-note solos or overdid the swooshes of his flanger. They weren't a good bet to stay together more than another three months, but they had something original in their inexperience and incompatibility. One in a thousand they would grow up together and forge a distinctive sound. A scene which encouraged that would make it more likely. Without one, they probably wouldn't stick with it, or they'd become boringly conventional after they learned how to play.

A skinny shorthaired kid wearing a t-shirt designed before he was born—the Circle Jerks one with the Orange County slam-dancer—glommed onto Underend. Tyler, the bassist for Pessimus Subprime, the next band, peppered Underend with questions about gear and the old days. "Did you know Black Flag? And what were the Circle Jerks like? The Dead Kennedys? Crackpot? The Minutemen? MDC? 900 Dead Cretins?"

"Hey, they were in California and we were in New York," Underend gruffed. Answering that many questions when he was trying to get his brain together for the show was like dodging a barrage of baseballs under strobe lights. Didn't want to diss and dismiss the kid, he meant well, but he was chasing chimeras, imagining a punk rock Camelot.

"What about the Ramones?"

"I met them. We opened for them a few times."

"Awesome!"

"Yeah, but I didn't know them that well. Joey was a nice guy. Johnny was the dictator. Dee Dee had a lot of heart, but he was really moody and paranoid." He didn't want to say where he'd most often encountered Dee Dee. Might as well not encourage bad habits to the next generation.

Pessimus Subprime turned out to be generic hardcore. A small moshpit formed. The lead singer simulated sex with a rubber chicken.

The Gutter Astronomers took the stage at 10:30, after some of the younger kids had to go home. "Good evening, ladies and gentlemen, cretins and perverts," Mick intoned. "We're the Gutter Astronomers, back from the grave and ready to rot." Scott hit a comedy-club rim shot. "Welcome to the Submarine… and let's submerge! ONE-TWO-THREE-FOUR!"

Excited, he'd counted it off a bit too fast. The song skittered by, too rushed for the band to lock onto a groove. They played in four different tempos until Scott got vexed and pounded straight beats on the snare, saving them from a trainwreck. They settled down during "Scratch and Claw" and "Radioactive Jellybeans." The bombastic noisefest of "God Made Me Shit" chilled to the dubfunk of "5:55 Babylon to Brooklyn" and clocked into the Krautrock pulse of "Selektion," and they knew they had the crowd. The kids surged forward, flashing cellphone and digital cameras, a forest of electronic eyes.

"Stop fuckin' recording it! Live it!" Mick snapped, as they paused before "I'm Sick of This." They burned through the last three.

Tyler came up while Underend was putting his bass away, told him "awesome show," asked what he thought of Pessimus Subprime.

"I hate to say it, but you sounded like a lot of other bands."

"Yeah, well, our lead singer says that's the scene, that's what we gotta do if we wanna get shows and sell merch."

"That is so far from what we were about… I mean, you gotta get shows, but…"

They schlepped the gear up to the van with the pleased fatigue of a job well done. It wasn't the best show they'd ever played, but they'd pulled it off. They were in a good mood, not kvetching about whatever had gone wrong.

"Pessimus Subprime's a good name, but they were way generic," Mick said.

"It comes from *Transformers*," Tina answered.

"How'd you know that?" Underend asked.

"Damian watched it. There's a good-guy robot called Optimus Prime."

"You pick up a lot of stupid shit having kids," Scott kicked in, singing a fragment of the *Teenage Mutant Ninja Turtles* theme song. "When Gene was little, I could have told you exactly what color bandanna Raphael and Donatello and the rest of them wore."

"This is a cool little town," Tina noted as they pulled into a gas station before the Garden State Parkway. That didn't stop Mick from telling a string of scabrous New Jersey jokes. They trooped into the convenience store and he picked a pine-tree air freshener off the rack and held it to his waist, declaring that he'd once bedded a not-so-fair Garden State maiden who'd had one hanging from her navel piercing.

"C'mon, that can't be true," Tina laughed.

"Well, maybe she thought Pine-Sol was a more romantic scent than essence of Exxon," Underend answered.

"Or she was paranoid you'd think the burning-rubber smell was coming from her instead of the refinery," Tina added. "Men can be like that, you know."

They knew enough to play along. Once Mick got going, the mockery of unbelievers could not shake him. He'd stick to his story as steadfastly as a religious martyr or a recalcitrant Mob witness.

"I swear on my mother's twat it happened. She was from Big Beaver Lake, Exit 69."

"Yo, Mick, you're busted," Scott interrupted. "Me and Alice went down the Shore a couple summers ago. Exit 69 on the Parkway is Barnegat Beach. We were joking about it."

"Whatever. You wanna put three points on my poetic license? My fellow Astronomers, as our late President Reagan said, facts are stupid things."

"And your mind is in the gutter!" the rest of them chorused.

"We are 148!" they sang as they ascended the on-ramp, to the tune of the Misfits' "138." There was an urban legend that "138" came from the exit number of the band's North Jersey hometown. The fact-checkers had debunked that one, too.

Saturday night was at Pulaski Hall, an old Polish ballroom on 14th Street. They'd all seen dozens of shows there, played there several times. Its new owner, a radio-chain subsidiary, had renamed it the Avalon. Soundcheck. This was it, the first big show since they got back together. Standing on the stage in front of the big empty room, looking out at the bar in the back. The sound guy bustled around methodically, long dark hair pulled back in a ponytail. He bent over, adjusting the mics, pointing a cigar-shaped gray one at the guitar speaker, an egg-shaped mesh one in front of the bass drum, plugging in the three mesh-balled vocal ones up front, then calling out the litany of sounds. "Kick." *Thump-thump.* "Snare." *Crack-crack.* It reverberated like a shotgun in the empty room, but that wouldn't be a problem when a full house of bodies absorbed the sound. "Hi-hat." *Tssh-tssh.* "Rack toms." *Bomp-ba-domp.* He sat at the board, making adjustments, adding or cutting lows or highs, touching on a bit of reverb. "All around the kit." "Bass." "Guitar."

A dozen globe-shaped lights blazed photons from around the dressing room's two mirrors. The opening act was on. Mick sprawled along the one couch, drinking tea with lemon and honey, wearing a calf-length, black and gold robe that made him look like a Buddhist pimp or the Maharishi of Atlantic City. Underend paced the room, chain-smoking, pissing every five minutes. "Cool out on the cigarettes. I need my voice," Mick told him. Scott stretched his arms over his head, rolling his neck to loosen it in convulsive bastard yoga. Tina strummed her unplugged Tele, tuning and retuning. Brain lightning flashed inside her eyes. Shit, a migraine coming on, at the worst possible time. She put on sunglasses, lit up a thin joint, smoked it by herself and massaged her temples, trying to shore up the levees and dissipate the storm. Mick got up and began warming up his throat, lightly singing "cee-ee-ah" and "Mommy made me mash my M&Ms."

The door opened. Two black guys stepped in, one the size of a linebacker, the other the size of a defensive tackle, both wearing the kelly-green t-shirt of the club's security. Breast-pocket badged with the OneWave logo, "1WAVE" with the 1 a radio tower and an ocean wave over the letters.

"You can't smoke in here," the smaller one said.

"The fuck you mean I can't smoke? I'm in the band. This is our dressing room."

"This is a smoke-free facility," the guy said politely but firmly. "And is that marijuana you're smoking, miss?"

"Yeah. Want a hit?" She held it out.

"No. Put it out. And if I catch you again, you're outta here. Band or no band." They pulled the door shut behind them.

"The fuck was that about?" Underend and Tina were fuming.

"OneWave bought the club out in '97," Mick explained. "They're a radio chain, they own sixty percent of the rock stations in the country. Then they went into concert promotion, they bought up venues in tons of cities. So they brought in their own rules, they're not as live-and-let-live as it used to be. And the cops are a lot tighter on bars and clubs now, after Giuliani and with Bloomberg's no-smoking law. It's bullshit that they'll kick us out, that guy's just woofing. They'd have to give people their money back, but they could be a real pain in the ass for us.

"Remember Bluebox from Seattle? They got pissed off because OneWave was taking a piece of their merch, takin' five bucks off the top on every t-shirt, so they had to charge the kids more. So they said 'fuck it, we're gonna book our own tour next time.' They wound up playing the fuckin' backwoods, the Cornhole County Fairgrounds in Coal Turd, Pennsylvania. They lost a ton of money, and OneWave blacklisted them."

"I never thought I'd miss the fuckin' Mob," Underend muttered. "As long as Vito the Ugly One could launder his money, they'd give us five hundred bucks and a case of Heineken and leave us alone."

"Well, it just goes to show, you're always fucked when you're a musician," Scott philosophized. "If you're not big enough, everybody pisses on you, and if you're big, everyone wants a piece of you."

They strode out to a sea of seven hundred people, the ones up front eager, the ones in the middle curious, the others drinking, chattering, and texting until the headliner came on. They opened with "Submerge." Underend immediately loved the house bass amp, a rented Ampeg SVT. It was an eight-speaker behemoth the size of a refrigerator, the head alone weighed eighty pounds, and even turned up to 3 it made his bass strings sound as thick as water mains. He felt like King Tong, a giant simian porn star trolling Manhattan for a Goddesszilla whose orgasms could send waves up the Hudson as far as Albany.

Tina was wobbly at first. She forgot the guitar solo to "Scratch and Claw," so she just played noise. Clawing out a splatter of random high notes, parlaying her migraine brainwreck into skronk. She needed it, getting blattered by a wall of noise. Scott and Underend caught it and rolled with it, giving her an extra chorus. Yeah, they were a band again. The healing power of music and herbs and tea. But it unnerved Mick, who jumped back in and then had to pull back, like he'd stepped off a curb that was higher than he thought. He caught himself in time.

They were on, picking up the energy of a big crowd. They could feel it turning toward them, the ones who knew them hanging on every beat, the others getting drawn and plunging in. They got through five songs before one of the stage crew raised a finger and mouthed "one more."

The fuck? They told us we had thirty-five, forty minutes. Nine songs. "One more," the stage guy repeated. A hasty conference around Mick and they cut to "Filth," the last one. Under the clock guillotine, they played harder and angrier, but it wasn't right. The drive was forced and the groove couldn't build to a hypnotic throb. Tina and Underend cranked their amps up to feedback as the stage guy slashed his finger across his throat and the soundman cut the stage sound and brought the DJ music up.

Backstage they were all boiling. Fuckin' disrespect. Treating us like we're a shitty kid band who got this gig as a gift. We're from New York, people from back in the day paid to see us.

Tina's migraine was now setting off improvised explosive devices in her temples. She couldn't see straight. Mick jumped on her. "What the fuck did you do on 'Scratch'? Maybe if we'd been tighter they wouldn't have cut us off."

"Fuck you, Mick. You just gotta blame somebody, right?"

"Chill out," Scott intervened. "We were great, it had nothing to do with us. Clubs pull this bullshit all the time. We didn't deserve it."

"Where the fuck is Rob, anyway?" Underend backed him up. "He booked us, he's supposed to have our backs."

900 Dead Cretins came on to a roar of adulation, opening with "Government Cheese" off their second album. The band sounded tight, solid, and unique as ever, but the lead singer aped Napalm's mannerisms like a six-year-old clumping around in his father's boots. The Gutter Astronomers drifted between the dressing room and the side of the stage, marveling at how bad it was. "They sound like a fuckin' tribute band," Underend said.

Scott seconded that emotion. "It's like seeing Scotty Moore, Bill Black, and D.J. Fontana backing up an Elvis impersonator. And calling themselves the Elvis Sun Sessions Tour."

9DC climaxed their set with "Jonestown Rock," the song that made their name. They'd debuted it in 1979 at the former People's Temple hall in San Francisco. It was a punked-out version of Bob Marley's "Trenchtown Rock," done at a fast chainsaw rhythm with the lyrics twisted, "One good thing about Kool-Aid/When you drink it you feel no pain." But the replacement lead singer missed all the black humor and rage of the original, catching none of the acerbic mockery of people twisted enough to kill themselves upon orders from a cult leader, and the inside-out sarcasm, the self-mockery of a suicide laughing at how fuckin' absurd he looked hanging from a bathroom plumbing fixture turning ugly colors. This guy sang it like a flat fun-fun-fun oldie. The crowd lapped it up. They were too young to remember, hungry for a touch of the intensity they imagined in the past. Were things really that fuckin' bland now?

Primitive, 9DC's drummer, né Alberto Primitivo Chavez, his cholo-plaid Pendleton shirt rolled up to show heavily inked forearms, buttonholed Scott after it was over. "Sorry you guys got cut short."

"Yeah, we were all fuckin' pissed about it, but it wasn't your fault."

"Well…" Primitive explained that Ike Blight, 9DC's guitarist and musical director, had told the stage crew to cut off the Gutter Astronomers. "He was afraid you were gonna blow us away."

They had the small revenge of knowing they'd actually been a threat to the powers that abused them.

They recovered and reassembled the next afternoon for CBGB, pulling up on the Bowery at dusk. They barely recognized the block. In their time it had gone from winos drinking Night Train to crackheads smoking Red Tops; now it was yuppies drinking Grey Goose. The yuppies had conquered. They'd packed the street with bland white condos, obliterating the scrappy ailanthus trees, the van-rental lot, the building that had housed suicidal 1890s hookers and feminist 1970s painters.

One last time the Gutter Astronomers carried the gear under the famous awning and across the pockmarked cement threshold. One last time they greeted BG and Brendan on the door, Hilly the white-bearded patriarch presiding, his face a lot wearier than they remembered. One last time they rolled Scott's trap case and lugged their guitars down the long subway-car alley by the bar, under the blackened neon beer signs hanging from the ceiling, inhaling the evocative bar smell—three decades of beer and cocktails soaked into the well-worn floorboards. One last time they schlepped back to the stage and dressing rooms, band names in spraypaint, marker, and stickers covering every inch of wall like urban kudzu.

Scott was jonesing for noise after last night's aborted set. He wanted to pound fuck out of the drums. He wanted to quake up a tsunami of sound, screeching, careening like ten thousand ambulance tires, a 1929 car chase with bootleggers hanging on the running board shooting at the G-men. Drums and amp cabinets piled like boulders on the jetties at Rockaway, big black waves crashing on the beach, swells and combers and outside sets. Yeah, I need it. Gimme something human. Boring just won't do. I wanna get my brain torn up. All we need is a drummer for coronary hypnosis.

They used the soundcheck to polish two new covers, T. Rex's "Monolith" and Zeppelin's "When the Levee Breaks." Mick had encountered resistance when he broached the idea at practice. Most of the band hadn't wanted to do any more covers, and Tina said she hated Led Zeppelin. "I got into punk to get away from jerks like that." But Mick had insisted. "What were you listening to when you were fourteen? We gotta respect our roots." He defended the two tunes. "It's a glam-rock doo-wop song, and we're from the city, we all got a little doo-wop in us, right? And I wanna do 'When the Levee Breaks' for New Orleans."

"I don't play like that," Tina interjected. "It's too leaden. No pun intended."

Scott took over. "Let him do it, but let's do it our way. Fuck doing it with all the changes, forget about them. Just do the riff and the turnaround. Relentless. Like a Swans version, you know? Underend, you take the riff, and turn the low end all the way the fuck up. Tina, you make noise on top. Remember how Lydia Lunch played slide with Teenage Jesus and the Jerks? Fuck it up like that." That worked. And they decided to have Janis sing backup on "Monolith."

A tall, gawky woman walked in with a heavy black leather bag. There was something oddly familiar about her, and she didn't seem completely female. "Mickey!" she exclaimed, hugging his neck.

Mick was bemused. Who was she? She looked like Berlin, who'd occasionally dressed in drag—red lipstick, denim skirt, leather jacket, and combat boots. But this one was more like a real girl. "Berlin?" he ventured.

"I'm Belinda now, also known as Daizy Phazor. I saw you were playing on the Net. No way I wasn't gonna come down."

"You're a woman now."

Tina interrupted, "That's what my mother said when I got my first period. She slapped me in the face and told me, 'You're a woman.' I was like, 'What the fuck does that mean, "I'm a woman"? And why'd you hit me? I didn't do nothin'.' I was eleven. I was still a kid. I was imagining a sappy Gary Puckett and the Union Gap song."

"Well, I haven't had my first visit from Aunt Flo yet, but I'm eagerly awaiting for the phone to ring," Belinda said. "I finished transitioning last summer, just in time to show off the marvels of modern medicine. And I'm designing delightfully destructive little sound effects now. I brought some for you."

That made sense, even though it was hard to wrap their heads around her sex change. Back in the day Berlin had been a sci-fi freak. He'd spouted grandiose fantasies about wiring the sewers for sound, hooking up a 100,000-watt PA system with octave dividers and giant arrays of 21-inch subwoofers, and when you hit the right bass note, one maybe below the 20-Hz limit of human hearing, it would set off an earthquake. The Avenue B Bass, four bridge cables stretched from Houston to 14th Streets and played with sledgehammers. Or putting ultra-high frequencies into records, ones people couldn't hear but cats and dogs could, and driving them crazy. He said there was a Von Lmo album that did that. Lmo was a metal-punk/art-noise singer with an extraterrestrial-übermensch sci-fi schtick. His record had annoyed Berlin's cat so much that she knocked the record player's needle off it with her paw.

Now she lived upstate and sold her effects pedals on the Internet. She presented Tina with a fuzzbox called the Purple Pubic Peach Fuzz, and Underend with a Cleopatra's Shaft, an automatic wah-wah envelope filter. She said she was working on an echo unit, the Cosmic

Mother Boxx.

The show sold out, but not many people they knew came. The $30 tickets kept them out. The crowd was mostly young history-seekers and fortyish suburban old-punk hipsters, with a sprinkling of vintage gay-arty types and noise geeks. They were on the bill between Flickknife and the Radiant Babies.

Flickknife was an early '90s intellectual grunge-hardcore-metal band, mathematical and abrasive. The Radiant Babies were an early-'80s noise-funk quintet who'd scored a couple minor left-field dancefloor hits. Their black/Latino rhythm section, drummer Trick and bassist Tania Caridad Rodriguez—a large, shaven-headed woman known to all as T.C.—gave them a groove that got them out of the art-scene ghetto.

The Gutter Astronomers ignored Flickknife's set. They were too busy getting ready to go on, and none of them had ever been into that sound. They were looking forward to the Radiant Babies, even though the new version was missing Trick and guitarist Keith Scooter. Both had died of AIDS in the early '90s. "Trick was fuckin' great," Scott eulogized. "He could do punk and funk, and you wouldn't see the seams on it like you would with anybody else."

One last time they ascended to the stage. Underend on the left by the frayed life-size portraits of silent film vamps, Tina on the right, by the black speaker box chained to the ceiling. She hit a Johnny Thunders corkscrew lick, slid up the neck an octave, held the note and let it feed back. Scott clicked his sticks four times, and they were off into "Submerge."

They rose to the occasion. Three shows in three days had them note-tight and smoking hot, lucid and lurid, flaming and fluid. They nailed the groove on "Selektion," the clock-tick speeded up and pushed just to the edge of losing it. They scorched through "We Will If We Have To" and "Filth," got the crowd rocking all the way back to the bar.

They easily got an encore, especially satisfying from a crowd of mostly strangers. They came back out with "Monolith," a slow jam with purple-prose lyrics and cosmic doo-wop harmonies sung by Janis and Scott's friend, Little Lisa. Scott switched to 2S drumsticks, the size of souvenir baseball bats, and Bonzoed the intro to "When the Levee Breaks." Underend followed, booming the riff in great slablike tones,

Tina did echoes and whines, and Mick splattered apocalyptic poetry about the hurricane and flood that had destroyed New Orleans, cooling down to a chant. "When the levee breaks you got no place to stay." Tina answered with a gaggle of no-wave squawks. "When the levee breaks you got no place to stay." Mick repeated the incantation.

"When CB's goes you got no place to play. When CB's goes you got no place to play. WHEN CB'S CLOSED, YOU GOT NO PLACE TO PLAY!" Mick screamed it one last time, and the band climaxed, spasming and milking their last licks. They stepped off the stage sweaty and satisfied. Underend ducked back in the alley for a cigarette. He didn't want to fight through the crowd.

Backstage was packed when he came back in, people crowding into the dressing room to say hi and congratulate them, others hanging in the hall, just trying to get a look. The Radiant Babies were setting up, trying to get the pulses on their synthesizer timed right.

Tina, Underend, and Scott went out to watch them from the side of the stage. It was a little anticlimactic after the Gutter Astronomers' set, and the crowd began to thin. The revamped version sounded good enough to the untrained ear, with T.C. putting out bass tones as big as her booty, but they were routine funk-rock without Trick's unique grooves and Keith's explosions of rhythmic dissonance, his trading vocals with lead singer Faith Black. They didn't flash beyond that until late in the set, when they did the Bobby Kane Syndrome's "Stop! Dancing! Fire!" It was an apocalyptic dance tune that sounded like discofied Velvet Underground. Trick had dated Bobby Kane somewhere between Max's and the Paradise Garage. Bobby was gone, too.

Mick stayed in the dressing room, seconded by Belinda. He was drained, and he had to represent. It was easier to deal with all the people wanting to talk to him when he could sit down and be semi-private, instead of being out in the crush getting accosted and jarred from all sides. Somebody asked him what he thought about CB's closing, somebody else about what's different about New York since he left. It set off a rant.

"You know what's different? No fuckin' street life. You can't just hang out on the corner talking bullshit, laughing, watching. That's sort of illegal now. It's all about buying and selling. If you're not spending money you gotta move, nothing for you here. I mean, it hit me when I was seventeen and I was in the Village on acid. It was supposed to be hip, but it was all about selling clothes, records, and bongs. So I'd go to Washington Square and hang out with the winos, and they'd tell me, 'You talk some crazy shit, boy.' And now it's really fuckin' outta control, it's like a fuckin' beast on steroids. And these fuckheads rule the country, the city, the world. Like, look at New Orleans. A whole fuckin' city got destroyed. Fuckin' thousands of people homeless, old people drowning in their attics, and they're looking at it like, 'All right! Now we can get some white people in there. Raise up the property values. Let's tear the hood down and build some condos.' Where the fuck do they think the music came from? Places like New Orleans and here. And a fuckin' theme park's NEVER gonna be the same thing."

But apocalyptic nihilistic prophets of doom were a dime a fuckin' dozen, Mick thought. Yeah, he'd indulged back in the day, spouting images of nuclear-blinded cockroaches scuttling through the radioactive rubble of Loisaida—the way some blocks were back then, how could they tell the difference?—and generals chortling "some of the crabs in your pubes are a little hot," but fuck that. Fuck that apocalypse-is-coming shit, the stock market's gonna implode and we're all gonna have to grow our own nuts and berries, pollution's gonna turn us into mutant hermaphrodites pissing out the sides of our stunted dicks, they've got a secret plan to implement martial law, and we're all gonna end up like the Road Warrior in fuckin' Somalia, jeeps full of jittery wired-up teenage gun boys patrolling every dusty corner. Or the whole galaxy's gonna go up in 2012 like a big fuckin' blob of white phosphorus. Shut up. I wanna know what the fuck you're gonna DO about it. The people who whine the loudest never do shit, you ever notice that? You think the people starving in Sudan are fuckin' pathetic? The women and children stranded in brown-grass refugee camps in the middle of fuckin' nowhere at the edge of the Sahara? They wanna LIVE.

Mick spent the week in Teaneck with his parents, Miriam and Louis. Every time he came east they looked older, *alte Juden*, his father fragile and creaky, his mom more hunched and less vivacious. This time his father was back in the hospital, in the intensive care unit following surgery to remove a tumor from his liver, with tubes jacked into his nose, wearing a flimsy blue gown, and toddling off in foam smiley-face slippers to piss with difficulty. He who always proudly dressed sharp, now clad in the height of bedpan-fodder fashion, and his hair was gone, making him look like a member of a New Age space-alien death cult.

"How're you feeling?" Mick asked.

"How the hell do you think I'm feeling? I'm sick. I feel like shit. There are vultures gnawing on my liver. Is that good enough for you?" He wasn't too sick to interrogate. "What are you doing with yourself?"

"I'm still working at the bar. And trying to get the band back together."

"You could have been a lot more than that."

"My music's taken me to a lot of places. People remember it. It means a lot to them."

"Louis, don't start that again," Miriam interceded.

"And now you're pouring booze for Hollywood shikkers. You could have been a lawyer or a teacher."

"I make more money than a teacher."

"Oy, it doesn't look good," his mom confided when they left the ward. The surgery had excised the visibly diseased bits, and they hoped the chemotherapy would scorch out any microscopic outcroppings of the disease. In the waiting room families sat in the solidarity of the bereaved, a three-generation set of Latinos with flowers and rosary beads, a Hasidic husband in penguin-black gabardine with his wife in wig and satiny green headwrap, their three little boys in matching plaid shirts and earlocks. Sentinels on separate watches praying for a reprieve. There are no atheists in ICUs, Mick mused. Everyone clutches onto magical thinking.

They got takeout Chinese on the way home. After dinner they drank tea and ate macaroons. His mom played records for him: a Mickey Katz CD, *Music for Weddings, Bar Mitzvahs, and Brisses*. Back in the day he would have hated it. Schmaltzy wedding-band riffs and corny Borscht Belt dirty jokes. Now it felt down-home, funny and soulful. Not like the wedding bands of his generation that inexorably played tame versions of the most hackneyed Motown and disco hits and treacly adult-contemporary inspirational ballads. Fuck, he was even developing a taste for Frank Sinatra—people often played "One for My Baby" on the jukebox as closing time neared. Yes, he who still thought the only good version ever of "My Way" was the one by Sid Vicious.

"Whoever thought we'd have a president that made Nixon look good?" his mom said. "He's worse than a murderer. He'll bomb people in Iraq, and then he'll go over there and pose for pictures with their kids, saying we're fighting to protect the lives of these poor orphans. It's disgusting. Someone should shoot him, but then we'd get stuck with that Cheney. He'd be even worse."

When did his mom become such a flaming radical? She was an old-school Democrat who didn't hold well with his older brother and sister's more incendiary attitudes. It had caused many a dinner-table argument when he was a kid. "Mom, one thing I learned in the music business. When people want to steal from you, the first thing they tell you is how honest they are. It's the same in politics. You can be a thief or a murderer, but as long as you look good, you can get away with it. Nobody pays attention unless they're a geek. People are so busy, so swamped with noise, that if they hear something often enough and loud enough, that's the impression they get. You can't shake it."

"Hitler's Big Lie," she said.

"Yeah, we don't live in a democracy, we live in a chutzpahcracy." They both cracked up.

She was thinking that Michael, the youngest of the three, was the "PAY ATTENTION TO ME!" one of her kids. Allen and Hannah had gone through their radical days in college, with the SDS and the women's liberation movement, but Michael had to have a different venue. He was a trombonik, tooting his own horn like there were seventy-six of him leading the big parade. Allen was now a lawyer with Brooklyn Legal Services in Williamsburg, Hannah a high school teacher in Holyoke, Massachusetts. She lived with her girlfriend in Northampton.

Brooklyn had felt suffocating when Mick was a kid, full of urban peasant rednecks. At least his parents read; they were interested in the world. Engaged … well, his mom was so engaged she had an opinion on everything, even if she didn't always know what she was talking about. Having a Brooklyn accent was like having a Southern accent. A certain percentage of people thought you were an idiot, a hopelessly ignorant cougine, the minute you opened your mouth. There were personnel agencies in the city with instructions not to send their clients any "dese, dems, and doses." The truth was that if you were smart, compassionate, and funny, the accent beefed up your lexicon, would help you say things that were pungent and pithy, rooted and profound, way more than the speakers of Midwestern Broadcast Standard English. But if you were a stupid, vicious bigot, then you really sounded like a fuckin' moron.

Selling the house in Brooklyn had provoked a family crisis. Allen and Hannah had called it racist, leaving the neighborhood as it was beginning to turn black. Louis had reacted angrily, "This house is the biggest thing I'll ever own. I worked all my life for it, and I don't want to hold on to it until it's worth bupkes and Mama and I are prisoners in our own home."

Mick had been more sympathetic. He'd been robbed for his favorite jacket, a lavender and black suede one he'd gotten in the Village, at knifepoint on Church Avenue the year before. He wanted to stay in the city more because moving to the suburbs would be a death sentence of boredom. Having to get a ride from his parents to hang out in the supermarket parking lot. The city was an amazing playground if you had the money to do a few things. You could ride the subway anywhere, to the Village, midnight movies, the Academy of Music, the Mercer Arts Centre, poetry readings at St. Marks Church, all-night restaurants in Chinatown. And girls, more girls than you could possibly imagine, from all over.

His father was in a better mood the next day. "You know, regardless of what I said yesterday, I'm proud of all you kids. Maybe I don't understand what you do, it's not what I wanted for you, but you stayed committed and accomplished something.

"I'm glad I retired when I did. The business is a lot more cutthroat now," he went on. "You know what they say in Yiddish? 'Oy, sa falshe velt.' It's a dishonest world. Allen and Hannah called me a capitalist pig, but I made an honest living. When I sold a line of suits, I was proud of it. They had good material, good workmanship, a nice cut, you could be proud to wear it. You wore the clothes, not the label. The label was on the inside. Now they take some piece of drek from a Chinese sweatshop, put a designer name on it, and sell a shirt for eighty-nine dollars. It's the same shmatte they sell for $2.99 at K-mart. Except the one from K-mart might be better made, it's not gonna come apart the first time you bend your elbow. It wasn't a bed of roses back then, I'll tell you. J. Edgar Hoover said there was no such thing as the Mob. Hah! I could have told you there was the Mob. The schvartzer kid pushing a cart for thirty bucks a week knew about the Mob. If business was good, they wanted a bigger shmear. If business was bad, they were there, too. 'Go to hell, pay me.' They put Weissman out of business in 1953."

That had been another family crisis, Louis being out of work. They were rescued when he got a job with GGG in '54. The job had gotten them a six-room apartment on Ocean Avenue and then a house off Albemarle Road. Mick remembered going to Mets games with his father a couple times a year, seeing the "GGG is MVP" ad on the outfield fence at Shea Stadium. There was the night in September 1968 when the ninth-place Mets had upset the pennant-winning Cardinals, Tom Seaver taking a perfect game into the seventh inning against Lou Brock, Curt Flood, Roger Maris, and Orlando Cepeda.

It's fuckin' scary, Mick thought. My dad's got fucking cancer. It wasn't too far off to say an evil spirit had invaded him. All these little cells that don't give a fuck about the rest of the body, about being liver or lungs or skin, they just wanna grow, and they don't give a fuck about what they destroy. They take over the pancreas or the nipple ducts or whatever and turn it into a big glob of nothing, this fuckin' monster inside you that's so big it's got its own blood vessels. And it does fuck-all besides feeding itself, and then it spreads to the rest of the body, sends out colonies in your brain or the knees or whatever, and that's when you're really fucked. And the only way people know how to stop it is to poison your system with radiation or chemo and hope it kills the bad stuff without killing you first. Hope the worst it does is make your hair fall out and you spend days puking because everything tastes like metal.

My dad bought into the system, he worked hard and succeeded, and now he sees how fucked it is. Society's got fuckin' cancer, too. The rich are out of fucking control. They're buying up everything. Their greed is like a really viciously aggressive kind of cancer. It wants the world and it wants it now; it's got tumors popping up in the bone marrow, the balls, the stomach, under the toenails. It's like we've been chain-smoking and inhaling radioactive waste for thirty years, and now it's metastasizing fuckin' everywhere, it doesn't want to leave any part of the body alone. People talk all this bullshit, about apricot pits or eating organic or having a positive attitude, but there's no sure cure. They're grabbing at fuckin' straws, and a lot of people are gonna be totally fucked before we see any kind of change. If we do. If we do before it kills us.

Tina was fried. She wanted to take the day off, but there was almost no food in the house. She maneuvered the shopping cart down the aisle of the Gristedes on Church Avenue. The PA played oldies. "Soldier Boy" by the Shirelles, the twangy guitar solo and the pledges of eternal love. Janis was working that night so she only had to cook for Damian. She did his favorite meal, stir-fried green peppers, mushrooms, and tofu over spaghetti. A quiet night at home. Damian's homework was a report on cat evolution. "Ma, did you know cats are descended from Middle Eastern wildcats, *Felis silvestris lybica*?" He read the species name awkwardly, lie-bick-ah.

"No, maybe it's pronounced more like the country, Libya."

"And cats adopted people," he went on, excited. "When people started farming, mice came to eat the food they stored. And the cats caught the mice."

She smoked a joint after he went to bed, watching the ember fade like a dying fire congealing to ash. Plugged her guitar in to the battery-powered baby amp. She remembered Terry taking her to see the Stones in 1965 at the Academy of Music, an old vaudeville theatre with cracked plaster on 14th Street. She'd been the baby sister chaperone, but she'd been mesmerized. She didn't want to be like the silly teenage girls screeching "EEEEEEEE" at their idols and making the theatre smell like pee. She didn't want to worship. She wanted to do it, to be like the ones on stage making that sound. The frenetic rush of "Not Fade Away," the deadpan cool of "Off the Hook," and the shimmering guitars and jungle drums of "Mona." A few years later she'd find out it was the Bo Diddley beat; many years later she'd learn it was an ancient African rhythm.

She'd been so quiet that Terry had asked her if she was having fun.

Yeah, she was, but it went a lot deeper than that. She'd been a misfit kid, neither girly-girl playing dress-up with her Barbies nor tomboy jock running with the pack and scrapping to be the alpha dog. The guitar under the tree on her eleventh Christmas, a cheap brown Japanese acoustic touting its Steel Reinforced Neck, was her way out. It had taken a long time to unlock its secrets. To play more than E A D G C chords, to cross the quantum gap between strumming song skeletons and playing something that sounded like music, to get the sounds she heard on records and in her head. To create music that flowed and said what you had to get out but couldn't explain.

Now she was strumming in a hushed, intense style, sculpted by years of playing electric guitar in New York City apartments late at night without infuriating the neighbors. Layering distorted arpeggios, a little bit of echo, dense filigree building up to a juggernaut of sound but delicate like a wall of finely wrought iron and humming with the force of Mother Nature underneath.

Janis had talent, she thought. Her direction was more traditional, in her own way, less seething. Well, she was entitled to be different. Tina's taste was changing. She was getting into more ambient-echo things. Most rock today had no energy. Loud but dull, nothing that made you want to move, to not be the martyred slave of time. And when it was fast it felt forced, artificial. It needed to be raw and subtle, like good sex. Let the groove build, then push it, and that's when the getting gets good.

She played textures, turning them into rhythms, letting them float. Somewhere in the urban jungle overgrown by plants. A steel cat's meow, magenta pin-trailed meteors falling from the sky, a wall of solar flame. She was glad she'd held onto her analog echo box. Digital delays sounded brittle and icy. This one was warm muddy waters, even with the most helium-metal tones she could get from distortion and a flanger and the fuzzbox Belinda gave her.

Cow curled up next to her, demanding affection, head-butting and rubbing and batting at her picking hand. "Kittygirl, how often do I get to play music, and you're bothering me?" she queried in light exasperation, taking a break to scratch the cat's white-furred ribs.

Underend woke up dreaming that a voluptuous homeless woman was flashing her tits at him on Manhattan Avenue. In this dream, he had just gotten out of jail, plucked up off a nameless waterfront boulevard and locked up on a cellblock where Iggy Pop and Bob Dylan were the wardens. She was in her late thirties, still fresh-faced and not too insane. Lifting up a striped top to show big soft floppy nipples. Her face was dirty but the rain was washing it off.

In reality, it was cold and raining hard outside. The worst fuckin' weather, dreary and insidious, dank socks and damp denim irritating your skin. The day dragged on under the dingy lights. Rayo stopped in at lunchtime, wrapped in drenched vinyl. "Mucho lluvia, poco dinero," he joked. There was no rain bonus.

It cleared up by late afternoon, when Billy called everyone together. "I'm sorry, but I couldn't get the lease renewed," he said. "We're gonna have to close at the end of the month. They want to triple the rent."

"Sheeit," muttered Black Dave. "In this economy?"

"Ay, dios mio," moaned Rayo.

"They think they can get it, so they want us out. They might end up sittin' on an empty storefront for the next five years, but that doesn't help us any. Sorry. I'm gonna do the best I can to help you all out. I'm gonna give y'all what would have been next month's rent for severance pay."

Underend and the other two office workers, Donny and Yvette, got two months' health insurance. The messengers got a couple hundred each. Rayo said he was going back to Mexico.

Ten years before, Underend would have gone for a drink or nine. Instead he went to a meeting, in a run-down theatre district building full of rehearsal spaces and headshots of minor league actors. He sat next to a skinny woman with cranberry hair and sleeve tattoos. She was hot in a weathered way, with mileage that intrigued him even as it tinkled the wind chimes that signaled lunacy. She started talking to him. They went out for coffee afterwards.

"You'll find another job," she reassured him. "You just have to visualize prosperity. If you really want something, you have to visualize it and ask the universe for it, and the Laws of Attraction will bring it to you."

"If visualizing things made them happen, I would have had a lot more sex when I was fourteen." You don't know the half of it. I would have fucked half the centerfolds in *Playboy* and *Penthouse*. The girl in the halter top at the Frank Zappa concert. The girl in the green stockings on the F train. Donna Spallone in my 9th grade math class.

"And I would have scored the winning run for the Mets in the World Series, when I was eleven." Beat out a bunt in the bottom of the ninth, stole second, and raced home on a bloop single by Cleon Jones, galloping around third with the coach waving go-go-go and screaming into the plate in a cloud of dust and glory.

Underend was on a roll. "I would have found a kilo of dope and $50,000 in cash in a briefcase on the street. Far enough behind the dealer who ditched it and far enough ahead of the cops looking for it to get away safe. And I can't even count all the dreams I had for the band."

"If you have negative thoughts, of course it doesn't work," she answered. "If you don't believe in things, it destroys your serenity. You're poisoning yourself with bad energy."

There wasn't much to say after that. You can get serenity from denying struggle, he thought, but it comes from delusion. You're doing the ostrich. Like a bratty kid thumbing his ears at the harsh voices of reality. *La-la-la-la I can't hear you! Nyah-nyah-nyah-nyah you never said it!*

Women seemed to fall for this shit a lot more than men did. Some could make a lot of things happen by artifice, with looks and moves, if they put out positive energy and the right signals. Or maybe she was just schizo, thinking the tiniest things were tiles in an ominous mosaic, a two-faced image that could flip from good to evil and back depending on how you looked at it, and you were a psychic Pygmalion who made it take life and wield power. The depressed have no illusions. It's more honest to admit you can't deal with it and blot it out, but the damage is too much. For every action there is an equal and opposite reaction.

You could fly like a Bird, winging it headlong into the realm of pure blowing, far beyond the charts and the changes, calling on the howls of the aether and the earthly juices of chicken grease and pussy. How long could you sustain that? How long could you ride the arc of alcohol or whatever, or how long would it let you ride? Then you were earthbound again, trying to walk on spindly debilitated pigeon legs.

They said brief goodbyes. He went to the bathroom before leaving. They want a drug-free world? We're all pissing our meds into the ocean, he thought. What are the fish absorbing through their gills? Ambien to make them sonambulate through the sea? Paxil, Prozac, Wellbutrin, Zoloft, Lexapro to elevate the mood of depressed dolphins? Lithium for bipolar whales? Vicodin to soothe the toothaches of sharks? How much fatalistic acceptance would keep you from blowing up with rage, and how much would sink you into despair? The effective dose wasn't much less than the lethal dose.

In the Times Square station boogaloo percolated from the salsa store in the mezzanine, a coro chanting, "I'll never go back to Georgia." A gaunt, bearded guy wheeled an upright bass like Jesus lugging the cross. On the platform downstairs a harness of baby dykes waited for the train to the Village, squat butch girls with cornrowed hair, calf tattoos showing under their baggy jeans, leaning up against the I-beam pillars by the tracks, caressing and kissing their slender femmy girlfriends with script names inked on their arms.

Mick came in to meet with Rob the booking agent one day. He hadn't been in Penn Station in years. It was an armed camp. A cop hung out at one end, assault rifle slung over his shoulder, wearing a heavy black-ribbed bulletproof vest that made him look like a Stormtrooper Mutant Ninja Turtle. A quartet of GIs in desert-sand camo gear patrolled the waiting room with their rifles; another four lounged by the information booth. What the fuck? Is Osama bin Laden's cave underneath the New Jersey Transit tracks? Now boarding on Track 17, the 3:22 to Islamabad, making stops at Kandahar, Waziristan Junction, Quetta, and Peshawar.

"Lookin' good, man," Rob greeted him. They had coffee.

"What happened at Pulaski Hall?" Mick asked. "They cut us off in the middle of our set. Scott said Ike from 9DC told them to do it because he was scared we were gonna blow them away. Nobody had our backs. We got jacked."

"Sorry, I couldn't be there. I thought it was gonna be smooth, no problems. They run things like a clock there, you know."

They paused. "So, is there any future in this for us?"

"Well," Rob said, "it depends." A drawn-out sign of trouble. "Let me be honest with you." Another bad omen. "You think you were something back in the day. And you were. You guys were the most original band on the scene, and you never really got your due. But you know what? That doesn't mean shit today. The kids coming to shows now got no fuckin' idea who you were. They were in diapers, or they weren't born yet."

"Yeah, but you gotta be able to do something," Mick pleaded. "Just put us out there, we'll prove it. I have faith in us. Put us on a bill with any band in the world, we can do it. We're good enough, we can reach them. We gotta reach the people. We give them more than bands that just wanna be product. They don't give a fuck. If somebody wants to use their song in an ad, they think it's great. They think it's cool to be known as 'the band from the Apple commercial.' Fuck! For any one of us, that was like selling your kid for child porn. Yeah, we wanted to make it, we wanted to be stars, but we had a mission. We wanted to fuck shit up. We wanted to lead an army of rebel pleasure-seekers. And we're sounding real good. I know we got another record in us."

"Mick, I believe you." Rob looked pained. "I know how good the band is, and I know what you stand for. I know you mean something. You're artists, you're better than the schlock and lamo bullshit out there. But that's not enough. That's not gonna get you good shows. The problem is, I hate to say it, you're not a guaranteed draw. Not on a mass level, at least. I want to work with you, but I can't do a whole lot for you." He shrugged.

"C'mon, I'm not asking promoters to lose money on us." Mick took a deep breath, trying hard not to sound as desperate as he felt. "Give us some credit. We're not a charity ball. I know we can do it." Slow down. Look him in the eye. "Just get us out there, people will respond."

"I can try, but it's not gonna be easy." A heavy pause. "How committed are you? Is everyone in the band willing to go out and do crap shows until you build up a following again? I mean, if you really are serious about wanting to do this, you've gotta go back and start at the bottom."

The honest answer was probably no. Was anyone willing to play Tuesday in Erie and Wednesday in Peoria, Thursday in a failing sports bar in Columbus, drawing crowds of twelve people and sleeping on someone's floor amid an armada of half-empty beer bottles? To chase some lottery ticket dream they'd already had a better shot at?

There was a message from Morena, that actress he'd been seeing in L.A., when he got home. Her period was still late.

Scott scored a session gig for Thursday night, with a singer-songwriter duo called the Wallabouts. A couple in their mid-thirties, they wanted to post an album on their website and were going to give him $100 for four songs, saying they'd use him for the rest if it went well. The tunes were simple enough, judging by the MP3s they sent him. He could pick up some extra money and sharpen his chops for the tour.

He drove down Flushing Avenue, past the Happy House, a loft-party space from the '90s, and the In the Drink Lounge, a boarded-up bar across from the defunct Brooklyn Navy Yard. He remembered sailors brawling at a rockabilly-band gig there, and the bartender telling him, "Those Navy boys, they get wild." That bartender was one of Alice's best girlfriends now. He turned left onto a lonely street of industrial lofts and ancient frame houses. The studio was in an old warehouse. It was called Heartbreak Hotel.

Paul and Martina, the Wallabouts—she sang, he played guitar—had told him they liked the idea of quick sessions. Hank Williams cut four songs in three hours, they said. Martina stopped the first run-through in the middle. "I don't want to do this song tonight. It doesn't sound right. There's something off."

We can't even hear ourselves yet, Scott thought. The engineer was still trying to balance the levels in their headphones.

"Let's try it faster," Paul answered. They ran though it again. Neither one liked it that way.

"Let's just drop it," Martina insisted.

Paul thought it could be salvaged by rewriting, by changing the key, shortening the chorus, and stopping at the end of the bridge. They blew a couple takes when he forgot those changes and started parts back in the old key. The two squabbled more while Scott and the bass player, a hipster named Josh with big geeky black glasses, tried to sort out when to come back in after the stop, finally figuring out that the wait was three beats. Paul kept hitting it late or early, on two or four. Getting "three" into his head was like trying to explain that "Who" was the name of the man on first.

"Why is this taking so long?" Martina whined again.

"Only married couples can bicker like that," Josh whispered. "They coulda been a bit more prepared, y'know?"

The studio engineer hunched over his computer, the sound a dense black EKG on the screen, two parallel strips thinning to a string on the quiet parts, flaring to the edges when it got loud. He was staying out of it. The four-hour mark passed at midnight. They quit at 2:30 with three songs down on the hard drive.

Scott got his money, but the session shortened his temper more than it sharpened his chops. It's good that people can get their music out now without going through a record company but, damn, somebody's got to filter out the flaming amateur-hour prima donnas. They clutter it up for the rest of us.

Everybody in the band took Friday off work. Tina cooked a big pot of spaghetti sauce to feed Janis and Damian for the weekend. They left at noon to beat the traffic, got to West Philly at four.

The show was in a one-room hall with a bar at the side. Some of the people who put on the shows lived upstairs. Somebody said it was an old Moose or Odd Fellows hall. Somebody else said it had been a jazz club in the '50s. It was a dive, but it felt promising. Comfort has its place, but rock'n'roll soul comes from schmutz, not glitz. Spraypaint on cracked plaster and walls ivied with band names, dubious toilets and dodgy legal status, beer in a garbage can full of ice.

"You should move down here," Jae, a slender dreadlocked woman, told them after soundcheck. "Rent's cheap, and we've got a good little scene. We'll even hook you up with a bicycle and a date. All of you."

At least they let you fuckin' smoke here, Underend thought. I'm glad I quit drinking before Bloomberg banned smoking in bars. I know it's bad for your health but I gotta have one vice left.

The show was well packed, and both opening bands were good. The Extra 13 from Baltimore played garage rock shading into psychedelic improv, a raw, frenzy-driving beat topped with splatters of dissonant fuzztone, a dragster engine revving into interstellar overdrive. Los Nuevos Anos were a Latino punk band from Allentown. Their guitarist showed metalloid roots, shredding on a sapphire-blue Ibanez, but it was more what-the-fuck chaos seasoning than annoying look-at-me heroics. They did a rant/song against immigrant-haters that sounded like the early Clash playing cumbia, and they turned a Mexican children's ditty called "Los Niños Que Comen Mocos"—"The Kids Who Eat Snot"— into a joyful ska-punk rave-up. *Si tú quieres ser feliz/Mete un dedo a la nariz.* If you want to be happy, put a finger up your nose.

The Gutter Astronomers got the room popping. They had the perfect loose-tight yin-yang, rehearsed enough so they weren't likely to fuck up and comfortable enough not to fear it. The gods of technology cooperated, too; the beats cracked and throbbed and the notes dripped juicy resonance. They gathered speed and scorch, and the crowd gave it back. A few were people who remembered them well from back in the day, some were kids who'd unearthed them through underground archaeology, but most had no idea who they were other than a name from history. This is what I was trying to tell Rob, Mick thought. Put us on with some good bands and some cool people, and we can't be stopped.

They stayed with Jae and her boyfriend, Zak, on a narrow side street of brick rowhouses. Zak was a scrawny guy with a wispy mustache and beard, Wobbly black-cat patches on his denim jacket. He was younger than she was. They brought back pizza and beer, sprawled around the kitchen and living room joking and philosophizing.

Tommy, the sound guy from the show, rolled a joint and passed it around. He was a scruffy white kid in his early twenties, a red P Phillies logo on his wool hat. Mick got on him for that. "I heard they booed Santa Claus at the Vet."

"That was nothin'. I went to an Eagles game with my uncle when I was a kid, and there were these two guys there, big beergut Godzilla and Rodan all decked out in green, pushing a guy in a wheelchair up the ramp. And the guy in the wheelchair's wearing a Dallas jersey. My uncle's like, 'I don't fuckin' believe it. They're helpin' a Cowboys fan.' But when they get to the top, they turn the wheelchair around, and one of them says 'Either that fuckin' jersey comes off, or you're goin' back down the fast way.' "

"That was fucked up, but people really hate Cowboys fans from here," Zak explained. "They're traitors. They got tired of watching the Eagles lose, so they switched sides."

"Like rooting for Goliath to crush that little putz with the slingshot," Mick rebounded.

"It's so great you could come here," Jae enthused to Tina. "Thank you so much."

"No, thank you for putting on the show," Tina said. "I haven't played out of New York in almost twenty years. I miss it. That's the best part of touring—we get to travel around and connect to people. There's people doing cool stuff all over the country, and you never hear of it."

Tommy rolled another spliff and put on a CD by his band, a one-man drum-electronica thing called Percussive Devices. Repeating echoes set the groove, then clanks, scratches, and crashes leapt out of the mix. A kalimba lilted on top, metal on the keys gently buzzing, then it twanged hard, the echo reeling like a stunned boxer. Tina, well charged, spaced out on it, caressing Sabotage, the black kitten that had gravitated to her.

"I like using car springs, weird stuff like that," Tommy told Scott and whoever else was listening. "Who says you gotta buy it from a store to make music?" He did it by attaching contact mics to drums, metal, and wood objects, then overdubbing odd sounds and polyrhythms. "I get the mics on the Net from a guy in Massachusetts. They're little red discs about the size of a quarter, they're like 85 cents each, but they're really fragile. I break a bunch of them every time I play. I like doin' stuff with electronics, but simple stuff, not computerized where everything's preset and it's like playing video games. I like when you push it to the point where it starts warping and fucking up, them you get a really cool sound. You can make a cowbell sound like it's goin' off inside a cave."

The Percussive Devices name came from the most notorious euphemism in the city's history. When the cops raided the MOVE house in West Philly in 1985, they dropped a bomb containing three pounds of C-4 explosive on the roof, starting a fire that killed eleven people and burned down two whole blocks. The mayor said it wasn't a bomb, it was a "percussive device."

"Was it a Ludwig or a Tama? A cymbal or a conga?" Tommy asked rhetorically. "You could do a lot of damage dropping a 20-inch ride cymbal out of a helicopter."

"They called us the white MOVE when we lived in West Philly but people were really cool to us," Jae put in. They'd been a bunch of dreadlocked kids, activists and poets and musicians, seven or eight or nine of them living together in a mostly black working-class neighborhood between the ivied, modern citadels of academia to the east and down-home neighborhood blocks to the west. "We didn't even have to squat, the city gave us a three-story abandoned building for $5,000. But Zak and I wanted to get some more privacy, so we moved up here."

They all slept well, on couches and cushions on the ground floor.

Tina and Scott were the first up in the morning, a bleary-eyed duo stumbling out for coffee while Mick and Underend languished in the arms of Morpheus. Having kids had put their body clocks on an unbreakable day schedule. The streets and houses seemed miniscule. The corner grocery was too brightly lit. A white-haired geezer babbled to them while they waited for the pot to drip full. On the way back they passed a house gilded with yellow ribbons, the windows festooned with "Support Our Troops" and "Freedom Isn't Free" stickers and a portrait of a young mustachioed cop, P.O. Danny Faulkner, 1955-1981. The black militant framed for killing him was still struggling to get off Death Row. In the middle of the door a poster proclaimed "ELVIS IS COMING!" Well, an impersonator at least, appearing at the Fraternal Order of Police Ball on December 9th. Tina shot a picture of Scott posing like a hunk of burning love in front of it before a dog barked and they decided a discreet exit might avert an encounter with a heavily armed resident cop.

After Mick and Underend woke up and had coffee, they collected their bags, loaded the van, and said their goodbyes, giving thanks and praise for the show and the place to stay, exchanging phone numbers and e-mail addresses, websites and wishes to do something in the future. Yeah. Definitely. That would be cool. Sounds like a plan.

Mick tried to call Morena from the road, standing in a rest stop parking lot on the Delaware Turnpike, dialing her number while the others got coffee and pissed. The D.C. show was in a space called the Pax Café northeast of downtown. A funky go-go beat, big bass drum and rolling timbales, boomed through a car window as they turned onto the block.

They arrived before the PA system did. They couldn't find Rodney, the contact person there. He was off "delivering a manifesto," someone said. They spotted him, a tall dude with male-model looks preaching to a host of volunteers and scenesters about the momentousness of the occasion, how this DIY show is "reclaiming our culture from commodification and reification." Someone else said he was the son of a powerful D.C. lawyer, gone anarchist renegade. It was supposed to be a collective but he was obviously the honcho.

"Be patient," he urged when they finally prised him away. "We're creating a space for people who think outside the box. We're creating and finding new ways for people to live and do business outside the system. It's not always going to be smooth. Don't worry. We've got a sound system coming that's gonna be off the hook. It'll all be good by the time you play." His artisanal t-shirt said Fuck Capitalism - Dumpster Dive.

The band immediately distrusted him. "This guy's like a bad version of me twenty-five years ago," Mick said. "Like he's the only one who ever put on a DIY show."

"Yeah, he sounds like a fuckin' cult leader, the way all those people follow him around," Underend put in. "And all his promises got plenty of wiggle room, you notice? Are they even gonna have a PA?"

"I hate it when people say 'think outside the box,' " Tina added. "It makes me think of my cats shitting on the bathroom floor."

Mick went outside to call Morena again. Scott unpacked his drums and started fitting them together. "Ya got a drum rug?" he asked one of the volunteers.

"A what?"

"A rug, like about that big," Scott gestured. "I need one to put under my drums, so they don't move when I play."

"You'll have to ask Rodney."

"A rug?" Rodney was incredulous. "Where do you expect us to find one? This is a grassroots show. We're not for rock stars."

"I'm not asking you for a bowl of M&Ms with the brown ones picked out. It's a fuckin' simple thing. Ask any drummer. If you don't have a rug, my drums are gonna be flying all over the stage every time I hit them. It's a fuckin' basic necessity so I don't feel like I'm taking a flying fuck at a rolling doughnut."

"This is a grassroots show, man. It's not a slick corporate music business production. It's the message that's important."

Scott stalked away, muttering "Fuck it, I'm not going through this bullshit sober." He went out to get a six-pack and a pint of whiskey, putting a good-sized dent in both before the PA arrived and got set up. The others waited around and simmered. They couldn't leave. Dinner was sandwiches on stale bread from a deli with bulletproof plastic around the counter.

The show started late. Only a few dozen people showed up. The space was in a sketchy neighborhood, the show was poorly advertised, and Nation of Dissonance, a big local band from the early '90s, was doing a reunion that night in Adams-Morgan. They should have been on that bill but Rob didn't have the juice to push them onto it; their name didn't carry much weight with that generation. Scott got more and more fucked up. Underend, Tina, and Mick were all irritated but he wasn't taking no for an answer. Tina's mood wasn't improved when she overheard a kid say, "What's she doing here? She looks older than my mom."

The other bands were mostly tenth-generation hardcore, except for Civil Decay. Rodney had pitched them to Rob as the main local draw, the co-headliner. They'd been on the *Raging Brainstorm* compilation that put the D.C. hardcore punk scene on the map in the fall of '81. The revived version was missing the original singer, bassist, and drummer. The guitarist was missing a couple teeth and several brain cells. He vaguely remembered the Gutter Astronomers and harangued them about how Civil Decay "blew away Minor Threat *and* the Bad Brains" back in the day.

Most of the bands went on far too long and the sound system was a mess, plagued with painful treble and feedback. The clock ticked toward closing time with the odds of the Gutter Astronomers playing a full set getting longer and longer. They didn't need ESP to be all on the same thought: Fuckin' hell, the same shit we went through back in the day, and we're WAY too old to deal with it now.

The kids with curfews and trains to catch filtered out as did the older people with shorter nightlife expectancies and babysitters to pay. As the last band before them went off, Rodney was introducing a video about "the truth about the most cataclysmic event in our history, the truth the government doesn't want you to hear. A conspiracy so immense it dwarfs any other in the history of man." The screen filled with repeated images of flames and smoke erupting from the sides of the silvery morning buildings, little specks of people plummeting to their doom, while an announcer droned on about thermite residue and Mossad agents, controlled demolitions and Building 7. Mick, Tina, and Underend were accosting Rodney, demanding, "Why do you have a video on when the show's running late? We're gonna go on two fuckin' minutes before closing time!"

"Some things are more important than schedules. I'm surprised, I thought you were a political band. I'm exposing the government's lies. We're following the way of Gandhi and Martin Luther King, and we all have to make sacrifices for the truth. People are dying because they covered up what really happened, that it was a false-flag operation. You really believe the official story, that those buildings fell down because a couple of Saudi students flew planes into them?"

Everybody in New York who was awake that morning saw the planes hit, Tina thought. Her cousin Al's name was on the plaque outside Ladder 115 in Long Island City. They hadn't been close but he was still family. This guy's pimping my cousin's death for his stupid conspiracy theories, like every sleazy politician in the country.

The 27-minute video cleared the room. Even the volunteers were outside smoking cigarettes and checking their phones. The Gutter Astronomers got through three songs before Rodney told them time was up. They tried to keep playing, but Rodney turned the overhead lights on and the sound guy turned the PA off. He handed them fifty dollars. Two twenties and a ten.

"Excuse me? We had a $250 guarantee." Mick was raging. "And Rob said you swore up and down to him that we'd do way better than that, that's why he came down for you. He gave you a break because you were a DIY show."

"Why are you being so materialistic? Money's only how they keep score in the corporate world, it's not what this space is about. I'm sorry more people didn't come but we got the message out and that's what's most important. I'd love to have a million dollars to promote awareness. But I can't afford to pay you any more because we have to keep the space sustainable." The spiel was juggernauting. It was hard to get a word in.

"Do you know what 'guarantee' means?" Tina was on the edge of screaming. "Look it up in the dictionary. It's a noun. It means something you promise to give under any circumstances."

"Sometimes things happen you don't expect. We have to keep the space sustainable. And none of the other bands demanded a guarantee. You're the only one."

"They're local. It costs us money to get here, you know." Not just gas money, it was strings and sticks and replacing cracked cymbals, the time and money they put into practicing and traveling, the years of work they had put in to make themselves worth listening to. "We gotta eat, too."

"What happened to playing to support the scene? You should support alternative spaces, man, that way you won't support the corporate system. And also, you didn't play a full set. You only did three songs." Scott came in on that line. He flung his beer in Rodney's face. There wasn't enough left to do much drenching, which made him madder. He flipped over a garbage can, swinging the bag and scattering drippy beer cans and food wrappers, stomping on empty water bottles. Then he took out his lighter.

"Okay, okay… chill out!" Rodney pleaded. "I'll give you a hundred bucks. I'm taking the money out of my own pocket!" They took it. "Was that necessary?" he asked Scott.

"Yes, you fucking asshole."

Scott was still fuming while they repacked the van. Rodney's car was parked nearby. Underend started the van and turned it outwards, Tina and Mick were in, they were waiting for Scott. He was selecting a half-brick from the driveway and fastballing it into Rodney's back windshield. Jagged little dice rolled onto the ground. Seven! He jumped in the van, and they cruised off.

They had a 7 1/2-hour drive to Mick's sister's house in Northampton. Scott passed out in the back. The other three debated in intense whispers. Underend was driving, with Tina shotgun and Mick leaning forward between the seats.

"He shouldn't have gotten so fucked up," Underend offered. "I mean, somebody needed to start a fire with that guy, but don't pour fuckin' gasoline on it and act stupid."

"It makes us look bad," Mick answered. "Unprofessional. If we wanna do more shows, gossip travels fast. I don't wanna think about how the story's gonna get twisted when it spreads around."

"I think he was right," Tina said. "You were outside, you didn't see what happened when Scott asked him for a drum rug. He was acting like we wanted an eight-ball each and separate limos."

"Yeah, and he certainly focused the fucker's attention," Underend chimed in. "If we just asked the guy to do the right thing, we'd have gotten bupkes outta him."

"And he would have told us that it was special organic fertilizer, that the Rastafarians use it to grow the best sinsemilla in Jamaica," Tina joked.

"I think," Underend paused, "he's just a rich kid playing revolutionary until he gets a job in Daddy's law firm. Why is it that the promoters who talk the most rhetoric always end up being cheap fucks who can't get the simplest things together?"

"He's not such a radical," Mick countered. "There's a weird right-wing smell to all that conspiracy shit. Everybody I hear talking says something about the Jews sooner or later. Of course, they all deny that they're anti-Semitic."

"Philly was great. Those people were really nice." Tina was trying to salvage something. "This guy, it was like he thinks he's too cool to treat people with respect. Common decency, really. We drove 250 miles to do his show, and he thinks it's 'alternative' to be disorganized and make us waste our time?"

"Yeah, and he used every weaselly excuse I've ever heard from corporate music-biz people," Underend threw in. "The bands were crap, too. In Philly, they were smokin'."

"It's ignominious that we've fallen so far," Mick sighed. "That's some sad Spinal Tap shit, second on the bill to a 9/11 conspiracy video. It's like out of town, we're fuckin' nobody now. We're back to where we were in '81, '82, only then we had a scene and word of mouth."

They kept at it. Fulminating and ruminating over the night's events and the injustices they exemplified in the larger scheme of banddom. Ranting and brooding under the fluorescent lights of a wee hours rest stop in Maryland or Delaware or South Jersey, their eyes zizzing at the black-and-white floor tiles as they drank more coffee.

"That guy from Civil Decay was fuckin' annoying."

"He looks fuckin' decayed. I don't think he was straight-edge very much after '82."

"They used to be good. They were the darkest, slowest band on *Raging Brainstorm*."

"So who conned who? Did Rodney con Rob that they were the real band?"

"No, I think that guy scammed Rodney, and Rodney doesn't know shit about music, he can't tell the difference. He just knew they're a name from back in the day."

Nick Cave crooned weary morbid ballads on the car speakers. The New Jersey Turnpike and the George Washington Bridge. It was strange to drive through the city without stopping. They faded into silence, mulling over each other's motives. Tina was sick of it. She wanted to play, it was reviving her, getting her out of a rut, but this was too much to go through for too little reward. Like having to get kitted out with hiking boots and a backpack full of ropes and pitons to climb two flights of stairs. It wasn't malicious, it was just tedious. She got enough juvenile melodrama from her own kids. And her cats were a better audience than they'd had that night.

Underend felt the same way, but what else had he got? It was still his secret unabandoned fantasy: yeah, if things broke right, I could get it. A dream deferred to arm's length, kept at a distance for fear of hoping too much. The azure lake could easily be a sidewalk puddle, the leap of faith a dry dive. But once you miss it, the glimmer shines twice as hard.

All lead singers are fuckin' drama queens, Scott was semiconsciously musing. They've all got a little Judy Garland in them. 'Oh no, I can't go on any longer. But I have to do it for my fans.' The point is to make fuckin' music. Mick still wants to be a star, he thought. And he expects a lot more than he's getting at this late date. He lives for the crowd. He knows what he wants but he doesn't know what the fuck it is. He wants people to worship him like he's David Bowie. A cult of himself, adored for his style and message, but then he rants about fascist celebrity, the cult of personality, Baal and Moloch on *American Idol*. Does this sound contradictory? Fuck yeah. It is what it is. Rock'n'roll walks a thin line between genius and insanity, between bread and roses and bread and circuses. Being in a band is a fantasy world, but it also makes you relentlessly practical, at least in the lower levels. The van's gotta run and the gear's gotta get to the show. I could be drunk as shit onstage, but I know I gotta tighten the lugs on my drums first.

Mick thought Scott had a donkeyish pragmatism. Eyes to the ground, believing that one gig isn't going to suddenly restore you to the throne of rock royalty that you never really had back in the day, as much as you might have thought you did. As much as you think you might deserve it, you're not going to be fucking Pamela Anderson Lee, the video image glitching from the blinding white light of your auras and the Andean ski slopes on your night table. You couldn't soar thinking like that. It was a small-time mentality. Never looking at the sky because you're too worried you're gonna step in shit. But fuck it, why pretend I'm a star any longer? Fuck staying in New York. They think Varvatos is hip because he's got a Ramones poster on the wall. Slap a designer name on a $30 pair of Converse All-Stars and sell them for $130. That's rock'n'roll? Fuck that, I ain't comin' back. Everybody who makes it goes against the odds. That doesn't mean that everyone who goes against the odds makes it. No matter how hard you work, how much talent you have, or how much you want it. There comes a time when you can't tell any more if it's perseverance or foolishness. He hadn't told anyone about the phone call from Morena Thursday night. If she wants it that way, if I gotta settle down and have a kid, I could do it. I've had my fun. It'll be a new chapter in my life. I'll be the best dad any kid could have.

Scott broke the silence. "You know what it is? If we do commercial shows, we get treated like piss, and if we do DIY shows, we're lucky if we even make back our gas money. And that motherfucker in D.C. was the worst of both worlds." They drove on, stopping for gas and coffee in Connecticut. Scott, bleary-eyed, emerged from the bathroom in a sudden good mood. "You know the red rubber thing in the bottom of the urinal?" he laughed. "I look down, and it's got a little nub on it that says 'SAY NO TO DRUGS.' The fuck? They tryin' to make sure all the stoners aim?"

They pulled into Mick's sister's driveway in Northampton just after sunrise. Hannah cooked them breakfast while her partner, Lynn, went out running with the dog. She played a CD by a local women's klezmer band called Zionist Plotz. A punkish guitar traded licks with a gypsy violin on the fast tunes; the slow ones sounded like Middle Eastern chamber music. With the light stabbing at their eyes, they grabbed a few hours of sleep.

Scott was badly hung over but able to drive as they headed south on the Interstate 91 ridge. They turned off into an abandoned swath of city. Miles of empty mills and factories, the roaring red-brick engines of 1907 stilled, no longer clattering, grinding, weaving, smoking, pouring out paper, cloth, machine parts. Silent and deserted, boarded-up windows, weed trees growing in the alleys. Faded paint signs for long-gone businesses high on the walls.

The sun glowed low over the old canal as they loaded in. It was silent even for a Sunday. Maybe it'd be livelier on a Monday morning or a Thursday afternoon, but just with traffic passing through. Nobody crowding into corner stores for egg-on-roll and coffee, nobody tracking slush into their bright and bleary bustle on winter mornings, no meatball-hero lunch counters, no workingman's bars where that first warm shot and cold beer brings instant relief, Johnny Cash and Aerosmith on the oxygen jukebox. An old movie theater sealed up with cinderblocks. Cement coins on a dead town's eyes. Yeah, they try to spruce it up with artists' lofts. It's cheap, they got a few refugees from the city, but it's an island. An isolated oasis.

Scott and Mick went on a coffee run, taking the van over to the non-white section in search of an open bodega. Tina and Underend went around the back to smoke. They stood wrapped in coats, tapping their ashes between rusted machinery and scrubby ailanthus trees, chainlink fence and crumbled concrete. It was a beautiful day, the sunglow warmed the spirit, painting everything a benevolent yellow, but it was still November in Massachusetts.

The old newsprint mill had different artists in each room, showing off their paintings, installations, and sculptures. Videos flickered on computer monitors, fish and snowy static and mannequins melting into colors. Ghostly robed figures doused with dusty grey paint filled one dark room. Another had a tape loop of scrapes and squeaks, the whine of a bowed cymbal, water dripping on orange-lit stones, the drops amplified and triggering electronic bangs and bongs. A sixtyish woman in red coveralls and a babushka held court in another, her eyebrows pierced and her eyes surrounded by geometric black and yellow makeup the color of a healing bruise. She pointed at her furiously spattered canvases, dark smoky eruptions and flaming oranges and reds intertwined with occult symbols and bleak black Xs. "Wilhelm Reich said that the only color an artist couldn't paint was the color of a dying fire," she told them.

Clouds blew in as the sun lowered, and a hard, cold rain befell from the sky. The band played an intimate show, eighteen people including Hannah and her partner. They burned but it felt like playing in a vacuum.

They drove south on I-91, the windshield wipers fighting a losing battle with the sleet. They dropped Mick off in New Jersey at two in the morning and reached Brooklyn at three, taking another hour to make the rounds of everyone's houses and unload the gear, the inevitable end-of-the-night caravan schlepping guitars, amps, drum cases, and clothing bags out of the van and into the building, loading elevators and lugging it up stairways, always keeping the pile within eyeshot. Then home at last. For better or for worse.

Chapter 8
The '00s / December

Underend's doorbell rang moments after nine on Monday morning. Who the fuck is it? The peephole revealed a black dude in a leather coat with a Jheri-curl mullet. He cracked the door open. The guy handed him papers. An eviction notice.

"What the fuck? I paid my rent!"

"Yo, I'm just doing my job. Your beef is with your landlord. Don't shoot the messenger."

Underend called the landlord's office. "What's goin' on? I paid my rent this month."

"It was late. Your lease says it's supposed to be in within five days after the first," the woman answered.

"I paid it as soon as I could. My job closed down last month, and my unemployment money didn't come through until Wednesday."

"Mr. Vicodini, we have rules for prompt payment and you agreed to them when you signed your lease. It's your responsibility to pay your rent on time. We're in business to make money, not to carry deadbeats."

Give me a fuckin' break. They probably pass out manuals on how to be an asshole when they hire people at that company. No, the smart ones already know. This is the last thing I need. I got no money to move. Well, let me get the pittance I have coming. The 800 number for unemployment had been busy all day yesterday. He dialed it. Busy. Try again. Still busy. He finally got through to the disembodied humanoid voice. *Welcome to the New York State Department of Labor. Remember, if you attempt to claim benefits for which you are not eligible, you will be denied benefits and may face prosecution for criminal fraud.* Yes, remind the fuckin' peasants to know their place. *Please enter your nine-digit Social Security number.* The other line beeped. *In the past week, did you work on any days? Press 1 or say yes if you did, press 2 or say no if you did not.* He pressed 2, and it beeped again. Shit, I hope it didn't screw up my answer.

The phone rang again the minute he got off. It was Billy Zap with bad news. From Black Dave, one of the messengers they used to work with. Jasmine, his poet girlfriend, was killed while riding her bike. She was twenty-four. She was riding from their place in East Williamsburg to her sister's house in Bed-Stuy on Sunday afternoon when she got hit by a woman driving in from Long Island in a Yukon. The *Real Free Press*, a budding leftist weekly with connections in the militant-bicyclist community, ran a photo of the mangled bike on its website, the truck's Bush-Cheney '04 bumpersticker hovering like a pro wrestler mocking a downed rival.

"You wanna play a benefit for them?"

"Okay."

"Can you practice tonight if I get time?"

"Yeah." He went out for a paper. A guy with long red dreads pushing a stroller rolled up to him.

"Yo, Underend, what's up? How you doin'? CB's was awesome, you gonna play again?"

Underend looked confused. The guy looked vaguely familiar and vaguely Puerto Rican. Actually, between his skin and hair color, he looked like an olive with an overgrown pimiento sprouting out of the top.

"Chris. You remember me? From B-CAT."

Oh yeah. Chris Ybarra. Worked at the Boricua Community Arts Temple when No Name Maddox played there, his band opened, he'd been the bass player. And he knew who I was, he'd seen the Gutter Astronomers when he was fourteen. John and Reed hadn't liked the place's political air, but Chris came by it deep. His father was a refugee from Chile and his mom a Queens-Irish professor.

"Yeah, now I remember. Los… it was a Spanish name, it meant the Dirty Ones. Thanks a lot. How you doin'?"

"Los Sucios. I'm doin' great. This is Emiliana, she's eighteen months. Say hi, Emiliana." The baby wavered her hand. "I didn't know you lived around here. I'm working for CTO, Citywide Tenants Organization."

"Yeah… maybe you can help me, then. I got an eviction notice this morning. I paid my rent. They said it was late. They wouldn't take it because it came in after the 5th."

"What kind of papers did you get?"

"Guy came to my door at nine with them, they said I had to be out within five days."

"Yeah, that's your basic dispossess notice. It's bullshit, it's total harassment, but you gotta go to court to answer it by Friday. They got nothing on you, but if you don't show up you're totally screwed. They'll evict you automatically. Call CTO if you wanna know more."

Underend called the number Chris gave him when he got back to the apartment. A Jewish-grandmother voice answered the phone. "Citywide Tenants, this is Rochelle Grossman. How can we help you?"

Underend pleaded his case. "I don't know how they can do this. Okay, I was a bit late, but I paid my rent."

"It's pure harassment, but unfortunately, that's the way a lot of landlords do business these days. What neighborhood are you in?"

"Greenpoint."

"How much is your rent?"

"$950."

"Oh, if he gets you out, he can get a lot more money for the apartment. Who's your landlord?"

"Asher Yotser Management."

"Oh, that's the Blutzoyger family, they're bad ones."

"Where's the justice? I mean, I lost my job, I was five days late with the rent, but I paid it." Mindful that he was talking to an elderly woman, he deleted the "fuckin's" that would have normally barnacled most of the verbs and nouns.

"I'm sorry, but the system is not designed to deliver justice to tenants. You can probably win, but if they want you out, you have to be prepared to keep going to court to fight it. Is it a dispossess notice?"

"Yeah."

"Then you have to go to court right away. Right away, you understand? This week. You need to answer the complaint. That's the first thing you have to do. If you don't show up by Friday, they can send it straight to the marshal to have you evicted. You don't need a lawyer—just file the papers and tell them you paid the rent and they wouldn't take it—but it would be good to get one. And be careful. It makes a big difference who the judge is."

"It doesn't say who."

"You won't know until you get your court date. Some of them are fair and listen to you. If you get Torres or Brandwein, you're lucky. Some of them are in the landlords' pocket. If you get Mason-Jackson or Colaneri, you're in trouble. They'll throw you out of the house like you're last week's newspaper."

Great. I'm unemployed and about to be fuckin' homeless. But, hey, I'm in a new band!

Billy Zap put together the band for the benefit. Underend, Wipeout, Little Lisa on vocals, and a drummer from Detroit called Dr. Q. They had two rehearsals to get a set together, a mix of covers and songs from their old bands. Billy got them time in a studio in the basement of a record store in Williamsburg. It was a dank room with the inevitable rickety drum kit and fried-speaker Fender Twins. The Manhattan alternatives would have been playing in a glorified cubicle with metal bands leaking through the walls or paying $32 an hour with a mandatory credit card deposit. Here they could hang out a bit instead of rushing in and out.

Underend came in with a cup of coffee. Billy and Lisa were already there. Lisa dressed in a mash-up of styles that would have hated each other in previous generations, a Social Distortion t-shirt over a long print skirt and motorcycle boots. A butterfly tattoo just above her right wrist commemorated an old boyfriend killed in a car accident. She was twenty-nine, with a blues-mama voice implausibly big for her 5'2" frame. She'd come up from North Carolina four years ago. Originally from a mill town in the Appalachian foothills, she'd gone to school in the Raleigh-Chapel Hill area and sang in bands there.

"I got tired of it," she explained. "I felt old when I wasn't even twenty-five. It was too much a college scene, even for the ones who'd graduated. Everybody had their little in-jokes and in-group rules and rivalries, and it was all so… superficial."

Wipeout arrived toting a sticker-covered Gibson case. "And you came to Williamsburg to escape that?"

"I didn't want to go back home and do bluegrass or classic rock. I could buy a house in North Carolina for the rent I'm paying here, and my cousin wants me to come and join his band, but I don't wanna sing ZZ Top covers."

"So what are you doing with this bunch of old wankers?"

"I don't know. I got into older music. Really old music, like the Carter Family and Son House. 'Death Letter Blues.' 'No Depression in Heaven.' You know it? 'St. James Infirmary.' Those songs, they've got a power, a soul, I can't put my finger on it, but I know it's out there. Like you know they really lived what they were talking about, you can feel it."

Dr. Q came in last, holding his five-year-old daughter Elvina's hand and apologizing for his trouble finding a babysitter. His real name was Quentin Odom. Brought up on Motown, he'd gotten into rock after hearing the MC5. He was in a garage soul band called the Ice Cream Clones, could rock hard and funk it up. Underend liked him instantly, he turned him on to Linton Kwesi Johnson's first album and Dennis Bovell's bass run on "All Wi Doin Is Defendin," sliding up an octave and playing straight eights while the drums pounded punctuation. Dr. Q also played lap steel, a swirly purple one with carpet on the bottom.

"That thing looks like a psychedelic toilet seat," Underend told him when they took a break. "I didn't know you played lap steel."

"What, you didn't think a black man could play country music?" Dr. Q sparked back. "My mom's from Tennessee. You oughta hear her sing Hank Williams."

"No, Daddy, you're wrong. Grandma Ivy lives in Mich-i-gan," Elvina interrupted. "She picks us up at the Mich-i-gan airport when we go visit." She was a bouncy, big-eyed kid in a tan t-shirt and jeans, a pink Dora the Explorer backpack, magenta marble ties holding her braids.

"You're right," he explained. "She lives in Michigan now, but she was born in Tennessee. She moved to Detroit when Granddaddy got a job making cars."

"And we drive on the highway with the big tire and all the broken cars," Elvina went on. Dr. Q knew that road well. It was like driving on ruptured cobblestones. But at least all the abandoned vehicles were American.

"Daddy?" Elvina pursued. "You told me all the people who made cars in Michigan were losing their jobs. Why doesn't someone give them jobs fixing all the broken cars?"

"You got a lotta sense, girl," he answered.

"You're so precious," Lisa cooed. She was all over Elvina, calling her adorable. "What's your favorite music?"

"I like Sun Ra Ark-kestra," Elvina said. "We went to see him in Central Park. They were all old men like my grandpa and they all had sparkly costumes like outer spacemen."

Dr. Q turned to the adults. "Yeah, last time I went home, I'm listening to the radio, and they've got a show where they play all the new local jams, and they got people calling in, rating the records. And all they're talking about is if they think they'd sell," he ranted. " 'It's got a good commercial feel.' That kind of shit. Fuck that! These people aren't in the business; they're not supposed to care about that shit. How about if it's good? How does it make you feel, does it make you want to dance, is it a three-in-the-morning record, a baby-making record? That's how you supposed to sell records—you make a record that moves people. I mean, this is Detroit we're talkin' about. The Home of High Energy. CKLW, the Motor City." He sang the last line as a radio jingle, then accelerated into spiel. "We got everybody on Motown, John Lee Hooker, the MC5, the Stooges, Funkadelic, a lot of jazz cats—Elvin Jones, Grant Green, Yusef Lateef, Alice Coltrane. And techno started here, with Juan Atkins and them, they do a humongous rave in Hart Plaza every May. So we got a history we wanna live up to, you know what I'm sayin'? What's the next chapter gonna be? But these people don't care."

"You hear they kicked the drummers outta Tompkins Square?" Billy interrupted.

"The Puerto Rican dudes?" Wipeout asked.

"Yeah, the conga players. The yuppies in the new condos on Avenue B called in a noise complaint, and the cops came in and kicked them out."

"Sheeit, those dudes have been there since Gondwanaland split from Laurasia. You cut them out, you cut out the neighborhood's heartbeat," Dr. Q orated. And they had been, playing bomba, plena, and guaguanco ritmos ever since the first Boricuas settled the land between Houston and East 14th, Second Avenue and the mighty D. A cluster of six or seven men—and the occasional woman or gringo good enough to sit in—gathered on a bench on the park's east side, tipping brown or sparkly congas to the side, bopping the beats on the hard cowskin heads. Now the bench was silent. One more devolution. One more turn of the screw.

"Yeah, well, the yuppies don't give a fuck. They don't wanna hear monkey music when they're eating brunch on Sundays," Wipeout cracked.

"They're doing the same thing in Harlem," Lisa chimed in.

"Where? In Marcus Garvey Park?" Billy wondered.

"Yeah."

"Shit, I jammed with those dudes." Billy doubled on djimbe and percussion. "They've been having African drumming there twenty-five years. The Parks Department's even got a sign up that says Drummers' Circle. Well, I guess they chase the crackheads out and now the fuckers who bought luxury condos don't wanna hear the noise. Turn off that jungle music!"

"Very bad when drumming stops. Very bad when drumming stops," interjected Underend.

Everyone cracked up, except for Lisa. "What's so funny?"

"Well, there was this English explorer in Africa who goes out to the bush, this pith-helmet motherfucker," Billy began, "and he finds this village, and they welcome him and give him some dinner and a hut to sleep in. Except they're having some kind of festival, some kind of ritual, and the drums are going all night. *Ma-ka-oom ma-ka-ma ma-ka-ma-ko-sa, ma-ka-oom ma-ka-ma ma-ka-ma-ko-sa.* So the next morning the woman in the hut next door asks him, 'How did you sleep?' and he very politely says he couldn't, because of the drums.

" 'Ohhh,' she says. 'Very bad when drumming stops. Very bad when drumming stops.' Next night it's the same thing. The drums are going all night again. *Gun do pa-pa. Gun do pa-pa.* So the explorer goes to the guy in the other hut next door and asks what's up with the drumming. And the guy says, 'Ohhh. Very bad when drumming stops. Very bad when drumming stops.' Third night the drums are really intense, they sound like a fuckin' army of 10,000 Bo Diddleys. *Boom-ga-doom-ba-doom boom-boom-BOOM! Boom-ga-doom-ba-doom boom-boom-BOOM!* And the explorer dude hasn't slept in three days, he's getting really cranky. So the next morning he goes to the village chief, who asks him, 'Are you enjoying your stay in our village?' And he goes, posh accent, 'Those incessant drums have kept me up all night.'

" 'Ohhh,' says the chief. 'Very bad when drumming stops. Very bad when drumming stops.' And the guy loses it and screams, 'WHAT THE FUCK COULD BE WORSE THAN THAT INFERNAL DRUMMING?' Chief says, 'Bass solo.' "

Dr. Q made a *b'doom* rim-shot sound. He could talk drum talk with Billy. *Ba-kee-ding ba-ka* African. *Thuk-thuk-thuk-boompa* British big beat. The polytheistic pantheon of percussive voodoo, St. Max of the Ride Cymbal. St. Clyde of the Funk. St. Keith, spirit of explosive propulsion and creative destruction. St. Tito the Timbalero, patriarchal protector of the barrio, keys, and bridges.

"C'mon, let's get going," Wipeout interrupted. "We got two practices to pull this together. It's either gonna be a triumph or a train wreck, and I don't wanna go down the Malbone Street tunnel. Robert Ray, you better watch your speed." He sang the last line to the tune of the Grateful Dead's "Casey Jones."

"What the fuck are you talking about?" Billy interrupted.

"Malbone Street was the worst accident in the subways' history, in 1918. They had a strikebreaker who'd never driven a train before working a sixteen-hour shift, and he took an S-curve in a six-mile-an-hour zone at forty-five." Wipeout was a subway buff. "Robert Ray was the motorman who came in to work totally wasted on crack and Scotch and ran the 4 train off the tracks." That crash, in 1991, had killed five people, night-shift workers on their way home.

"Yeah, like I want to be really solid on these tunes, too," Underend put in. "It's like Billy and I just got laid off from our jobs, I got an eviction notice yesterday morning, I got no girlfriend anywhere in sight, but at least I got a show." He paused for the punchline. "So if we suck, it's really gonna be a fuckin' bummer."

They laughed and reshouldered their axes. Dr. Q gave Elvina earplugs and told her to get her shekere out of her backpack if she wanted to play along. "Now, don't you mess up the time, you understand?" he instructed.

They ran through two songs, "Cyberhog," Dr. Q's quasi-electronica/ drum'n'bass number, and "Shake a Tail Feather," a self-explanatory soul jam penned by Andre Williams, a 1967 hit for James and Bobby Purify. Elvina shook the beaded gourd studiously—and in perfect rhythm.

"Daddy, you were messing up," she said when they were done. "You were playing too many beats. You should have been playing the song."

Everybody cracked up. "Damn, you taught her well!" popped Wipeout.

Underend shaved carefully the next morning. He put on a shirt with a collar, a tie, and the black jeans that looked least like denim. Caffeinated, medicated, and prepared his pitch for work. Rolled a few cigarettes, even American Spirits cost $9.50 a pack now, and Top was making mentholated tobacco for $2.25. He got off the subway at Grand Central and gave a quarter to a panhandler, an old bag-of-wire guy wrapped in a blanket and clinking his coffee-cup coins in motorik spare-change riddim.

He made the rounds of the temp agencies on Fifth Avenue. Showed his ID and signed into the building. Remembered doing this sometime in the early '80s when the band was between gigs. Then he'd been up on speed, trying to be perky and alert, but when he looked at the men in suits and the women in designer jeans and crescent plastic nails, he got the message. No place for you here. Now he was on Madison, in an office that looked like a giant candy cane with red and white stripes and logos. Career Creators. He inhaled, prepared his spiel about being an experienced phone dispatcher. "We'll just get you set up on a terminal here, and you can fill out the forms," the woman said, ushering him into a side room. "When you're done with that, there's a test we want you to take so we can see where to place you."

Okay, an aptitude test. He filled in his name, address, and job history, and clicked on the next screen. "Be honest in your answers," it instructed.

"I always do my best in a job situation." Always, often, sometimes, rarely, never. Oh, a personality test. Do they think I'm fuckin' stupid enough to say Never? "Workers need to be supervised or they'll slack off." Always, often, sometimes, rarely, never. "If I was offered a better-paying job before I finished my assignment with Career Creators, I'd take it." How about how fast would they ditch me if they found somebody who could work cheaper? "I have days when it's difficult to be cheerful and energetic." Always, often, sometimes, rarely, never.

How about every fucking single day? "I am quick to find problems in a situation." Yeah. I've got a problem with this one. He clicked Often, logged off, and walked out.

Guess I failed that one. The only thing this test measures is your ability to lie convincingly. Well, that's an indispensable skill in the corporate world. To spew what they want to hear without being obvious about it, without being too perfect, and to guess what flaws you can admit to that aren't fatally damaging. And anything you said could be used against you. This was not a decade to be a fuck-up, unless you were a Teflon celebrity or a billionaire big enough to own the bank. Then you could stage a tepid expiation ritual and be accepted as someone who had Grown.

Ordinary people had it harder. There wasn't much between you and the ulcerated-leg ragpiles begging for quarters in I Love New York coffee cups. No, there was a lot. You had four walls and a future beyond scrounging enough change for a slice of pizza and a pint of wine, a forty of malt liquor, or an airline bottle of whiskey, whatever was the most cost-effective way of getting alcohol into your body. But even if you were a hardworking solid citizen with 2.3 kids, they could chute you very easily. And then if you slipped into the neurochemical abyss, there was a lot less padding once you fell out of the machine lattice. For those who landed in the gutter they didn't give a fuck if you marveled at the three stars in Orion's belt, followed the curve of the Big Dipper's handle to orange Arcturus, could digress about Antares, the aging red giant stretched out for millions of miles of cooling inferno, or white-hot Sirius a mere nine light years away, its partner a burnt-out dwarf collapsed a thousand times denser than lead. No. You were a bum. A worthless useless eater. Born under the ass of Taurus the Bull, and they were telling you it was the Pleiades plopping on your head. The depression wasn't doing him any good, but reality wasn't helping him get on either. There was no way out he could think of.

He walked down a street where lurid pink religious-fanatic flyers covered the lampposts and mailboxes. DOCTORS WARNING = GAYS GIVE SYPHILIS OF THE BRAIN. THAT CAUSES BLINDNESS. AND ALL THE DOPE FROM MEXICO IS POISON. ALL DOPE FROM MEXICO MUST BE IN REFREGARATOR OR

DOPE TURNS TO POISON. YOU WILL DIE JUST LIKE JOHN BLUSHIE DIED. And small stickers: HEAR SEXY GIRLS TALK. 9-11 WAS AN INSIDE JOB.

Billboards loomed overhead, four-story signs filling up the sides of buildings. A silvery paean to vodka: LUXURY FLIES ABOVE THE FLOCK. Yeah, and it shits on their heads like a diseased pigeon. In the subway it was the same. More giant vodka ads, ULTIMATE LUXURY over a red-lipped woman kneeling in front of a yuppie's fly, a '70s pervert leering in the background. Fuckin' hell, is anybody having sex except for money any more? Anybody other than escort services, porn stars, and celebrities? Everybody else is stressed-out drones expected to live vicariously. "Aspirational," they called it. Lives of envy, and when one of the rich and famous messed up, they fell upon them and tore them apart like a fucking pack of jackals. A nation of self-righteous closet cases. Platinum or plastic. A whole new world of über-chic glamor. The middle-aged yuppies got $6,000 custom-made Les Pauls so they could do half-assed classic rock covers. The kids growing into the music, the fourteen-year-olds in black t-shirts, got to go to guitar stores and sneak a half-hour on cheap computer-sawed sweatshop copies.

You have a choice, they tell you. There is no alternative. You pay your money. You get the deal. You do the deed. And the only thing you feel afterward is the empty space in your pocket. The sweet aftertaste of fake champagne. There was a void in his veins that wanted to be filled, to feel the chemical love train rushing up his spine. Or the warm sparks of whisky rippling out to his extremities. No. The days were shortening, rushing toward their dark afternoon nadir. Outside, the damp cold soaked his bones. Inside, his skin dried out like parchment from the winter heat. At least he had heat. He had to go to court tomorrow.

The G train took him to Hoyt-Schermerhorn. He walked the last few blocks to Housing Court along the back streets of downtown Brooklyn, new luxury condos rising above parking lots and welfare offices, a store barker chanting, "Step right up, getcha cellphones, every cellphone on sale."

At the court entrance he dropped his keys and change into a gray plastic tub and walked through the metal detector, climbed the stairs, and joined the line. They gave him a ticket and told him to wait. He scanned the room, looking for a place to sit. There was an obese-armed woman, a burly shaven-headed man in a cream shirt, a neck-braced woman in a wheelchair, a mother trying to keep a preteen girl and a little kid in a pink stroller calm and entertained. The only other white person was a woman with a familiar-looking head of black hair. "Tina!"

"Underend! What are you doing here?"

"I guess the same as you. I was five days late with the rent, and my landlord's trying to get me out."

"Me, too. I got an eviction notice that said it's not my primary residence. I've had that place since before Damian was born."

Island-accented voices rippled around them, interrupted by the clerks calling out "Yellow 47, window three. White 36, window seven," like the announcers in a game of Eviction Bingo.

"You know," Tina said, "it was great to do the band again. I just can't deal with all the bullshit of the business."

"I know. Those kids in Philly were really cool, they were doing something original, trying to find something real, but that guy in D.C. was a royal fuckin' dickhead."

"And we're adults now so we've gotten beyond a lot of the immature ego crap. I had more energy when I was young. I don't have ideas bursting out like I did then—I used to have nights where my brain was racing like Lenny Bruce on speed—but I feel like I've got a lot more depth now. I feel like I know what I'm doing, even though I was really rusty for the first couple shows. I wish I had more time. Between working and the kids, I'm so fried by the time I get a minute to myself."

They finally filed their papers and got dates to come back in January. "Wanna get lunch?" Tina asked.

They walked down to Atlantic Avenue, past bail bondsmen's offices and the looming slab of the county jail, past low brick buildings with antique shops, real estate offices, and Muslim stores selling African soap. A cold wind blew in from the harbor, under a smoky gray sky.

"I hate going to court," Tina said.

"Who doesn't?" Underend answered. "I haven't been in court for around ten years, since I got busted for my girlfriend's bag of pot. I'm not like you, I can't smoke that stuff. It makes me paranoid."

"It's got the opposite effect on me," Tina smiled. "Sometimes I think I might kill my kids if I didn't get high. It makes me more tolerant. I appreciate them instead of getting cranky."

They got falafels and went across the street to a coffeehouse with a UFO motif. It was quiet, the only other customers an old white lady with antiwar buttons and a couple hipsters pecking on their laptops. A curly-haired, poet-type girl in a leaf-green I ♡ BK jersey worked the counter. Ambient electronic music wafted, swelling and receding.

Shelter from the cold. That's how New Yorkers survive winter. People who malign us don't understand us. They think the city is all elite predators, that only the most accomplished cutthroats can make it here, the baddest killer whales in the stock market or the crack trade. No. Outside the bitter winds rage, the arctic air bites into your bones, the lampreys of greed hunt for fresh bodies to chew and eviscerate. They want you wired up like a terminal patient with IV tubes, only hooked in reverse so they suck the life out of you. The rest of us have to survive. We need each other. It's a fuckin' cold and hostile world. All we have is hope and solidarity. A little temporary relief. We'll take it. It makes it worth walking the twenty blocks or climbing the five flights of stairs. Inside we've got coffee, the radiator, hot soup, each other. Like cave dwellers around a campfire but with guitars to play rings of fire and redemption songs.

"They told me my apartment's not my primary residence. They said I lived in Queens," Tina related. "That's my parents' old house. My mom doesn't even live there anymore. I've lived here almost fifteen years. So I call the landlord, and all they tell me is, 'The matter has been referred to counsel. We can't discuss it with you.'"

"Did you call CTO?"

"Yes. The lady asked who my landlord was, and then she said, 'Summit? They're notorious.' She said they're buying up buildings around Ocean Parkway and trying to get people out. She called it 'predatory equity.' I never heard of it, but she said it's happening all over the city. They buy up buildings in neighborhoods that are nice but aren't gentrified yet and they try to drive out all the old people, the rent-stabilized people, so they can jack up the rents."

"That's evil," Underend answered. "I paid my rent late because my unemployment hadn't come through yet and I didn't want the check to bounce. But they're after me big-time now. You know I got laid off? The messenger place closed down. Billy's covering my health insurance for two months, but after that, I'm fucked."

"You can get COBRA, right?"

"Yeah, but it's $450 a month. I'm barely making the rent now, and my meds are $120 even with insurance."

"I haven't had it in years. I get it for the kids through the government. The S-CHIP program."

"I fuckin' hate this. I got enough problems trying to survive and stay sane. I don't need these assholes cutting another pound of flesh out of me every time I turn around."

"I know. I just wanna live and raise my kids and play music." A red gobbet of rage grew in her gullet, a hot goo somewhere between snot and lava. No, you'll never have it. You weren't born to it. You did your striving and grinding in the wrong places. This is private property, and we're sorry your throat is in the way of our knife, but they slaughter cows, don't they? We're artists, too. It's creative destruction. Hate. People say that if you hate someone, you're attached to them. You see what you hate in yourself in them. Sometimes. But you also hate people who have power over you. Who use it to exploit and abuse you. Who enjoy their cat-killer sadism or conceal their cold callousness behind phony apologies and glib euphemisms. Who are convinced of their superiority and smash you down the minute you question it.

Their thoughts raged in and out of warped unison like an out-of-tune 12-string guitar, in dissonant call-and-response like a No Wave opera chorus. How can you not hate people who'll spend $5,000 on football tickets, $2,000 on a blowjob, or $300 on a bottle of vodka, and then fire their workers for wanting a $10-a-week raise? How can you not hate people who buy your building deliberately planning to throw you out? Who'll put out old people, people with AIDS, put single mothers and their kids in the street four days before Christmas? It's toxic, but it's a body's natural reaction to evil in power. You can't escape them unless you overthrow them. There were some crimes that hadn't been outlawed yet.

"Yeah, the pressure's dropping on all of us these days," Underend grumbled.

"I'm tired of struggling," Tina sighed. "I just wanna live in peace. I'm sick of this." She realized she was quoting a song title and sang the line again. They shared a laugh.

"Seriously, you know what my ideal city would be? I'd love to have a place in a brownstone, somewhere near Prospect Park, with a little backyard and a wrought-iron gate in front, with purple geraniums and asters blooming. And a stoop where I could sit and play on summer nights, with Janis and our friends, with a big glass of iced tea and a joint. Watching Damian play ball in the street, little girls playing hopscotch on the sidewalk and chanting rhymes, teenagers flirting, neighbors stopping by and saying hi. And maybe some cute guy would come along and check me out."

Another one of her sister's old records jukeboxed on in her head. The Crystals, "He's Sure the Boy I Love." A broke-ass boy collecting unemployment. A love song for the new Depression. In real life he'd be another mouth to feed and probably more immature than Janis or Damian. And she'd have to be a millionaire to afford that life.

"You're dreaming, Tina."

"Yes, but I'm not the only one." She'd been a fourteen-year-old with an acoustic guitar and an Army jacket with peace signs the first time she heard that couplet.

They kissed goodbye, lingering a bit. They both felt a spark of romance, a flickering, a glimmer. Maybe, Underend thought. She understands what I feel, she's been a lot of the places I've been, and she's still hot. But he wouldn't know the first fuckin' thing about being a father. He hadn't even had a cat or a dog since he was a kid. Tina felt the same thing. They had a bond, a history, a warm connection. But bring him into every part of her life? They'd reconnected and made some peace, why risk fucking up the friendship?

She couldn't make it to the show Saturday. They promised to keep in touch. They took the train home from opposite platforms.

Dr. Q came by Underend's to pick him up, Billy coming in to help him get his amp down the stairs. The mix CD in the van morphed from the space gospel of Sun Ra's "The Satellites Are Spinning" to the more secular sentiments of Lee Shot Williams' "Everything I Like to Eat Starts with a 'P.' "

"You teachin' Elvina the alphabet?" Wipeout inquired, as the record tabulated pork chops, peaches, pears, pasta, and potato pie. "It's like *Sesame Street*, man."

"Not with this. She'd be asking me, 'Daddy, why would anyone want to eat cat meat? That's mean and nasty.' "

They rode on, their destination the benefit, a loft party in Bushwick. They navigated the one-way streets of a gentrifying ghetto/industrial neighborhood.

"Is Dave comin'?" Wipeout asked.

"I don't think so," Billy said. "I talked to him this morning. He said he wasn't really fit for public consumption, he was too fucked up to deal with being around a lot of people. I'm gonna see him tomorrow."

A procession of somber cyclists retraced Jasmine Spencer's last route through northern Brooklyn. They locked a white, seatless "ghost bicycle," flowers wound through the spokes and chain, to a No Parking sign at the scene of the accident, in front of an abandoned mansion on Bushwick Avenue.

The rubber-tired horde cruised in just as things were getting underway. A rather sanctimonious leftist singer-songwriter finished a tune about driving to the mall and wondering what it's like to be a Palestinian suicide bomber. He yielded the stage to a DJ spinning hip-hop, dancehall reggae, house, and '80s funk. A handful of people danced. The MC, *Real Free Press* city editor Sid Berkowitz, introduced the next group, a punk band called Plutocide. They had an oddly arty sound, like Sleater-Kinney or Sonic Youth.

"How you doin'?" Underend greeted him. "I thought you were working for the *Eye*." It was hard to believe he'd been in a punk band, Underend thought. He now looked like an archetypal middle-aged New York Jew, a balding, gray-haired man with glasses, a beard trimmed just at the point it began turning pubic, and the remains of last summer's Brighton Beach tan.

"No, I got laid off last year. The paper got sold to a chain, and they axed almost all the old staff. The *RFP* pays shit, but at least I got a job, and I can do good work there, I got a lot of freedom."

"Hey—you know about housing, right? My landlord's trying to get me out." They went into a back room so they wouldn't have to shout monosyllables over the music. Underend told the story. Sid uncapped a vial of pills, swallowing two with a small sip of water, and lit a joint.

"I got a bad fuckin' migraine," he explained. His eyes were pinned, Underend noticed. Between this guy's intake of pot and pills, it's amazing he can function, he thought. Sid's wife and teenage stepdaughter floated around outside. "Asher Yotser? Yeah, that's the Blutzoygers, those people are ruthless fucks," Sid rasped. "There's a whole family of them, they own a couple hundred buildings. I could do a story on them every week. And as soon as they buy a building, they want the people out. That's their business model. It's happening all over the city. They're not the only ones. There's Summit, NextStage, Jaguar, the Economalakas family."

"How can they do that? I'm paying my rent."

"They'll find a way if they can. That's what they pay their lawyers for. You're paying what? A thousand? They spend a few thousand in legal fees to get you out, they can get $1,700, $1,800 for your place if they fix it up a bit. They make their investment back in a year and then it's clear profit after that. And if they get the place over $2,000, there's no more rent control on it. Those fuckin' people look at kicking you out the way you'd look at killing cockroaches. You're a fuckin' parasite to them. And you're a fuckin' parasite who's in the way of them making more millions. And they control the city now. The assholes have won. At least until people get off their asses and do something about it."

"That's fuckin' evil." That feeling had been coming up a lot lately, he thought. Well, it slapped his face every time he went out in the world these days.

"You want evil?" Sid told Underend. "If there's one thing I learned writing about politics, it's how many rich and powerful people are complete sociopaths. It would scare the shit out of you. At least the junkie who stole the Demerol suppository out of his dying grandmother's ass had the excuse he was dope-sick, but health insurance executives deny medication to ten thousand people they've never seen just to make a few extra bucks. They're not stupid. They don't wanna look bad in the public eye but bottom line is, they don't give a fuck about anybody but themselves. Everybody else is a pawn or an obstacle.

"You know what gets me about the Blutzoygers? They claim to be so religious they won't press an elevator button on Shabbos or listen to music seven weeks out of the year, but they're total scumbags to their tenants and workers. I don't understand how they can do it."

The next band on, the Dioxin Flowers, was noisier, the guitars a wall of distortion. No bass player, the drummer playing Keith Moon explosions, the singer screeching and snarling in classic "SOCIETY MADE ME GARGLE WITH TOXIC WASTE AND NOW I'M PUKING IT UP!" hate-rock style. Not much songwriting, Underend thought, not much in the way of tunes, but they've got something. The kids want escape. Adventure stories. Fuck the fist of blandness, pounding us all with its incessant inanity. Freedom in a wall of noise, two guitars splattering through vintage fuzzboxes, stretching the boundaries of sound on a small stage in a black room, the far end of a loft. Even in December it was miasmic with sweat. The singer slugged whiskey. When the band was off in their own worlds, the drummer lost, they wavered, floundered, a loud puddle rainbowed with gasoline dreams. When they caught themselves and the drummer locked in, they were a juggernaut.

A rapper named Atoke the Iron Belle followed, her short set hampered by a glitch that cut out the sound from one turntable. The DJ came back on, spinning reggaeton, a rapid-fire chant over a simple electronic beat, congas and kick drum, a Spanglish wrestling-announcer voice growling "Quema, motherfucker, burn. BURN!" The dance floor was corked, the room throbbing. The *RFP*'s two editors—Vijay, an acerbic, bearded Buddha in a monster-collared Superfly suit, and Erin, a dark-haired Irish-Argentine woman in her mid-thirties who managed to be both driven and goofy—boogied behind the makeshift bar, uncapping beers and pouring mojitos from the blender.

The band bent over in the jumble of instrument cases by the back wall, tuning up and scrawling set lists. Underend was edgy. They'd pulled a lot together in two practices, but they'd still need luck and their best listening instincts to fly. Damn, he thought, I hope this isn't another shitty show, the band ragged or uninspired, the audience as responsive as Mount Rushmore. That's the last thing I need. I don't wanna come away feeling like we half-assed our way through a set to people who couldn't give two shits about what we're doing. If we don't burn, tomorrow morning's gonna be really fuckin' bleak. Then Sid was introducing them, "I want to thank you all for coming out and supporting us. We've got a special band together for tonight. You know, most of you don't know this, but a long time ago I used to play in a punk band called the Bad Words. And there was a band we played with a lot called the Flaming Roaches, and that's their guitar player, Billy Zap.

"And then there was a guy from Queens who played guitar in every shitty dive bar on the Lower East Side, and that's Wipeout O'Connor over there.

"And then there was a band called the Gutter Astronomers we opened for a couple times, and we're lucky to have their bass player here—Underend Vicodini.

"On the drums, from the Motor City, the fantastic Dr. Q. On lead vocals, from North Carolina, the fabulous Little Lisa Ashbury. Ladies and gentlemen, give it up for the Detroit Sex Pistols!"

They opened with a couple rockers, simmering and scorching into "All Wi Doin Is Defendin." They chilled it out with a dub coda, then hopped into "Cyberhog." Underend's long, low bass notes set the keel, the drums skittered like a hyperactive kid, and Billy quocked it up with a wah-wah, Lisa scatting dancehall chatter over the top. Billy switched to drums so Dr. Q could play lap steel for "Wreck on the Highway," dedicated to Jasmine. A tune Lisa had brought in, off an old Louvin Brothers album. Wipeout and Dr. Q knew it, too. They took it like a gospel song, which it was. Slow organ-like deep bass notes, Wipeout's reverent, keening waltz picking coming through the distortion, the lap steel dripping tears, and Lisa, Dr. Q and Wipeout singing the chorus with desperate harmony. None of them had that old-time hardshell religion, all of them despised its queer-fearing bastard of a son, but they got the spirit. Is there no one righteous enough to care about these crushed souls? Is there no one righteous enough to stop this carnage?

They followed that with a more homegrown weeper, Johnny Thunders' "You Can't Put Your Arms Around a Memory." If they were going to lose the crowd, it was going to be now, during the slow songs, Underend worried. How many of these people cared about Johnny

Thunders? Most of them weren't even born when the Heartbreakers did their last rent party at Max's. Some people weren't paying attention, they were drinking and socialating, a background static of chatter. Fuck it, can't please everyone. Some people looked like they were really moved, including the small cluster of crusties. Back in the day doing a corny country tune to punk rockers like that would have been like being a gay Red Sox fan in the Yankee Stadium bleachers. And then the groove hit, he pulsed the bass like a hippo heartbeat, locked in with Dr. Q on the drums. It wasn't really a groove song, but they felt it, people were up and dancing, a girl around twenty swaying in the front line, wearing hot pink sweatpants with Fuck Off printed in Gothic script on her ass. And Wipeout, Lisa, and Billy were torching the vocals like a trio of Joey Ramone, Ronnie Spector, and Johnny Thunders, the first and last of them ghosts.

They jumped into the homestretch of rockers and up-tempo soul jams: "Shake a Tail Feather," the Clash's "Garageland," Gateria's "Give Me Back My Brain," and a couple from Billy and Wipeout's old bands. The dance floor packed, bodies back to back. Dr. Q pounded the drums in tribal hypnosis. Underend locked in, his fingers rippling off notes, rhythms popping straight from the synapse. His brain clicked. He couldn't remember the last time he'd felt this good. It was fun. Pure pleasure, no melodrama. Music didn't have to be grandiose, like if you weren't a rock star you were a failure, if you didn't save the world and burn all illusions you were a failure, if you just played for pleasure you were mindless disco fluff. Like the blues, the mother root of everything. It was the alchemy of the blues: You take your pain and pleasure and the community's pain and pleasure, and people could feel their pain in it, but still get off.

Why the fuck didn't he figure that out sooner? It's us and them, and we need our own culture. Something they can't hijack and sell back to us with all the flavor leached out. I don't want to live in pain but I don't want to be numb, he thought. Living as an adult means being numb most of the time. Blanking out the boredom and slow decline that's your fate, blanking out the scabby-legged homeless in the streets, blanking out the six people killed by a car bomb in Iraq yesterday, lives reduced to dead meat like a smashed guitar is scrap wood. Sonambulating through the daily routine, petrifying in slowly setting glue.

I don't want to be fucking numb any more. I want to feel alive. I'm looking for the scream, the life force. The Puerto Ricans called it the aché, Dr. Q said. The force that comes from the beat, the drums. It illuminates everything. Something to transubstantiate this faceless city of chain stores and banks.

Why does food taste good? Why does sex feel so great? Skin on skin, licking and wallowing in the slippery warmth, screaming wordless invocations to the spirits that possess you. Every note he hit felt like that. Every note tasted like city soul food, oozy juicy molten mozzarella and fresh-fried mushrooms, salty roast pork lo mein, rice and beans savory with olives and cilantro and greasy sweet platanos.

Connection. Community. Nothing could stop the inexorable night-fall of decrepitude, but it was a lifeline to ease it. Something that could pull you out of a fate as an achy old geezer with clogged bowels, sitting alone in a room full of detritus watching reruns on a sputtering TV. The tendrils of your life would spread a net through the city, curving and ovulating and coming back bearing fruit. Even a ten-minute conversation on a street corner plugged you in.

Ain't no substitute for flesh. Contact. Fingers on strings, tongue on tongue, electron on diode telegraphing speaker to move air, soundwaves cracking on eardrums, hip shake, earthquake, hope the cops are on the take so they won't come in and raid this joint just when things are getting good. No. It's alive with plasmatic powers that amaze scientists scribing observations in the Book of Life. They found no formulae for this. You gotta grab it and ride the wave, the roar, the ecstasy of flexing helixes.

Yeah, and you better appreciate it when it comes around because you can plant, water, and plow—and nothing happens if you don't—but you never know when it's coming up again. A living, breathing thing in all its sweaty efflorescence. Give people a community, not a commodity. An exorcism and refueling that carries on, sustains them, gives them more than the empty tristesse of another transaction. If you buy it, it sits dead in your hand, a worthless fetish. You got to live it. Feel it. It's impalpable but more real than you've ever been. Get up.

It ain't over till it's over. Not until the breath no longer fogs the mirror, the EEG flatlines as the auditory nerve shuts down, the pulse drops from 48 to zero and the EKG beeps its last. And no matter what kind of fascist fuckwits rule the world, it ain't over until some jackbooted prick slams the shower door shut and seals it.

Fuck you, Death. I'm cheating the actuarial tables. I'm sticking around as long as I can just to get in your face. I'm gonna be doing stuff as long as my fingers can move.

But somehow Underend couldn't escape the feeling that the assholes were winning. Fuck it, maybe he'd call Tina this week, see if she wanted to hang out.

Acknowledgments

The author thanks the following people for their help and support: publisher Jennifer Joseph of Manic D Press; literary agents Gloria Norris, Kent Wolf, Deborah Carter, and Gary Heidt, for their encouragement; lawyers Angela Bocage-Lemerise and Helen Richardson, for expert advice.

Writer friends who read early versions: Marci Davis, Lynn McSweeney, Lee Williams, Nina Karacosta, and my brother, Ken.

Friends, musicians, poets, and actors, including (but definitely not limited to) Mac & Kathy, English Steve & Miranda, Matt, Faith, Dave & Angela, Edwina, Antrim, Magenta, Kim & Austin & Jacop, Trish, Meabh, Gateria, Silent Chris, and one single mom I have sworn to keep anonymous.

The labor and radical movements of the 1930s, President Franklin D. Roosevelt, and Senator Robert F. Wagner for unemployment compensation.

And my family: my parents, brothers, sisters-in-law, son, nieces, and nephew. Specifically, my father for his list of Yiddish epithets; my mother for Mercury and Venus; Karen and Leah, for filling my apartment with art-girl spirits; Ken, still hard-to-top competition for the best writer in the family; and Ian, whose love, generosity, and wise-assery enrich my life.